MR. LUCKY

Nigel Bray. © April 20th 2022

This story is dedicated to

Gill, my sister,

Who was there at the start of the journey,

To my lost friend Chris,

And

To Simon, my husband,

Who will be there at its end.

"Oh, I am fortune's fool!"

William Shakespeare, *'Romeo and Juliet'.*

"But, he thought, I keep them with precision. Only I have no luck anymore. But who knows? Maybe today. Every day is a new day. It is better to be lucky. But I would rather be exact. Then when luck comes you are ready."

Ernest Hemingway, *'The Old Man and the Sea'.*

"Are you what is called a lucky man? Well, you are sad every day. Each day has its great grief or its little care. Yesterday you were trembling for the health of one who is dear to you, today you fear for your own; tomorrow it will be an anxiety about money, the next day the slanders of a calumniator, the day after the misfortune of a friend; then the weather, then something broken or lost, then a pleasure for which you are reproached by your conscience or your vertebral column; another time, the course of public affairs. Not to mention heartaches. And so on. One cloud is dissipated, another gathers. Hardly one day in a hundred of unbroken joy and sunshine. And you are of that small number who are lucky!"

Victor Hugo, *'Les Misérables'.*

"You own everything that happened to you.

Tell your stories.

If people wanted you to write warmly about them,

they should've behaved better."

Anne Lamott.

Chapters.

Mr. Lucky!

Mr. Lucky? Is that a good title, a good reflection of what is contained herein? I think so, though it might not appear so at times.

This is my autobiography, my life thus far.....

There's lots of swearing and shagging and jolly japes to keep you entertained, lots of sorrow – no 'memoir' would be complete without a dollop of sorrow....but my life has been pretty funny too so I have included some stuff to make you smile.

Everything here is the truth, the whole truth and nothing but the truth. Or at least as far as I remember it. Half a century – a lot to remember! Strange how some things – tunes, places, voices and conversations are all so clear in my mind even now, easy to recall.

All the people are real, everything described, happened.

All seen from my point of view.

I want to leave something – I can't paint, draw, write novels, invent stuff so this will have to suffice. Maybe it will end up on someone's bookshelf, passed around to friends – in that case, I WILL have left something and that will suffice. It will be good to know as I am scattered – in the land that, in my heart I never left, in all my wanderings: Kernow, back to the wild, wild sea.

Enjoy.

MUM: Sorry for swearing.

PS. I have referenced songs that were in the chart on that day, at the start of each chapter.....look them up, and see how they interpret what follows......if you want. It's a kind of interactive thing.....

Please yourself. See if I care.

Part One

Mr. Lucky Opens The Door.

CHAPTER ONE.

A STAR IS BORN, REDRUTH, CORNWALL.

'Our hero comes in to the world – and what a world he finds......'

'Que Sera Sera'

By Doris Day. No1. The week I was born.

'Whatever will be, will be
The future's not ours to see..'

How very apt.....

~ ~ ~

I was hoping to have started this on August 27th, my birthday so with a fanfare I could have announced; "FIFTY SEVEN YEARS AGO TODAY......", but I didn't get round to it. I went to Paris instead.

I was born, 'mewling and puking' at about half past three in the morning, on that date though, in 1956. I was born six weeks premature, 'sans teeth, sans nails, sans eyebrows'; apparently a horrible colour...and completely silent and stary.

This was 'Up 'Druth' as we used to say when referring to Redruth Hospital, where it seems, everyone I know, was born. Clearly, I don't remember much of this period. I was a baby, a tot, an infant, a yet – not – sentient being, so not having any memories from these first years is pretty normal.

I don't believe people when they say: "Oooh, I remember when I was two and I went to Yarmouth..." No. you don't. You were *told* you went to Yarmouth. Then, it was just emerging colours, scents and sense, breasts or bottles – Yarmouth wasn't part of your drive for life, I don't think, so nor would you remember it.

We have photos; those odd, square, not – quite – in – focus snaps that we had then, grainy obsolete memories, chucked into tins or squirmingly posted on Facebook....I have one of me where it looks like I have shit myself – my pendulous nappy hanging down the leg of my little shorts. They're funny those photos. You know they're YOU, your past, but somehow, they belong to someone else – certainly not the 58-year-old homosexual writing this. That toddler was intended for Dadship and kids, that's for sure. Why would my Methodist father have expected anything else?

Nappy Full.

I was born into a very weird set up. I had a Mummy (who apparently had to stay in hospital as they thought they'd found a shadow on her lung or something. Don't know; I was only 0), a Daddy and two sisters - no wait, four sisters and two brothers. No, that's not right....who did they belong to?

To explain: (and this is apocryphal; if you ask my cousins in Oregon, they have the exact opposite story. *Their* mother won't talk about it and the only people who TRULY knew what happened are all dead.) So, my Dad was married with four kids and he was away at war, which really lucky for us! Cornwall would have been invaded by the Germans if it hadn't been for my Dad. There was this giant German ship (must've been off Porthtowan or

Portreath), and he swam out to it with a tin opener and cut a big hole in the side so it sank, thus saving England from being overrun by the Hun. It's true; he told me. He was my absolute hero.

Anyway, my Dad's version of events, who I didn't even know had been divorced until I found the divorce certificate when I was about 17, in the lift up bit of one of those vile telephone table / seats everyone had in the 70s, is that he came home (I'm presuming, on leave) from the war to find the house where had lived with his wife (not my Mum), his two daughters and two sons to discover – and there are many variations on this theme and unanswered questions, because the dates don't add up and anyway, my Father was a lying bastard who always only told 'the truth', according to his version of events – that his old lady had been having it off with someone else (how would he know this? Maybe she told him?) So what did he do? Allegedly, this: he took HER, vile traitorous bitch that she was, and the two girls to Redruth railway station, put them all on a train (to where, I have never been able to discover) turned his back, walked down the platform and never saw his wife or his daughters again Then, (again, an assumption) he went back to France, left the eldest boy Michael with his mother, and presumably Barrie was either IN Tehidy with his polio or he went to Gran's with Michael and then got sent there later. He never saw his daughters again. Ever. Well, actually he did, but that's a tale for later....I was 17 and at my aunt's wedding when my brother said; "It's lovely to have the family together isn't it? Shame the girls can't be here...." Girls? What girls? This was the first time I ever discovered I even HAD two other sisters. Talk about a fucked-up family.

Anyway, I digress....

I was born into a pretend Methodist family, which used God and his wrath when it was convenient. My very early years were spent in a titchy house, a small stone Cornish cottage which belonged to my gran, a formidable, unpleasant woman, but who apparently my parents had to put up with as she'd agreed they could live there – I don't know why we didn't have a house of our own. We did have a cat though. Fucking great ginger thing (no, I don't REMEMBER it, I've been told!) that apparently was placed once, on my face by a usurped sister. This is the house where my exploding nappy picture was taken.

Redruth was a small granite Cornish town, faded glory from its tinning days then struggling, in the late 50s to re-merge from the war, the lack of menfolk and no jobs. I've been back since, of course; it has new shops, a 'Precinct', natch, but still the air of failure, not quite really making it work, clings to it. The places I remember as a boy (the little alley where I went to go to have my hair cut, at a proper barber. I had to sit on a plank, put across the arms of the barber's chair so I was high enough up. I DO still remember, now you come to mention it, deliberately rubbing my arm or elbow against the lump in his trousers, as he worked; this was a kind of frottage I have used many times since – the dentist, the doctor, the hairdresser when I went, all very (or maybe, not so) subtle, but electrifying nonetheless) are there but now coated in new brick, the department store where I once got lost is now something like Poundland, the cinema where I was taken to see 'Lawrence of Arabia' and fell asleep, is now gone...you get the picture.

We lived in Sparnon Terrace with my gran for a few years, though it must have been less than four (after my birth) because we had moved by the time I had started school. I went to school early, being a smart – ass, but also because my birthday, being late August and therefore so late in the educational year – September to September – meant that I was the youngest in my year group; all through my school career, in fact. If mum had managed not to have me six weeks early, I would have been the oldest as I'd have been born in September.

I know very little of those very early years – I have been told I was a beautiful baby, and that my sister loathed me, a fact borne out by three attempts to murder and / or maim me:

1.   Suffocate me with Beelies, the cat.

2.   Sprinkle cracker crumbs in my eyes while I was lying in my cot

3.   Put the gas poker from the old cooker up my nose and switch it on.

The Scene of the Crime.

Clearly, I survived these assassination attempts. Gill, however, barely survived my Mum's dreaded Golden Ear Whizz, which came out of nowhere, was unavoidable and hurt like hell. She received several as a consequence of trying to murder or disfigure her little brother. I love her now, but throughout our childhoods, we were at war. I once even threw myself down the stairs, top to bottom and said, as I lay screaming and wailing on the hall floor (it had those beautiful cream and maroon mosaic tiles), when Mum came out to see what "all the bleddy racket was", that she had pushed me. At this point, Gill came out of the kitchen and stood behind Mum and watched in glee as I was administered a G.E.W. to add to my pain.

I will come back to the mystery of the other siblings later; at this point I had no idea of their existence. I knew of Gill, and Sandra (who also it seems might not be my sister after all!) and about Barrie (who had been in hospital, up Tiddy, for nine years) and a mysterious, exotic other brother who had gone to America allegedly with only 1d in his pocket and a metal plate in his head. How fantastic was that? I want one!! I don't remember seeing him too often – I know there's some of those photos with Granny Bray, him, me and Patch. I am wearing the CUTEST little dungarees....... Anyway, that was our little family – Mum Dad, two and a half kids (Sandra being a bastard, I'm beginning to think) and a dog. Perfect, eh? Oh, no. No, no, no, no. Far from.

You don't know all the bad stuff until you're older, do you? Until they begin to tell you stuff, confide in you, tell their pain; until you begin yourself to notice things, add things up.....la *famille* Bray was FAR from perfect, nuclear or not.....

We moved to 68, Albany Road, when I was four. It was a proper house, all Cornish granite, with a beautiful stained-glass panel in the front door, blue and red and it made endless variations of deep blues and crimson patterns on the hall floor. There was a small front garden and a path to the pavement. The front door had a step where Mum used to stand and have a fag, standing on one leg, ankles crossed. I had the little room, above the stairs, Gill and Sandra shared next door and Mum and Dad were at the back. The kitchen was out the back, a middle room and the Front Room. We never went in there, god knows why – what's the point of having a room if you can't go in it? Anyway, them was the rules until, Granny Bray came to live with us.

Fag Break

My Gran came to live with us then because there were too many of us in her little house. I imagine she missed going to her Funerals…….our next door neighbour at Sparnon Terrace was called Edie, (she was Head Mistress at Trewirgie, the school I would go to), and she and Gran, or sometimes she and her friend Lylie, would just go and gate-crash all the funerals in town – or more specifically, the 'do' after. They'd get all dressed up and then go and eat all the grub and drink sherry. More front than Selfridges, as they say.

I'm guessing we had no choice but to have her with us as she had allowed us to live with her. There had been a conflab with Dad and his siblings and -

…I feel a digression coming on…

Do you want to know their names? Check this:

William James Kingsley

Thora Ethelinda

Ronald H. 'Roy'

And, my Dad:

Invenar Redvers. (I am not joking! No wonder he changed it. AND he used to be in AmDram. I have old photos of him, looking very camp.)

......and they all decided they it should be Dad's 'duty' to look after his mother. Her husband, my granddad, William, fucked off to South Africa – there are records of him sailing out of London on the SS Borda, bound for Australia, but stopping off at Cape Town. He became a miner in Kimberly, South Africa, mining for gold and didn't come back for years. That's why, I guess, that Gran, deserted at 38, with four kids, was such a miserable bitch, bitter and spiteful. At the time, Mum and Dad had a little grocery shop in Gloucester. I don't know but I am guessing they might have rented a flat or something above it. Nobody tells me anything! Nearly anyone who WOULD know is dead, I'm not speaking to Sandra and Gill was only a baby. As I said, the deal was that they (I was as yet a sperm), the four of them, would go back to Cornwall and live with and look after Gran – a decision, I suspect, forced upon Mum and one which caused massive repercussions for their marriage.

My memory of her is that she WAS vile. She had what was the Front Room (the one that was never used, for some reason – always clean, tidy and ready for guests that never used it), and she had her bed and a commode. The room, on the rare occasions I was allowed in to it, always smelled of rotten apples and piss. I used to be summoned sometime and have to sit on her bony knees while she sang 'Little Sir Echo' to me and I would have to do the echoey bits. She used to sit there like some wizened old crone and she SHOUTED so much. Meal times were awful – she used to take chewed up food out of her mouth and just hurl it across the room to the dog. I know now that she made my Mum's life an absolute misery but Dad either had no choice or just didn't have the balls to do anything about it. Gran treated Mum like a skivvy, as if she didn't have enough to deal with – an eight year old with a police record, a sister who was always out shagging up the park and a husband who, as you will see in the fullness of time, was a bastard. Gran, she just didn't need. There was a great deal of pain in our house, things going on that I didn't understand but felt nonetheless. I know now there were many unspoken hurts and grievances that festered – my parents never spoke about 'stuff'; Mum suffered in silence and Dad just refused to acknowledge anything was wrong, or if it was, it certainly wasn't his fault – the default position of his life and the tool with which he beat us, all our lives.

As I said, I started school. Early, 'cos I was a smarty arse. I could read at four – small books, obviously, but still pretty good. I went to a nursery class, but have little memory of it.

I then moved up to the Juniors, and this meant, aged 7, I was able to walk to school on my own, - can you imagine!!- about a mile through the town, across two main roads and past Nan Tuckett's sweetshop, which was (and still is) opposite the school gates.

Trewirgie juniors. (Front row, right)

Ah, sweet joy! It was her *house*, looking back now, and she'd turned her front room into a shop. Those pink shrimps. Flying saucers. Black Jacks. Rhubarb and Custards. Sherbet Dabs were my favourite and you could buy little bags of various coloured sherbet (pronounced 'SHERBERRRT') from big glass jars. We ate it with our fingers and it stained our tongues and made them feel rough. I don't remember how much money I had, but enough to buy a couple of each on the way to school. We never bought them after school as we were likely to get them nicked by the older boys on the way home. We used to walk home via the Back Way and I remember my one and only experience of being bullied occurred here – Mark Venton (who was SUPPOSED to be my friend, the bastard; third row, 2nd from the right) and Andrew Parsons (back row, 5th from right) grabbed me and kept punching in the stomach. All these years later, probably 50+, I can remember him saying, *"Is he crying yet?"* and Mark saying, *"One more punch and he will be."* So, I feigned it, so he'd let me go and ran home. When my Mum heard my story (bigged up a bit, naturally) she put that look on her face and knew, I KNEW, what would happen.......Mark lived opposite us, and the next evening when he came over, he stood on the doorstep and said: *"Is Ningel* (bit of a speech impediment, you see) *coming out to play?",* she just gave him a Golden Ear

Whizz. Just like that; like a cobra strike it was. While he was holding his ear, she gave him another one, on the other side – she did back hands as well. *"That one's for Andrew Bleddy Parsons when you see him."* Mark left, crying. I was mortified though – glad he'd got his just desserts, but a bit worried as to where it might lead. Nowhere, as it happened. I think they were both so scared of my Mum, they left me alone.

Mummy's boy. Hahaha.

Mark and I were ALWAYS in trouble, and the best of friends, as you are at that age. FOR EVVA!! Behind our house was Victoria Park – it's still there, but seemingly much much smaller – and this was our land.....we roamed it like William and the Outlaws, causing mayhem wherever we went. We broke windows, snapped tree branches climbing them, put dog poo in the sand pit.....what japes! Once though, we went a bit too far – well twice actually....we lit a teeny bonfire in someone's garage. It was winter and we were a bit cold. Unfortunately, the owner saw the smoke and caught us. He was fucking LIVID. A bit OTT in my opinion – it wasn't THAT near his car.....

Another time was when Mark dared me to put my head through the railings of the park gates.... (Actually this COULD have been Gill....just as likely, given her history) where, because of my big ears, I got stuck. Proper stuck and my Dad had to get the Fire Brigade who came and cut the railings. Oooo. Embarrassing. I'd like it now though, of course.......all them big burly fireman and me, trapped, bent over in the park gates....

Here they are folks! Victoria Park Gates...!

In town there is a church, St. Andrews, which has beautiful stained glass windows and someone threw stones through them. I swear on my LIFE, it was not me. Nor do I know who it was but, one evening, there was a knock on the door and it was the police. I am only recounting this story because it marked me, for life. It had a profound effect on my relationship with my Dad and on the whole of my life and it's still something I wrestle with often. As I'd already been in trouble, I had an immediate guilt reaction – I didn't know what he had come for even, but I was scared. My Dad asked him in and we went into the middle room, the one with the table with the green chenille cloth, its fringes long since unravelled and pulled by little fingers; it was the table we used to hide under when 'Dr. Who' came on...we'd hear the 'Woo-OOOOO' and get underneath. I don't think I was scared actually - it's just that everyone else did it and I did love a bit of drama....

Anyway, we were there, the three of us, Dad angry and embarrassed, me afraid but bewildered. The policeman was fucking HUGE, all in his black uniform, towering above me.

No foreplay, straight in:

"Did you break the windows in St. Andrew's church?"

"No."

"DID you break the windows?"

"No, I didn't."

"Did you?"

"No, honestly, I didn't."

"Who did then?"

"I don't know."

"It was you, wasn't it? Eh?"

"No, sir, honestly, I didn't. I didn't."

"Yes, you DID."

This went on for what seems like hours and I just wanted him to stop so I said, *"Yes, I did. I did it."*

Snot running, tears now, fear. Dad was just staring. I DIDN'T FUCKING DO IT!!
WHY DON'T YOU BELIEVE ME? WHY AREN'T YOU HELPIING ME? WHY AREN'T
YOU SUPPORTING ME? I DIDN'T. FUCKING. DO. IT!!!!

"I'll deal with him, Officer. Thank you for coming round." I couldn't believe
what I was hearing, what was happening. I didn't do this thing. Why are you
saying this? I just said it to make him stop....

The policeman left and Dad said, *"Get upstairs."* I ran, snivelling and crying to
my room, knowing and not knowing what was coming. A shouting, a bawling,
his red and angry face, fag breath, pushed into mine. I heard him coming up
the stairs and he came in.

"I didn't do it, Dad, I swear," was all I managed before I felt the fire of the
belt he had taken off, as it ripped across the air to my arm which I'd held up
to protect myself. This was incomprehensible to me – I hadn't done anything.
He had asked no questions, shown no support and here he was, weapon in
hand and I was being punished, harshly, wrongly.

"I'll teach you to embarrass me!" he said and came towards me. After the
beating, I realised it wasn't even about the windows but the embarrassment
of having the police on the doorstep. The cunt, the absolute CUNT. I realised
this after, maybe long after, but at this particular moment I was screaming
and crying and trying to avoid the belt that kept roaring towards my legs, my
arms, my face – anything that he could reach while I careened helplessly off
the walls of my small room.

Then he stopped. He just turned, breathing heavily, and left. I was in pain,
such pain. Not just from the welts he had inflicted, but from the injustice, the
overwhelming sense of wrong, of not being believed, of not being supported
by my Dad....it was unbearable. And the worst thing of all maybe was that he
forbade my mother to come and comfort me or even tend my wounds. This
was the default for our lives with him – all the wrongs, injustices, pain he
heaped upon us, all of us as children, teenagers and adults came down to not
being supported, believed, cherished, loved enough. It's no wonder we're all
so damaged.

Germoline could not heal the wound he left that day, and it never has. The
agonies I suffer when I tell the truth and am not believed send me spiralling
back to that room and the scars he left on my heart never heal.

On a lighter note - Victoria Park saw a lot of action actually. At one end was (is?) a glass pavilion type thing, which you could get behind if you pushed through the rhododendrons. This is where my older sister used to go and shag. Always at it, apparently. This of course is all hearsay, but facts delighted in by me who of course told all my friends, and I remember taking them to see 'the Place', the bushes where my Big Sister used to have it off, whatever that meant. Actually, I ALSO used to go in there and do 'sex'. By this I mean that Yvonne and I used to behind the glass house and kind of fiddle about - she used to lie down pretending she was tired and I used to come home from work and lie on top of her. Nothing happened more than that, I don't think. I was seven or eight. I DID know the bloke had to be on top and that it was nice, and actually it was. Then we used to go home and have our tea.

Unfortunately, that didn't go quite according to plan, because Sandra got pregnant. It was bound to happen, given the regularity she went 'up the park'. Now, she was 'up the duff'. I knew nothing about this, (LO! I have ANOTHER relation I have never met!!) but I was told she was 'going away on holiday to Falmouth for a while, to stay with a friend.' Do you see a pattern here? My Father, when they need some support, some understanding, discards his children to remove any ugliness from his life, something that occurred all throughout our lives. I don't know, but I guess she was scared and alone and being forced to live with a stranger, in a strange town until this inconvenient baby was born. She, for it was a girl, named Ann, who in fact still lives in Falmouth, was taken away and Sandra reappeared in my life, back in Redruth. The effect this must have had on her is unimaginable; just another day at the office for him. Maybe. Maybe he did feel the agonies of sending his daughters away – that was the third – but was unable / unwilling / afraid to show it.

School was OK. In the year I was in (maybe the equivalent of today's Year 2) I became MILK MONITOR. Oh yesss.....it gave me a chance to get the little shits that had caused me great offence in the playground or went off with someone who was my Best Friend Ever etc.

There was one of those great back cast iron heaters in the classroom where the milk used to get put. Hello?? Heat + milk = curdled......anyway, it played to my advantage. When Miss Richards said. *"Bray, it's time for milk."* I would rise, majestic, to my feet and look around the class.....who? WHO shall I choose today? Who wants to do......? THE STRAWS? I could choose each day and the opportunities for revenge were endless.....HA!! That'll teach you to knee the backs of my legs in assembly.......Not YOU......not YOU......Yes, I choose.....A girl. Always a girl. So, then I'd get the crate and go along the desks, giving the cooler milk to my Best Friends and leaving the warmer, more revolting bottles which had been nearest the fire, to the end, making sure the bullies and the cads got them. Actually, this was quite good insurance - they knew they'd get the curdled warm milk so it protected me a bit. Until, that is, my tenure was over and I became, once more, nobody, a little fish back in the big pond, looking for an identity.

There's not much else I remember from Primary School – Gordon somebody punched me in the mouth because I got to the top of the climbing frame first and to be beaten by me was something not to be borne, so he upped the macho bar and smacked me in the face. I responded – by crying and telling Sir. He got a bollocking, I got an enemy.

Went to school, went to Nan Tucket's, went home, and went up the park, all pretty normal stuff (except when Mark Venton was involved). We had a dog called Patch by this time and he was so disobedient – he chased cars, he disappeared for days...one day – and this is BRILLIANT! – he went over the wall into next door. Our neighbour, Mrs. Eddy was having some kind of party – a wedding reception or christening or something and she'd laid all the food out before she went and left a window open. Patch got in and stole a whole chicken from the centre of the table – I remember seeing him legging it out of her back gate, the whole chicken in his mouth. We couldn't catch him of course. Mrs Eddy was in tears – it was all very dramatic.

We used to go and visit my Nan and 'Poppie' too, in their little miner's cottage. And it was little, a tiny granite box, full of fag ends and dog hairs. I used to quite like it though; I got to eat biscuits and watch my Nan play cards. She smoked Capstan Full strength fags, no filter and I can see her now – grey hair with a yellow streak running up the centre, stained with nicotine, legs splayed at the little coffee table, bloomers agape with her fag packet stuffed up one leg. They played for hours, for matchsticks, and a little company. There was a lovely lady who used to live with them, a friend of Nan's I think, who judging it now, would be classed as living in slavery. She did EVERYTHING around the house. I suppose she lived rent free, and was even frying chips in the chip shop when they moved to Devon, late into the night. Poppie had to sit out in the other room, in the dark because she wouldn't let him have the light on. Why did nobody say anything? Like *"Fuck Off and get it yourself, you lazy old bag"* or *"My house, my lights!"* but no one ever did and she continued to rule from her nicotine roost. Her daughter, my aunt, was similar and although she TOO is another story, I will just tell you this: she married Fred (who burned the hairs off pigs for a living, while she stuck her hand up chickens' arses and gutted them – lovely dinner conversation, I'm sure!) and somehow, they had taken in a friend of Aunty Jack's first husband. He was called Phil and he'd moved in for a couple of weeks. He stayed for forty-seven years, until he died, amongst the dog shit and fag ends in a house that had never been cleaned.

Oh, before we leave Redruth, I must tell you about our car... It was a pale green Ford Anglia with one of those seats in the front you could get three on. I was an AWFUL passenger, really really car sick. One time I recall throwing up in the hood of Dad's duffel coat which was hanging over the seat as we couldn't stop in time. Often there'd be pools of vomit in the seat wells. I think the fact they both smoked, chuffing away as we drove didn't help. Anyway, this day we were driving along the cliffs, by Hell's Mouth, singing *'I Love To Go A'wandering'* and just as we got to the rousing *"Fal – de – reeeee, fal – de – raaaah"* bit, the fucking car blew up! Bang! Smoke coming out of the engine, knackered. I helped immensely by having hysterics. We were miles from anywhere, no mobile phone (ha ha) and it was tea time! I don't know how that was resolved but I only have to hear that song, or have a 'knapsack on my back 'or I'm on a ...erm 'mountain track' and I am transported back to that moment. It was funny / terrifying in equal measure, though at the time, the terrifying bit was what I remember most.

There were many things from those years. My family had what seemed like a massive extended group of friends and neighbours and usually on a Sunday, we would ALL pack our cars and head of to the beach for the day, to swim, to play, to make kites (though the last one was usually taken out of my hands by my dad as clearly I couldn't be trusted to tape a bit of brown paper to a bit of stick......) but I DO remember once: he was as usual in charge, we were 'standing back' as instructed as he went racing past, trying to get the kite into the air, along the top of this sand dune which suddenly ran out, disappeared from beneath him and after a bit of a Fred Flintstone – legs frantically cycling in the air moment, he plummeted out of sight. Hilarious. I have this picture in my mind of all us kids, heads just peering over the top of the dune and him, what seemed like miles below in an undignified heap with a broken kite. That was the end for today. Bit frosty thereafter.......

Sand, sandwiches, bottles of pop, baggy swimming trunks, sun, rounders...all of it wrapped up n the halo of Summer and the warmth of belonging.

Just another Sunday....

Another time, he broke his leg showing off on a boogie board, pushing us out of the way. He drove home with a broken leg. He was so arrogant. And stupid. He used to turn the car engine off when we were going downhill, "to save petrol". Never mind that also meant he had no control over the car until he turned it on again.....

Lucky me?

Looking back, I reckon I can say I had a pretty good start – I was fed, I had both parents, a nice house, a dog, siblings, I was quite good at school.......perfect recipe really. Except......except.....it was all bollocks of course, a veil, a conceit.

~ My grandmother was a fucking bitch and was putting intolerable strain on my parent's marriage.

~ I had hidden sisters I knew nothing of, just discarded like trash by my Dad.

~ My brother was in hospital for NINE years with polio.

~ My elder sister was a slapper and probably a bastard, and maybe not even my real sister.

~ My other sister was sad, lonely, scared of her parents, her life and had an imaginary family she preferred.

Secrets and lies, secrets and lies.

But I was only 8 - cosseted, spoilt and self-centred – what did I know? Nature or nurture? The jury's still out but if the nurture argument stands, then THAT'S why…..Mummy's Boy.

Right now, on the verge of leaving everything and everyone I knew (though not living over the road from Mark Venton didn't stop my criminal career), all I could think was me me me…How will I live, I would just *DIE* if we move…..

I didn't know then, the reasons: if we moved, SHE wouldn't be coming.

So. We did.

Butter wouldn't melt.

Granny Bray (with two mysterious bullet holes in her head).

CHAPTER TWO.

SUMMERCOURT.

<u>'In which our hero is betrayed, but finds his inner muse.'</u>

'*You'll Never Get To Heaven'*.

By Dionne Warwick. No23. 20th August, 1964.

I wasn't Sure I wanted to…

~ ~ ~

I don't know for sure, but after asking about what things were like at Albany road, for the grown-ups, I know now the decision was as motivated as much by the hope of getting a new, better and different life as much getting shot of the Woman with the Commode……

Because we were moving, Gran had to go into a nursing home. What she, or anyone thought about this, I don't know. She was just gone. It turns out that she was so monstrous, home after home threw her out, passed her from one to another. She ended up in the notorious Blackwood House – a kind of Alcatraz for the bewildered. It was there that she fell and her broke her hip; she never fully recovered from this and died from pneumonia in 1974. It is unknowable what personality traits she passed on to her children – my memory of her daughter, my Auntie Thora (Thora Ethalinda!) was just of a kindly, white haired old lady and Uncles Roy and Kingsley were always good fun to be with, but that may just be rose-coloured Summers. I do know that my Dad and she were very similar – as he became a very old man, he became her: vicious, spiteful, and full of hatred for his lot, for what his 'kids had done to him', a distant echo of Granny Bray. My Mother's sudden death in 1995 was a blessing really. Though it was the most terrible thing you could ever imagine, I understand now that she was spared the onset of her husband's fury and bile at how life had treated him. He never, EVER had any recognition or understanding of how he had treated US……

My Dad had been working for a small, but locally significant clothing firm in Redruth. I don't know what he did there but we had food on the table, a car, we went to the beach on a Sunday etc etc. Mum worked there too as well as looking after us (and Her) so I imagine her life was pretty shit. Gill tells me that there was a massive row once because some money had gone missing from work. I don't know if he was accusing *her* or they were fighting because they were in trouble, but she says she saw them, over the banister shouting and then he grabbed her and ripped her dress....she says she went into her room and drowned out the noise. I guess *'Whiter Shade of Pale'* is a difficult song for her to hear, even now.

When the news broke that we were moving, because we had BOUGHT A SHOP, my tears and tantrums receded, and it didn't seem such a bad idea after all. It meant SHE wouldn't be living with us although I was never told why. Looking back, I am guessing that Mum had finally had enough. Probably, it had become a 'her or me' situation. She'd already walked out once over the missing money thing so it was likely she'd been pushed to the limit – the move was to be a clean break; completely clean.

We didn't go to Newquay straight away though. I know now that we couldn't find or afford a house there, so we had a little house in Summercourt, a small village, seven miles away. I was put into the local primary school, two classes, about 50 / 60 kids. It was a bit strange as I was used to a big school, hundreds of us where, I could lose myself, blend in...

1, Wyoming Villas, Summercourt. My bedroom, top left.

Anyway, it was quite nice as it turned out and the beginning I think, for me, a budding homosexual, for 'twas there that I discovered.....DRAMA!!! Oh YES. It was Christmas, 1965 and we were doing a Nativity play. Obviously. I was cast as Herod. Well, that was it! I was AWAY.

Picture this: Black satin trouser suit, with big pantaloons trousers wiv dragons on! A sparkly bolero, SOOOO First Century, darling. And my turban! To die for. Designed it all meself! It was like I was channelling Lacroix / Vivienne Westwood. I had one line, I think, but my God, did I milk it. I was marvellous, dahling, marvellous..... I had to clap my hands and say something like: "Bring him to me!" Can you imagine? The pathos! The anguish! The wringing of hands....

I'd rehearsed for the longest time, trying to decide the most effective, the most powerful, the most commanding way to order this Christ Child, the Son of God to be brought before me:

"BRING him to me....."

"Bring HIM to me...."

"Bring him to ME....!

"BRING HIM TO ME!!!". . This last one was in stentorian tone and I deemed this to be the most effective and realistic. My Mum and my sister were in the audience (I could see them when I looked through the curtain at the side of the 'stage'.) I only had one shot and so the time came: CLAP CLAP CLAP. *"BRING HIM TO ME!!* I bellowed, which unfortunately for the Mums in the front row, was a wee bit too much and all the babies they'd brought started crying, shocked from sleep by my Olivierian tone. My part was quite near the beginning, so most of the rest of it was drowned out by wailing infants. Actually, it might have added to the realism – I had after all, just ordered the Massacre of the Innocents....

So. That was IT. Touch paper lit.....Unfortunately, my next brush with fame didn't go so well, and is another of those incidents from my tender years (I was very sensitive, actually...) that has left me with a nasty scar, to go with ChurchWindowgate.

My best friend, who I sat next to that year, was called Angela. Angela Woodley. She had a cousin who was killed in the Aberfan Disaster, which happened In October of that following year, 1966. I remember her coming into school crying and I put my arm round her and was her Best Friend. We had an assembly about it too, when we had to have a two-minute silence. Really? 50 or so small people all trying to remain silent? Maybe someone farted, but whatever, somebody (not me!) started giggling. You know, that behind clenched fists, snorty, squirty sort that you try desperately to keep in but only succeeds in making the two people behind, in front and to each side start too. The result was the whole room was snorting and gasping and Mr. Tothill was apoplectic with impotent rage as there was no clear culprit and his moment, when he'd planned to be all morose and give a speech and that had been snatched away by a hall full of wobbling, snotty children.

I'm not making light of what happened; it was truly terrible thing, but we were 10, Wales was on the other side of the world and we were only really interested in ourselves and the four streets that surrounded the crossroads in the village. I mention her though because she was pivotal in my pain, my betrayal in my next Stage Appearance. Fucking little bitch, who I'd helped through her tears the morning of October 21st, the day she promised me she would be my Best Friend. For Ever. And actually, your yellow jumper was SHIT, in spite of telling you I wanted it.

One of the delights of primary school was recorder lessons. Decades later, a teacher myself, I can still remember the joy of getting 'Hot Cross Buns' right, then progressing to 'Little Bird'. As that teacher, however, there was less joy, trying to mark books when recorder club was on.

I digress. We were getting recorder lessons, and I was quite musical (you see the way we're going here?) and got on with it quite well. After a while, there was a chance to play in assembly. *"Who would like to play in assembly on Friday?"* Totters asked. In front of everyone! On my own! A SOLO!! *"MEEEEE!! I'll do it Sir. ! ME MEEE!"* I asked discreetly and Sir said OK and it was arranged for Friday's 'Show and Tell' assembly. I wanted so desperately to get it right and spent playtimes and lunchtime practising. I forget what it was now, but *'London's Burning'* comes to mind because that uses a 'half – hole' note on the *'FIRE FIRE!'* bit and I was rather expert.....

So, against school rules, on the Thursday night (can you see how clearly I remember? This was forty-seven years ago, and what happened scarred me so deeply I can see it as if it were yesterday), I smuggled a school recorder home. I put it up the sleeve of my coat, hoping nobody'd notice I couldn't bend my arm, and went off home and spent all evening practising, much to the delight, I'm sure, of my family.

The next day dawned, my day of glory, the day I was to play 'London's Burning' in front of all my peers. Remember, I was the youngest in the class and this was my chance. We sang the song, Mr. Tothill read some notices and stuff. I was beside myself with nerves and excitement and pride. Finally, after waiting for what seemed like YEARS, he said, "OK, it's now 'Show and Tell' time and this morning we have a musical item." I stood, I blushed, I think I might even have bowed, and walked up the little stair to the stage (actually it was more of a platform really, but it FELT like a stage).

He then turned to the table and picked up a gym shoe. What? This wasn't part of it. What was happening?

"Someone tells me that you have broken a school rule and that you took school property off the school premises. Is that right?"

My face burning, eyes stinging, I said, "Yes, but it was only to do extra practice, to get it right, to be perfect....."

"You broke a rule. Turn round. Bend over". Just like that. I front of everyone.

I couldn't believe this was happening. He must've known he was going to do this, all through the hymn and the notices. What about my solo? What about my chance to be good, to impress my friends, and my enemies? As I bent, I turned my head, and there she was, a small smile playing on her lips. Angela Fucking Woodley. Angela Fucking Woodley, who wasn't chosen to do the solo. Angela Fucking Woodley who must have seen me put the recorder up my sleeve and instead of being impressed by my resolve to be good, and be my Best friend Ever and be pleased for me, grassed me up.

As the slipper came down, it hurt. Oh god did it hurt, but that pain was nothing against the pain of the injustice being done that day and that has stayed with me, in this detail, ever since. I was only trying to be better and it was taken away; instead of receiving praise and accolades from the teachers and my peers, I was humiliated and beaten in front of the whole school.

I write the above conversation as if verbatim, but I think it is only the gist – my head was roaring and I am guessing I didn't really hear that much. Betrayal. Injustice. Shame. Rage. Today, I feel the same if I am done to unfairly and suffer disproportionately. Thanks Angela. And thank YOU Mr. Tothill, for not pausing, not taking a moment to wonder WHY I had done what I did and, though I did break a rule, give me some credit for trying, being proactive, trying to be better. You could have chosen that way. You could have taken me to your office. You could have let me play. Instead, you beat me, humiliated and marked me.

Not much else happened here; a one horse town, well, village. Crossroads, pub on one corner, corner shop on the other (naturally) the hairdressers ('Audrey's', where my Mum used to go to have hers done), church, school, garage (owned by Ivor Kessel whose daughter Susan, was the love of my life, and WAY out of my league), row of council houses, where Terry Archer lived (they were interesting because they were a bit...you know....coloured and therefore talked about.) Small village life where nothing much seemed to happen. Probably everyone was shagging everyone else, but I was ten and completely self – absorbed, so I didn't notice.

I had a few friends, long since lost. I do remember being quite an odd child, playing strange games in the playground, always with girls. At one time, Michael L and I pretended to be koala bears; all the time, speaking in a really high pitched voice to each other. Gooby Bear, I was. What a twat.

I stayed away from the 'rough' games, and with good reason: once, some kids were playing Chain Tig and the chain had about a dozen people in it, and the poor sod on the end was beginning to reach supersonic speed and then, the inevitable happened. He (and I think it was actually Michael L) was going so fast, he lost his footing and literally took off, horizontally and smacked head first into the playground wall. Ambulance job, that was, but he was OK.

I DID join the choir though. It was run by Ivor, so I thought I might get to see the fragrant Susan more often though, as it turned out, I was quite good. We had to audition and that – I think I sang 'The *Hills Are Alive'* (Yes, really...) and it turned out that I had a good treble voice. Clearly my bollocks hadn't yet dropped; I hadn't even discovered the joys of masturbation – so, perfect choir boy material. We used to practise in the Community Centre; it was bleddy FREEZING; as we sang you could see our breath. I loved it (and still do) and was with them for a few months, quite happily, until I got kicked out. Yes, really. KICKED. OUT. And I didn't do THAT, either. We were due to move to Newquay actually so it didn't matter too much, but again....the feeling of being blamed, and being blameless. It was hell of a funny though......

3rd From Left.....

We were doing a concert in the Methodist chapel and the choir was up in the balcony. I don't know if it was full in the audience or not; I just remember it being freezing cold. Anyway, we'd done a couple of songs and were sitting, waiting. Then, just as we were motioned to stand, Marilyn Coles let out this ENORMOUS fart. Being a chapel, and silent, it echoed, nay, RUMBLED and bounced off the walls in a thunderous clap. Or so it seemed to me. Can you imagine ANYTHING funnier to a ten year old boy? It was just textbook, and I started to giggle. A lot. And continued to giggle uncontrollably through our next song. Possibly it was inaudible, but to the audience below it was unmistakable – the soloist, the boy soprano, beetroot red and crying with uncontrollable mirth, in the middle of the second row. It was also unmissed by Ivor, the conductor, who after the concert had finished, took me to one side and gave me a massive bollocking for ruining the concert and 'giving his choir a bad name'. Notwithstanding it wasn't me who'd farted, he was quite right. I had made a tit of myself, and deserved what happened.

Another thing that happened at this time was that Gill met Ian. This book is MY story, but the impact of that meeting resonates and matters deeply; the behaviour of my father around that meeting changed forever the way I viewed him.

For whatever reason, he HATED Ian and forbade Gill to see him, an order that she refused to obey. She loved him, she was a teenager, and she wanted him. She began to see him by climbing out of the bedroom window at night (How utterly ROMANTIC!) but I assume she was caught.

This time, the order of things, is a bit hazy for me – I imagine it was all kept from me, or my head was so far up my own arse I didn't notice anything. I'm not sure of the order of events, and when talking to her and asking for information, she says this period in her life is too painful and refuses to talk about it.

But I DO know that he beat her. I don't know if this was over her refusal to stop seeing Ian or her refusal to 'obey orders'. Whatever the reason, I sat at the top of the stairs and watched him beat her to a bloody pulp. He began punching her and hitting her and shouting; eventually, he beat her to her knees, and then she fell on to her back in the hallway. The photograph I have in my mind is the one of him, kneeling astride her, her on her back, punching her over and over in the face. There was blood and screaming, and my Mother pulling at him, trying to get him off her, saying *"Stop. Stop Trevor. That's enough. You'll kill her."* I saw all this, I heard all this and I could do nothing – I was frozen, there, on the top stair. I don't know if they even knew I'd seen, even until they died. Another family secret, locked away.

Worse, he made her go to work the next day. By now, we had the shop in Newquay and she was made to sit outside where all the display stuff was, her face cut and her mouth split; her eyes swollen shut, telling people, as instructed, she'd fallen down the stairs.

Fearful times, happy times that year in the village.

The last thing to report is that, unknown to me, I had been entered for the 11+, which I passed and so booked my place at Grammar School. This was 1966.

I also, fuck knows how or why, was called out in assembly at the end of the year and presented with a certificate, announcing I had won the 'Bishop Philpot's Bible Study' award. Who? What? I'd never even read a bible. How bizarre!

So, there I was – 10 $^{3/4}$, a grammar school boy, an awardee of the Bishop's prize, an ex-chorister, a slippered and humiliated pupil of the school, a recorder player and witness to the savage beating of my darling sister by my father who had changed from the hero who had sunk the battle ship to a man of insane violence and who in my eyes, would never be the same. Quite a year, eh?

Oh, and Mr. Tothill.....

Do you believe in karma? He's dead. He hanged himself. What pain in his heart caused that?

Summercourt JMI School.

The big white windows are in the hall, the scene of my betrayal.

CHAPTER THREE.

GRAMMAR SCHOOL. NEWQUAY.

Where our hero finds himself at the bottom of the food chain, but finds his true vocation.

'I'm a Boy',

By The Who. No.20, September 1966.

'Paint your nails, little Sally Joy
Put this wig on, little boy'

This was to become a moot point.

~ ~ ~

So. I'm eleven, scared and looking like a twat in my school uniform. Maroon blazer with gold braid, shorts. SHORTS. Mother, I DO forgive you, but fucking hell! Have you any idea what that MEANT??, and a maroon cap.

"Awww, don't you look smart?" No, I fucking didn't. I looked like someone who will get the shit beaten out of them. I never made it as far as the school gate before my cap had been nicked and chucked around the bus, then trodden into the ground as people got off.

I learned later that this was in no way personal – they did it to all the new boys. And the girls' straw boaters, actually which went Frisbeeing wildly up and down the bus.

At first, I travelled into Newquay on a school bus from Summercourt as our house still wasn't ready and I couldn't go in the car because it was too early. So, there I was, on my way to Grammar School, blazer shouting the fact, and so it began. I wasn't used to it – I'd been pretty much like everyone else (Herod aside – that flame was just simmering) and now here I was, gold piping shouting *"NO LONGER ONE OF US......."* I didn't even know I was DOING the eleven fucking plus – they just said do these tests and I thought it was just routine. I don't think mum and dad knew either; I'm not sure they cared either way about it – they had far more pressing concerns – how to stop their daughters getting pregnant for one. The Summercourt – Newquay trips didn't last very long and we finally moved into our new house. Right the other side of town. Great. At least though I could blend in – we all looked like twats, and we all got bullied so that was alright. It was *de rigeur*; the older boys (what 12? 13?) were supposed to be shits to the Sprogs as we were so lovingly known, and I in my turn was equally vile to those who came after, although not with quite so much relish. I could remember how crap it felt – I know it wasn't malice, in most cases anyway, but is bullying ever 'harmless fun'? It wasn't exactly Eton or Harrow; we weren't flogged or made to be fags (?!) it was just constant harrying, cap – nicking, pushing…..

Official School Photo. Aged 11.

I think it might have been a bit more intense for me, as I KNOW, looking back that, I, to quote Geoffrey Willans, did tend to *"sa Hullo clouds hullo sky hullo sun, and skip about like gurl"* I knew I wasn't like the others. I wasn't rough or loud and was quite clever (this led to agonising decisions about whether to answer in class or not – choose Sir's approval, or risk the jeering in the playground?) and this marked me out. Nothing overt: barging was a favourite – why not barge into Bray rather than walk through the massive space next to him? My days were spent avoiding the 2nd years, who in turn avoided the 3rd years. There were no gangs, nothing serious, just mosquito stuff.

P.E. was, as I'm sure many readers will sympathise, the worst of times. It was the time when I was most exposed, most skinny and most shit, apart maybe for maths, but that drama, the red marks and crossings-through was in secret and in my books and therefore not mockable. This was the time when my failings were most obvious. And as such provided a hierarchy for the playground and the future, marking me out. I didn't hate P.E., per se – it was quite fun. We had those big fat ropes, tied up to the walls during normal class times, but two sets hung vertically during P.E. They had big knots on the end which really hurt if someone swung one into you.....actually, come to think of it...bastards....

Those 'balance benches', worn and flaking, with the hooks underneath, for jumping over, walking along, balancing on...hardly Olympic training, but I could DO it without looking like a prick. I could 'vault' over the musty old leather horse ('vault' being a loose term for it!); do somersaults both forwards and backwards; climb the wall bars; cartwheel more or less in a straight line, big shorts flapping.....I did what I was asked. I watched both in awe (I wanted to do that) and boredom (why would you want to do that? The rope was all hairy and burned your thighs and it was bleddy hard work) as the bigger boys climbed the ropes to the top and down again, hung upside down from the wall bars, flew over the horse without catching their legs and going ass over tit – I watched all of that from the safety of the *"He won't ask me to demonstrate as I'm obviously too crap"* corner. And he never did. Am I grateful? Relieved? Disappointed? I know of teachers who would have done just that – humiliation for a laugh, and boys with broken hearts and a lifelong shame of the unsuitability of their bodies.

(Bizarre to recount though – later on that year I somehow found myself in 'Gym Club', where we met for an hour after school one day and did somersaults on those awful green mats, the kind with the honeycomb rubber backs which were really scratchy and shit at breaking your fall, and threw ourselves with wild abandon over the old suede topped vaulting horse, safely into the arms of Sir.....hmmmm. Not sure; no recollection of anything pervy but could've been. No, the point of this digression is to say that that after Gym Club, a couple of us found ourselves being 'volunteered' to put the equipment away in the cupboard in the corner of the hall. This was a bit shit at first – we'd ALL benefitted from the equipment, such as it was, so why do I have to be the one…..but we found that after all the rest had gone home that I could get my scrawny little arm through the wire mesh of the stock cupboard at the back of the cupboard in which, just within reach, was all the stuff left over from school camp and was able to get my hand into the box of Cadburys fruit and nut. RESULT!! We loved Gym Club and went every week…….)

Not much of note happened for a while. We worked hard, and I found areas which compensated for my skinny legs and weak arms; I was excellent at English and it was this that saved me I think in those early Big School years. As much as I grudgingly respected the boys shimmying up those hairy ropes, they noted that it was ME who knew what a past participle was, ME who knew how to parse a sentence, ME who knew what an adverbial clause was….not realising that none of that mattered in real life, only in the chalk scented arena of the classroom did it become currency. It was where I was most rich. And I traded my wealth – I did people's homework sometimes and they left me alone. They got wall bars, I got pentameters.

When, as 2nd Years, we were shitty to the Sprogs, we discovered that stamping on an ink cartridge near a group of girls could spray a multitude of white knee length sock at the same time. (Girls, of the year of '69, if you're reading this: I apologise. NOT doing it was a more difficult option; needing to belong was the driver. But I AM sorry…) Another wheeze was when you dropped your school bag off the balcony on to the head of the boy (usually, sometimes a girl, and me, often. 'Belonging' was sometimes expensive.) who had been made to stand under the hall clock during play and / or lunchtimes. If you got the backward swing right, the bag would land squarely on the upper portion of the body who was a) not expecting it and b) unable to do anything about it as you had to keep your hands behind your back. Funny, I suppose. If it wasn't YOU under the clock.

Once, we locked the History teacher in the map cupboard. Well not actually ME, but I was in the class. It was an old school, 1888, and full of walk-in cupboards. He went in to find a wall map, they shut the door and locked it. And we just sat there. A bit longer, until it dawned on us that we're now in deep shit and had no idea how to react. Eventually, the boy unlocked the door and raced back to his seat, Sir came out and said, *"Sorry class, we'll have to manage without the map. I couldn't find it."* I don't know to this day if he knew or not. It was probably the line of least resistance….

Another time, the rest of my class thought it "would be a laugh" (for that, read *'Do it, or else you're a poof'*) if a girl and I hid in the cupboard during a supply teacher's lesson. We climbed in and sat on the top shelf, intending to come out before she came but she arrived early and we were stuck. Worse, she kept coming in to the cupboard, looking for things as she didn't know where anything was. All we could see from our top shelf, from behind our held – up knees, was her hand and arm groping around for chalk, paper, pens.....praying she would look no higher. Who knows if she knew? Probably, but as she wouldn't be back, thought it would have been more trouble that it was worth. The result was we were in there for an HOUR, squeezed up on a hard wooden shelf, in total darkness and in silence. Nice one, rest of 2A1 – it wasn't YOU that got cramp, arse ache etc. Still, massive set of Brownie points, to use in the future.

Assembly was great fun. It went like this:

Two people, usually lofty third years and chosen termly (for Fucks SAKE! It was only pushing a lectern! It wasn't a Nobel Peace Prize, or the death mask of Tutankhamun!) had to fetch the lectern after we'd all filed in and stood in straight quiet lines. Then there was a crash as the doors blammed back against the walls as they hurtled in with it through the swing doors, screeching to a halt at the foot of the stairs which led up to the balcony and half way up which, where the stairs turned, was the Grey Door. The Head's Office. After silence had resumed, she'd come out and walk slowly down the stairs; all you could hear (and I still can) was the swish of her black gown as she descended to come to rest at the lectern. It happened the same way, every single time. Now, if you were in the third row, that is, behind the row of first years, the lowly sprogs, it was at this point, when her gaze was somewhere else in the hall, that you kneed the backs of the knees of the boy in front, who would involuntarily bob down. If you were lucky, he would be SO uncoordinated, his knees would hit the knees of the boy in front of him and HE would go down too. The best result was a 'doubler' and we always tried for the Big One. This risked being caught of course but it was hard to tell, from the rows of serene faces, whose fault it was. If you WERE caught, not quick enough to regain your own posture and the air of *"Woddn me Miss"*, you'd be under The Clock, where the very 'mates' who had had part in the crime, then dropped their fucking bags on your head. Only for a laugh, obviously.

At some point during this time, the old Luvvie bug started to itch again; we had proper music lessons, where we sang a lot, mostly badly, but at least it wasn't Maths....it must have been my second year (as we moved to a new school in '67) that I got cast in the school play! YES! Proper actin and stuff. We did a bit from *'A Midsummer Night's Dream'*, the Pyramus and Thisbe scene with the wall. This was 45 years ago now and I still remember: *"I kiss the wall's hole, not your lips at all"*. I was mahvellous, dahling, MAHVELLOUS, even more fabulous than Herod, dressed resplendently in me Nan's wig and green bouclé.....and it was done on the Hallowed Steps, from whence the High Priestess Jeffreys descended each morning for assembly. It was probably complete shite (did I do falsetto? God, I hope not...) but there it was again....the spark for performance, lit and burning bright.

All this time, actually since before now, I had developed this wonderful hobby: I collected and assiduously wrote into notebooks, the lyrics of every song you have ever heard! From the Charts, the shows, films and everywhere and when we went out in the car, I took these books (which, for FUCK'S SAKE I still have!) with me......looking back now, my parents did have enormous patience, or selective hearing, because what happened was I'd be in the back seat with my books (there were FOUR, full from cover to cover!) and I'd yell, "NUMBER!!!" and they'd say "26" or whatever and...yes, I'd sing the chosen song, right through, all the verses, loudly and, I might say, rather magnificently. It must have been bloody awful for them – tuneless and bellowing from the back seat in a wobbly soprano (bollocks were dropping), remembering my Glory Days in Summercourt choir...on and on, song after bloody song. It must have been insufferable, but it was me, the Golden Boy, and I did what I liked.

So, our school was due to move to a new building, brand new and the old building, 1909, was to be vacant. It is now a Primary school, much modernised, but the façade remains, protected status. Our new school was adjoined to an existing secondary school populated by what you would now call chavs.....WE were Grammar School and deserved respect, WE had passed our 11+.......there were walls half way along the corridors, dividing the two schools, schools behind which lurked all manner of thugs and oiks, designed, sometime in the future to be removed and the two schools would become one: Newquay Tretherras; I had left by the time that had happened, but I can imagine what it was like: Fotherington Thomas- Bray *'skipping about like a gurl'* and getting mown down by hordes of unwashed SECONDARY SCHOOL kids. Actually, it was OK, and as far as I understood it, the transition when it happened went as well as could be expected.....

So. Top stream. Go me. My English skills (and associated disciplines of cheating when I could, copying other people's homework and general toadying) ensured that I was in the top stream for the 'Arts'. I languished in the middle sets for Humanities (or Geog. and Istry as they were called in the Olden Days) and nearly always in the bottom for Chemistry (which I hated), Physics (which I hated more and couldn't understand; what the fuck's a Wheatstone Bridge? Who uses one? Not me, that's for sure) and Maths...oh Maths, you labyrinthine beast, you holder of the Dark Arts. Mystified, totally mystified. I could do Sums ok, even quite difficult ones (even by Set 4's standards) but...really: logarithms? Quadratic Equations? Not something I've had much day to day use for. And then, the unkindest cut of all to a young man, sad, alone, desperate, lost......SUMS WITHOUT NUMBERS!! I mean...WTF?? How can you have sums without numbers? You can't add LETTERS, for God's sake! So, Algebra, you Satan, you destroyer of boys.....you won. At that point, any success I WAS having just flew away, along with my confidence, and any desire whatsoever to be involved with numbers again, if I could help it. Ever. (Obviously naïve, but scared and hopeless enough to think such a future would indeed be possible.) Later, I was entered in to CSE Maths, where I scored 8%.

Were my schooldays 'the best days my life'? Well, no, but they were pretty good and I look back fondly. There were hateful things, see above, but also good things, things that fed me, nurtured me and made me point toward what would eventually crystallise into my future. There were certainly people, most dead now, but living on through me in a funny kind of way – the fuel they gave me, the energy, the love of rich things in art and music and literature – these gifts were immeasurable and I have always been grateful.

I got involved in the Drama lessons as soon as it was possible. There, I was safe, successful, myself. No failures, no embarrassments or under-minings. THIS, I could do. Apparently as I discovered much later, THIS was the moment that everyone (except me, that is) decided I was gay; doing Drama (and Cookery; more later) AND Drama Club...IN MY SPARE TIME!!...clearly meant I was a big poof. One time, I was late for Chemistry (stayed a bit to pack up after Drama – not toadying, but staying as long as I possibly could) and as I went into the room, Sir was calling the register. I was always first, being a 'B' and I heard him say; "Where's Bray?" and someone (I know who it was, actually, you little shit) replying, *"Probably in the hall, Sir, flower arranging!"* They all laughed, and I was just trapped, between the doors, exposed and ridiculed. It didn't MATTER that they were joking, that I was their peer, their colleague – they were laughing at me for doing what I loved (I hadn't quite clocked the poofiness of the comment, I thought they were denigrating the dramatic side of my nature.) I think I just swep' in, as if I'd heard nothing, saying *"Sorry I'm late, but I was helping Sir clear up in the hall."* But. The damage was done. If that's what it was, it was my first experience of what is now called 'homophobic bullying', although of course, as I wasn't a Gay, it couldn't be. Could it? People just don't THINK, don't KNOW what damage they do....I'm 57 now, I was 14 then. Go figure.....

As a nascent homo, I think I got off pretty lightly at school during those years. This might be because I lived pretty much in a world of my own, where there weren't any sticks and stones. Apart the incident with Andrew Parsons and Mark Venton, I seemed to lead a charmed or at least, naïve life – there probably was all kinds of stuff going on behind my back, but I was blissfully unaware, just kept right on luvvying, cooking and generally being a dick. The drama lessons were my refuge where I knew I was safe, successful and popular. I didn't care that I couldn't add the valences of hydrogen and helium...*'a valence is denoted using a positive or negative integer used to represent binding capacity. For example, common valences of copper are 1 and 2'*. Who knew? Who gives a toss? Not me. I didn't care about Wheatstone's fucking bridge either, or oxbow lakes.....it all seemed meaningless. I did my homework, got it in on time (also not such a clever move) got sent out of Latin repeatedly and was made to stand in the corridor with alarming frequency. Actually, there was a little bit of kudos in this – people passing thought you must've been irritating / rude / uncooperative to Sir and this was obviously a cool thing. The truth was nearer to just being such a useless twat that I was a hindrance and it was easier if I was sent out.

Amo, amas, amat, amamus, amatus, amant,

Nominative, genitive, dative, accusative, ablative, locative, vocative,

Declension,

Blee, bli, blo, blum, blum, blum... (HAHAAAA. That sounded like BUM!)

That's it: the sum of my Latin education. My heart was very selective – I knew what made it sing, and what made it beat with an ominous thud....the sciences (although as you will later hear, Biology and the little room in the lab was pivotal to me….) were just meaningless. The only thing even remotely enjoyable about Chem. was filling the Bunsen burners with chalk dust – you could scrape the chalk on the edge of the tube and the dust would go inside and then when the gas was turned on there would be an amusing shower of chalk dust which attached itself to your blazer, quite often mine. We would get hit with the rubber tubes that were for the Bunsen burners, whipped with them like dogs by the passing teacher. I also liked staring at Sir – he had floppy browny hair and blue eyes. It was an arresting combination and one I found compelling. Not in a stiffy kind of way, but I liked him; he was handsome and kind, in a world where not much else was. Maths held its own horrors (and I am certain that this, ironically, was what helped to make me a pretty good maths teacher later – I understood, so clearly, the misery engendered by not understanding, the feelings of total inadequacy at just not knowing what to do, when everyone else apparently did – I found it easy to be totally empathetic and consequently the children that passed through my hands were served better because of it. So, thank you, actually, Mr S., you sadistic cunt.)

The years passed. Fell in love once a week. When, I hear you ask, will you get to the sex part. Not yet gentle reader, not yet. Got dumped. Wrote tear stained letters ('Gail L, My heart broke when I saw you with him and knew you didn't love me. Tears poured down my face and I will be alone for ever'. Yes really! What a knob). I don't think I was even wanking…..a late starter. When I was in the third year though, I went on school camp, to Dorset and there, there was a seminal change (pun intended).

Health and safety? I don't think so! We went in a furniture lorry, the kind you could leave the top half of the back open. All the equipment, the food, all the luggage and all of us, all piled in the back of a Pickford's lorry and off we went, hanging out the back waving to weeping parents, as well they might – who knew how many of us will have fallen out before we even cross the Tamar bridge? As it happened, no one did, but they COULD'VE….that's what made it so exciting!! We were away, alone in the world, some of us (me) for the first time ever. We were under tents and had a campfire and everything, just like in the films. It was totally awesome and bit scary, as it began to get dark, but we 'rowed the boat ashore', 'kumbyahed' and 'Ging gang goolied' ourslelves into exhaustion and were happy to go to sleep. It was a completely surreal experience for me – where was my squares of cheese on toast with a sliced pickled onion, for a start? People wouldn't shut up, shouting and punching each other. I hated it and immediately wanted to go home, but of course....to show fear would be inviting trouble ('ha ha, poofy Bray wants his mum') so I did the best I could and hid in my sleeping bag and hoped no one would step, fall or fart on me.

One night however (and this was a seminal moment for me – no pun intended this time - and one that opened many doors and slotted barely recognised jigsaw pieces into place), everyone decided to have a wanking contest. Well, not everyone, as I wasn't really sure what was going on. I don't remember now how many actually got involved but I DO remember with absolute clarity, being invited to look into HD's sleeping bag and to watch. His cock was enormous (it seemed – to a boy whose cock was still a willy) and he was going at it and grunting and then he came, great thick gobs of it in his hand. I, and some of the other boys, stared in astonishment, at the size of his knob which got even bigger at the point of orgasm and at the copious amounts of semen which he then wiped off in the grass. Astonished, because I really think that this was the first time we had seen a proper wank, in all its panting, spurting glory. We KNEW about it, some of us had even had a go but I think we were amazed at the reality of it. *"Look"*, he said, *"it's the same size as my torch."* And it was. And I can see it now as I write, in the dark of that sleeping bag tent, glistening and slick with spunk, as we called it... You see, for me – and who knows who else out of those goggling boys? – this was more than an illicit sex-wee; more than a bit of fun that lads got up to. It was suddenly incredibly important to see that 'event' again, to be able to summon up at will such a wonderful thing. It was the beginnings of desire, of my lifelong love of cock and male bodies, though HD was still technically a boy, he had a man's *thing* and I wanted one, wanted to touch one, make it do that 'thing' again.

One of the few, and there were very few, perks of being force – marched two miles to the rugby pitch, as we didn't have one at the school, was after the match had finished. I'm not sure if you can call a miserable gaggle of skinny boys listlessly running after a ball, being knocked over constantly and trampled into the mud by the big ones or running out of the way if they or the ball came in your direction, a match. Anyhow, we survived the pummelling, the mud and the cold and then had to shower. Any gay man reading this will know the agony and ecstasy of shower time; the longing to go in and see the Big Lads lathering their cock and balls, or, swoon, even Sir, watching them soap between their legs, seeing cocks hanging (and not hanging) in every direction; that longing directly opposed to the fear of being caught looking, of being found wanting – skinny, shrivelled willy, like a fool amongst gods. It was hard to stay out of the shower but it became the way to survive – not being able to find my towel / clothes / shoes until the others had finished then dashing in and dashing out again just in case I missed BR showing everyone his dick – he used to poke it out the leg of his shorts and then get a hard on and walk around the changing room with it swinging or slapping against his leg, depending on the state of erection. I remember this, dear reader, 40 years on. Breathless with desire, burning with envy and understanding neither feeling. It would be interesting to know how many others of us sprogs were feeling just the same things, but hiding, guilty, embarrassed and ashamed. Rugby was to be looked forward to, endured, for that one shining moment when you got to see BR's todger. It was a sad day when he didn't flop it out, or wave it around, which sometimes happened. Muddy, bruised and todgerless, bereft of our thrill of seeing BR's dick, we then traipsed back to school. Not much reward for the bruises and the mud.

That digression was a brief time shift, but only to illustrate that BH's dick had set up an unstoppable motion in me, towards what I knew not, until that night in our school camp tent, full of beans, sausage farts and semen. Something massive had changed, but it lay dormant for some time to come. A day or two after that, I was handed the most precious gift – I got to hold HTs cock! Oh yes! For one glorious second, I held my breath and held his dick. There it lay, in my hand, dark brown, broad and silken, hooded, before he took it away and resumed activities.....

......we had decided, HT and I, to walk down into Swanage, on our afternoon off – it was a bit like going to Hogsmeade but without the butter beer. Anyway, we were walking along the road when H. suddenly said, *"I need to pee,"* and went into the field. *"Come on."* So I followed him (I couldn't not; it was like I was attached) and there he was, cock out, having a piss. So far so normal. (ish) Then he said, *"Do you want me to teach you to wank?"* His dick was sticking up now in the way that only a 14 year olds can, thick and...oh, so inviting. *"You can hold it,"* he said and so I did, with no hesitation and there it was, for the first time, an enormous (remember I only had 14 year old eyes and probably everything seemed bigger that it really was) penis was in my hand. Someone else's admittedly, but a penis, nonetheless...... I didn't know what to do then, and that's the truth. I just stood there, like I'd been given a gerbil or a kitten, motionless while its heart beat in my palm. I don't know what he intended but he soon said, *"Oh give it here. This is what you do,"* and he began masturbating. It didn't last long, I don't think and there it was again – glistening, slippery, gobs of semen. Miraculous. He wiped it off on some dock leaves, put it back in his pants and just went off back to the road. I joined him, aware of a throbbing in my groin, and I do think, looking back, this was my first erection borne of proper desire, proper sexual feelings. But it was a strange thing – we were back on the road, walking down to the village as if nothing had happened; some weird X File thing where time had stood still, stuff occurred and then you were back where you'd been, without a pause. He never spoke of it again.

The next night (or the same night, I don't remember now – I was in such a heightened sexual state, it could have been anytime) the wankers were at it again, and I had a go! I had a hard on, I knew how to hold it (although I have actually developed my own style over the years.....H.T's grip wasn't for everyone! He held his with a kind of...well, never mind.), and I joined in with gusto. I don't remember whether there was an 'ending' – I suspect not – but I did get to see H. do his stuff again – and I was the only one he let watch him shoot this time. Now, what did THAT mean?

Whether or not the nocturnal emissions continued throughout the whole camp, I cannot say as I was sent home, in disgrace on day 3. What happened was, GR and I went into Swanage, a little seaside town in Dorset, about an hour's walk from camp (past the wank field, with its secret, jizz covered dock leaves) as it was free time again. We walked around a bit and then saw a newsagent with a couple of those wire carousel things outside, for holding paperback books. We went in and bought something, a, drink probably, and then on the way out, paused to look at the books. RUGBY SONGS! MORE RUGBY SONGS!. EVEN MORE RUGBY SONGS!, each book fronted by a bint with massive boobs and frilly knickers or some such 'enticement'. It wasn't the boobs that enticed me, but the thought that if I could take these back to the camp, I would be so fuckin cool, so hard, that I would be popular forever. As we didn't have any money, we decided to nick them. Genius! GR went back into the shop to 'distract' the shopkeeper (what his plan was we never really clarified) while I stuffed all three books up my jumper, where they didn't show. At all. Then I started walking nonchalantly away. I may even have been whistling in an insouciant manner, waiting for GR to catch up, and we'd walk back to camp and say "Look what we got. Songs with swearing in. PROPER swearing. *'Twas on the good ship Venus, by God you should've seen us! The figurehead was a girl in bed, sucking the captain's penis'!* How rude! How thrilling! 'I *MIGHT* let you have a look. Stand back, you varlet, until I invite you..." or something grand, thus demonstrating my control of the whole, eager camp population.

What actually happened wasn't quite so good: the next thing I heard was fast – approaching footsteps (GR's) and slower ones and a voice shouting: "COME BACK HERE YOU LITTLE BASTARDS, I'LL FUCKIN SKIN YOU ALIVE….." or some such thing – the words got scrambled by the rush of pure adrenalin that surged through my body when I heard them. We'd been betrayed, probably by that old cunt who had been staring at me by the books and then went in the shop….he was chasing us, and closing. I just dropped all the books, saying, *"Here, have them back! It was only a joke!"* when GR said, *"QUICK, DOWN HERE! DOWN THIS ALLEY…!"* So we veered left, down the alley. Into a *cul de sac*. With a Police Station at the end. Fuck. Mr Shopkeeper was gaining on us now and then a copper came out of the station, saw what was happening and just said: *"Chase them in here and leave it to me."* FUCK! Fucketty FUCK! Not so 'Mr. Lucky' at this point.

We were taken inside, snotty and snivelling; well, I was, anyway. You know what, I don't actually have any memory of GR being there at this point. Maybe he'd escaped? Anyway, I was scared, *REAL* scared – all my terrors of that earlier time came roaring back, fangs bared to sink into my heart. There were 2, I don't know now, 3 policemen there, all in their terrifying black uniforms. The worst thing was that nobody said anything to me. I was put on a chair, crying and shaking, covered in snot and fear. After what seemed like hours, the copper came over and said, *"Stand up."* I did. And then I pissed myself. I was 14, and I pissed myself. Hot, like my face, I felt it filling my pants, then in the trousers legs and down, down where I knew it was going to make a pool which was going to make things worse. I just wanted to die, to be spirited away – I had no idea of the consequences, what would happen and I knew of course, unlike the fucking church windows, I HAD done this. What would happen? I didn't know. I was numb with fear and wet with my own piss.

The rest of that afternoon passed in a blur and I can't recount it – I don't remember. Maybe I had to mop up the piss? I don't know. I DO know that Mr. D came down form the campsite and spoke to the police and then we (so GR MUST have been there) were taken out to his car and driven back to camp. When we arrived, covered in shame, me in pants still damp with my own piss, we were told to pack. One of the teachers, who had only been there for a few days was due to go back to Newquay that day and he was told to take us back home to our parents. It was at this point I KNEW what was to happen. My mind just shut down and G and I got into the car, everyone staring – and I looked at them and thought 'why did I want to impress THEM? Just a bunch of wankers……..' and I hated them for no reason – they couldn't defend me, protect me or change the outcome. The car doors closed and we drove back to Cornwall in silence.

When we got home, my terror was absolute. Sir rang the bell and my dad came to the door, smiled, and they spoke politely together, as if they were old friends. Neither glanced in my direction; I briefly wondered what was happening to GR who had been dropped off first but in reality, I was too full of fear to really think about anything other than what was about to happen. I was summoned and I got out of the car. Dad stood to one side, not a word was spoken and I waited in the hall. The door closed; the fear increased. *"In the kitchen. Now,"* he said and there was my Mum, standing at the sink, sobbing. I had never seen her cry. It was the most painful thing I could ever have imagined and I HAD CAUSED IT. My feeling of self-loathing engulfed me and I opened my mouth to speak, but she said, *"Don't. Don't say anything."* My dad was standing there and by this time had his belt wound round his hand, with the buckle end hanging loose. Silence. Beating heart; mine. Sobbing; Mum. Heavy breathing; Dad. Then mum said: *"Don't Trevor. Please. Don't."* The silence stretched out to eternity, me standing there in my dried-piss trousers, my badge of shame, he breathing hard barely able to contain his fury, his shame, his embarrassment, she standing by the sink, in her apron, gasping for breath……

"You've already beaten my daughter to a bloody pulp. I am asking you, Trevor, not to do the same to my son".

The silence was the biggest silence in the world, punctuated by his panting, her sobbing.

He walked across to me and with is face right next to mine, his temples bulging with unexpressed rage and said: *"If you ever, EVER bring shame to my door again, I will kill you."* And he turned, threw the belt to the floor and left the room.

I don't know what happened after that. I'm assuming I went to my room, and stayed there for months……ignored, ashamed. I know now what it was about – the same fury when the police came about the broken windows was ignited when 'authority' had come to his door. It should have been about my Mother's pain but it wasn't. It was about HIM. Always, about him. Darkness in his soul.

On a lighter note, my life wasn't all doom and gloom and shouty dads! No! Things at school were Looking Up. School play time Ta DAH!! It wasn't quite *ME SIR ME SIR PICK ME SIR PLEASE SIR,* although I DID employ my stealthy superpower of subliminal persuasion to make him stop at me when he went along the line announcing who'd got a part. And it worked! It had been decided to DO Shakespeare, with my beloved Miss H directing and......

......anyway, there we were, on a Casting Call (well, lined up in the hall) for announcements for parts in *'A Winter's Tale'*. I was cast as Florizel, a rather fey young thing, in love with Perdita. I remember skipping around a lot, in some old sack thing, representing sheperdism but it was probably a bit pants. Although.....I had a legitimate excuse to say *" hullo clouds, hullo sky!"* and skip about like a gurl.

The following year, we did Macbeth, again directed by Her Maj. This time I got cast (I always did now, and NOT, I'd like to think, because there so few boys interested. It was for my immense thespianism...) as Donalbain. (NB: when I told my Mum, she said she'd never heard of Donald Bain and that it didn't sound a very 'Shakespeare name'. THIS, from the woman who shouted at the crossword compiler that that there was no such word as SCRAPIRON. Scrap Iron, Mother, Scrap Iron. She also wanted to know, when I played her Simon and Garfunkel's *'The Boxer'*, why there 'was a horse on 7th Avenue'....Honestly......).

Anyway, I got to say *"Thou liest, abhorred tyrant; with my sword I'll prove the lie thou speak'st!.* (SPEAK'ST!! How professional and Shakespeary!) and a few other things, and I had a great big sword! No matter that the photograph shows wrinkly knees in my tights and that I'd had to colour in the scuffed bits on my plimsolls with black felt tip....none of it mattered! I was Donalbain and fled to Ireland AND I was YOUNG SIWARD and that Macbeth had better bleddy watch out. Oh, yes......arrghhh I get murdered. But! Ten lines, ten glorious lines. No matter I had to wait about four hours in between (practising, practising...*Thou liest...! Thou **LIEST**......*backstage, where Miss H. as it turns out was in the changing rooms drinking gin.) I HAD TEN LINES. That's ten more than the twat in the Chem lab had.....

"Thou liest, abhorred tyrant; with my sword I'll prove the lie thou speak'st!"

We did a circus too, as end of year show, this time I was 'CREW', natch. Up in the balcony, in charge of lights. All these little things, not that I yet knew so, were forming me, creating me. I was far away yet from acknowledging that I was suited to the Theatre, in more ways than one, but I knew I loved it, that it was what made me whole.

At Drama club, I was introduced to Pinter (not literally obviously. Can you imagine: *"Hello Sir Pinter. I'm Nigel"*. Four minutes of silence….ha ha) in short sketches I did with my besty, Liz. Then I moved into the rarefied world of opera…OK not opera exactly, more operetta. And also I didn't sing. At all. Not even in the chorus, but I was a page to one of the Kings wot brought gifts to Baby Jesus. It was *'Amahl and the Night Visitors'*. Pretty well done actually for a school production.

P. and E. Two letters to strike dread in the hearts of most boys like me. You will of course have read in other memoirs, about the shame, the embarrassment and finally the sighing acceptance of always being picked last for the football teams. There we stand, the line diminishing, along with my hopes, as the burly boys, the ones with muscles, B.O. and bum fluff get picked, one by one…..the line and the masculinity of the population of it gets smaller and smaller until I once more hear the words; *"We'll have Bray then."* And *"You twat, if you'd picked heads, we would have had first choice and not ended up with him, although the other one's just as shit.....blah blah blah."* No wonder my kit kept getting eaten by the dogs / stolen by big boys on the bus / shrunk in the wash. Unfortunately, there was always a 'spares' box so we, the few, the pathetic few, ended up in someone else's skanky old socks and shorts with only ninety minutes of boredom, cold, abuse and showers to look forward to.

There was one time, and this like all the other moments of shame so far described, has seared itself into my memory as the ultimate disappointment, the one chance at redemption that, once more, passed me by. We were in a match, in most of which I had managed to avoid any participation whatsoever; I tried my best to appear wraith - like at the edge of the pitch, unseen and uninvolved, when suddenly! Fuck me! There was the ball!! Right at my feet. Dribble. DRIBBLE, that's what to do (apparently) so off I went.....dribbling! Not very well as the ball kept going faster than me. However, I could hear the cheering, and shouting and I must have looked really fierce as the others were falling back, terrified of my skills obviously and then, sweet Jesus! There was the goal! I drew back my foot as the cheers got louder and BLAM! There it was, in the back of the net – the goalie didn't stand a chance! It was in the silence that followed that I computed that the cheering was in fact shouting. It was many years ago now, but I suspect it was along the lines off NO YOU IDIOT!!! WRONG FUCKING WAY!!! STOP! STOP! YOU STUPID CUNT!! Etc. Yes, dear reader, it was our goal; the boys weren't actually terrified, they were letting me past.....my one and only chance at glory. Own goal. You can imagine how popular I was – not only did the captain have to pick me, I had just lost the match for them. This was my one and only foray into The Glorious Game. If ever I WAS picked to play, everyone made sure that the ball was NEVER passed to me. Ever. Suited me just fine.

In the sixth form (apart from the chance to see increasingly hairy cocks, even Sir's, in the showers) the PE options changed and I opted like there was no tomorrow. I became the world's most prolific opter. ANYTHING that didn't involve fields and mud and getting hurt was good for me. And so I discovered that I was in fact a pretty good swimmer. I had always swum, right from those early beach days and now, living in on the coast, summers were spent more in the sea than on land. So, when the two schools amalgamated, we had use of a swimming pool in which, time and time again, I proved myself to be very fast, very competitive and gained some grudging respect from my peers. I also discovered I had a particular skill as a diver. I also became something of a gymnast (and got to see the other older boys, and Sir in tight white gymnastic trousers. Adding, adding.) Flick flacks, back sommies.....I could do it all. There was also a trampoline and, believe it or not, I became school champeen! So you, see, there's a place for us all. The Neanderthals could have their ball and field, I had my pool and my pommel horse. So fuck you, and shame on you for making me (and so, so many others) feel worthless. Go on – get *YOUR* fat arse over the horse! Ha! Do a back layout and a barani. You can't, can you, so fuck off.

CHAPTER FOUR.

A NEWQUAY LAD.

Where our hero becomes a facilitator, and gets humiliated.

'In The Summertime'.

by Mungo Jerry. No4. July 1970.

*'In the summertime, when the weather is fine,
You can stretch right up and touch the sky…'*

Ah, sunlit days, though it was not as bright as it seemed.

~ ~ ~

Outside of school, things were good. I lived in a wonderful place; beaches, the harbour, the river. Very Tom Sawyer. We were always near the water in some way – on it or in it and school holidays, right from age eleven, when we moved there, passed in much the same way. Sun soaked and salt caked, golden summer children. Things were OK at home. The shop seemed to be doing OK, although things were a bit tougher in the winter as it was only open for the summer months. But we sold enough shit to people to feed us through those cold months.

We had neighbours who had a son, a bit younger than me, JJ, and he was pretty much my constant companion for the years between 13 and maybe 15. This small story that I am about to tell you is significant, though it may not seem so, but I realise, tracing the course of my journey to Homodom, it was the first proactive thing I did and it was kind of tacit admission, though at the time I never thought of it as such.

There is a cave on Towan beach, not very big but not usually reachable when the tide is up.

There, down there, on the right.....

One morning, down on the beach as usual, we went in and we were sitting on some rocks and talking. I said to J, *"Do you know where babies come from?"* This was the early 70s, remember and sex ed. wasn't very high up the school curriculum, though of course we all had our own theories. Anyway, he replied, *"You have to give her a biscuit, with some stuff on it."* Dear JJ. This was one I hadn't heard, but being the elder and therefore much wiser, I said, *"No, she has to have some spunk juice."* Ah, teenagers, eh? So he said, *"Where does that come from then?"* And, dear reader, I showed him! I got my cock out (which, by this time, was no longer a willy) and it was hard! I told him to get his out and that I'd show him (debt of gratitude HT) and said, *"This is what you do."* I began to rub it, mine I mean, and he did the same, although as I recall he didn't have very much to play with. Anyway, quite quickly, I came – I really think this was my first proper load, in a cave, on Towan beach, people! *"Do you put that on the biscuit, then?"* JJ asked........no, that's what happens after rugby matches but I didn't know that then. *"No, JJ,"* I said, being older and wiser, *"You have to put your thing INSIDE her then this comes out and you get a baby."* Shocked is the word I'd use to describe his look. And a teeny bit disgusted. We both put them away, my cock and his willy, and never mentioned it again. Clearly, he got over his disgust – he is long married and childrened up to the eyeballs.

I mention this incident for two reasons: one, I initiated a sexual act with another male (kind of) and two, I had my first proper orgasm, which I liked a lot and decided from then on I was going to try to have as many of them as possible, either by myself (I had played with myself, hard, but nothing more than a dribble had occurred. At some point, the manufacturing plant had opened so by the time we got to the cave, I was fully operational) or with others. I would definitely play well with others. It was a significant moment, where I crossed over from a passive starer and wisher, to an active wanker. Thank you JJ. Though you never knew it, you were a major contributor to my career.

Next door also had a dog, called Timmy. I tied to bum him once. I held on to his tail and tried to insert what was by this time, having been awakened like some dragon in that cave, my somewhat rampant penis into his asshole. I got just the tip in before he broke free of my grasp, leaving me kneeling, pants down, on the floor dolefully calling, *"Timmy! Timmy come back..."* but he didn't. He buggered off over the wall. He was somewhat cooler , towards me, less eager to be petted, after this. I guess I was lucky he didn't chew my face off....

Around this time, as I was actually quite a social lad, I joined the local ATC. It did provide some companionship PLUS a uniform, but I didn't stay that long. I got tired of being shouted at. Why couldn't they just say *'Fall In!'* in a normal way instead of bellowing all the time?

Two things worth reporting though. One, due to my swimming prowess, I was chosen to represent 781 Squadron in a National diving contest! We travelled off to RAF Lyneham where we stayed for a couple of days, to go the event. I came second. My fault. I was leading, until my last dive, which was supposed to be a plain header, piked position (hardly Greg Louganis, I know, but HE must have started somewhere, and anyway, I was the best we had) but as I took off, up graceful as you like, a nymph in flight, I forgot what the dive was, thought it must be 'tucked', then, plummeting towards the water, remembered it was 'piked', didn't have time to recover and entered the water in the 'bomb' position, also drenching the officials poolside. Simple mistake, but it cost me the competition and Graham Strawberry (see how my shamings live in my head?) went on to win.

The other, less successful, anecdote concerns a visit to anther camp, RAF Scampton in Lincolnshire. I have no memory of why we went – it was a hell of a long way so it must have been important. Maybe it was an annual meet of the South West squadrons? No idea, but there were HUNDREDS of us there. I don't remember much about this event, but the incident that lives on in my House of Mental Horrors concerns the parade square and drill practice.

Early morning of the first day. Up, dressed, ready for....I had no idea. I didn't even know why I was there....

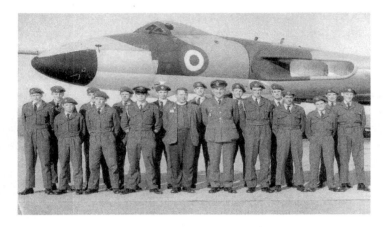

781 Squadron (Newquay). Front, 2nd from right.

I quite liked this drill thing; the orderliness, the precision – wasn't too keen on all the yelling, mind, but that seemed obligatory and as long as you did what you were told you were left alone. On this occasion, we were on parade, as I said, hundreds of us, on a massive parade square. All was going well. Then the Drill Sergeant yelled:

"SQUAAAAAD...........TURN.........RIGHT!!!!"

And several hundred boys all turned right, with a stamping of feet. Except me, who turned left. Just me, in a sea of right – facing boys, facing left and staring, horror struck directly into the face of the boy who had turned the right way. It must have been like a synchronised swimmer sinking, or a Red Arrow (who's base this was) sending out green smoke instead of blue. He noticed. About four million boys held their breath as Sergeant Shouty Bastard walked slowly towards the mass. He reached the outer row, took his baton from under his arm, levelled it straight at me and said, quietly to my amazement (maybe he was going to be nice and whisper, *"You turned the wrong way, sonny"*)

"You. Here.

Now!!!"

I threaded my way between the ranks, all my old demons descending, the police, my father, the succession of unimpressed PE teachers – here they all were, crowding round, rubbing their phantom hands with glee – until I stood before him. A small, grey clad boy, praying he wouldn't piss himself, like last time, the entire massed ranks of my 'colleagues' waiting in silence to see what would happen, a thousand eyeballs all swivelled as far round in their eye sockets as they would go without them having to move their heads. He leant in, like my Dad did, the day he said he'd kill me, and breathed: *"You turned the wrong way."* Quietly, almost secretively. Any hope of escape was fading fast now. Then he yelled: *"Six times round the square. On the double."* The final nail was when he bellowed: *"That means running. Go."* And then he screamed *"NOW!!!"* in my face; I was blown back by his breath and his malice and just turned and began running. *"NO! THE OTHER WAY!!"* What fucking difference did it make? I set off again, passing the massed ranks of the other cadets, who had been standing motionless while this went on, but with grateful eyes following me as I passed them on my first lap. After they were back drilling, while I, stupidly, in panic, had started off far too fast to be able to sustain the distance, got slower and slower, eventually grinding to a teary panting stop. I don't remember how this ended. Whether he made me finish, or he let me go or the drill finished I don't recall, What I DO remember is the burning shame, the embarrassment and the feeling of pure hatred I felt for that man. He could have just told me to turn round, to let it pass. We were boys, a little kindness, a little understanding of the fact I hadn't MEANT to turn the wrong way and that it DIDN'T REALLY MATTER, DID IT? There I was again, back in assembly, being beaten for trying too hard. Scars, scars. They heal, but never fade.

I left the organisation shortly after that (too much shouting) because I was developing other interests and they were more pleasing to me. I discovered that RT, who live in the next road along, liked having his cock sucked. So we used to go out in the evening and break into the bakers, next door to the ATC hut and I'd suck him off amongst the flour sacks. This wasn't every evening – what do you take me for??   - because things were gearing up in school, homework was increasing and exams were getting near.

By now we were in O Level territory (remember them? They were the things before the last 193 Education ministers fannied around with the curricula), and things were getting serious. Unfortunately, Phys. Chem. and Biog. were compulsory, as were French, and English. I did my Eng. Lang. a year early, and passed, grade 3! Go me! I did Eng. Lang. (Modern Authors) and dear God, was it boring. If anyone asks you to read Edmund Gosse's *'Father and Son'*, don't. You'll be mummified before you reach the end. And as for Jane Austen's *'Emma'*. Who reads this stuff? Actually, in hindsight, it was probably SO badly taught, I was forever put off Austen and her bloody ilk. I cannot to this day, watch anything that involves a bonnet or a heaving bosom. For fuck's sake you lot! Just say what you mean! Get a room!

But there were choices too, and I chose......COOKERY!! Oh yes. I couldn't decide whether I wanted to be a famous actor or a famous chef so I thought I'd better hedge my bets. Actually, I was the first boy in the history of Newquay School to do O Level Cookery (or 'Domestic Science' as it was loftily known). Phuuleese. It consisted mostly of Mrs J reading from some text book, sitting behind her desk, trying not to fall asleep while we just wrote down everything she said. Actually, that's not true - we just fucked about, passing notes, doodling etc. She never asked to see our books – which was just as well! Acres of empty pages....

Anyway, exams came and went, results came and went and I did as well as expected. Bit of a result in French – CSE Grade 1 which was accepted to be an O level pass so that was one more in the bag. Mum and Dad were pleased (they bought me a Malibu board, which was so huge it wouldn't fit under my arm. Instead of being a DUDE, strolling down the beach to Hang Ten with the others, I was a KNOB. They were all in the surf by the time I got there because I had to fucking DRAG my board by its fin through the sand. Why is it that I always ended up looking like a twat?), I was pleased, some teachers were pleased (as I validated their teaching), others didn't give a shit. After O Levels, I was able to NEVER EVER have to go into the labs for Phys. Chem. or Bio. again (well, the Bio lab, just once more....). Nor did I have to go to the Slough of Despond, to be diminished and crushed by inadequacy, to do quadratic equations, logarithms or algebra again. You know - all those things that would have been oh so useful in later life. Not.

I was free!! FREE!

I entered Sixth form, heading towards A. levels, full of hope and flushed with success.

CHAPTER FIVE.

SIXTH FORM.

<u>Where it becomes clear to our hero that the worlds of Fine Dining and football are not where he should be, but in the Groves of Academe. And in people's pants.</u>

'Children of the Revolution'.

by T.Rex. No2. September 1972.

*'Well, you can bump and grind, it is good for your mind
Well, you can twist and shout, let it all hang out*

But you won't fool the children of the revolution...'

The man in the women's shoes and me – we were as one, it seems.

~ ~ ~

Here is wot is chose: English. Cookery. That's it. And we had P.E. for 'our health', but more of that later.

This is where it started to get serious. Maintaining a place in top set English was going to be harder, especially as this meant we had...MISS H. She was exceedingly scary, one of those teachers who (in me at least) inspired fear and love, in equal measure, and a fierce will to do well in her class. She was about 107 years old and was the scariest woman ever. But she taught Top Class English and, apart from being a luvvie, that was the only thing I was really good at and so that's where I found myself. It was a funny thing – we'd all be out in the corridor, talking, laughing, giving each other dead legs and love bites (to ourselves – it was important to have a hickey, even though everyone KNEW you'd done it as it was on your bicep)... and then... a rustle, an approaching force... and she'd materialise, with her cloak billowing and with her grey hair coiffured like a steel helmet of an avenging goddess on a smiting mission. We'd fall silent, eyes downcast in case we were singled out for anything (which we all secretly longed to be of course) until she'd swep' into the room. We'd all file in, stand patiently at our desks waiting for her to say *"Good Morning Class. Won't you sit down?"* and we'd all mutter, *"Good Morning Miss H.......*" and plonk gratefully to study.

We did 'Shakespeare, Chaucer and Classic Lit.' with her and I. Loved. It. I will always be grateful for what she instilled in me. I used to spend the week waiting for Double English – we'd have to read out loud in class, chunks of unprepared Bardy bits, stumbling and blushing, but always encouraged, gently corrected. My love of Shakespeare, without a doubt, came from her. And when she read Chaucer aloud in OLDE ENGLYSHE......fuck! It was the most amazing thing EVER.

'Whan that Aprill, with his shoures soote

The droghte of March hath perced to the roote

And bathed every veyne in swich licour,

Of which vertu engendred is the flour;

Whan Zephirus eek with his sweete breeth

Inspired hath in every holt and heeth

The tendre croppes, and the yonge sonne

Hath in the Ram his halfe cours yronne,

And smale foweles maken melodye,

That slepen al the nyght with open eye-

(So priketh hem Nature in hir corages);

Thanne longen folk to goon on pilgrimages

And palmeres for to seken straunge strondes

To ferne halwes, kowthe in sondry londes;

And specially from every shires ende

Of Engelond, to Caunterbury they wende,

The hooly blisful martir for to seke

That hem hath holpen, whan that they were seeke.....

(Geoffrey Chaucer, from 'The Prologue', The Canterbury Tales)

It was alchemy, it was the deepest mystery, and I adored the sound of it and adored her for making us do it. She's dead now, but she lives on, you see, in me, and hopefully some of the others in Top Set English who devoured her and set her in our hearts and memories. She was the only one who, when she called me *"Bray!"* I didn't mind.....

I'm not really sure what I did in these years. I mean I DO, but how it was ever good enough to spend all week doing TWO subjects, I'm not really sure. We had loads of 'study periods'...how naïvely sweet.... where we were allocated carrels, two in a unit, adjoining, where we were supposed to be doing research and studying our subjects whatever they were. I'm pretty sure the only thing that got studied were genitals and porn mags (I remember seeing one once around about this time, a really hard core Danish one – it seemed to have lots of nooks and fanny crannies, and everything was just really really *pink...).*

These were the days of Monty Python and on a Wednesday, we'd spend most of our 'study periods' re-enacting sketches that we'd memorised from the night before. *"Wake up POLLYYYYY!!"* could be heard emanating from the booths*; "I'd like to start an argument, please"; "Does she GO? Eh? Eh? Nudge nudge, wink wink"; "OOOOOH Hello Mrs Conclusion..."* Ah, all these long years on, I can quote pretty much lines from any sketch – this we did instead of preparing for our golden futures; discussed wanking, fannies, tits and the Gumbies.

OK. I know you're DYING to hear – I've dropped enough hints - about the biology lab technician's room, and I think it's time to spill, so to speak...It was just before the end of our O Level year and, as I've said I was always a bit of a teacher's pet, always offering to help clear up after, and in Bio., I was allowed to 'set things out'. There was a small annexe to the lab where stuff was kept – frogs in jars, scalpels, ammonia – the kind of stuff which was brilliant, but long since banned. I was allowed in before and after the lessons. It did sometimes become a refuge, an escape from the corridors stuffed with hormonal pushing boys and (apart from the Animal house where me and LR used to look after the gerbils – I know, I know – are you getting a picture, here, the way things are heading....?) it was a bit prestigious too. 'Creep!' 'Ass – licker!' and worse, but it didn't matter – it was a good thing to have. Anyway, I was in there once and Mr. G, the lab assistant came in. He was a nice man, was always nice to me anyway, but this day he undid his white lab coat and he had a stiffy! There it was, bulging in his trousers. He just stood there, facing me, staring at me. Lab coat open, legs splayed, as if.....as if what? I didn't know what to do ...I knew what I wanted to do, but in fact didn't do anything, just stared at it, and him (more at it, actually.) Then, he did up his coat and got on with preparing the 'dissection of frogs' lesson, or whatever it was that day, as if nothing out of the ordinary had happened. He never spoke of at all, even though we were alone together quite regularly all that year. After I moved up in to sixth form, we had no need to see each other anymore. I just read that back and I realise I made him sound like a dirty old man – he wasn't; he was about 25 (only seemed ancient, and I was 15). I don't know why it happened, or how – there was a massive risk, I guess. It was, looking back, a very surreal moment.

OK. I'm gathering evidence here, collecting all those clues together......HD shining his torch on his cock; BR letting his stiffy flop around the changing room' HT showing me 'how to wank' and letting me 'hold it'; masturbating with JJ in the cave; Mr G showing off his erection in the Bio. lab......I remember these incidents SO absolutely clearly, with a delicious sense of ownership (they were all pretty much private, 'given' to me especially) and they were, looking back, absolutely pivotal, defining moments. They all seemed to be pointing one way – I was, in fact, a homo! Yes, gentle reader! Surprised? Well, if you'd told ME that, I would have been – because there's no way I could be, silly – I had a girlfriend and everything! I knew the texture of breasts! I had visited The Kingdom of the Jubblies, fiddled in the Fanny Folds......

In her wisdom and pride for her Boy Child, my Mother, for the start of the term, as being in the Sixth Form, we were no longer required to wear the old maroon uniform, bought me a new blazer and new shoes. The shoes, fer fuck's sake, were black PATENT leather and the blazer (Blazer? What was she thinking?) was navy blue barathea, with gold 'sailor' buttons with little anchors on. *"Don't you look nice?"* she said the first morning as I got ready for school. No, I didn't, I looked like a cunt, and a clear target for slapping, name calling and sending up, all of which happened. I began to 'lose' the blazer in various places as soon as I got into school, having run the gauntlet of the walk TO school. Once, the bastards threw me out of the (ground floor) classroom window. As I hit the mud outside, our form teacher was walking past and he gave me the punishment. ME, the ejectee! I had to write an essay on 'why it was foolish to climb out of windows'. Hardly fair, I felt....

We had moved house by now. I no longer saw JJ (or Timmy) or RT – although I did once suck him off in the toilets down on the harbour, but that was later, and just in passing – and I was now a serious student of literature and pastry.

I had joined (and left) The Pasty Club, which was a shame as the pasties were very nice (it was a recruitment thing for the church, in a little hut near where we now lived). All you had to do was turn up, make some things out of paper, read some verses from the bible and then you got a free pasty! Result! It was boring though, and as I said, my extra-curricular activities were becoming more important. Homework, and loins.

By the time we moved into the Upper Sixth, there was, actually, a sense of time beginning to run out, important decisions needing to be made and, I for one wasn't ready for that. As Upper Sixth formers, we at last, had moved into that Elysium, attained the goal we had been moving towards for years – the Common Room. One enormous room, with armchairs, full of a whole year group of pubescent hormonal teenagers. It was just asking for trouble. And I'm sure there was, aplenty. I didn't notice however; I set up my corner, gathered my coterie around me – we were the Arty corner and we didn't have much to do with the rugby playing morons that populated the Other Side, who sat on the cupboards and not the chairs, who pulled their girls up against their groins, for all to see. No, we interested in higher things. I was writing reams of (shit) poetry...shall I show you some? No, maybe not...., doing drama, and singing in the choir....long gone were the blazer and patent shoes. I now sported, as evidenced in an old photograph, a lemon shirt and red flares, set off by a pair of blue clogs. And white socks. And a leather thong tied around my neck. I was *gorgeous*. I was doing OK in class, and more than OK out of it.

Wot a stunna.....

One of my friends had a car.....that put him in the super league and we became bum chums or more 'friends with benefits'. Yes we did (though of course I'm not gay – you can ask any of my girlfriends in the Common Room, whom I have fondled) and we spent quite a lot of time together.

At this time, the shit shop having long gone, Dad was working on RAF St Mawgan air base (we lived off stolen aeroplane meals all through the winters) and in the Summer we did bed and breakfast. As a result of this, I had a shed in the garden so that my bedroom was available. Suited me fine. Had my HUGE old brown wooden radiogram, my Marc Bolan posters (with whom I had become obsessed – I was fascinated by this man who was brave enough to wear women's shoes in public. I used to sit, in panting expectation on the floor in the lounge, in front of the telly, hoping he would be on Top of the Pops that week) and was allowed to write all over the walls. There was an intercom so I could be told when meals were ready or if a friend had turned up. It was quite a cool place to be and I could listen to '*Electric Warrior*' and '*Deep Purple In Rock*' and '*Atom Heart Mother*' in peace. In fact, these were great as I could have it on quite loud and there was a lock on the inside so when PB came over, we could have sex without the risk of being caught. Sometimes, he'd have my cock in his mouth, the intercom would go and I'd say, "*Just coming*" and we'd roar with schoolboy delight. This went on for some time, either in my shed, or in his car, parked up in farmyard gateways, in laybys and on cliff tops. We never went any further than this, gear sticks notwithstanding, because of course if we did, that would make us gay and, obviously we weren't.

On one occasion, which actually turned out to be another of those 'moments', clarity shone though and was missed. He and I were in my bedroom in bed; it must have been winter as I was back in the house. I was under the bedclothes, noshing away on his knob, music playing, when he said, "*Fuck, someone's just come in!*" I surfaced and heard my dad in the kitchen. I was familiar enough with the sounds of the house. In a total panic I ran, naked, stiffy suddenly not so stiff, to the door and locked it, just as I heard him coming down the passage. PB was desperately struggling to get into his pants (rather than into mine), the bed was in a complete and clearly-just-been-occupied mess, I was naked, with my clothes over the other side of the room. "*You in there?*" he yelled and tried the fucking handle!! "*Yes*" Just coming!" which actually, now, wasn't funny at all. "*We're just recording some music. That's why we locked the door.*" What? Jesus, what now? "*I'm just*

going down to the shop, to tell your Mother I'm home early, won't be long."
Slam, door banged.

What? WHAT???

"QUICK! Get dressed and go, quick, before he comes back. Quick! QUICK! FUCK OFF!!" Apart from the fact his bright yellow car was standing in our drive, there was no evidence of anyone else being there....and the stink of teen spirit in my room. PB roared off, I tidied the room, opened the windows to let the fug of teenage sex out, got out my 'recording equipment', and chucked a few LPs around in prominent positions. And waited.

The old dread returned the same time as he did, with Mum. It was Tea Time, Five O Clock. He said, *"I need to get some fags. Come on, let's go down the shop".* Clearly, not true, and anyway, he'd just been down the shop. We went outside, and got in the car, even though the fag shop was a 3 minute walk down the road and he began driving out towards the cliffs. In silence. I really had no idea where this would go. He must've known what was going on, he must've allowed PB to escape....I had no idea what was next.

The cliff path was deserted, the sea was raging. *'Next time I'll kill you'* was the only thing I could hear, in all its sibilant horror. But, he turned to me and just quietly said: *"I know what you were doing."*

The horror of those moments is hard to put in words.

Silence. Seemingly HOURS of it.

"Do you enjoy that sort of thing?"

Fuck, what am I supposed to say to THAT? I decided that lying would be ridiculous, as I clearly DID.

"Erm, yes. I do".

"Even more than when you do it with Mary?" How did he know about that? I supposed he must have assumed his son was bound to be porking somebody, as I was a teenager...ergo....He was offering me an escape route, or maybe a way for him not to believe he'd bred a monster.

I took it. I lied. *"No, of course not! It's just a bit of fun."*

"Then we'll say no more about it."

Right answer! We drove home and it was never mentioned again, until 1982. November.

I didn't stop of course. Free dick was hard to resist, and anyway, as he'd said, there WAS Mary ...

Mary was a good Catholic girl, to whom I had lost my virginity at 15, up against the washing machine in the outhouse while her darling mother, whom I adored, was in the next room cooking up Dublin Coddle or colcannon or something very pungent. They lived opposite us when we first moved into Newquay town from Summercourt until I moved to another part of town at around 15, so it wasn't quite so convenient. We used to shag, quite unprotected of course, being a 'good Catholic girl'. Then after, she'd wipe her fanny, and leg it down to St. Mary's church to give confession, so she wouldn't have a baby, and so we could do it again, as she was washed clean of all sin. When she wasn't available, I used to blag my way into the swimming pools of local hotels, with Paul, who lived next door to her, and we'd suck each other off in the changing rooms. Just filling in time, obviously, until the Real Thing was available again. And NO BUM FUN. You know why. SO, Mary was my smoke screen from what was becoming increasingly urgent in me, in my heart. Later, I had another girlfriend, whose parents owned a hotel. We used to play cards and I'd finger her and she'd put her hand down my pants and make me cum. It was all very confirming: I CANNOT BE GAY! Ask Mary! Ask P.A.! They'll tell you. Going to parties and getting monstrously sick on Woodpecker cider, wearing white loons, a blue nylon vest, a headband and cloak meant NOTHING. All my friends were girls. I like girls. Obvious.

As my education proceeded, so did the horror of my sisters' lives.

Sandra had had enough apparently of being found in ditches, reeking of vodka and lime, after a night out down the Flamingo. Once she'd shagged Gene Pitney's drummer, roaring away on his motorbike, but mostly she was drinking and fucking, which I didn't know about but it seemed to fill the hole left by the baby that had been ripped from her arms, and having been abandoned by her Father and by a Mother (who I am sure was obeying orders. Probably her heart was breaking too) when she needed their arms, their understanding, their forgiveness. So she sought refuge in numbness and sex. How she didn't end up pregnant again, I have no idea. Maybe she was on the pill? Anyway, do you remember Ian, the man the Gill got her face pulverised for? Well, he was still around, and he had a mate, Derek, who met

Sandra somehow, and they got married. She was pregnant at the time, presumably with HIS baby, but this time it was okay(ish) as she was being made 'respectable' and anyway, it wasn't showing yet so Mrs Johns wouldn't know – horror of horrors. It wasn't long after this, the three of them went off to Australia, where Derek's parents already were and who'd agreed to sponsor them. The three of them left from Redruth station one morning, in a cloud of black smoke. I don't mean in a Harry Potter way, I mean on a steam train bound for….actually, I don't know. I suppose they went from Southampton. I know they had 'an assisted passage' and they only paid about five quid or something. It was, of course a disaster and not long after, after getting into a shit load of debt (nothing new there then) and Derek drinking himself into oblivion and beating the shit out of her, she and Debbie, now three, came home, back to Mum and Dad's in Newquay. They found a flat soon after and there begins another tale of failure, abuse, and theft of such epic proportion which cannot be told here. It would make a book on its own – a thriller, a porn novel, a crime novel, all three, as she continued to live out the life of an abusee. And still does. As does her daughter. And *her* daughter too.

As for Gill, while I was careening around school, with John Cleese and Geoffrey Chaucer, wanking in caves and trying to bugger dogs, her lot was even worse, worse than you can imagine.

She stayed with Ian, who made her pregnant. She moved out of our house and got herself a flat, and eventually married Ian, much to my Father's fury. She, pregnant, went to live with Ian's folks, in a house just along the road from where Sandra was living at that time. We used to go and visit Sandra on a Sunday afternoon, and as we drove along the road, I could see Gill, watching us pass, and we, never stopping, never acknowledging her. The sound of a breaking heart is one hard to bear. My Mum knew she was there, watching, but was forbidden - *forbidden* - to look in her direction. I had no idea any of this was going on and wondered why we never went to see Gill, and her new born child, *HIS* granddaughter. But I knew enough not to ask. Once, we were walking along the High Street in Redruth, or Camborne, I don't remember which, and Gill was coming along the road, with Samantha in her pram. My Father took my Mother's arm, and pushed us into, and across the road and continued along on the other side, eyes ahead, not pausing. He crossed the road, to avoid her. And her child. I can't imagine who was hurting the most, my sister or her mother. Or maybe even him. Samantha was SEVEN before they met. What a bastard. What a FUCKING

BASTARD. Blanked his grandchild, crucified her mother, stabbed her so deeply in the heart that she has never been able to leave it behind. And as he was old and dying, she STILL cared for him, hated him and wiped his ass. That's FOUR children he had discarded now. It would be some years before it was my turn.

Tales emerge over the years, tales that would feed Ayckbourne for decades. Stories of things going on behind the nets of 70s suburbia Redruth and Camborne.

Here's some for your delectation. I'm not sure of the chronology but I present to you: Family tales which explain Why 40 years later, when we get a chance to meet the sister who was sent from us decades ago by my father, we can't because someone else in the family fucks it up for us! 'DISFUNCTIONAL' was invented just for us.

La Famille Bray, Butlins, c.71

~ Barrie and Rosemary. Sandra and Derek, her husband. Cousin Gerald and Harvene (Another name to conjure with!). Playing strip poker, in the middle of the afternoon. Mum Dad and I arrive, as we happen to be in the area. We walk in and there they are; mysteriously Rosemary was the only one with no clothes on. I have no memory of what happened next. Probably my brain shutting it out.

~ Rosemary and Gerald caught shagging in the cupboard under the stairs.

~ Rosemary, caught in bed, with the electrician (God, this could be a movie, eh?) when Barrie comes home early. Apparently, he saw them, went downstairs, got his shotgun (?), went back upstairs and told the man that if he wasn't gone by the time he got to ten, he'd blow his bollocks off. I imagine he got to 3 ish.....

I know all this because, in his later years when Barrie and I used to sit out the back of my house, and have a fag and he began for the first time ever really, to talk to me, treat me as an equal. Maybe he'd never said all this before –it was pretty out there, with his wife at home as we spoke. Dad, of course, used all this as ammo – he used to call her a slag to his face and tell him to "get shot of her". I think the point of him telling me was to illustrate his feelings for my father, which were pretty similar to mine. He told me that if my Dad EVER insulted his wife again, that would be IT. He called him a vicious, miserable poisonous old man. All true. Several times over. I didn't go round his house for tea or have him over to mine for Christmas every year though. Or maybe it was his way of admitting he'd been cuckolded by his missis all their lives together and he just needed to fess up? I don't know and now he's dead, choked by his own vomit in a hospital bed. That doesn't seem right does it?

When Sandra lived in Camborne (round the corner from Peeping Gill, Heartbroken Gill), she lived initially with Derek's parents and his brother, David. We stayed over one night (or just I did, can't remember) and David and I were in separate rooms upstairs. In the dark, he whispered, *"Come in here."* He decided that we should share a room. A bit nonplussed, I went. Then he decided we should share a bed. Hmm. OK then! In I got and he had an enormous hard on. Just like all those summers years before in Dorset, I can remember it. Its girth (large), hardness level (extreme). He said, *"Let's pretend we're queers!"* and he just rolled me over, got me under the hips and hauled me up and positioned himself behind me. *"We have to be really quiet"*, he said and then started pushing his hardon against my arse. Now I won't pretend it wasn't nice, but I wasn't really sure what was going on, what was expected of me and what to do? So I just knelt where I was and let him do it. He made no attempt at penetration, just kept thrusting his hard dick against my arse cheeks. Did he come? I don't know. Did we have a wank after? I don't know. I imagine so, but I was about 15, 42 years ago, and the memory of the incident is naturally a bit hazy. But the shape of his cock isn't. I can feel it now....

I often wonder about these moments in people's lives. Does HE remember that incident? When he's in bed with his wife? Does J.J. remember wanking in that cave? Does Timmy......hahahah, never mind. But they are the things that make us; burned memories that construct our adulthood. It is interesting to me when I look at old family photos, people smiling out of those Polaroid squares – how much pain is hidden there, the stories the pictures are not telling. Now, I know so much more of the truths, the lies, the intrigues and scandals and I am intrigued by the duality of them. Look at you! You Lying Duplicitous Bitch! Arms round his neck, while you're shagging your cousin! Look at you all - Mum, Dad and beloved daughters, smiling, laughing.....the bruises faded, the baby adopted.....

The school years were drawing to a close. A levels were looming, meetings with careers advisors were scheduled. Please. Does anyone actually get PAID for that? That's not a proper job. Anyway, I was told I had to be a teacher. I wanted to go to Uni, to 'do' Drama, but in the end, my grades weren't good enough, or actually, 'of the right sort'. English and erm...Cookery. So, College it was then. I went off to Hertford for an interview, was awarded a place if I passed my English A level (which I did, with a B, thank you very much); it seemed a pretty flimsy thread on which to hang the next three years, but it turned out, I discovered, that at the interview, Hamlet, the Principal's Great Dane "really liked me". Apparently, that was the main criteria.

So, Miss H's wisdom was put to the test. The *'Shakespeare and Major Early Authors'* paper contained everything I could've wished for, and there I was happily translating Chaucer as if I'd been born to it, and the Shakespeare questions – well, I could have answered any or all of them. Miss H. I bless you.

The cookery exam didn't go quite as well. The question, out of four, that I chose was to cook a 'four course meal for my parents' silver wedding anniversary.'

I can do that.

Menu:

Starter: Cold Pasta with garlic and herbs. (Not really cooking, but whatever)

Main course. Shepherd's Pie.

Dessert: Ice cream with chocolate sauce.

Coffee. (Not really a course, but nobody said anything).

Result:

Starter: So much garlic in the pasta it was inedible.

Main Course: I'd actually forgotten to switch on the oven so it was cold and congealed.

Dessert: I'd put the ice cream in the OLD freezer, which was switched off, and it had completely melted.

Coffee: I hadn't put any coffee in the percolator, so it was just hot water, really.

Hmmm. As I served this to the teachers, course by course, I saw my cheffing dreams vanishing in a swirl of smoke as flimsy as that coming off the surface of the 'coffee'.

Result: (out of 1, 1, and 1 for three elements of the course) 6, 6, and 7. That's a fail then.

So Drama at Teacher's Training College it was then. Scheduled for October, 1972.

One final thing, before I leave Newquay, my home, my parents and my adolescence – to take us back to the beginning of this story, it was during this Summer break that I found Dad's divorce certificate. I'd lived all these years, unaware of it. Such a massive thing – how could NOBODY not mention it? I asked, but my question was met by silence from him and, *"He doesn't like to talk about it, dear,"* from her.

So there we have it: Gill, now married and living with her husband and a baby. Sandra in Australia, and me in my fur coat, sitting on a railway station, with a ticket for my destination, um –aaha, suitcase and guitar in hand, awaiting the train that will transport me to my new life - a world of actors, alcohol and sex. Oh yeah. And teacher training.

CHAPTER SIX.

COLLEGE.

Where our hero discovers boobs, beer, bollocks and blowjobs, and officially becomes a Luvvie.

'Knock on Wood'.

by David Bowie. No.10. October 1974.

"Cause your love, is better
Than any love I know
It's like thunder, lightning
The way you love me is frightenin'...

It was. Like thunder. And lightning. But in a good way.

~~~

We had, I recall, a 'buddy' system set up at the College for which I was bound; a student already at the college from a reasonably close home location was assigned to all the newbies, to ease them in, allay their fears and, as mine was from Cornwall, supply me with pasties. Elaine was mine, she of the ginger mane and ample bosom. It WAS a useful system I guess as it was pretty scary. For all the bravado, it was the first time, ever, I hadn't been at home (apart from School Camp, but I think we'll not mention that...) and of course didn't have a fucking CLUE. As predicted.

We, Martin and I, my comrade, my friend, my fellow countryman, travelled up to Hertford, a foreign land, up England......it was exciting, fearful, but mostly full of expectation. We had all, of course SEEN the College before when we'd gone for our interview but the thought of being there, permanently was...well, just WEIRD.

On our arrival, there were various socs. to join, none of which were particularly attractive to me, so I didn't sign up for any. 'Debating soc'? I don't think so. We all gathered in the hall and were welcomed then our buddy took us off to our Halls of Residence. I, apparently, was lucky as I was living IN for my first year. New Hall. Shared room. Not much else to say really.

New Hall, Fire Escape, the scene of many a jape.

Problems began to arise soon enough. Graham kept bringing 'birds' back to our room; the bookcase dividing us offered little or no protection either visually or aurally so I stayed out quite a lot.....

Also there was the question of pants. Namely, used ones. What was one supposed to do with them? They were accumulating and there didn't seem to be anyone coming to collect them for the wash. All over New Hall were heaps of pants – yellow flied and skid marked and no-one seemed to know what to do with them. There was a top loading washing machine, which we peered into but had no idea how to use. Or, perhaps, one of us DID know how to do it but wouldn't own up in case it appeared a bit gay. In the end the stench got so overwhelming, once the socks had been added, that somebody probably said, *"I'll have a look and see how it works. Doesn't make me a girl though"*. In my eyes it made him a superstar.

The same kind of thing was happening in the 'kitchen'. I use the term 'kitchen' loosely – there was a Baby Belling. And a bin, which was usually full of paper towels and rubber Johnnies, as we used to call them then. After a night at the bar, much cooking of beans on toast and eggs, barely recognisable, went on. It was pathetic. Probably in the girl's Halls there were five course meals, mounds of profiteroles and roast suckling pigs but here – poor wretched, zit – spattered boys – there was no clue. It was becoming clear the magnitude of the plethora of secrets our Mothers had kept from us: plates and cutlery and cups do NOT magically reappear in the kitchen cupboards – they grow mould. The clothes scattered on the floor of the room just STAYED there, and were still there the next day, and the next – how did they get to be all Daz sparkly and hung up, just like that? The toilet seemed to gather a collar of pubes – how did it suddenly get all glistening white and smelling of Dettol? What alchemy was this? We'd always been cooked for, pandered to – we took to eating beans from the tin as it seemed too complicated to factor in a saucepan and having to watch them.....too many birds to chase, beers to drink.

The College Bar was the hub of our Universe. Its where we sighed wearily after having had to attend a lecture...humping our colossal bags, full of never-to-be-read books on Educational theory, bemoaning the length of the lecture (usually half an hour, if you count being 10 minutes late and switching off 20 minutes before the end, having scribbled down some random notes, some pearls that might or might not have been wisdom, written a few notes to me mate in front asking if he's going to the bar after etc), wondering how we'll ever make it through another day.....

The best time of day was just after dinner (or TEA as a proud Cornishman I steadfastly called it, refusing to be lulled into the middle classdom of DINNER, or worse, SUPPER) as that was the time we weary educational travellers gathered to discuss the woes and travails of our day and then get wazzed. Lager was 11p a pint, so....you do the maths.

The bar was run by students (I never did know HOW you got that job, who you had to suck off to reach such an exalted position) and of course favouritism was rife – their mates were always served first, and me being such a weed (a role I repeated very successfully in a play years later – very Method, very Stan.) usually ended up being elbowed to the back of the heaving, gasping throng. Anyway, lager was purchased, crisps were scarfed, and vomiting ensued. Once, my mate Chris and I were SO drunk we fell in the hedge on the way home and apparently passed out; wrapped in the arms of Morpheus and a cradle of privet, the next thing we knew, people were passing us on the way up to breakfast. NOT our fault, though. The barman had bust the tap on a barrel of lager and announced that if you bought a pint, you could keep filling your glass for free. Looking back now, I wonder why he didn't charge – they were still pints...... Anyway, Chris and I happened to be

IN the bar when the shout went out and got a head start. Oooft. Good job it was only *'The Child's Place in Early School'* the next morning......

The bar was also Folk Club; there was a piano there (of sorts) and all the Music students used to get on it and play the opening bit of Rachmaninov's 1st Concerto. I gave 'Chopsticks' a pretty good go.... But came in to my own the when I decided to actually play at folk club one night. I had (and still do, sporadically when the hard water here allows me to grow enough nails that don't just drop off when I so much as look at them) been playing the guitar since I was about fifteen; there was a guitar club that the Chemistry teacher ran after school, (you know, the one with the floppy hair that I fancied but didn't really realise it?) and have been playing the same 4 songs for the last 40 years as I am too bone idle to learn any new ones.

Anyway, Folk Club night......hadn't a clue what to wear (not having noticed, at the previous ones, that people just arrived in what they'd been wearing all day. Or week). Should it be a woolly Arran Jumper with leather elbow patches? Maybe a tie-die vest? In a fevered delirium of nerves, I finally decided on a – I hardly dare write this – kaftan (the kind with the reeeely reeeeely long flared pointy sleeves) white loons and my clogs (one of which clattered to the floor when, perched magnificently on the bar stool, I crossed my legs to play). I thought I looked stunning in a kind of hippy cum Woodstock cum new age twat kinda way. I can only imagine I played my Four Songs and, fortunately this was before paparazzi days, I pushed my way to the bar and......Robin bought me a drink! ROBIN! HEAD OF DRAMA! I was fucking well IN!! He was one of those men that you just admired. There were 3 lecturers in the Drama Dept; one was useless, one was weird and one was...well just ROBIN, whom I worshiped. And he just bought me a drink!! I drank it, kaftan sleeves flapping wildly, and then offered to buy him one back. He said YES!! OHMYGODOHMYGODOHMYGOD......he wanted lager....and then he uttered these immortal words, when I asked him if he wanted lime; *"Christ, no! Do you think I'm a girl?"* (FUCK! What was I thinking – I might as well have offered him a cherry, some cucumber, an umbrella...calm down you fool! Calm down!!!). *"Oh! Erm....no, of course not...here you are..."* I don't think I backed away bowing, but its how I felt. I. JUST. BOUGHT. THE. SENIOR. LECTURER. A. DRINK. Hey! Look! EVERYBODY.....And nobody did. Nobody noticed. Nobody commented. No-one gave a toss. Gutted I was, gutted.

The time at Balls Park. (BALLS! BOLLOCKS! KNACKER'S PARK! BOLLOCKS PARK!!!My how we laughed!!) sped past. Good times. Now forty years have gone. I was a Drama student and therefore, by definition, a bit suspect. We were only allowed to mix with the Music Dept, who were also, by definition, a bit suspect. And hairy. My GOD, were we hairy! Crystal Tips (for all you older readers!) was my twin! But I looked soooo goddam cool, man. And groovy. Loons. Bri – nylon vests and we were IT. I look at the photos and smile now -- those days when the biggest worry was having 11p for a half a lager. The REASON for being there, i.e. to train to become a teacher and a part of the next stratum of people who would have absolute power of the lives of children, seemed to belong somewhere in Unicorn Land. For now, it was Acting (loosely, in a MAHVELLOUS seventies student type of way), drinking lager and girls. And cock, but I'll come on to that later.

Not long after arrival, in fact it might have even been the first day proper, having checked out all the Socs, and not joined any, we were lining up for dinner and I spoke to the girl behind me in the queue and it was she who was to be my companion, my love, my best friend and the girl who would be laid low, in the wreckage of a relationship when we finally admitted that her lover was a homo. This though was seven years in the future. For now, I asked her why she was covered in flour. Because she was. I have no idea why, and no memory of the reason she gave but it was the Coolest chat up - line ever…..*"Hi. You've got flour or something on your tits"*. Class, eh? Fortunately she thought it was funny and introduced herself.

"Hello," she said. (Not "Hi" like a proper student. But "Hello". A bit posh then, probably.) *"I'm Juliana."*

Cool! A foreign name.

"Juliana Slododian." (Julie – if you're reading this – please forgive me. I include it because it's important to readers to get the idea of what a total knob I was.)

"Slob…..what?"

"Slobodian". Sighs. Rolls her eyes. …… *"It's Ukrainian."* She's probably had twats like me all her life sniggering.

"Nice. Nice name." Pfffft.

Anyway, as we moved down the queue, we talked and talked some more and that was the start of our affair. I fell in love. I didn't mind that she had a funny name. She was wonderful. She didn't mind that I called her SLOBBIDBOBBIDDY all the time (probably. She never told me not to...) - and she had wondrous boobs. Slobbidybobbidy boobs. We went about our separate studies, she to her English books, me to prancing about, declaiming and projecting, still tending to say ' "Hullo clouds hullo sky hullo sun", and skip about like gurl', only in a more manly way, with a deeper voice.

I DO know that I was there because Hamlet liked me, but I like to think that wasn't the ONLY reason. Back at school, when I realized I wasn't going to be a World-Famous Chef, I had decided I wanted to 'do drama', but in the end, I only got one A Level (out of 2; we'll draw a veil over the Cookery result, shall we?) and so wasn't 'University material'. Cheeky bastards. Anyway, College was the next best thing. *"So, you're going to be a teacher?"* Yeah, whatever. I just want to 'do drama' so do your fucking job, Mr. Careers Officer, (What? That's not a JOB!) and find me a College. Which he did. The drama studio, newly built, looked exciting, the principal's Great Dane liked me, I got a 'B' for my English so I was offered a place at Balls Park (pfffft!) and so here I am, in the queue for dinner, blowing flour off Slobbidybobbidy's tits, flicking my hair out my eyes, with the whole world in front of me. It was October 15th, 1974.

As I said earlier, this was the first time away from home for most of us, and to be honest, we were like fish in a basketball game – utterly bereft of any knowledge of how to do anything. It was I'm sure, utter chaos. Minging, in fact. Unwashed behind our ears, literally this time, cheesy knobs and lank hair. Nobody saying: *"Nigel! Go and have a shower."* *"Oh but......"* *"No buts. You're not too old for a Golden Ear Whizz you know..."* and so it went. At least we'd got past her washing my hair while I held my underpants over my face....

Actually, the last wasn't true in my case. New Hall stank like a possum's armpit, rank with the bitter sweet smell of unwashed male students and their clothes, hormones gushing from every pore and stagnating in the air. But, I had a girlfriend (Sorry, wossname, back home. Needs must, and all that) and that required a certain amount of cleanliness. In fact, I probably appeared to be a bit of a fop – always making sure my tresses were just so – they were pretty long then – my loons were pressed and my packet adjusted accordingly.

College days were halcyon days, that's for sure. Lectures were few, and short, and the 'Education' bit passed pretty seamlessly. Julie and I were an item, shagging nonstop, wherever we could, often getting caught in rooms where we had no business being. We were stardust, we were golden....beer, sexual shenanigans and no Golden Ear Whizzes...We played hard, we worked hard. No! Hahahaa. We didn't. We played hard, we went to a few 'compulsory' lectures, took the aforementioned notes and blagged our way through.

We were fed, we had money to spend - I had £169 per term! Sounds nothing, but in 1974 it was plenty. Copious amounts of Lager and Spring Roll and chips from the Chinese Takeaway on North Street. These were the days when going to College was free. Actually FREE.....and the bank of Mum and Dad topped it up if you were poor. Brilliant! So there was NOTHING to worry about – no bills, clothes if you need them, your responsibility though as I've said – nobody seemed to change very often. Then when the hols came round, especially at Christmas, you could just ring up from the payphone in the hall and say, *"Sorry...I'm REEELY disappointed but I won't be able to come home for Easter / Christmas....I've had to buy so many books I don't have enough left for the train fare..."* (Cover mouthpiece – *"Mine's another pint please"*). *Everything's so expensive these days, so I'll probably have to stay here on my own. Everyone else is going home, I think. But, I 'spose I'll be alright....."* and Bingo! A cheque would arrive, enough to buy a few more lagers, chips n' curry sauces and get a lift part way, say down to Plymouth to get the train from there. Genius.

We DID eat more than just Chinkies, as we non PCly called them. We were also fed three times a day, meals of mind-numbing repetition. Breakfast was usually toast, done on one of those rotary toasters and stacked in big steel trays, gently steaming and wilting, so, depending how far down the queue you were you got crispy toast or something with which it was possible to do origami. Jam. There was jam and a mahoosive tureen of tinned mushrooms. Not much choice; eggs sometimes glistening or congealing, again, dependent on your place in the queue. Breakfast was always overseen by Luigi, a mad Italian with leettle English but a massive wooden spoon with which he smacked you if you tried to take extra...anything. Too many mushrooms. *"NO!!"* SMACK. Another piece of toast? *"NO!!!"* SMACK.....He was even known to have chased people through the dining room to retrieve what he considered to be stolen goods.....but he was always outrun though as he had a wooden leg. True. He used to hobble after you, and yes, me, on occasion, shouting *"NO!! TOO MUCH TOAST! BRING BACK….".* Run Luigi Run!

Lunch and tea were much the same, except for Sundays when me and my coterie used get in to tea early, bolt it down so that we could get the comfy seats in Black and White Hall to watch The Muppets….MANA MANAH.

It was a strange time looking back at it. We were hermetically sealed, protected, kept away from the Big Bad Wolves. We rarely saw a human who wasn't someone at the College. We ate, worked, drank and shagged in perfect isolation from the world outside, which was why, when it was suddenly July 1977…well it was a bit scary, frankly.

But before that, before reality came crashing through the glass wall of our Utopia, there were tales aplenty, adventures, dares and japes…..

These are probably not – and please forgive me - I'm trying to recover a time line written forty years ago, most of which was lager doused – in strict chronology but they are real happenings with people I know, loved, loathed, and still think of so far far down this line.

There was a boy / man called Mick who was older than us and therefore a) brainier, b) had had loads more sex and c) HAD A CAR!! Mick had the biggest hair you ever did see – a massive ginger afro style, which was unlike anything we had ever seen before. I don't remember what his Main Subject was, but he became my friend. I still don't know why, but it gave me massive kudos – I was FRIENDS with Mick, who did sex at home with his girlfriend and smoked pot. (POT! Ha! That's what we, wide – eyed, called it then.) Anyway, we spent time together, made some really shit *'Music with Objects'* and recorded them on a cassette recorder. Banging bits of wood, dropping things in to the piano (thanks John Cage. How cool were we?), pissing into saucepans, snoring into paper bags. It was SOOO amazing, man. It was so shit actually but seemed very fabulous at the time. The most amazing thing with Mick, (apart from once, when he let me suck him off. It was OK though, because we both had girlfriends) was when he decided to go to Stonehenge to watch the sunrise…BOOM! Just like that. Get in his van, drive through the night, man, and get to Stonehenge man and watch the Dawn. Man. And that's what we did. Five of us, I think, although when we got there we couldn't get near, but we climbed Silbury Hill and watched the sun come up. It was magical. It was adventurous. It was unique. I am forever grateful for it and wherever you are now Mick – I thank you.

College was three years of joy, looking back. Cocooned from anything nasty (work, bills, responsibility), we played and drank and shagged, those joys only interrupted by the annoyance of Teaching Practice, once each year. I look back in astonishment, knowing what I do now and having been involved in Education for all the years I was, at how lax it all was. Presumably, there were conversations like:

College: *"Hello is that the school?"*

School: *"Yes. Oh hello College".*

College: *"Its TP time again. Any chance you might let a malodorous student in for a few weeks?"*

School: *"Yeah, OK."*

College: *"They won't know anything much – just let 'em do what they want, disrupt any timetable you might have, upset your kids, be a bit hung over, and be without any lesson plans that have a hope of working."*

School: *"That'll be fine. Just like last year then? It WOULD be good if the males could get rid of their bus erections before they come through the gates......"*

[Dear Reader – it's TRUE! Being a bit sleepy, always horny in that studenty kind of way, vibrations of the bus in the mornings invariably led to a stiffy. [This is NOT an urban myth.]

Teaching Practice. 1975.

And so it went – bus loads of minging students, barely able to tie their own ties, would descend on the classrooms of Hertfordshire's Schools, wreaking havoc, feeling annoyed at having to get out of bed and face Luigi before eight a.m. I don't remember anything much about them; they increased in length over the three years as we (apparently) increased in skill. That was at least the theory and I may be doing a disservice to many of my fellow students – they may have been brilliant and had wonderful TPs, as did the kids in their care for those periods. This was 1974, 5 and 6 – 40 years ago now, and these children will be nearing 50. I wonder if they remember me? That strange man that came and made a massive hot air balloon collage that covered the whole back of the classroom? I have photographs from the first two schools I went to – one, where I look particularly gorgeous, in my caramac coloured flares, blue nylon shirt and hair down to my shoulders. I don't KNOW how well I did. Nobody said....I wasn't thrown out or anything so I am guessing it must have gone OK. I'm not sure if either party actually learned anything and it wasn't long before we were back doing the things we were sent to College to do – drinking and shagging, mostly.

It was around about this time I was introduced to a Canadian woman, with whom I struck up an utterly profound relationship. She was wise, perceptive, utterly beguiling. She was – and still is – one of those people you could turn to when things were bad, when the world had turned to shit and her gentle words would soothe me, mend me, seal up the wounds however small or profound. I am still in love with her and call upon her when I have the need; not too often now, as my life is not so painful. But I know she's there, with her words shining bright, ready to enrobe me and dry my tears.

Now, dear reader, I must introduce you to Chris, who features heavily in my story (and whose mug, that he made at College sits on my desk, right now, holding my pens and my heart's kind thoughts for a man who saved my life later), with whom I spent a drunken night sleeping in a hedge, and tell you of his impact on my entire future.

He was a music student, a composer, who would later compose the score for 'The Common Room', the piece I directed for my Finals and for which I was awarded a Distinction, in no small part helped by the brilliance of the music. And, as a music student, he was not, most definitely NOT, one of the rugby players / geographers / mathematicians etc, and, as such, fell in with the 'other crowd'. You know ...THAT one, with the drama students, with my old mate Martin (who I still am in touch with, whose road was so very different from mine) and we (Chris and I) became very close. Particularly for the following reasons: a) he was very heavily involved in my finals production as MD; b) in the third year, we lived on the same top floor corridor in Halls of Residence (with Martin next door but one – I wonder if he ever heard anything? He's never said......) and c) he was a HOMOSEXUAL!! Yes really! A proper, I - don't - give - a - fuck homo!!

He was very dear to me, was Chris – pivotal in my life and it is still painful to me that I no longer see him.

Chris, as 'Wilfred Weed' in 'The Common Room'

He was older; he'd been on another course somewhere before he came to Balls Park (fnar, pffft, snurggle) and, as I said, we were kind of thrown together by circumstances of Art and by my, at a subliminal level, being utterly captivated by him and his attitude to himself. I had never met anyone like him before and because he was so (in)famous around College, a bit of his stardust rubbed off on me. I knew a real HOMO! And I didn't CARE! I was like, totally cool with it – not really realising or admitting to myself as to why that might be....

So, the plot thickens. During the day, between lectures (or during lectures skipped) in rooms in various parts of the College, you could find Slobbodybobbidy and me fucking; in locked bathrooms, me ejaculating on her ample hooters or on her arse cheeks, in sheds, in attics. During the evenings, you could find us in the bar, or back in either of our rooms, maybe shagging again, maybe not. And at night time (because I just could not stop myself) you could find me in room 7, at the end of the corridor, sucking Chris's cock, and then maybe shooting on HIS arse. TMI? Sorry, but I promised to tell the truth, the whole truth....

Obviously, it didn't MEAN anything, as I had a girlfriend. We were shagging like bunnies, so clearly, I wasn't like Chris. Bisexuality never came into it – he was queer, I was straight, but I just liked him sucking my dick. (Actually, experience has since shown me – he was rubbish at it! But as my experience had been pretty limited, it was better than nothing – and it was only a bit of harmless fun. Wasn't it?)

Julie - if you should ever come to read this, please forgive me. I was NOT, in my fucked up mind, being unfaithful to you – I wasn't doing it with another *lady* or anything so it didn't really count. I wasn't having a relationship with him and I loved YOU. I did, truly. But, I couldn't help it.....and it wasn't doing any harm. Or so I thought. Seeds were sown in room 7 of Ashbourne House – both literally and emotionally. But this came to fruition many years later.

Add to this potent mix, Jerry, another music student, who also had a girlfriend so what we did dint mean nuffin. Chris was besotted with him (think Brideshead) and as students in the same department were able to be legitimately close. Jerry used to visit Room7, after dark too....probably for the same reason. Chris always said they discussed music (and rubbed each other's crotchets, I'll be bound); Jerry was a talented pianist (and had a quite talented penis....oh stop it!!) and Chris and he used to write together and obviously they needed to discuss the 3rd movement after midnight, in his room with the lights off.

However......Jerry would leave no.7 and tiptoe along the corridor (past no.5, where Martin was sleeping soundly. Or shagging Karen or whatever she was called) to no.3, where he would tap oh so gently and creep in to where I would be lying, in the dark, with a raging hard on, waiting....

.....an added bonus to this nocturnal activity was that Jerry had had a rugby accident (Public School you know, probably used to this sort of thing, what, what?) as a result of which he was able to take his top front teeth out..... An extra skill. A happy ending.

This went on, I would say, for most of year 3, whilst I was 'seeing' Chris, making love to Julie and planning our future for 'After College', the spectre of which loomed ever larger.

I was a DRAMA student. Did I tell you that? Did I, dahling, did I? I ADORED it. For the first time in my life, so far – Herod and Thisbe, Donald Bain and Florizel notwithstanding – I could legitimately be as fey and luvvie as I wanted, with no real repercussions other than *"OH, he's in the Drama department"*, and to weather the sideway looks and rolled eyes. This was luvviephobia, I'd say! But it was OK because there were lots of us, three years deep, and so I was in no way special (well, actually I was) and didn't stand out (well, actually, I did). My behaviour during this time was, looking back, so camp, so queeny it is not surprising that things turned out as they did! I WAS good at what I did though, and the Drama Studio was the place I felt most alive (except for in Jerry's pants but that's another thread) and I worked. Worked hard.

The three lecturers we had were as different from each other as it was possible to be and I suppose they were purposely employed to provide a spread of knowledge and technique. Diana was all silly and wobbly and did 'backstage' stuff for those who wanted to be crew in the future (No! Actually the government was paying for you to be a teacher. Remember? Whatevvaaa...), David, who was a complete twat, did 'acting' (God preserve us) and then Robin, dear dear Robin, on whom I had a kind of mancrush, who I hero worshipped (that's why I bought him half a lager and lime, readers!) did Drama in the way I understood (and hoped one day) it would be. Difficult, demanding, rigorous and worthy of study and conflict. He did the academic side too, setting the course work, the assignments (which I loved doing – it was like having Miss H. back again; special. And it seemed like he spoke only to me)

'Analyse the Skill with which Middleton Develops the Relationship Between Beatrice – Joanna and De Flores in 'The Changeling'. A sound analysis! **B-** (Robin)

"Something's Rotten in The State of Denmark". How Far is Hamlet's Tragedy of his own making?' "Some perceptive ideas here. Impressively organised" **B.** (Robin)

'Discuss How 'As You Like It' Combines Aspects of Romanticism and Reality'. "Nearly....." **C+** (Robin.) (He obviously didn't quite understand what I mean here.... Fool.)

'Discuss the dramatic elements in 'He and The Hundred Slaps' [A Russian play] and say what you consider the element to be and how they are best treated by the playwright, producer and performer'. "Your comments concerning cruelty and humour are most perceptive and are very interesting ideas in this essay" **B-** (David)

'How far is 'The Revenger's Tragedy' a Macabre Comedy?' "Your analysis of the play is distinctly good" **B.** (Robin)

These were rigorous plays; plays that have challenged scholars and students for a long time and so I feel, looking back at these titles and the grades I was awarded, as I scan through the actual papers, crinkled, handwritten and smelling musty with age having lain in the folder now for almost 40 years, I did good. I also understand now, even though there was a gap of decades that that rigour, that encouragement and challenge was what enabled me to do what I eventually came to, with Phoenix Drama.

We did all the usual ridiculous drama luvvie stuff that only students do – but we thought were FABULOUS, darling. Actually, looking back I spent a lorra lorra time in the drama studio, either directing plays under the aegis of 'Drama Club', which actually quite well supported and allowed ME to practise on real people. I was also IN loads of sketched, plays, 'happenings'.....one of which I am proud to say was performed in the Royal Albert Hall.

One of the third year students – the redoubtable Chrissie Willows – became involved in an event which was 1976, for 'International Year Of The Child' and there was to be a mahoosive entertainment spectaclier at the Royal Albert Hall. The 17th of October, 1975 – my X Factor Moment! She had been asked to produce a dance piece using to some students from Balls Park (Phahaaaa. BALLS PARK. Oh grow UP!!). It was be a 'dance – drama', if you please, something the about the Creation of the Universe, with lights and smoke and music by YES and shiny fabric and swooshing about and, and.....I think I did a wee when I heard. There were auditions for parts, as yet unknown, but I didn't care!! I'd do anything, me. It was my chance! I was being given permission to "spend my time to skip about and say *'Hullo clouds hullo sky hullo sun'* legitimately!!' Fabulous!! And nobody could say anything because it was ART. And therefore inviolable. In my eyes, anyway. So they could just fuck off.

The auditions, as I recall, took place in one of the lecture rooms, upstairs in Mansion. I'd like to say there were hundreds, queuing round the block, but there weren't. I am guessing the consensus was, amongst the majority, that it was way too gay and they certainly dint want nuffin to do with THAT! Anyway, though, there was a goodly number, as we needed *'People of the Earth'* as well as the leads: The Child of the Universe, The Sun and The Moon. I don't remember what we had to do – something about running around like a dick and emoting...the slow passage at the end of *'The Gates of Delirium'*, from 1974s LP, *'Relayer'* by YES, was the theme music used, and still when I hear it, I can see the massive cheesecloth circles the People of the Earth laid reverentially on the hallowed ground of the Royal Albert Hall. Anyway, after much emoting, Chrissy said, *"All those in the front row, come back tomorrow"*....a call back!!! As we say in the business......

The next day came, more Jon Anderson, calling me to exotic places and Steve Howe being twiddly, and I emoted SO much, I can't tell you.....galumphing about, arms flailing, hair blowing as I hurtled about....and, panting, sweating, trembling with anticipation, we were lined up again. *"Ann – Child. Chris – Sun. Nigel – Moon. Thank you very much. Rehearsals start onnbbfbbbbbfppppfffffmmmtrnn"*.

OHMYGODOHMYGODOHMYGODOHMYGODOHMYGODOHMYGOD OHMYGODOHMYGODOHMYGOD. I heard nothing of what was being said. Rehearsal what? When? SQUEEEEEEEEEEE! I was going to the ALBERT FUCKING HALL!! A blur, darling, a blur.

'Mr. Lucky', indeed!

So. Rehearsals began in earnest – it was, actually, a pretty big deal, and we took it deadly seriously. We rehearsed in the gym (the first time I'd been in one since Grammar School with its gnarly ropes and tortuous wall bars) and we hit it full on, ignoring the gangs of jeering colleagues who regularly came and watched through the glass walls, making wanking gestures and holding each other up, helpless with mirth. Did I care? Not a jot! Were they going to the R.A.H? No they were not! Were they wearing blue tights and a blue satin kaftan with big yellow moons on? Erm…no they were not, which is why they were pointing, and mouthing 'POOF' and 'CUNT' through the window…..

Dress Rehearsal, 'Child of the Universe'. College gym.

Anyway, the day drew near, dress rehearsals were had, and Ann and I stayed after to practise the lift (Dirty Dancing stylee); got the feet positions right, adjusted our centres of gravity……if you listen to the piece, there's a wonderful crescendo, where Anderson's clear voice soars, *"Soon! Soon the light….."* with the band ramping up the backing – glorious, heartlifting stuff, and on that crescendo, I hold Ann aloft, offering her to the Universe, as 'Desiderata' began over the top. I know it SOUNDS shit, but really, it wasn't. It was a wonderful moment and one of which, Chrissy (choreographer and Jim, sound man who seamlessly mixed it) were very proud.

Royal Albert Memorial, Just before we Went Up……

It was SUCH a big deal that my Mum and Dad actually travelled up from Cornwall to come and see it. This was exceptional. It meant getting a train, then a tube and then walking through the London streets. They were staying for a long weekend; I'd booked them a 'guest room' in Mansion for two nights and then I'd planned to get them back to Paddington for the journey home. It was SO weird having them there. I was genuinely moved that they'd made such an effort, but riding back to College on the coach with us was, well – a bit style-cramping, to say the least.

There were two performances – afternoon and evening – and they were due at the evening one. I just hoped for the best; that they'd find their seats. Find the R.A.H. Find London…..

I had much more important things to worry about. My Performance! I was going to be SPECTACULAR!! Cossy all ironed; no ladders in me tights; hair blow dried, a la Farrah Fawcett only manlier. We all, bug eyed, wandered around the labyrinth that is the 'backstage' at the Albert Hall; miles of tunnels with signs to 'Door A', 'Door S', 'Stage Left'……we all lined up, actually struck dumb when we were led out on to the floor to mark out the dance – it was fucking HOOOGE! We'd only rehearsed in the gym back at Balls Park (BALLS!!! KNACKERS!!! Hahahahaaa……) and this was about 200 times bigger. Well, four maybe, but it felt like 200. We needed, obviously, to cover far more ground and move quicker to keep up with the music – at least we wouldn't be poking each other in the throat or stankin' on each other's feet, but still….it suddenly became massively scary. We walked through the piece, had a few meltdowns, luvvy attacks, but Chrissy was satisfied, our allotted time was up and we were allowed to go to lunch. We pratted around for half an hour on the Albert Memorial, watching with growing pride / horror and the hundreds of people filing in through the doors across the road. Pride at what we were about to do……ONLY DANCE IN THE ALBERT FRIGGIN HALL!! And horror at the thought that a) we might fuck up and b) Ma and Pa were in the audience. Did it matter? Why was that an issue? I look back at this event and realize that, still, at 21, I was STILL seeking approval. Arse.

Anyway. 2.00 pm came, and there we were, nervous, shimmering creatures, queued up in the appropriate entranceway, waiting for our cue. We could see the audience, rows and rows of faces, each growing more indistinct as the serried ranks of seats ascended. Up, up up they went, seemingly forever, up into the Gods where, it seemed they were hanging horizontally out in to the auditorium. Somewhere, out there, were my parents, who had travelled up London to see their son perform. I probably tried to find them – two familiar faces, no doubt glowing with pride, amongst the 5,272 strong audience. Twat – they weren't even going to the matinée! DUH!

The music swelled. The 'People of the Earth' did their thing, laying their tie – died muslin cloths in the correct sequence, on the vast arena floor. Then. Then it was time. Ann Childofhteuniverse came sweeping down the centre from the back and, on the nod, Chris Sun and Nigel Moon made their entrance, stage right and stage left, UP ON THE BLOOMIN REAL STAGE OF YER ACTUAL ALBERT HALL! SWOOOSH! we went! We twizzled and swooped, and the stars all came on, from the tunnels, making the allotted patterns that only the audience (Clever *CLEVER* Chrissie!) could see from above.

"You. Are a Child of the Universe. No less than the trees and the Stars, you have a right to be here..." said the voice. YES began.... (great fade Jim!) and 'Gates of Delirium', with Steve Howe's majestically soaring guitar, and Chris moved, in a mighty solar kind of way. I moved, in a fabulously lunar kind of way, and there we were....in alignment – the stars, the Sun and the Moon in their given places in the Universe.

Ann turned. We locked eyes.....

"And whether or not it is clear to you....."

Turn. Swoop. Look Moonly. Keep her in sight....

".....no doubt the Universe is unfolding as it should...."

Jon Anderson's angelic voice cut in, high, clear over Steve Howe's guitar....

"Soon. Soon the light........"

And hands under hip bones. ...And....Adjust balance. And....Lower centre of gravity and.......LIFT!!!.....

FUCK!!!!

I dropped her.

My shiny kaftan and her sweaty leotard made contact, stuck and then she slid down my front, to land in a heap at my feet.

UTTER UTTER silence in my head. I dropped her. I FUCKING DROPPED HER!!!! The climax of the whole piece and she was kind of sat on my feet, with my moon suit trapped under her, pulling me forward so I couldn't stand up straight. I really don't know what happened next – all I remember was thunderous applause and us all standing, holding hands and bowing.

I dropped her. I. DROPPED. HER. I DROPPED HER IDROPPEDHERIDROPPEDHERIDROPPEDHER.....why were they clapping? I'd RUINED it. It was a DISASTER.......it was shit. I was shit. EVERYTHING WAS SHIT. STOP CLAPPING!!!!!

We filed off, everyone grinning and bursting with joy and pride. Apart from me, obviously. Did I tell you I dropped her? I THREW, nay HURLED myself on the floor in the dressing rooms, sobbing and wailing....AAHHHHHHH IM SORRY IM SORRY, FORGIVE ME, I'M SHIT, ARHHHHHHH, FORGIVE ME......

This went on until Chrissie came in and slapped me one. Bam! Right in the face. She said nothing, but the shock and embarrassment soon shut me up. I apologized to Ann – who said it had been her fault!! For some reason, she'd not jumped high enough and it was NEVER going to work as our clothes, once touching, would become the slippiest thing ever. Really? Ah, well, I KNEW it wasn't my fault! I graciously forgave her and said she'd better get it right tonight.....

And we did. Gloriously, as high and as perfect as Jon Anderson's voice. There she hung, presented to the Sun and the Stars and all the People of the Earth. Just wonderful. Now, 38 years on, I can see this moment, hear the song, and imagine my parent's faces.

Euphoria, such as you only get after doing a good show – this became my drug of choice. This relit that damp squib, that quiet light, under my bushel, ignited by Thisbe *et al*. The quest for that feeling and for validation has followed me all my life.

We all rode home on the coach back to BPC, stopping in Muswell Hill for fish and chips. My Mum and Dad were on the coach, sat at the back, vainly trying to divine what fresh hell this was. Wrapped in their Best Clothes, which hadn't been updated since the sixties probably, trying to understand what was happening all around them – 60 or so students, drunk on success and glamour and cider, singing, screeching, falling over, snogging, shouting, laughing......it was only an hour and a half, but it must have felt like an eternity, trapped in the Seventh Circle of Hell. I was flitting about like a tit, trying to play the dutiful son and then rushing off for a quick snog, or to interfere in something that was none of my business, in case I was missing something. 'Pokey Geeky', as my Mum used to call me....

We arrived back and I took them to their room, said goodnight and went back to Asbourne for a MASSIVE party. Not much memory of the weekend other than Mum, Dad, Slobbidybobbidy and I went out for a Chinese at the Salisbury Arms, where I had sweet and sour pork balls, the dish of which I jammed my elbow into, thus sending them all cascading to the floor, where they rolled about under people's feet and chairs. Well. I was bloody paying.....I crawled about and collected them back up, every last one. A quick blow and into the sauce. Sorted. No-one said anything.....

We went down to London with the parents, bunged them on the train back to Cornwall, and headed back to catch up on some much needed shagging. Nice of them to come; really it was, but man.....NOT cool to have them around......

Oh. FUCK.

Julie's pregnant. With a baby. In her belly. That I put there. A baby. A baby in her tummy. A slobbidybobbidybaby. Oh fuck fuck FUCK!! Well, yes actually, you twat, you did. Unprotected as usual. In a hurry, probably between '*Major Authors*' and '*School Development*' up in Mansion. Yes, you pulled out and jizzed on her bush, like usual, but this time it didn't work did it? You fucking IDIOT. You dopey CUNT. What were you thinking? Clearly NOT about your finals, your teaching career, Julie's finals and teaching career, or what your Dad is going to say......

She's NEVER late. Ever. In fact she used to be quite poorly so when she wasn't moaning or puking, we knew something was up. Or rather, HAD BEEN up, and not removed in time.

After the shock and horror of all the implications of what had happened, we decided we needed to make some plans. Plans. Me. I couldn't even plan when to wash my own pants. The first thing was to get some money to pay for 'the operation'. Like where? How? Who by? No matter – we needed money so I would write home and get a hundred quid, because "we had a massive load of books to buy for my life when I was a teacher and making you proud".......maybe we won't have to tell anyone? Maybe we can 'get it done' and go back to normal.... Like, back to the bar for instance. Julie, meanwhile, went to the College doctor. FUCK! Now he would know. Though, actually, come to think of it, I AM a bit of a stud, all fertile and that....

Fuck Fuck FUCK!

She WASN'T pregnant. Doc said it was probably all the stress of the looming finals or something. Anyway, she was back on the blob, as we so charmingly called it! YAY! Her stomach was hurting! She was feeling proper poorly! Hurrah…..

I look back with shame at the cavalier attitude with which I treated this incident. No care for her, the baby, and her career – just really REALLY wanted to avoid a MASSIVE Golden Ear Whizz. But I was 21 and scared shitless – not sure whether of the wrath of my Father *("Look at what we've done for you!!! Worked all our lives to send you to College….blah blah!"* (Actually, you DIDN'T - I have a grant, but never mind) or the thought of years of poo and crying and not being able to consume vast quantities of lager. Call me shallow…..

Anyway, the duff, she was not up and it was normal service(ing) was resumed.

Slobbidybobbidy, My True Love.

Oh drama, drama, DRAMA! What else is a boy to do? Yes, of course, we did have to jump through all the Pavlovian hoops for exam purposes, but the idea of being a Teacher seemed more and more of an alien concept – it was like being prepared to be a gynaecologist or a mountaineer – something that had NOTHING to do with my aspirations. I was doing OK – getting good grades, mostly Bs and A-s, getting work in on time *('How far do you consider the village you visited a Community?'* [I didn't – I made it all up! Teehee!]. *'A Machine for Living in – Discuss this in the Light of your Studies'; 'What is involved in the claim "I KNOW"?'; 'Discuss the concept of labelling and its implications for school success or failure'*.....blah blah blah.......and on and on. I have just looked at these papers, now, taking them from their musty folder where they have resided these some 40 years (Wonder why I keep them.....?. Though, if I hadn't, I wouldn't have been able to source them for this book, and read them and gasp in amazement at how shit they were, and what the fuck is that HANDWRITING about? ....) and I know now that I was adequate, that I was always going to pass. What I DIDN'T know then though, was that my grades in my yet-to-be-sat finals and my 'aptitude' (pfffft! Whatever THAT was) would be enough to earn me an offer to go on to Cambridge University to study for a B.Ed.

I turned it down.

I know, I know....Cambridge; all very Brideshead; would have suited me perfectly, I'm sure. Fopping away like mad, on the Backs, boater askew.....but.....the Siren Song of the leg warmers was getting louder as the year drew to its close and I opted – much to my Fathers delight, I'm sure – to go to The Laban Centre to enrol on a 'Dance in Education' course, at Goldsmith's University, London.

Here is how it happened.....

There were several productions in the course of the years, both mounted as course work (and directed by MEEE!) and as part of Drama Club. More and more, in these there was 'movement' incorporated. I hesitate to say 'dance', because we were all shit – nobody had had any training of any kind. Sylvia Young's it was NOT! But – we did some interesting pieces; Some Pinter, some Beckett, some Shakespeare. We also did a full production of *'The Boyfriend'*. I, of course auditioned for the lead but it went to some scrote who wasn't even a bloody student at the College. Rex. Rexy....probably felt up the director's jubblies; something I wasn't prepared to do, even for the lead.....but I did get one of the 'boyfriends', *Alphonse*, and a little *pas de deux* with my cherie (the character, obvs.) to ourselves and Rex. Rexy Rex. Rexy Boy didn't really get a look in. HA!

A significant event occurred in my final year too. As well as being given the honour to direct 'The Common Room', written by Dr. Sangster himself (he'd probly had a conflab with Hamlet to check) which was to be my final assessment piece. The music was written by Chris – real proper, 'Musical' music, in partnership with Jerry (those late night sessions. So THAT'S what they were doing....) and I had the pick of the music department for the band and for the lead singers. It was really VERY successful. It's a pity that there is no record of it now – no music, no video. I DO have some photos which I lovingly preserve for.....for what? Actually, when I'm gone, nobody will know what it is or who those faces belong to. Still, it lives on in people's heads – mine, Martin's, Anne's......all of those people who sang brilliantly (and acted to the best of their ability) and acted (and sang to the best of their ability). It was a triumph, and a very proud moment. It was also reflected in my final end of course grade: 'Drama. (Distinction). It was like all my horses had romped home, my numbers had come up, Mr Lucky's number had been called out.....wonderful.

Sorry, yes....the other thing. Robin, dear Robin – did I tell you I bought him a drink? – had collaborated with this friends 'in the business' and had pulled together a collection of short plays, by such luminaries, of the 70s at least, as James Saunders ('A Scent of Flowers', 'Next Time I'll Sing To You'), Olwen Wymark ('Speak Now'), Vivennne Welburne and N.F. Simpson ('A Resounding Tinkle'). They donated two plays each, and they exist as anthology, called 'Play Ten', nothing if not original.

They were chosen as the third-year drama department's acting assessment piece. Brilliant. I managed to get into four of them – due to the usual dearth of male drama students, though I like to think it was because of my versatility, skills and all round arselicking and my "ME! I can do that" ness.

Anyway, it worked. They were very good, in a 70s sweary, absurdist kind of way. We did them at Balls Park (HAHAHHAAAAA) for four nights but then...deep joy. We went on tour. On tour, dahlings! We went to The Orange Tree Theatre, Richmond, Upstairs, which was WAY cool. We also did the plays at the Cockpit Theatre in Islington, when it was under the aegis of the Inner London Education Authority. After, we went into SoHo, and remember I was 21, and had never SEEN such things...The Raymond Revue Bar? What was that? Why were those men standing outside those little doorways? Ah, the innocent abroad. Anyway, we went to a pub, where Olwen Wymark was waiting to meet us. I think she liked it, what we'd done with her work. I bought her a Bloody Mary! Oh yes indeedy! I was in Heaven. Star struck, full of adrenalin.....Not the National, or the Old Vic, but hey! A PROPPA London theatre and drinky- poohs with the playwright. AND Robin, on whom I had the biggest crush, was with us too, patting my back and saying *"You were marvellous, darling!"* 'n stuff. I have used several of these plays myself as director when I was teaching in schools, back in pre-history. In fact, N. F. Simpson came to see one of the productions I did. That was a bit of a thrill, and he was very complimentary. Or maybe just polite.....

'And After Nature, Art' – Olwyn Wymark

'What's Acting? '– N. F. Simpson.

My dissertation, for my written finals was *'The Growth of Modern Dance'*. See? I was hooked, drawn in by me leg warmers, with no wish to escape. I would like to tell you of one more thing I did — you may make a judgment, around the opposing thoughts of *"Wow, that is so happening, and brave"* or *"What a fuckin KNOB! Who DOES he think he is?"* Most people, I fear, came down on the latter side, but never no mind! During these last months, I was drawn more and more towards 'expressing myself in Modern Dance'. Really? We, usually Julie and I, had been Up West to see some pro companies, some of which have lodged themselves in my mind, my photographic memory — Pilobolus, at Sadler's Wells; Nureyev at the Coliseum, Merce Cunningham, Ballet Rambert, The London Contemporary Dance Theatre (with the GLORIOUS Kate Coyne — I loved her, adored her, dear reader, and actually met her once, years later, but was too struck dumb to manage more than a gurgle) but most astonishing, most truly unforgettable was The Martha Graham Dance Company. They were utterly mesmerizing. Everything I'd seen before became 'the past'. This was dance of the most tribal, feral, technically awesome, powerfully beautiful......I knew in that moment that my life — or the next year for sure — was decided. THIS is what I wanted. I wanted to do that, make those shapes, learn that technique, and feel the agony that surely it must entail. Cambridge and its B.Ed can just FUCK OFF!! THIS is what I want. I applied for a year's Dance Theatre course at the Laban Centre the very next day.

I watched a film round about this time (How? Long before YouTube. Must have been on telly?) of the Graham piece, entitled *'Lamentations'*, (1930) where the dancer simply sits on a wooden bench inside a cocoon of stretchy material and dances the pain in her heart. Astounding! (Actually, whilst writing this, I just watched the original — I didn't realize what a bloody racket the soundtrack is! Horrible! Kódaly — bloody Hungarian composers! And you, Bartók! Away with your discord!!) Anyway....I thought: 'I can do that! Can't be too hard. Bench. Bag. Bit of blue lighting'..... Peggy Lyman, if you are looking down on me, forgive me! I know: TWAT of the highest order. You trained for twenty years to be able to do that. I apologise. I was young. What can I say?

Anyway, off I trundled to Berman's in London to purchase a piece of stretchy material, blue, like the original. Was hers a bit of old offcut from a leotard making roll? Probly not, but it seemed perfect. So, back in the studio, and I was to find out just how difficult it was to make all the right bits poke out at the right time, without having the whole thing ping off, or unravel like a giant condom....

Did I hear sniggering....? This is ART.....

I'm sure you can see the extraordinary similarity....

I, did, however, persevere and between us, Jerry and I sorted out a 'piece'. I dispensed with the bench and just 'made a piece' where I emerged, bit by bit, from the bag – sorry 'WOMB' - until I was BORN fully. Geddit? Actually, I shouldn't mock it, as it was, in a studenty kind of way, not bad, and different, if nothing else. 'STRETCH' (phulleeeese) was my first foray into choreography; I 'made' the 'piece' 'on myself' (see how the terminology of we, in the business, trips off my tongue...?) and something, though mocked mercilessly by the *what a fuckin knob* contingent, I am proud to have at least attempted. Bruised, I was. BRUISED!

All these events, all these luvvy – ins were pushing me as inexorably in one direction as surely as finals, the need to find somewhere to live and a job were pushing in the other. These salad days were soon ending. How could this BE? It was supposed to go on forever. THREE YEARS! That was a lifetime. A utopia of lager, shagging, running around like twats, playing croquet, shagging, going up London to see Tangerine Dream, shagging, putting on plays and 'happenings'.....this was Promised. To US, the Golden Ones, but.....but it really was ending. Finals were looming, decisions were having to be made, heads were needing to be pulled out of our arses.....

Croquet on Mansion Lawn.

......it was, and to my eternal gratitude, a wonderful time. Everything I'd hoped. I'm not clear of the chronology of it all now; which plays went where; On 2nd of March, 1978 , having been 'trained' by Jerry, to 'be a counter – tenor', I sang two duets by Purcell from *'Come Ye Sons Of Art'*, in a candlelit black and white hall (a wonderful occasion, welded fast to my huge golden memory ingot of Wonderful Things), and carried it off with, I have to say, some moderate success; with two weeks training as opposed to twenty years, it wasn't bad at all!

Black and White Hall. c1637.

'Come Ye Sons Of Art', Henry Purcell.

In what order *'TO GOTHAM'*, *'INTERVIEW'*, by JeanClaude van Italie 'A *Flea In Her Ear'* by Georges Feydeau', *'Last To Go'*, by Pinter, *'He and the Hundred Slaps'*, by Leonid Andryev, *'The Boyfriend'* by Sandy Wilson, *'The Common Room*; by Paul Sangster, *'The Cagebirds'* and *'Little Brother, Little Sister'*, both by David Campton, and others long forgotten, occurred I am no longer certain. It, they, all blend together in this golden web — faces appear that I can name and that I can't; memories of occasions that brought sorrow and joy; places visited; relationships made and lost with time......all of it was wonderful, a privilege that I guess we didn't quite appreciate at the time. It was free, it was heady, it was beer washed and sperm coated and most of all, and it was the only time, for me at least, at last, to have the chance to begin the discovery of who I really was.

'He and the Hundred Slaps'

You, dear reader, KNOW, who I was already. There have been many clues, so if you've been following, how it turns out will come as no surprise.

So. June 1977. The morning after the final piss up. The morning after we'd all sat, drunk and weeping on the floor of Martin's room while Clare sang Fleetwood Mac's '*Songbird*', clear and plaintive and unable to finish so thick was the sorrow in her throat.

> *'And I wish you all the love in the world.*
>
> *But most of all, I wish it from myself.*
>
> *And the songbirds keep singing, like they know the score'....*

There it was. All done, bar the shouting. Long panoramic photo taken of Balls Park - no sniggering now – bit sad... Summer 1977, with a tall skinny bloke at both ends; Look there's me! In the front row. There's Luigi with his wooden leg stretched out in front of him. There's the Doc. There's Robin...Robin (who by now had completely abandoned 'The Old Bag' and was shagging one of the 3rd year drama students.) There's Slobiddybobbidy. There's Malcolm "It's the chicory that give you 'eadaches" Coppen, Jerry, with his teeth in.....on and on, faces with no names now; some dead no doubt, most married, divorced, remarried; how many became Teechars in the end? Are they still there? Gary and Milly, still dear friends and still married; a black and white moment, taken this month 37 years ago. Folks I loved, folks I hated, folks I lost with the passage of time, but all folks who added tesserae to this boy/man mosaic and sent him out into the world, wide eyed, shagged out, holding tight to the hand of the girl / woman he loved and headed South, south to London, to a new life, to the future.

Oh look! I'm right in the Centre....there's a thing....

CHAPTER SEVEN.

LONDON.

<u>In which I 'Dance away the heartache', and our hero discovers he's not as bendy as he thought. Just bent.</u>

'Jilted John'.

By Jilted John. No.13. October 1978.

'I've been going out with a girl
Her name is Julie….'

I *was* going out with Julie, but she was more of a man than *I* turned out to be.

~~~

I was 21, full of hope and spunk. I had plenty of pubic hair, a girlfriend and a Cert.Ed (credit). The world, allegedly, was my oyster. Except that for the first time I was entirely without support. Not even College to lean upon. London, and the bleedin East End an' all…..what if I got shot by a gangster? What if I got mugged or knifed or severely murdered?

Someone in the Drama department, my year, so she'd left too, had a boyfriend who had a flat where she'd used to bugger off to at weekends, with a room going spare. Looking back, I realize they were subletting but hey! London! Rock n Roll! We had a mattress on the floor in the front bedroom, and we'd lie, Julie and me, listening to *'Wuthering Heights'* and watch the damp run down the wallpaper, turning its already skanky green skankier. The flat, first floor of a typical London Victorian row (25 Cann Hall Road, Leytonstone E11), with a pretend balcony which was outside the room that became our room. There was a rabbit that lived there too, in the flat. A Dutch dwarf rabbit that shat everywhere and we were forever cleaning bunny shit out of the carpet. Also, its teeth always grew too long and after a while it was unable to feed properly, so there was the ceremonial Rabbit Teeth Cutting ceremony every so often, where Phil would snip the protruding yellow incisors off with a pair of nail clippers. PING they'd go, flying across the room, PING!, behind the sofa, anywhere. The place became littered with bits of rabbit teeth. But as they ADORED the bastard thing, there wasn't much we could say. It stank too as it never went out. Ewwwwww.

25 Cann Hall Road, Leytonstone E11.

Phil and Ali, for that was their names, were some kind of weird vegetarians and seemingly only ate cabbage (though I did share a Marathon with her once, and we had a kebab one night when HE was away. Can't trust 'em….). He used to cook these vast pots of cabbage and onions with *tablespoonfuls* of turmeric in; *"I'll do loads, so it'll last us a few days…"* was the worst phrase of all, the one we dreaded to hear. Julie and I fed ourselves which as actually quite hard as we weren't allowed to have FLESH anywhere near the kitchen……

The lounge (apart from shards of rabbit fangs) was always spotless and in the pride of place stood a record player. Nay, A DECK. A LINN record deck, which we forbidden upon the pain of death to touch, breathe on or even look at. I don't recall him ever actually playing anything on it himself, and really, I did consider it quite a waste, especially as I had Joni Mitchell's 'Don Juan's Reckless Daughter' burning a hole in its cover…….

…..there sat the deck, in its shiny Perspex cover…..'Play me……PLAY ME!…….' Day after day until, I could stand it no longer! I tiptoed towards the deck. Breathe.

Don Juan's Reckless Daughter.

(That's Joni in blackface at the front - caused quite a stir in '77)

I eased the black shiny LP from its paprika and blue sleeve and placed it on the deck…..

'I'm Don Juan's reckless daughter,

Been out two days on your tail……'

Her clear and vibrant tones soared out across the room, across my heart – my Canadian mistress who had stuck with me through times, good and bad…..

She pissed a tequila anaconda

The full length of the parking lot!'

Oh MY! She swore! What a gal! I adored her; I risked my home to hear her! After the disc had finished, I put the holy artefact back in its sleeve, closed the lid of the deck, forgetting to replace the needle cover and went back to whatever I'd been doing – picking up rabbit teeth probably.

What happened next doesn't need to be explained really – the next day we were homeless. That is all. At least I wouldn't have to eat anymore fucking cabbagenturmeric. That was something.

Getting turfed out of that house was when a WHOLE lot of trouble began.

The July before we left BPC, I'd attended an interview at what was then called 'The Laban Centre', in order to pursue my dancing career – I'd done a cover version of *'Lamentations'* don't forget! I don't remember too much about the day, actually, other than I was wearing a to-*DIE*-for hooded knitted cardy with toggle duffle coat buttons, in darling shades of brown. Lush it was, if a little shapeless. I have no memory of any kind of audition. There was an interview at which I was obviously good enough (maybe the Doc had told them Hamlet approved...?) but anyway I got in, one year, 'Dance Theatre in Education' aka 'Still not having to get a job', and maybe more shagging experience but in a more bohemian kind of way – I was an Artist now, after all. And there was obviously going to be a bar. What's not to like? So I'd left Balls Park with my next year planned. Slobbidybobbidy unfortunately hadn't, so she got a job working in the Shaftesbury Hotel in Piccadilly. Good for her. She can go to work, and I can say *'hullo clouds, hullo sky'* and skip about like a gurl'. For a YEAR!! Result.

It was, actually, bloody hard work. For a start, I'd had no training at all, and half the class had, at some point in their education. Consequently, I didn't know what anything was called – I knew plié and entrechat (God knows how) but that didn't mean I could do them, although in our first class (think Sorting Hat with Leg Warmers) Maggie White, a dance teacher, seemingly constructed only of bones and muscles, told me that *'I went down very well'*. How she knew that, I don't know.....

I hated hated HATED Ballet class, mostly because I looked like a complete twat. Who KNEW it hurt so much to put your leg THERE, or your feet like THAT? I just felt like a fool, in my cut off dance pance and stupid leg warmers....I couldn't *jeté* or *ronde* me *jambes* properly, *a terre, en l'aire* or any fucking where. I couldn't accept that this takes years of practice, *"This is where you start payin' – in sweat"* to quote Debbie Allen's immortal line and includes lots of hurty bits.

So. There we were: two fat American babes, who could get their legs anywhere they bloody well wanted, while chewing gum and talking at the same time; 20 or so others, lithe as whippets, ethereal, effortless snatchers of air and grace. And me. Some mutant stick insect who could do nothing, not even 'walk', in my too-tight dance support, me bits all crammed in at odd angles – Nureyev's never looked like that, and I KNOW, being a lump *connoisseur* - belly sticking out, knees knobbly and my locks all awry (I never *went up*, you see) doing my very best to turn out into second, third, fourth, fifth….no wait…that was fourth….hang on…….and on and on…

So, ballet and I chose to disagree.

I was proper bruised and scraped as most of the Modern Classes were on the floor to begin.

Now, THIS was different. I still couldn't really do any of it for toffee. People all around in effortlessly turned out second, foreheads to the floor. I looked as if I was trying to suck myself off – and not even succeeding in that! Nowhere near! Like a gadfly or a transformer that had been mis-assembled. Me bits just didn't go where I wanted, and where everyone else's seemed to. Debbie Allen was right – sweat and pain, but also the feeling that you were walking on hallowed ground. These teachers, these great, wonderful, powerful people had MADE this technique, had GROWN it from their bodies, their cores, their fierce determination to make a change in how the world saw things. SO I accepted the agonies; accepted the thwack of the cane on my shoulders when I raised them as I raised my arms; accepted that I would not, in a year, achieve a miniscule amount of the physical skills needed to master the Graham technique – how pure, how visceral it is! – because I was just grateful to be part of something bigger than I had ever experienced before. LUCKY Mr. Lucky.

I'm not sure what I learned, mind you. I DO know that I had a fabulous year, full of adventures and new things – I LOVED this world, with its nearness to skin, its associations with pure bodies. What I lacked in skill, I more than made up for in enthusiasm and I did, in the end, acquit myself well in my final assessment. I made (as we say in the business) a dance based on Mere Cunningham's ideas of chance, random choice informing the dance – and it worked, really well. I was pleased, they were pleased. It was in the days before video...all that remains is the hand drawn program.

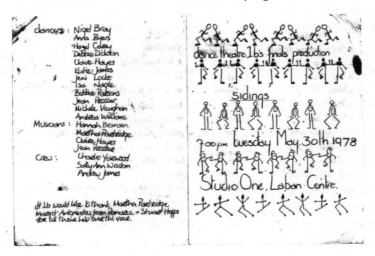

Dance Theatre in Education B1, Finals Programme.

So fast, so fleeting went the year, that it was done before I was ready.......
now what? No more the cocoon of 'being on a course'; no more the certainty of 'Graham at 09.00 sharp', of refectory lunches, Labanotation with Walli Meir followed by more Graham (standing class) with the extraordinary Bonnie Bird (google her!) watching from the barre and making notes. Going home, aching, scraped and scabby but warm with the satisfaction of effort and knowing you'd be back the next day......

Carpe Diem. Did we? Probably not – we didn't prepare for anything, I don't think. Jobs? Nah? I'm not sure what any of us did after Laban. Certainly, none of us became dancers; clodhopping things we were, made of meat and gravity and not trained. Not really, not enough to make any inroad into that ethereal and sublimely beautiful and hellish world. No, I guess we all ended up married or teaching – two certainties in an uncertain world.

There was a sense of impending doom, of horror, that soon we might ACTUALLY be required to do something like, y'know.... *workwise*. Wait! Stop! This wasn't part of the plan! I thought, we all did, those amongst us who'd led such charmed lives so as not have had anything expected of them ever, we could continue doing...doing...well, anything except getting a job. Pay back our debt to society, make our parents, whose noble sacrifices had made all this possible, proud, as we sallied forth into the workplace, with our degrees / Cert. Eds / B.Eds / LCDMs (delete where applicable) .....to change society for the better, to make a difference...I just wanted to carry on shagging, drinking cheap beer and not thinking about it.

But, May came around, with its talk of preparing our final – FINAL – dance piece for the showing, so I began to hatch a cunning plan.... another course! Another year (or maybe three!) of saying *'Hullo clouds, hullo sky' and skipping about like a gurl....*

What if I phone up Cambridge and say: "Hello? University? You offered me a place last year to do my B. Ed, but I told you to go fuck yourself. Is it still available, maybe?"

Maybe not. Didn't matter; they're all too faw faw faw and stuck up their own arses anyway. Boating on the Cam? Tossers. Me, I'm a Entertainer! A dancer! A actor! Cambridge wouldn't be able to handle me! *Footlights*? Load of old bollocks! That'll never amount to anything......

No, I needed a place, a special place, a place for someone who had re-enacted, nay, *reinterpreted* Graham's *'Lamentation'*! Who had met Olwen Wymark! Who had danced, spectacularly lunarly, in the Royal Fucking Albert Hall! A school, where all my skills will be stretched to fantastic places.....so I began to search in the Yellow Pages, covertly lurking in the Uni phone boxes, lest my cover should be blown.

"What are you doing next year? I've got an interview for a job in Manchester," said Jenny. *"Going back home, like."*

"Oh, not sure yet. Still looking around..."

"Well you'd best think on and look sharp.....not much time left now...."

I fucking know that, *JENNIFER*. And stop talking like you're Ena Sharples.

"Something'll come up. Strange to think we won't be here anymore, eh?"

"Yeah. I fookin hated it. Fookin ballet. What's that all about. I only came here so I didn't have to get a job. Nick didn't mind. He's sound, is Nick."

What's going on? You never used to talk like this....like bloody Brian and Michael and their bloody painted matchstalk men. Salford born and bred, Jenny Penny. Shit I'm gonna miss you, with your gangly legs, your roll – ups and your foul fookin gob. And Bobby, and Jean (were they Lezzers?.... Jury's out on that one) and Andrea....and the marvellous Martha Partridge: if I wasn't a homosexualist, I would've lusted after those magnificent boobs that she kept getting out, whilst changing her sweat soaked leotards, after teaching her Graham class.

She liked us, did Martha, and in the Summer, as it goes, we formed a Dance Troupe! Oh yes! Specially chosen from amongst the group – she chose only the 'unusual' (shit) dancers and we had this routine, which she taught us and then performed 'out in the community'.... Weather Permitting. That was our name! Clever eh?

The Opening Procession, Greenwich Park, Summer '78

It was, of course a load of old bollocks, but we thought we were MAHVELLOUS! Just so DANCEY! And COMMUNITY-Y!

'The Farmer's Solo', Greenwich Park.

The Farmer's solo...really? Well, the good folks of Greenwich and of Blackheath applauded and whistled so it must've been good. Or maybe, not for the reason I thought. No matter! It was a beautiful ending for us.

While this was being prepared – me learning how to do a barrel roll! Oh yes! - my secret plan was developing. I had found a place that I was SURE would snap me up, with me skills an' all. And now, I could add, 'Community Dancer (soloist) to my C.V.....

.... It must be a sign! Divine providence! Being *so* close to Bonnie Bird (well, she'd told me off once for 'not contracting deeply enough' in a Graham class; so that's close enough) must've directed my finger to the B section of 'Courses for crap dancers with overinflated egos and ideas above their station' and found.... The Doreen Bird College of Performing Arts! See? Bird and Bird! Two birds! With one stone! This was definitely my way in. Once I tell the people there, I actually know the actual Bonnie Bird...well, deal done. Really? Was I always such a twat? Looking back now, some 40 years, it seems I was. Doreen Bird, well respected, dead in 2004 from leukaemia, did in fact found a very well respected school, one that is still flourishing, in her name and it was to the bosky groves of Sidcup that I was bound as I had applied and been given an audition date, with instructions to prepare 'a piece of dance, self-choreographed, and something musical to perform in front of the panel'.

I didn't, dear reader, want to have to remind you of this, this glorious re-enactment, this movingly powerful piece of dance theatre, but I needed to look at it myself again – but...could I? Could I get away with it....? Would they recognise it instantly as an *homage* to the incomparable Graham? Probably not, on reflection, and anyway I could neither take the risk of being accused of artistic plagiarism (How very dare they! This was MY version, original in its stunningness) or find the bit of blue cloth. I know I still had it (I kept it just in case I was ever asked to give the piece again, which actually, I was, some years later, although it was cut into four and used with the dance class I was teaching) but I knew not where 'twas. So, I was going to have to make a new piece on my own body (see how the dance lingo just trips off my tongue?) especially for the occasion.

Now this is where it became obvious that my own vision of myself as a dancer and the reality of such a thing became a bit of a chasm.....anything balletic was OUT (Fuck! What if they asked for a demo? Tested me on me *port de bras* or me *développé?* I still couldnt tell me *rond des jambes* from me *entrechats*....and this was after nearly a year!) Well, I'd just have to tuck my bits in, and hope for the best. I'd like to quote from Wiki at this point:

'Dance belts were developed and considered desirable for male dancers and others to wear because various choreographic moves can otherwise result in

pain or possibly even injury to the male genitalia which are not supported nor held snugly in place against the lower abdominal area, as well as skin-tight, body-hugging ballet tights would otherwise reveal the contours of the male dancer's anatomy to a degree of detail which could be considered distracting to the audience.'

I would just like to say that that is rather counterproductive in my view. I like this kind of distraction.

Sorry, I digressed. I'll look the part, that's for sure: spandex goolie pouch, so as not to 'reveal the contours of my anatomy' and distract the panel. (..actually, that might be a plan...maybe if I don't wear it at all, or have one bollock hanging out the side, they'd be so busy looking at 'the contours of said anatomy', they'll not notice the quality of my *fouetté*), knobbly knees notwithstanding. Anyway, they'll be so impressed by the other components I'd prepared, I'm sure they'd overlook that part.

So, what to do? I'd heard of someone called Merce Cunningham, who apparently just ran about on stage a lot, at random, flapping his arms. You see? *See?* THIS is just how much of a twat I was. Cunningham, the genius of 'choreography by chance', the developer of a rigorous technique, every bit as demanding and cunning as Graham's, the lifelong changer of perceptions. So, no, Bray, he didn't just 'run round the stage, flapping his arms', you knob. But, anyway, I reckoned if I designed something, using the aforementioned technique of 'running around the stage, randomly, flapping my arms' (aha! But no! All designed, in a Cunningham-ey way!), then I would be seen to be at the cutting edge of modern dance, using all the influences of the master teachers and incorporating their techniques, honed and developed over years, in to *my* piece and the panel would be overwhelmed by my work ethic and barely supressed talent. Then, just the music thing and BOOM! I'd be up for at least another year of shaggin', beer and no job to piss me off. Sorted.

So, my work began in earnest. I found some music – I read that Merce, (Merce! See, close already) used John Cage as his musical inspiration. To my foolish 22-year-old, know – it – all ears, this wasn't really *MUSIC*. It was just silence for hours on end, or else a fuckin' racket, with pennies and nails and bit of wood in his piano or some other bollocks. Music? I don't think so....Silly boy! Not knowing how those spaces was where the dance fitted, that the discords were the impetus for change, for precision, for daring. Watching his work now fills me with wonder – the newness, the skill, the competence and economy of movement. Watching it, back then, just filled me hope that I might be able to blag my way into another year of not getting a job.

I nicked my own idea, actually. I had developed, as you know, a piece to be included in the end of year show, based loosely on Cunningham's idea of chance informing the dance. Meant for 6 dancers, it eventually went on to be really quite a success, garnering fulsome praise, from the fulsome Martha, she of the fulsome bust. Anyhoo....I decided to use this germ of an idea for the audition. Unfortunately, it was just that really – a germ. Winging it with the pros is not a great idea – what they saw in the end was rather like my ill-fated A Level Cookery final – undercooked, badly conceived and unappetising.

I however, thought it would be FABULOUS.

The date was approaching and I still needed to sort out some music. I had no idea what was expected, and so I decided on the 'intimate' approach and that I would take my guitar and sing something noble, something heartfelt, something that showed I understood the frailty of life, the ephemeral nature of beauty and loss....that'll show 'em.

Oooh! Look at me, on the train! My suitcase and guitar in hand (hmm - hmmm), all adrenalined up and off to er....Sidcup, for the first day of the rest of my life! These places are HOTBEDS you know, people being *discovered*......

Hither Green...Mottingham....New Eltham....Sidcup...and there I was. On the platform, not having found out where the College was beforehand. After I'd asked a rather nice chap, I discovered it was a 15-minute walk and I was already late. Well, I'd missed the first train....I had to make sure my hair was OK, and sew up the hole in the armpit of my darling brown cardy, the one I'd worn at the Laban audition. Lucky cardy, I reckoned, so I needed to repair it. It had been like that for months but....you know me! We artists, honestly.....far too busy being creative to indulge in something as Earthly as darning one's cardy.

So, there I was sweating like a fat bird's fanny, on a beautiful day in May, humping a rucksack, guitar case and a great thick, hooded, knitted cardy, marching towards either my doom or my liberation.

Now called 'Bird College'

Which, dear reader, do you think it turned out to be?

I arrived in time, thankfully – 'fashionably late' wasn't really a good idea at this point and I didn't really want to make an 'entrance'; for a start, my beautifully bouffed hair was now sticking to my head and I was puffing. Puffing? You're supposed to be a dancer and you're puffed, after 15 minutes' walk? Maybe a vomit bucket by the door for you? So, I walked in, and was ushered with about a dozen others into a room, where we were told to change and begin a warm up. Ballet class in ten.

WHAT? NOOOOO! They never told me this. Fuck! FUCKETTY FUCK!. I looked around....people already with their legs above their heads, doing the splits, triple pirouettes.....I was doomed. DOOMED!

Dismally, I began to change, wondering if it was even worth it. I didn't even get distracted by the men tucking their bits into their dance belts, fiddling, arranging. Normally I would have considered asking if they needed help – (joking; that was all in my mind. I thought of being a professional fluffer once, but not many openings...) but all I could think of was the oncoming humiliation. Of a ballet class. A bloody bastard ballet class.

"TIME PLEASE, BOYS AND GIRLS. PROCEED TO STUDIO 2" ......boomed the voice of doom.

The girls were quickly Going Up, the boys adjusting their knobs, just so, so it looked as big as possible but didn't show the outline or a bollock. My supportless, goolie peeping plan would never work now. I thought I'd be auditioned separately, you know, one on one stylee. But not this. Not THIS….

We arrived in the studio, all mirrored, where my inadequacies would be repeated into infinity. Some were already at the barre, (I just wished I was at the bar), legs all over the fucking place, full of grace and power. I took my place, behind a really tall bloke, hoping he might block the view of the Ballet Mistress or Master, so I wouldn't stand out too much.

Have you seen the Trocaderos? Well, *they* do it on purpose and it looks funny and its very clever. I looked like some kind of crane fly trying to avoid being stepped on. My limbs just would NOT cooperate; she said one thing, they did another, its hideousness clearly marked out by the line of perfectly poised humans on either side of me, pointing and bending, stretching and *reléving*, full of grace and gravity, all perfectly in time with the piano and the Ballet Mistress's beat. And from the corner of either eye, on the mirrored walls, I could see myself, reflected into nothingness, which is exactly where I wanted to be.

The class lasted about three years, and then it was over. Nobody else was even panting. Actually, neither was I as I hadn't actually done very much – a few vague arm waves, a *plié* or two…..hardly exhausting work. But it was over, and so were my hopes of not having to find a job. Back to Laban for a couple of months, squeeze in as many shags as poss, actually *move* into the bar and wait for July. Julie wouldn't mind, I'm sure. She must see how important it was to me – not the shag bit, obviously, but the need to remain at my *alma mater* for as long as poss.

"BOYS AND GIRLS. Good class; everyone did well. Thank you very much…." she said, and everyone clapped, as is the way. 'Everyone'? Really? We all picked up our towels, girls letting down their hair, and the boys pushing and pulling at their suffocating bollocks, and me…..me, trailing disconsolately behind, towards whatever horror was waiting for me next.

"AUDITIONEES. ATTENTION PLEASE. ORIGINAL CHOREOGRAPHY, STUDIO 4, FIRST FLOOR. ORDER OF CANDIDATES ON THE LIST ON THE WALL IN THE MAIN CORRIDOR. THANKYOU. HAVE A GOOD DAY".

Oh, fuck right off. And stop shouting. How could it get any worse? Anyway, I wasn't here to bloody do ballet. They didn't say that in the letter, the bastards. Any idea how shit that made me feel? No, you don't. do you. Well just you wait! My Merce is up next…ha!

I looked at the list. B. Second, after some girl called Ann Anna? What sort of name is that? So, I went up to the next floor and took my seat outside and waited.

Ann Anna came out of the room, sometime later, leg warmers sadly pleated and crying. Crying. This was getting worse by the minute. OK, breathe. Think… count….12 before you move. 12! Oh yes, not on 4, or 8, but 12! How daring! How original! *Jeté,* hold for …5!! They'll be overawed with the cleverness of the counting, the apparent randomness of the piece, but it was all cunningly crafted, like *Cunningham* crafted…!

No, wait. Was it 5 before I move, then hold for 12? Errrr ….now I can't remember….clock ticking on the wall. Tick. Tick. Tick…Beads of sweat began to accumulate in my rather fulsome eyebrows, from where, in the middle of the piece, they would probably be dislodged and run directly into my eyes, stinging like fuck and rendering me blind…

Tick. Tick.

Come on. Come ON…

Door opening.

"Next. Bry. Miss Bry?"

"No", I replied, in a manly tone. *"Bray, and its Mr actually"*

"Do not matter for me. Come in. We are been waiting since ten minutes."

"What? Why didn't you come and tell me sooner?"

"The girl who come out, she say you to come in".

Oh, fuck. Poor Ann Anna, who was sobbing too much to breathe, let alone speak, had just run away, down the corridor with her hands over her face….

"Come in now, pliss. Dance for the people. They waiting."

Not an auspicious start, but once the music began, and I began to enchant them with my superlative grace and startling originality, they would of course be forgiving; after all, it wasn't exactly my fault they had reduced poor Ann to a suicidal mess..

"Er, hello. My name is…."

"We know your name. You are late. You will have to begin. The schedule is already behind. Because of you."

"OK, er, sorry , but the girl that...."

"Are you ready?"

"Yes! Yes! Ever so ready! This is so important and thank you SO much for inviting me. My piece is called 'The Deal' and is inspired by the wonderful Mr. Cunningham of the New York City Ballet. He is so inspiring and such an inspiration to me and he inspired... (What? Why do you keep saying INSPIRED? Breathe.....). Anyway, the music is a very clever juxtaposition to the dance. It was made (see? MADE!) to a Bach fugue which runs in opposition to the dance, which is inspired by the random dealing of a deck of cards, which......"

I trailed away into silence as I looked up at the panel of six, six Nazis, all silent, all motionless, except the one in the end who kept tapping her notepad with her biro...

"Erm...yes, so. Yes, well, let's begin. I'll just put the cassette in the machine and then we can"....the cassette, with the Bach fugue, recorded from my LP of Bach fugues and cantatas, which was not, in fact, when I peered in, in my bag, but still in the cassette machine, back at home, in Tony's flat.

The world narrowed down to a tiny pin prick of light as the room span away and I was at the bottom, mouth agape, silently screaming....

"..So, after, erm, devising the dance, to the erm, erm, fugue, yes, fugue, by, erm Bach – Johann Sabastian, not the other one – I decided it would be even more original to then showcase my, erm piece by dancing it....in silence! I will retain the music INSIDE my head and so that you will experience a more, erm, unusual and original erm.....thing.

SHUT. THE. FUCK. *UP!!!* Maybe I should just leave and run screaming and sobbing down the corridor after Ann Anna, stepping in the pools of her tears marking the end of our careers? I turned back, and still they stared, *die Oberst gruppen führeren* of the dance world; tap, tap, tap, went the biro, booming off the concrete walls of the studio...

So. ... count....12 before you move. OK, so far so good....8 *chassés,* hold for 5......*plié,* run, blah blah.....actually it began to go quite well. Fuck knows, I'd

rehearsed it enough, so.....hold 12.....hold 5, into 2nd, extend
....leap...land.........shake head ....dislodge sweat waiting in my eyebrows.....

Ahhhhhhngngggggggg STINGING!!!! AH AHAAHAAAA FUCK!! AHHHHHH and
then, caught up in the *jeté* section, unable to stop or see, I crashed into the
table where the panel sat, watching in sheer astonishment (on reflection, I
wasn't sure if it was in wonder, or horror), at this albatross in leg warmers
and what seemed to be a wig, as my legs slid away from underneath me,
such was the momentum and flailing of my arms, just like Merce, and I
disappeared from view, beneath the table and in amongst the panel's legs.

"Erm, I said, once I'd stood up again and swiped the stinging ichor form my
eyes, *"that bit isn't actually in it. It was the sweat, you see......"*

"Next."

And so there I was, in the corridor, but determined, unlike Ann before me,
not to weep. It wasn't really my fault....the floor was probably polished or
something, or that woman with the biro distracted me.

Still, there was the music section to come. Unlike my Cookery A. Level, where
I wasn't really aware of the result at the time of the exam itself, things
weren't looking too good. At this point, however, it was looking pretty
similar. At the mo. But....

Actually, having to wait around for hours for them to finish the 'original
choreography' section didn't help. People going past saying things like:
*"Ooooh, they loved my dance; it went relly waahl....my take on the 'Bayadère
was ver wahl received,"* and *"all the judges were just so lovely to me, they
made me feel really really supported and didn't mind when I fell over and had
to start again. So sweet...".* OK, so it might've been better with the music, but
it wasn't *my* fault I forgot the tape. And if it hadn't been so hot, if the
windows had been open – it was bloody MAY, after all, I wouldn't have had
all that sweat in my eyebrows. And my dance belt wasn't in the right place
and my bollocks felt like they might've fallen out which was at the back of my
mind when I had to do the slow splits bit...

*"STUDIO 6, SECOND FLOOR. MUSIC AND SONG. RANDOM ORDER, ALREADY
CHOSEN, NAMES IN BOARD IN CORRIDOR. THANK YOU."*

Right, this is it. Last chance to impress. And I was 7th, not bad! Home early
and in the bar by 6!

E, A, G, D, B, E...oooh, top E a bit flat. That's it. All in tune, in my comfort zone now. Seasoned Balls Park Folk Club aficionado, me! Do that finger warming up thing. Look at them go, fingers flying like...flying things – such dexterity! I could see the envy written all over their faces.

No 1 sang *'Maybe This Time'*, from *'Cabaret'*.
No 2 sang *'Don't Rain on my Parade'*, from *'Funny Girl'*
No 3 sang Puccini's *'O Mio Babbino Caro'*
No 4 sang *'Ole Man River'* from *'Showboat'*
No 5 sang *'What I did For Love'* from *'A Chorus Line'*
No 6 sang *'Something's Comin'* from *'West Side Story'*
Then it was me. OK, so maybe a song from a show might've shown off my vocal skills, range and power, like the first six, whose voices soared and swooped and rang like bells from the hall. Applause from the panel each time. Impressive.

But, I think my choice showed, daring, and originality and a deeper understanding of the meaning of life.

7!

In I went.

The hall seemed very very long as I walked in and took my place in the centre. Tap, tap, tap went the bitch's biro. Her again, though the others seemed to be different and maybe not aware of my slight mishap earlier (though I bet that vile cow has already grassed me up. I didn't MEAN to take the skin off your shin with my body weight as I hurtled into you, trapping it against the chair leg. I said sorry....) I sat, just played a couple of chords to make sure the tuning was right – top E was down again, tut –, took a breath, remembered all my lines, rehearsed so meticulously, and said:

"I believe my song today has a very serious message of hope, of compassion and is about accepting that, sometimes, no matter how hard you try, it is important to accept that some things are just not possible. And that's OK. About the turning of the world and the hope of new seasons. About...."

"Will you sing? Please.

Now."

I looked at their faces. It was a Mount Rushmore of blank disinterest. Bastards. I'll make you weep....I will melt your hearts and you will let me into your school.

"So. I give you: 'Percy the Penguin'. By Stackridge. In case you don't know."

1971

Three minutes later, after the last chord rang out, and Percy, who had cucumber wings and could never have flown, despite seeking the wisdom of the Polar Bear, lay dead, all alone on the ice, I began to question my choice. Erm....Up against *West Side Story* and *Funny Girl* (*'Eye on the target, and wham! One shot, one gun shot, and BAM!!'*), it didn't seem quite so strong...judging by the look of astonishment on the faces of the panel, I think they tended to agree....

"Um, well, yes thank you. That was very, erm...unusual"

Unusual! That's good!

A silence. A long one. Then the man in the middle said:

"Mr Bry.

"It's Bray, actually..."

"Mr. Bray. Do you have any idea, at all, what this school is? What we expect? What the standards are?

"Well, I....."

"I have had reports from the other two panels (Biro Bitch, no doubt) and I have to say that either you lied on your application....let me see...yes here it is: 'I have studied intensively under Merce Cunningham, and have an excellent grounding in Graham Technique. I have some ballet experience though it is not my strongest suit. However, my vocal training allows me to tackle almost any genre of song. I am looking forward etc etc....' OR you have a completely unrealistic view of your abilities, OR, and I suspect this to be the most likely, OR – you see this course as a way of prolonging your life as a student.

Well. Not here. Your ballet class was appalling..."

"No! She said 'Good class everyone'! I know, maybe, I'm not as bendy as some, but..."

"SILENCE! Your own piece of dance might have been interesting, but you have most certainly NOT studied under Merce Cunningham and.."

"No, I meant to put 'studied Merce Cunningham, not 'under' Merce Cunningham. My..."

"WILL YOU BE QUIET!! Then you come in here and give us a ridiculous piece of whimsy about dead penguins. You couldn't even get your guitar in tune. The top E was flat.

 The whole day has been a fiasco, young man. As you can probably guess, we will not be offering you a place. You will have to find a different place to continue your studies. Good day to you."

As I was shown to the door, the lackey said, sotto voce,

"I was in dance class. I just wanted you know, as you do the splits thing, one of your bollocks, he fell out."

So, that was the ultimate fail – I couldn't even put a jockstrap on properly. Percy had finished me off, cruelly expiring on the ice, as surely as my chance of studentdom had, as my day of reckoning played itself out. I don't know what happened to Ann Anna. Much the same as me I suspect, but at least she hadn't exposed her gonads in 2nd position.

Back on the train, homeward bound, though not as full of hope as Paul Simon apparently was, embarrassed, and full of righteous indignation. You're a *SCHOOL!* You're supposed to recognise raw talent, pluck it from obscurity and nurture it – well, you don't what you missed here, lady! What slipped through your net! Nah, I reckon Mr. Lucky's luck actually held out, by NOT being picked. They might have destroyed Ann Anna, but not me. *I'M* made of sterner stuff. They might have seen my bollock, but they didn't see all the talent deep inside. Call yourselves judges? Pah. And you! Yes you! Woman with the biro. The red and the orange *really* don't go.

I decided to stop off at Laban – after all, the train did stop at New Cross – see me mates, spin a yarn or two and partake of a flagon or six of the Student Bar's finest ale.

"How'd it go? Was it poncey?, asked Jenny. *"Full of soft poofs, like?"*

"No, it was great actually. Everyone was really nice"

"Well......?"

"Oh we had a ballet class, which was OK, but they just loved my Cunningham."

"They did? You just waved yer fooking arms around and tried to do the splits"

"Actually, that's SO rude. It was very carefully made."

"Made? Made of what? Made of shit."

"No Jennifer. MADE. That's what we dancers say when we build a dance. Oh never mind. Pint please."

"So, it went OK, then? asked Bobbi / Jean, the possible lezzers.

"I said already."

"What about the song? What was it? Some bollocks about a dead penguin? Bet that went down well.", snorted Jenny.

"Actually, the panel was very moved, actually".

"So, when do you start not getting a job then?" she asked.

"I decided not to accept their offer actually."

"What? Why?"

"Because I don't feel it's the best environment for my particular skills, that's why"

"You're a fookin dopey cunt then", Jenny said. *"I'd go if it were me. Oh. Meant to say: I got a fookin job interview."*

"I know. Manchester. What for? Sweary twat?"

"Teaching. Fookin teaching."

The thing we dreaded, if truth be told. The thing we were all trained for, ready for, had been subsidised for....

"Oh, so that was a waste of a day then.

"Well, I think for the best. It wasn't really for me."

"Oh, and..", said Jenny, *"And you missed it - Martha had her tits out again."*

I had, on the train, decided not to mention the *barre de ballet*, my fucking up the timetable, the flappy armed dance, the missing cassette, the sweat in my eyes putting an abrupt end to it, skidding on something (probably my sweat), sliding under the table, skinning one of the panel's shins, the out of tune guitar, and most definitely my bollock falling out, though this would have provoked much hilarity and earned massive kudos, I suspect. But I was amongst my coterie – I simply couldn't let the rest of them know, although I'm sure Biro Bitch and her gang will have reported back to the Laban staff. Ah well. One has standards you know, and lying is always the best policy.

Mr Lucky's Day Out – ended happily, surrounded by friends and full of Harp. Mum's the fucking word, eh?

Running alongside the tale of my leg warmers and dance support, of *jete*-ing and *rond de jamb*-ing, is a parallel thread, one just as significant to this tale; one of discovery and pain.

After the debacle of being chucked out of our flat, Slobbidybobbidy and I had a bit of a problem, i.e. nowhere to sleep. We were going to miss that mattress, the skanky walls and its tiny smattering of rabbit's teeth, but.....luckily, or not so luckily for Julie, as it turned out, a friend on the Laban course knew a friend who had a room to rent in a flat. In *BLACKHEATH*, natch! Well, we leapt at it and left Cann Hall road, the following weekend, tout suite, flickin' the Vs and trailing the stench of cabbagenturmeric as we headed ova the rivah. Sarf.

This was due to the fact that on the course was this rather wayward hippy chick called Jenny, whom I adored, mostly because a) she was as shit at ballet as me, being all gangly, and b) she smoked her own rollies and swore like a navvy - two things that this impressionable young gel adored. I had mentioned to her that Julie and I were going to be homeless, again, and she said that she had a friend who was looking for someone to share and help with the rent at this house. In Blackheath. BLACKHEATH!! And what's more...he was a HOMO!! Yes, dear reader, a proper homosexualist. Jenny mentioned our position to him and we agreed we'd meet at hers for dinner. Julie was unable to come to the dinner as she had a shift at the Piccadilly, so I went alone. After all, what harm could it do? Ah, how sweet the gift of hindsight...had she been there, our entire lives may have turned out differently. Or for a while at least, until the Problem returned, which inevitably it would have.....

Anyway, along I went. Jenny had cooked nut roast or lentil cobbler or whatever vegetarians had in those days, and had provided rather a lot of wine. I arrived, and they were there....Jenny, Nick....and Tony. Fuck. Fuckity fuck. He was GAWJUSSS!! Large, solid....like a sort of statue. We ate, drank (too much) Tony flirted outrageously, though I found out later, that was his normal behaviour - silly girl that I was, I thought it was all aimed at me. I was flattered, I simpered and gushed, no doubt and generally behaved like a prat. I probably thought I was making sure he offered us the room; subconsciously I was probably asking him to jump me, as he was, as I said, now with my wine goggles on, a tiny bit GAWWJUS.

So, the next morning, interview over, I saw Jen at the warm up, and she said, *"Tony says it'll be fine for you and Julie to move in. He did say the room was a bit small, but the rent isn't much. You can move in at the weekend".*

"Coo! Thanks Jen. I'll tell Julie when she gets home."

So, that weekend, we packed our stuff and went to Blackheath.

When he said 'small', he forgot to mention 'dark', 'dank' and 'windowless'. On the plus side, it was near the station for Julie to get up to town and near Laban for me to get to College. The flat was a basement flat, with its own back garden, one bedroom (his) and a small kitchen. Our room, when I say 'room', was UNDER the road - presumably a former coal cellar – but you couldn't tell as it was completely dark, no windows, no light other than a table lamp, by the bed. When I say 'bed', I mean mattress. BUT! Still we were YOUNG! We were happening! We were living the London Life. Sort of.

At first, all was well. The days passed. I went off to skip about like a girl and Julie went off to clean up condoms, stiffened sheets and worse in the hotel. But. But......the Problem was in my peripheral vision, always just there, just out of sight. As long as I could keep looking straight ahead, and not down to crotch level, all would be well, but of course, that was never going to work was it? A cock, near, every day, and probably available if I wanted it.

He certainly was an Adonis, that Tony. He had one of those delicious belly hair trails that led mysteriously down in to his pants (which of course, increasingly, was where I wanted to go). I don't remember the exact sequence of events, but I do remember that I had got 'shin splints', from jumping on unsprung, and even concrete, floors at Laban, and I was 'off sick', unable to dance. Julie was up town, at work and it was just Tony and me at the flat. Oh. Dear.

The only place to sit in the flat was on the bed in his room – there was no sitting room – and so there we were, and the next thing was he was kissing me, pushing me back on to the bed. I was alarmed, thrilled, and immediately hard and I instantly forgot the promise I'd made to myself –'NO COCK. It gets you into trouble'. That afternoon passed in a slither of sweat and body fluids. I realise that some of you are of a sensitive disposition, so I will just say this: it hurt. A lot. But not so much that I didn't want to do it again. So we did.

Every afternoon, in fact, as the golden light streamed into the window and lit our rutting bodies. He was a big boy, Tony, but also very experienced and he soon turned the feeling of spending 24 years pushing stuff out, into the very weird experience of allowing things IN.....and I LOVED it. I loved the feeling of being 'taken'; loved the physical sensation of being entered; I loved the slip and slide of our bodies; I loved the release that we shared, in varying positions and endings; I loved the utter exhaustion of that release and the calm that followed. At these times, I had no guilt, no shame, only the rightness of that moment. My argument of *'I can't be, because I have a girlfriend'* was beginning to look less substantial, a shade *insubstantial* in fact.

I don't know whether she could smell sex on me or in the air when she came home, but I do know that Julie loathed Tony, and maybe, in retrospect, that was the reason. Me? I was oblivious to any undercurrent, but just waiting for the time to pass until I could be once more in his arms, and once more have him inside me.

My shin splints lasted far longer than was necessary (or true) so, although I DID have to go in for notation classes and theory, I was temporarily excused class in the afternoons. Tony, who worked for a long since defunct organisation called GALS (Girls Alone in London Service – anyone remember?) he could take off what time he wanted. So. We were able to fuck every afternoon (it never became 'making love', as that was reserved for Julie. I know, *I know*....) and it was GLORIOUS. He had a nice fat dick (though I didn't really have much of a benchmark...it FELT fat) and a lean hard body, and that, oh! That little trail of belly hair, which 'fetish' remains with me to this day, and we relished our illicit times together, writhing and slipping on his silk bed cover in the Summer sun light that streamed in through the blinds. We were never caught, not even nearly, though I do wonder if I was, somewhere, hoping that might be the case – it would force to the front an issue that I could no longer ignore...my Father's words came back to me; *"Which do you prefer then?"* and it was becoming undeniable which it was, and was NOT what I'd told him, and Julie, poor Julie, was fast becoming a girlfriend only in name.

Tony's flat had a small back garden and he grew, to head height and in full view, a complete garden full of marijuana....just a path down the centre, along which he used to move, with scissors, cutting of leaves to dry under the grill and then roll up a few joints for the evening – for whoever might be dropping in, for himself, and yes, dear reader, for me too, although I preferred being pissed – I understood it better, having had years of long experience. He used to sell little bags too, which was probably how he was able to afford a flat in Blackheath (and later, an amazing house in Whitechapel) and to take so much time off work to fuck me.

He had a friend, a theatre director, called something improbable, but I shall call him Luvvie, for fear of being sued, if he were ever to read this (and when it becomes a world bestseller, he just might...), although every word is true, to the best of my memory. He was awful – loud, opinionated, arrogant, and he always turned up when dinner was just about to be served...*"Oh sorry, loves, don't mind me, I can wait in the other room Oh really? You sure? I don't mind. Oh, O.K. then if there's enough..."* Every fucking time. And Tony would always set him a place, and feed him – some of my, and Julie's, dinner. Then they'd get stoned, he'd get even more awful and wavy and luvvie and drink all the drinks, the wine, whatever we had planned for our dinner.

I only mention him because he does play a small part in this story.

He used to come at random times, sometimes in the afternoon. He never caught us but he knew we were fucking. He never said anything, but he looked at me in a spiteful kind of way, as if to say: '*I know. I KNOW....*' and it was always worrying as with him, as with most of us, *in vino veritas* and he could quite easily open his big gob and tell Julie about Tony and me. But, you know what? He never did. He seemed to prefer to have the secret intact – it was more powerful that way. Bastard.

He kept saying *"Go on Tony love, you have to tell her, it's not fair,"* and Tony would reply, *"No, I can't do that. Shut Up Luvvie - I don't want to rock the boat."*

The boat, however was foundering, heading inexorably towards the rocks. Poor Bearsy and me rarely shagged these days – too tired? No. Wrong bits. She must've known, but bravely bore it, looking no doubt for a way out.

And then. One night, Tony had invited Jenny and Nick for dinner, just the five of us. We sat down, round the tiny table, hip to hip, and then...guess what? Fucking Luvvie arrived, gave Tony the usual old bollocks about not minding him, oh go on then if there's enough and proceeded to squeeze in. Next to me. Ewwww. He was clammy always and his hair was greasy and just...just....unpleasant.

The wine got drunk, WE got drunk and then Tony went a-picking in the garden, came in, grilled the leaves and started rolling joints. At this point, sensing how things were going to go, Julie left the table and said, *"Shall we go to bed now? Work in the morning."* Knowing full well I wouldn't, she waited at the door, hand outstretched...a test, a plea; both.

"No, I'll just stay up for a bit. Won't be long. Night night."

So off she went along the little hallway, through the blue door and disappeared in to the dungeon.

The booze flowed, the mara wove its spell and Jenny and Nick were soon unconscious, leaning on each other, like some kind of hairy pieta. Suddenly, Luvvie grabbed me with his pasty arms, and dragged me onto his lap.

"Want me to fuck you, do you? Eh? Like HE does? Come on…. I've got a MASSIVE one, and I will…"

"SHUT THE FUCK UP, LUVVIE!" said Tony, sotto voce. *"Leave him alone. GET OFF HIM!!"*

"She's got to know some time, you know. It's not fair on the poor girl….."

"Mind your own fucking business!" said Tony and pulled my arms, and Luvvie lost his grip around my waist and we tumbled, Tony and I, backwards down the two steps from the kitchen and lay sprawled, me on top of him, in the hallway.

The blue door opened, and Julie came out. She said nothing, but looked at me with such sadness, such sorrow, that my heart squeezed shut for pity.

Then, still with no words, for she had none, smiled sadly, turned and went back to her wide wide bed.

We lived on, sadly, silently, with no words to say. The event that evening ended Tony's and my 'affair'. It seemed clear at this point that the damage was too great, and he had a good heart. Even though it was never reciprocal – and now certainly more so – he respected Julie, and now that what we had done was laid bare, in all its painful detail, he knew we could not continue. And so, that beautiful yet deceitful and sorrowful chapter ended. But the fire and desire it had started would never leave me; the need and the absolute clarity with which I now knew what my future was, shone bright, laced with fear, shame and confusion, but with certainty too. I tried to say the words: 'I AM QUEER', but only to myself. I wasn't ready to say them aloud. It was some time before I did, and then, what catastrophe that brought…

As if to save us, out of the blue, an offer of *another* flat came – friend of a friend….and we, or rather, SHE, grabbed it. Mr and Mrs Lucky found an escape route – she from the hopelessness of knowing her lover was, bit by bit, vanishing, and he from a situation that was, like crack, truly awful but not possible to give up.

So there we were. Proper bedrooms, North of the river again, near a tube, and most importantly, no homosexuals in the house. (Not quite true, but we'll let that pass).

We packed our meagre belongings – plus my Epiphone guitar – and moved out, moved up, moved on. The horror was done. Though, of course, it wasn't.

Tony's little piece of Heaven.

CHAPTER EIGHT.

LIVING IN THE MATERIAL WORLD

In which our hero goes to Carpetworld and enters another one, accidentally.

·

'Do Ya Think I'm Sexy?'

By Rod Stewart. No.3 December 1978.

'If you want my body and you think I'm sexy
Come on, sugar, tell me so (tell me so)
If you really need me, just reach out and touch me
Come on, honey, tell me so....'

I'm not sure he DID think I was sexy, but that wasn't really the point...

~ ~ ~

I was told, by my 'Careers Advisor', the bastard, that by the time I left college in 3 years' time, there would be 'teaching jobs for everyone'. Pants on FIRE! In 1978, there were NO jobs, or at least only shitty ones that no one was willing to do. So I got meself a proper job. In Harrods.

HARRODS! I have no recollection of exactly how that happened. HOW would I have got a job at HARRODS? I have a vague recollection of knowing someone who worked there and said they needed staff for the Christmas period. I'd left Laban in July, I had no job so anything would do and.....well...HARRODS......

So I ended up in the charcuterie department, selling posh spam to people with more money than sense. We also doled out caviar. This was 1979 and it was £45 an ounce THEN! That can't be right, surely? Actually, it might well have been – I've just checked their 'Caviar Bar' and it's now £110 for 30g. And people were buying it by the bloody bucket load. I'd never met people like this before. "Fur coat and no knickers" my Gran would've said. They were so fucking *RUDE*. Arrogant, pushy, imperious, loud. I was a country boy – I never heard the like. In me LIFE!

There was one woman, who after pushing her way to the front, unluckily picked me to serve her (I was too slow at pretending to be slicing me bratwurst with olives when I heard her foghorning her way through the throng). She needed, simply MUST HAVE her caviar, now, *NOW*, because she was going to a desert island for Christmas and her flight was leaving and she STILL had to get to Heathrow, and the traffic was TERRIBLE, loads of FOOLS on the roads, and she NEEDED caviar, LOTS of caviar and she would miss the plane if I didn't hurry up. As if ANY of this was my fucking fault. She should have started out earlier – it was Christmas Eve, fer Chrissakes. Anyway, she spent about £500, and this was '79 remember, and off she went, trailing a cloud of arrogance behind her. FIVE HUNDRED QUID??? As my Mother would've said: "More money than bleddy sense.....

The Charcuterie. (photo: Niels Jørn Buus Madsen)

Mind you, I did develop quite a taste for the black stuff (caviar, not Guinness) because, at the insistence of having to wash the serving spoons every 20 seconds, we'd have to go out to the little kitchen where the open tins of caviar were kept. Spoonful for you, one for me...... (that's fifty quid, thank you very much! Merry Christmas Tiny Rowland!) one for you, one for me (dessert spoonfulls, straight down the gullet). We must have eaten hundreds of pounds worth during that Christmas period. I served Russel Harty, David

Bellamy some mackerel pâté (no of course it doesn't have any bloody bones in it. This is fucking HARRODS) Joanna Lumley had several portions of olives, and a terrine of duck to the Queen's Lady in Waiting, but these were small delights amongst the maelstrom of over privileged, over indulged, rude 'customers' , who were most certainly not always right....it was chaos, it was fun, it was money, it was Christmas!

Below the shop floor is a warren of tunnels where stock is stored, where the staff rooms are, where the toilets are and where I had my first cottaging experience! I didn't even know what it was! Honestly, guv. It wasn't intentional, but it WAS fun/scary/filthy and very very powerful. It set me further along on course for disaster, did I but know it. Forbidden fruit....

I had gone on my break and went down, through the warren of corridors, to the toilet, for a poo. I was just sitting there, minding me own business and someone came in to the next cubicle. So far, so normal. I had put some paper down; I was hoping I wasn't making a splash or farting (my 'cone of shame' moments – something I have never conquered). Then, his foot, just the tip of his shoe, appeared under the partition. Just enough for it to look accidental if the person next door WAS just having a poo. Well, I *was*. But, it didn't move. (The shoe, not my bowel). What was this? Some kind of arcane ritual? Some system of messaging? Some set of coded responses I knew nothing about? What to do? Well, here is what I did do...I put my shoe next to his! Obviously, this was the right response, as the pressure from HIS foot increased a little. Didn't retract, just pressed against mine. By now, I knew what was happening, and I was both scared and exhilarated. What now? What happens next? I felt that familiar surge of lust, in my groin, the rush of blood to the head and loins when there's the possibility of some sex. Animal, unbidden, male, unstoppable.

Next, he withdrew his foot and slipped a piece of bog roll under the partition. Scrawled in biro, nearly illegible (have YOU tried writing on toilet tissue, with a pen, resting on your knee? No, I thought not!) were the words *'MY BRAKE IS OVER. HAVE TO GO. HERE. AFTER WORK. 5'*. Flush, bang of door and he was gone, leaving me breathless and with a hard on. I was appalled, but caught like a mackerel on a spinner. There was NO way I wasn't going to be there at 5, to meet with this man, this axe murderer, this ugly person, this man who couldn't even spell 'break'. I felt sick, I felt adrenalin, I felt.....well, randy.

The day passed in a pâté smeared haze. Wrong amounts weighed, lids not shut properly on containers, meat trays not restocked – I even forgot to go and nick some caviar, that's how preoccupied I was. Thinks...must remember to take my hair net off.....must remember to get the salmon mousse smell off my hands......must remember to not smell of meat / fish / anything pertaining to charcuteric artefacts ...Christ! It was like going out on a first date! The floor manager kept staring; I could ACTUALLY lose my job, they were that strict on customer service. I just couldn't concentrate – bockwurst paled into insignificance! Ham, on or off the bone? Who cares? Chicken breast, skin off.... Actually quite ironic to see these words....'sausage', 'bone', 'skin'......all I could think about was, with trepidation and wet pants, was the mystery cock waiting, at 5 pm.

The time came. I signed out, washed my hands, cleaned my nails (Look, he isn't going to want to marry you....we all know what it'll be....calm down you fool.) and descended the stairs to the Second Circle of Hell, reserved for those condemned with Lust. And there he was. Middle aged, not bad looking, black hair, all his own teeth.....

....and next to the loo, where the deal had been brokered with a knock-off Reebok trainer, was a door. A storeroom. No words, just a tilt of the head, and we entered the room. I don't know what I was expecting – soft music? Dimmed lights? Plumped up cushions, in front of the fire, some candles and chilled champagne with a little Mantovani playing? Or even *'Another Brick in the Wall'*, number one at that time. Er...no. It was a carpet store. Rolls and rolls of carpet, making avenues, down which he propelled me. Judging by the expert way we found 'the place', away from the door, out of line of sight should anyone come in, I imagine that was his shag-lair, the place he went when he copped off. Anyway, down to business. He was already hard by the time we got past the shag pile (hahahaa geddit?) and lost no time in getting it out. He leant up against me and starting noshing on my neck (no kissing – them, apparently is the rooles) and rubbing my crotch. I wasn't quite sure what to do. It was all a bit sudden, a bit animal – no foreplay, no talking even (How naïve! This was a cottage pickup! This is what it's like – you don't chat over a cup of Lapsang Souchong first. Cum and go, mate. Cum and go). I think, looking back, I could be forgiven my gaucheness - after all, I'd never done this before, and he clearly had. But, despite my confusion, my baser instincts took over and my erection soon appeared, willingly or not, which he swiftly whipped out and wrapped his mouth around. Oooof, FUCK the smell of carpets! FUCK the weirdness of the situation! Suddenly nothing else mattered – and he was good. I felt myself beginning the rush, over the crest of that wave, but he stopped. He knew, to the second. *"Now you"*. These were the only words spoken. So I got on my knees and sucked his (rather impressive) dick. Not very expertly it seemed because he pushed my head away and started tossing himself off. I just joined in – it suddenly didn't seem very nice any more – too quick, too harsh. So we came, me spurting onto a pile of carpet offcuts and underlay, binding the tufts together with semen – presumably, the place he usually used, as it seemed to be a bit stiff, a bit matted. Wankminster, probably. And he – he shot in my hair. FUCKING HELL! I had collar length bouffy hair, a la Nick Rhodes, at that time and now it had great globs of jizz in it. He wiped off, zipped up, and fucked off. Charming. I did the same, szhooshed across the corridor to the bog, which fortunately was empty, and….dear reader, I could see no other option as the sinks were small and my hair was large…I ran into a cubicle, locked it and flushed my own head down the loo, rubbing my hair furiously as the water cascaded over my face and upturned nose. Choking and spluttering and dripping, I grabbed a massive handful of paper towels and scrubbing furiously at my hair, sneaked out of the bog and returned to the (fortunately) empty staff room, collected my fur coat and my thoughts, and walked along the OUT corridor, got felt up by security who every night checked you hadn't knicked anything (like a quarter of ham in me pants? Really?) and stepped out in to the Knightsbridge air.

It was snowing, and as usual, Julie was waiting.

"Hello Bearsy," I said.

"Had a nice day?" she said, turning round, from watching the snowflakes falling through the neon-coloured air.

"Erm,…. Different, certainly."

"What on earth have you done to your hair?" It was about three feet wide and tangled like an exploded bale of hay.

"Oh. Um. I um…got some.. er…caviar in it so I had to wash it quickly."

"Doesn't smell like caviar. "

"Oh," I said.

She looked at me, in that odd way she had. And said no more.

Ho Ho Ho Harrods.

CHAPTER NINE.

THE DISENTANGLING.

<u>In which our hero faces the truth. And hates what he sees.</u>

'You Don't Bring Me Flowers'

Barbra Streisand/Neil Diamond. No.7. January 1979.

> *'You don't bring me flowers*
> *You don't sing me love songs*
> *You hardly talk to me anymore*
> *When I come through the door at the end of the day...'*

I wasn't really bringing anything anymore. I had nothing left to give.

~ ~ ~

And so. Our days went by. Christmas came and went and with it a burrowing sense of dread, the feeling that my 'encounter' was one more step along the road that was leading to catastrophe. I had kind of put Tony and all the bum fun down to 'opportunity', a chance to 'explore my bi side'; certainly, service had been resumed in the how's-your-Father department and Slobbidybobbidy's lady garden was being well attended to. We had our flat, some friends who 'came for dinner'. We listened to *'Diamond Life'* and they said *"How nice"*, and *"I like your sofa"* and *"We have a plant like that."* They even liked my first attempt at a fish dish, even though it looked a lickle bit messy on the plate. This was on account that it had slid off the grill pan and when it hit the kitchen floor, disintegrated in to its constituent parts. Undeterred, and gin fuelled, I just scraped it back up, and served it 'in a different way'. No hairs were reported. The flat was nice. We had a telly, we were near the tube, and Paul Hardcastle's house (NOT number 19 hahaaa) and off we went to work, like jolly little twenty – something commuters. Because...

I had a job! Oh yes, I did, dear reader! Mr Lucky had a job. Again, I don't know how it came about. I was laid off from Horrids because Christmas was over and I somehow found myself heading for the Town Hall in Enfield for an interview. All a bit Star Trek really – one minute sucking a knob in a carpet warehouse, the next – on a train, in a suit, going Into Education. In my memory, it went something along the lines of:

Man*: "Hello. I hear you're looking for a teaching job?"*

Me: *"Yes".*

Man: *"Have you had any experience?"*

Me: *"No, I qualified in 1977, did a fourth year of study* (I didn't mention Laban, in case it was too poofy) *and then worked in Harrods because I really wanted to work and pay my debt to society and my parents for putting me through College, where I learned so much*".* (*right answer)

Man: *"What did you do in Harrods?"* Guessing he didn't want to know everything I'd done, I responded,

"Interacted with the public and improved my people skills." (*Right answer no2)

Man: *"Oh, very good. Here. Have a job. Go to Bush Hill Park JMI School and tell them you can start on Monday. Bye."*

I look back at this with great amusement and fondness for the simplicity of the system then, having been grilled for hours, by panels sometimes for two days, for jobs I applied for later in my career. I didn't even have to have a kiddyfiddling form.

Bush Hill Park JMI School, Enfield.

So, there I was, Monday morning, 8.30 sharp, in my first job. The first thing I saw was one of the teachers dragging a boy down the corridor by his ear, stopping, rolling up his trouser leg, slapping his legs hard, 4 on each and then sending him back to his room. *"OH! Hello!"* she said, cheerily. *"I'm the Deputy Head. You must be the new one. That's your class, in there"*. And that was it. No introduction, no induction – I could have been a child rapist for all she knew. 'Here! Here's 30 for you!' Luckily the Head came along, and introduced herself, and me to my class – but it was still a baptism of fire. Kids being smacked, dragged to the hall for detention, stopped from actually having lunch.....all things being a sackable offence now (even if the little buggers deserved it, which they often did).

I was there a year – my 'probationary year' as it was known then. All the kids thought I was shagging Miss Winehouse (I would have, just for her name.....) in the stock cupboard, of which I was In Charge, having been given a 'Stage Two, Art Coordinator' (a.k.a. keeping the Art Cupboard tidy). It was quite fun, quite grown up, rattling past Ally Pally every morning on the train from Liverpool Street. Nothing to report from school really.

However.

I was at home with my lady love one half term, and a letter came through the door. The clap of the letter box was the harbinger of doom, did we but know it....

It was from Chris, who had gone off after Balls Park (Oooh! A thought! Talking about Balls Park, I don't think I told you: the first band that played at the Student Union were called Thunderbox. The only memorable thing about them is their massive hairy lead singer bellowed: "BALLS PARK? BALLS PARK? WITH ALL THE FUCKIN MINGE HERE, IT SHOULD BE CALLED CUNT PARK. HAR HAR HARRRR"......) sorry, yes...Chris. He'd to do something musical but had also got his first teaching job, in Forest Gate. Was that near me and could we meet up for a pint the letter said? Well, the answer was Yes and Yes! My favourite homosexual was back! He had a flat within walking distance – a 'Teachers Flat', provided, for free, by the borough! (Yep, for real!)- right on the crossroads in Leytonstone at the Thatched House – one of the four roads issuing forth from there was Cann Hall Road, where Julie and I had been force fed cabbagenturmeric and picked up shards of rabbit teeth! Oh, what synchronicity! Anyway, I wrote back and said we'd be delighted to see him again and arranged to meet at the Thatched House pub, on the crossroads at the bottom of Leytonstone High Road, and not far from our flat, long since gone and now an Estate Agents.

The Saturday came, and I excitedly, and Julie reluctantly (she had a nose for disaster, did Julie) toddled along to the pub and there he was. My Nemesis. The man who was to change my life for ever. We got drunk. Hopelessly, and I couldn't stand, let alone walk back to Pearcroft Road, so Chris said, *"My flat's just round the corner. Stay there if you want."* So we did.

Thus began the time I shall call 'The Disentangling'. The time when it was possible for me to still be a coward, to use her and to still hang on to the last vestiges of my relationship, when I could be too drunk to get home so *'I'll just stay with Chris'*. Not that there was anything between us, Chris and I, other than a fierce and abiding love. I just felt freer there. I could be a bit poofy, and know he wouldn't mind. I could be, what was becoming increasingly and painfully clear, myself there; what I really was.

It was a terrible, sad time for us. For her, especially. She was facing forces she couldn't control or change. We still hadn't talked about it, but my behaviour over the first few months of 1980 was both despicable and painful for her and I am sorry. Truly sorry. I was doing things I could not stop, then lying in the face of clear evidence to the contrary. It was ghastly, and messy and I look back with shame at the way I handled The Ending. It was full of blood and tears and gin, my anaesthetic of choice. It was just so HOPELESS – we said bad things, very bad things and sweet hopeless things, to stave off the inevitable. She wished she had bigger tits, smaller tits, longer hair, blonder hair, prettier dresses, but we both knew none of these things mattered.

We both needed fucking. Aye, there's the rub.

My tending of her Lady Garden had long since stopped; I was staying at Chris' more often, usually drunk, but more because I couldn't face the sorrow, the deathly silence of my house. Then, one night, the tipping point was reached. I didn't come home. To either place.

77 Pearcroft Road, the beginning of the end…

CHAPTER TEN.

A NIGHT IN TURNPIKE LANE.

In which our hero finds 'you should be careful what you wish for', and suffers an almost unbearable loss.

'Breaking The Law'.

by Judas Priest. No.12. June, 1980.

'Feel as though nobody cares if I live or die
So I might as well begin to put some action in my life….'

This was *so* not part of the plan; I broke every promise.

~ ~ ~

Chris said one day that he was going to a pub in the West End called the Salisbury. He had to go 'Up West' for something to do with school and we could meet for a tea time bevvy. Good idea, I thought, not knowing that this, this of all things, would be the thing that brought my house of lies tumbling and break my Bearsy's heart.

June 27th, 1980. The night I did a BAD THING. It was horrible, it was frightening, it was unstoppable, it was the sum of all the ridiculous things I thought would be right and they turned out to be wrong.

So. I got the train down from Enfield, marking all done, to fill in time until The Great Adventure. I wandered down Tottenham Court Road, past Centre Point, along Charing Cross Road, along St Martin's Court to The Salisbury.

FUCKFUCKFUCK……the place had homos and queers all around the entrances, the side, the corner and the big double doors at the front. Just standing there, talking, smoking, and laughing. Like real, normal people. The doors kept swinging open, people went in, and people came out, kissed each other hello, and kissed each other goodbye. ON. THE. LIPS! I crossed the road and stood opposite the main doors, those famous stained glass deco doors, and watched, and waited for Chris. And there he was, all homo-y and not caring, like he was at College, but now in a place where no one would judge him. HE WAS JUST LIKE ONE OF THEM BY THE PUB!

"COOO –EEEEE!!" he yelled and I looked round in a panic in case people were listening, looking. Nobody was. *"Come on, you twat, I need a pint. It's your round"*. It always was, I seem to remember. Always in the pubs and bars, he wasn't 'quite finished, go on, you get yours', or he needed a slash, spotting we were nearly dry….anyway, I crossed the road, he'd already gone in and the doors had swung shut in my face.

'The Gateway To Damnation'. Salisbury Arms, W1.

I stood there, transfixed. Someone came out, and I could see in – into the pit, into the place from where there would be no escape. The doors swung shut. Still, I stood. I knew, I KNEW, that once I pushed open those doors, once I crossed that threshold, I would be lost. Lost to sin, to lust, to flesh and sweat – all the things I both crave and feared. The air gusted out again, as a couple, older, came out arm in arm. *"You going in love?"* one said and he held open the door. 'Love? *LOVE??'* *"Um, no. No, thanks"* and once more the doors swung closed, a barrier between me, here on the pavement and a new life. Once I stepped in, EVERYONE WOULD KNOW. EVERYONE....

Then the door opened again and it was Chris. *"Come on you dozy cunt, I'm fuckin PARCHED!"* (he always had a way with words) and he held open the doors.

"Come on! It's your round..!"

I stepped in.

No bolt of lightning. No crack of doom. No Satan, no pit of hell yawning at my feet. Just Chris, saying *"You OK? You look weird. I'll 'ave a lager, please"*.

No one stared. They just carried on drinking, laughing, kissing, smoking, just being gay in a gay pub. So, I bought the beers, we found a seat, and thus began a chain of events that changed my whole life in one night.

It was about twenty past five; all the office drinkers were in. Long before the days of the Hooray Henrys, people were just drinking pints. Normal pints. Like.....beer. How could everything be so normal? Apart from a couple of blokes snogging, which I found utterly unreal and found myself unable to stop staring. *"Stop staring, fer fuck's sake,"* said Chris. *"Haven't you seen two blokes kissing before? I'll have a lager."* Well, no actually, I hadn't and found it repellent but also amazingly seductive. *"STOP FUCKIN STARING AND GET THE DRINKS IN!! I'm going for a slash".*

I ordered more beer.

The evening wore on, people came and went – theatre people, people who were dancers, actors and this was THEATRELAND! I WAS IN A GAY PUB! WITH ME BEST MATE! MORE BEER LANDLORD!!!!!......

We continued to drink, and the fact I had a fiancée waiting at home, not having told her where I was, became less and less relevant and important. Mobiles hadn't been invented, so what was I supposed to do? Ring? Nooo!

That would mean having to find a phone box and make sure I had some 10p pieces. No time! MORE BEER LANDLORD!!

The evening wore on and by now I was pretty pissed and EVERYONE seemed really *really* attractive. A bit blurred, but very lovely all the same. Especially, THAT one, over there, on his own. But what to do? I had no tool kit, no 'methodology' other than sticking my foot under the door, clearly not the appropriate method here. What to do? *"Chris, look at him. Look, over there. GAWWWJUS, eh?"* But Chris, the bastard, was up at the bar with his own 'bit of trade' (as it was called. Who knew? Not me, at that point, certainly). *"Chris."*

"Chris!"

CHRIS!

CHRIS!!

"Oh fuck off! I'm busy. Obviously. Mine's a lager."

"Yes, but…. Chris…. …CHRIS……CHRISSSS!!....."

"Oh fer fuck's sake….." and he went OVER to the bloke, said something to him (Please don't let it be 'my friend fancies you…') and returned to his 'trade', taking my pint as he went past. *Don't look up. Don't look over.* I kept my eyes focussed on the table, where my drink used to be, totally torn and bewildered as to how to deal with this – wanting it, being fearful, and not knowing the rules…..

I became aware of a crotch, at eye height, next to my table.

"Mind if I sit down?" Northern. Yorkshire, maybe or Lancashire. I wonder why he's in London? Maybe he's got a job here. A bricklayer. Maybe he's a plumber. Working to send money back to Poland. Maybe he's a teacher. An actor, and that's a pretend voice. Maybe…

"MIND IF I SIT DOWN?" The music, once very loud, seemed to pause mid song or maybe the barman was turning the record over, but the voice dropped like a bomb in to the silence.

"Erm…that seat's taken, I'm afraid…."

"No, it's not. It was your mate's. But he's gone."

Uh, no, he's at the ....."

No, he fucking wasn't!! My only point of reference, security, way out of this situation I was in, which had suddenly escalated into something terrifying / amazing had copped of with Miss Chaps and gone! Bastard!!

"Oh, well, yes OK...."

"Ta".

Dear reader, the rest of the evening in the pub passed in a kind of lippy blur....I'd had about 40 pints of lager and no dinner and now he was even more gawjuss.....

I was about to say: *"Have you come far?"* (like the bloody Queen!) when he launched himself at me, pinned me against the banquette (HAHAHAH BONKETT) and started snogging my face off. I was really pissed, and so was he, so we just snogged and snogged and then the barman came over and ACTUALLY SAID: *"Drink up now, it's getting on time to close....,"* - if THAT wasn't a sign...actual Joni words from an actual Joni song, registering dimly in my spinny head, though he wasn't actually wearing fish net stockings and a bow tie, then what was???.......and then we were out on the street, drunk, flushed, sore lipped from scraping stubble, and still in my work clothes and with my briefcase in my hand.

"Come on. My place," he said and started dragging me up the road to the tube at Tottenham Court Road.

I was utterly torn – sex, cock, everything I wanted was here on offer, right now, but my brief case was a mocking reminder of my other life: boyfriend, teacher, and responsible adult.

"OK." O and K.

The End of My Life as I knew it came with those two tiny letters.

We lurched along the Court; he was, actually VERY drunk, more than I'd realised. He kept stopping and pressing me up again the wall, trying to kiss me. For FUCK'S SAKE!! We were out in public! I kept pushing him off, he kept staggering – I was, by the time we reached the Tube, beginning to wonder whether this was a good idea.

'Kenneth Ockenden, 23, was Canadian student on a tour of England; Ockenden encountered Nilsen in a pub on 3 December 1979. He was escorted

on a tour of Central London, before agreeing to accompany Nilsen to his flat for a meal and further drinks.' Hmmm, sounds a bit similar. Dennis Neilsen was a nice bloke, too, apparently. As was Jeffery Dahmer. But STILL I kept walking....the lure of his cock overrode everything else – my fiancée waiting at home; my lesson plans still incomplete in my case; the fact I had work in the morning; the chance this man might murder and dismember me.....all of this mattered less, at that moment, than the chance of having sex with him. A man I didn't know, who was so drunk he could barely stand. But a man, who I had seen when he'd stood by my table, had a big bulge and he had a hairy chest, tufts of which poked out of the top of his shirt and made me helpless with desire.

We got to the tube, and went down to the platform. It was pub chucking out time and it was pretty crowded. And he kept grabbing me and snogging me, there, right there on the platform. I didn't really know what to do – I kept pushing him off, he kept lurching back in – but luckily the tube came, slid to a halt, the doors opened and he got on. NOW!! Run, you twat! RUN! It was the only time he'd not been mauling me since we left the pub. – Just run away!! Now!

I got on the tube.

We sat together, and still he kept launching himself at me, all slobbery and majorly embarrassing. HE, all denimed – up, me looking like a preppie – I still had my jacket and tie on, fer Chrissakes!

Somehow, we negotiated the change of lines on to the Piccadilly Line at Holborn and we roared on, on through Russell Square, Kings Cross, Caledonian Road, Holloway Road, Arsenal, all flashing by while we hurtled north, we strange soon - to – be bedfellows, towards Turnpike Lane. Somewhere between Holloway road and Manor House, he said, *"Nnnngggg. I feel sick"*

As the train began to slow, he vomited. Right there. On the floor of the tube, gallons of lager and bits of whatever he'd eaten prior to going to the pub. BLUURRGGHHHHHH. The stench of sick started to fill the carriage and people began to look disgusted/annoyed, partly because of the smell and partly because the sick was running round the carriage floor and getting on their Louboutins and Gucci bags.

I just smiled weakly, trying to look as if I'd never seen him before – clearly untrue as he'd been tonguing me for the last twenty minutes – and prayed to be struck down dead, right there, right then.

Just then, we slid into Turnpike Lane station. The doors opened, letting out some passengers, gasping for air, the stench of beer and vomit and him. He stood there on the platform, swaying, and looking at me.

In the moments it took for the passengers to get off on this busy train and to allow the new ones on, I could have just stayed in my seat, feet pulled up to avoid the swilling pool of vomit on the floor, allowed the doors to shut, and slid off into the tunnel to the next station, got the next train south, then east and been back with my dearest love. In those moments, that was my window of opportunity to escape what had turned into a fucking nightmare.

And it was in those moments, he looked at me, and rubbed his crotch.

I got off the train and followed him like a crack whore.

We walked, my Nemesis and I, through the night streets of Turnpike Lane and reached, after some stumbling and colliding, his flat. No.19. It had a dark red door with one of the numbers, the 9, having come un-nailed and hanging upside down. 1980 and the ghastliness of this night is imprinted in my memory as if it was yesterday.

What was no.19.....now a restaurant called 'Paradise'.

How deliciously ironic...

We got upstairs to his flat, top floor, with a probable view, in daylight, of the place I was to be murdered. He drew the curtains and I had no idea at this point what was going to happen to me. Were we going to fuck? Was he going to kill me? Were we going to have a coffee and then I could go home....I didn't know. I had no tool kit for this. How did I ever end up here?

He began to undress, fumbling with his belt, pulling at it, but not enough to disengage the buckle. He fell backwards on to the bed. AGAIN, I could have escaped. But what did I do? I crossed the room and helped him undo his belt. Then his shirt, which was covered in great patches of sick (nice, eh?) but as I did this, I revealed his beautiful hairy chest and he had the same trail down, down, down as Tony had, and I was lost. The balance between feeling lost and scared was being replaced by the feelings of the possibility of sex, of touching this chest, this man's flesh, and my dick was telling me I was right.

He sat up, sort of, and I managed to get his shirt off, and then I put my briefcase, holding all my real life, on the floor, near the door, then I took off my shoes, my tie, my shirt, my trousers, my socks and pants, all in one go, like a man possessed, not pausing to weigh up the consequences of my actions. Stark bollock naked, and hard, I stood before him and he seemed to come round a bit – obviously his lurve juices were running now too as that bulge, that had dragged me across London, was looking decidedly larger and more inviting by the second.

"Let's get in bed," he slurred, and stood up, and pulled back the covers, and I tried not to mind the tissues that tumbled across the floor.

"Um, OK," I said. O and K. Two little letters. How can they cause so much harm?

So I lay on the bed and he wobbled to his feet and allowed his jeans to drop. *"Pull them down,"* he said and I took the waistband of his pants and eased them over the ridge of his cock. Look, I am not intending to make this a 'sex bit', for you to perv over. I'm just telling you what happened, that night, Turnpike Lane, June 27th 1980. (I know this, because in my disgust, I wrote a poem, as you do, and that's the date on it, but as its utter shite, I'm not including here).

His cock was the fattest cock I had ever seen. I'd not seen many at that point, as you know, but logic told me that, no fucking way would that fit ANYWHERE. Mr. Fatcock said, *"Right, come on then"* and tried to force it in to my mouth. Well, honestly, I couldn't open my mouth wide enough. It was like a fucking fire extinguisher. Only pink. I pulled away, and he obviously misread my meaning because the next thing I remember was that he'd managed to hoist me up under my hips and suddenly, I was on all fours ('doggy style' hadn't yet entered my vocabulary) and he was trying to poke it up my arse. Well, clearly it wasn't going to go, any of it. Not even the tip, which was fatter, wider than most people's entire arms. I tried, valiantly to guide it, but as I couldn't even get my hand round it that was pretty pointless.....

He tried a few more pushes, moaned a bit and then I suspect, he reached the brick wall where all of these encounters must end for him. I have often thought back to that night and how his life turned out – did he ever find a lover? Was he destined to be rejected at the very point when he really would have wanted validation, approval, acceptance, and not just have to have yet another wank, filling the bed with accusing tissues? He stepped back and sat on the bed beside me. He suddenly looked very sad and very lost. And still very drunk.

"I need to sleep now," he said, so I lay down beside him, pretty pissed still myself, and shut my eyes. Sometime later – minutes? Hours? – he stirred and the next thing I knew, he was sitting astride me, staring down at me, his massive cock rearing up in front of my face. Oh god, not again! I thought but the next bit of this utterly surreal evening was about to happen.

"WHOOOOO ARE YOU.........WHAT ARE YOOOOO......WHERE ARE YOUOOOOO.........." he said, but in a really spooky wailing kind of voice while at the same time waving his arms above his head and in front of my eyes, like Kate Bush but with a stiffy. *WHAT....??*

"Erm.....I don't......"

"WHOOOOOOO ARE YOOOOOO? WHAT ARE YOOOOOOO? WHY ARE YOOOOOOOO...." Fuck, this was getting weird.....maybe he WAS going to kill me after all and they'll find me in his freezer in six months' time.....

*"Look, erm..(*I didn't even know his NAME!), *"why don't we go back to sleep now?"* I said, patting his arm, and trying to avoid touching his giant knob. *"It's really late....."* And I have......OH FUCK!!!!! I. HAVE. WORK. IN. THE. MORNING!!!

My brief case stared at me, accusingly....

"BUT WHO ARE YOOOOOOOO? WHEN ARE YOOOOOOOOO? WHY ARE YOOOOOOO?...."

"Listen, maybe we should stop doing this now. Why don't you just get off?"

By now, he was in full 'Wuthering Heights' mode, with his arms and his knob all waving about out of synch, and he couldn't seem to hear me. That and the fact that he was pressing on my bollocks something awful, with his gyrating, made me just push him backwards, and he tumbled off me, off the bed, and cracked his head on the floor. And lay still, his big ole cock lying over to the side and his eyes shut.

OH FUCK! OH FUCKFUCKFUCK I've killed him. He's dead. That's MURDER. That's life imprisonment. That's oh FUCK!!!!!

I went over to him and knelt down. Silence. *"You OK, erm......thingy?"*

Nothing. I was crying now, the alcohol suddenly wearing off. What to do? What to do? I am in Turnpike lane, with a dead naked homosexual with all my lesson plans not finished. I was screwed. A dead man walking.

I leant over him, and then, like something out of 'Carrie', he suddenly shot out his arms, put them round my neck and, can you believe it, started trying to snog me again! Awwwwhahhhhhhhhhhhhh.....

I pushed him off, and he let go.

"Let's go to bed now," he said. I didn't know whether he intended to attempt some more cock and bum fun or just REALLY sleep, like he said. But, I got up, not really feeling particularly horny at this point, and got back on the bed. Within seconds he was asleep. And I watched the dawn filtering through the curtains.

You couldn't have made this up, and I haven't. Every word is true, including the next bit.....

I gently sat up, and he didn't stir. He had a morning woody but I managed to avoid it (just) and slipped out of bed.

I stank. Of sweat. Stale beer. Vomit. I had the headache from Hell and a mouth like Gandhi's flip flop. What time was it? I searched round the room and there was the clock, saying 6.50. So, I had to get a bus or a taxi, go home all the way to Leyton, shower, shave, eat something to counteract the acid in my stomach, do my lesson plans and get out to Enfield by 8.00. That was SO not going to happen.

So, dear reader, to my eternal shame, I had a quick wash there, knicked 40 quid out of his wallet and got a taxi to school. Later, *MUCH* later, Chris asked if I'd had a good night. I wasn't sure how to answer that.

The scene of my downfall...

CHAPTER ELEVEN.

THE RECKONING.

<u>In which our hero breaks a heart. And that's all.</u>

'Love Will Tear Us Apart'.

by Joy Division. No.17. July, 1980.

*'And we're changing our ways, taking different roads
Love, love will tear us apart again....'*

We most certainly were torn apart.

~ ~ ~

I DID make it to school, filthy, sweating from the alcohol, covered in shame and remorse. I went straight there, descending into the tube, remembering that not eight hours ago, I had passed the other way, vomit on my shoes, heading towards the worst night of my life. The kids stared a bit, some went *'POOOH, SIR!'* but the day passed. Ironically, nothing had actually happened, but only for reasons of physical incompatibility, and yet everything had happened.... I'd lied, I'd been unfaithful, I'd been totally unprofessional coming to work the way I did – I should have thrown a sickie – I had stolen, I had put myself in possible danger......as I said, that **O** and that **K** had wrecked my life and I still had to go home and face all the hurt and betrayal I had caused there. All for a shag. Which actually was awful and never actually happened. What a price to pay.

On the trains home I tried to devise what to say. And failed. What could I say? There WAS no excuse, there was no other reason for my not coming home, not finding a phone box and calling, and returning dirty, exhausted, stinking of stale booze and fags, and unable to raise my eyes. It was at this moment that the truth of my situation really became clear. THIS is what I was, and for too long now we had shut our eyes, turned away, tried again, hoped it would go away, hoped it would stop.

Well, it would. Stop. Now. My night in Turnpike Lane – what a catalyst, what a deal breaker! So, I would NOT make an excuse, I WOULD tell the truth and I

WOULD accept the consequences, although we both knew what they were going to be.

"Hi, Bearsy," I said.

"Don't fucking call me that ever again, you fucking fucking SHIT. Where were you? No, don't tell me. With a man. Having sex with a man. Again. Like that fucking Tony? (she did know then….) *Who else? EH? WHO FUCKING ELSE???? YOU BASTARD…….."*

I'm s…….." I was going to apologise (as if that would have made a difference) but I didn't finish the word because she punched me in the face. Bang. Just like that. Like a Golden Ear Whizz but with a hundred time more pain. For us both. *"Get your fucking things and fuck off. NOW! Go on! GO TO FUCKING CHRIS'S! GO ON!!!"* she screamed, as I tried to see through my swelling eye.

I managed to look at her then, at her beautiful face, all puffed with tears she'd cried through the night, now narrowed with anger and sorrow. That face, that was supposed to have been the last thing I'd see as my final breath left my body, now all pummelled and hurt and overwhelmed with grief and the hopelessness of the situation she had found herself in.

"You have to know. Bearsy. That I love you. And that I cannot help this. Or change it. You have it know it is not your fault. You have to know that there is nothing you have done wrong. You have to know that there is nothing you can do to make it better. Or less painful. Just know that it is not. Your. Fault."

I was sobbing now, unable to form my lips into the words I so badly needed her to hear, so whether or not I did actually say these things, or they were just an unintelligible scramble I don't know. But she understood the import, that the meaning of her life had gone and that she was powerless.

I include a poem here. Not very good, but it shows how we were with each other and what a sad sad thing this was.

Once upon a day

There were two bears.

One was big and the other was small

And they loved each other a lot.

Now, the Big Bear had a problem,

That was bigger than him

And sometimes bigger than both of them.

The Problem used to come at night

(which is the time when Bears should be thinking about each other) and it creeps up,

with its black hands stretched

and the Big Bear joins hands with one black hand

and sort of likes it but

he holds tight to Little Bear with the other and holds oh-so-tightly.

Sometimes the Big Bear can't be interested and Little Bear

Feels very sad and hopeless.

(He feels very sorry for her

Because he needs her to feel sorry, such a lot).

But sometimes though

Little Bear Feels as big and tall as Big Bear

And at those times he puts his long white hands

Round the neck of the problem

And slowly squeezes its life away and its nasty black blood.

And then he takes Little Bear's hands

And they are very close and they run away laughing

The sad thing is that the Problem

Has more lives than a cat

And it keeps coming back

So Little Bear is thinking of seeing a man,

A man with eyes as big as plates,

Who will chase away the Problem

Because maybe Big Bear

Can learn to hate ALL of it, instead of only half

And then get on with loving Little Bear

With all his heart,

In peace.

The End

July 25th 1980

Beaten, and bruised, I went to get my 'stuff' – all my life packed into a holdall, whilst knowing I would have to come back for the rest and face her wrath and agony again; it was not an idea I relished but......I needed to man up here; it was HER who's life had been wrecked, irrevocably altered, and now had nobody to hold, to break bread with or to tell her heartmost secrets.

Hang on. That was me too.

It was far from satisfactory, me dossing most nights at Chris's and Julie living on her own (though, not, I hasten to add, alone, as she was being repaired by friends), but I moved, completely, with all my worldly goods, such as they were, into the bedroom vacated (by fate?) by Chris' housemate, and so began my New Life. I hadn't really ever considered a life without Slobbidybobbidy, and the thought of being her boyfriend, then fiancée then husband had been a given. Obviously the 2.4 children bit was going to be an issue, due to the Problem, but we were STRONG! We could face it down, or at least live alongside it. But of course, dear reader, we all know that that way disaster lies.

In my life since then, I have lost count of the number of stories I have been told by men who married when they knew full well they shouldn't have – they thought 'it wouldn't matter' (it always will), that 'they could get through it together' (you won't), that it 'would go away' (it doesn't); sad tales of sad men and even sadder wives. I've lost count of the number of 'straight' men I have had sex with; I've lost count of the number of married men that I have talked to on line, who can 'host, between 2pm and 5pm' (when poor wifey is at work).

Yes, it's hard. Yes it's unbearably sad to break up but believe me.....it saves a whole lot of heartache further down the line.

So, weeping for days and drinking enough gin to sustain a distillery, my new life began. And it was shit. I had nothing familiar to sustain me. The thing I wanted was in E10, in my flat, surrounded by my smell, my imprint – was that of comfort to her? Or worse? I went to work, I came home, I drank gin, had some beans on toast and went to bed where I cried some more. Chris, in his wisdom, didn't offer comfort, or say it'll be OK – he knew I had to go through this; he knew it would lessen as the time became right. He just bought beans and gin and let me go cold turkey. Days passed; it was still shit. Silence and staring. I knew every curlicue in the lounge carpet. Was THIS what I had crushed Julie's spirit for? Broken both our hearts? This endless flatline of emptiness?

One lighter moment came, when in despair (and maybe trying to justify my actions to myself as having been the right ones) I had sex with Chris' ex-housemate who had come round to get the remainder of his things. We had a drunken shag (well, I was – he probably wasn't but saw an opening. So to speak). Anyway, a few days later the phone rang and it was him to say he'd got syphilis. Yay! All of his recent contacts were to report to the clap clinic, pronto. Brilliant! I knew there'd be a good reason for me leaving my beloved and breaking everyone's hearts....

So off I went to Whitechapel, to the charmingly named Clap Clinic, furtive, embarrassed and ashamed. Could it get any MORE shit? I was called in (eventually) and told to get upon the trolley as they would need an anal swab. So, there I was, on my elbows and knees, my naked arse in the air, burning crimson with embarrassment, waiting for it to be over when his pager thing went off and he said, *"Don't go away, I'll be right back"* and just fucked off! Just like that. *"Don't go away"??* And to make it worse, it was one of those long rooms with a passageway at the back so that all the nurses and doctors had access to all the equipment and drugs and stuff they'd need and they just kept passing backwards and forwards, talking amongst themselves fetching things while I just knelt there, my ring piece exposed for all to see....

How long this took, I can't remember; about a month, I'd say and then the doctor returned, stuck a cotton bud up my arse and said, *"Thanks. We'll be in touch"*. All that humiliation, embarrassment for THAT?? Redder than a red thing that won first prize for the Best Red Thing in the 'Reddest Thing There IS' competition, I snuck out back into the streets of London, wondering what ever had become of my world? Heart broken, single, drunk most days and now down the clap clinic, riddled with syphilis with half of the NHS having seen my asshole.

THAT'S what I felt like. An asshole. I could've beaten it, I could've lived beside it, I could've been happily there. I could've, could've, could've......I should've tried harder. I should've stayed. I should've treated her better. I should've told it to JUST. FUCK. OFF.

But I knew. I knew in my innermost place that I couldn't have and certainly shouldn't have....*this* was me. Outside the clap clinic.

So, welcome to Homodom, Bray Boy, the land of Plenty. Yeah - plenty of heartache, mistakes and utter confusion.

So, Mr. Lucky opened the door and stepped out. Or in. Depending on your view of where I've ended up.....Free? Or Trapped?

Did I leave safety for THIS?

I knew not where to go....

Lucky Mr. Lucky. Turned out I didn't have syphilis. Actually, I had fuck all. And, how the bloody hell was I going to tell my Mum and Dad that their golden boy wasn't going to provide them with 2.4 grandchildren, after all? OK. I need a Plan B.

Nigel Bray, where did you go....?

Part Two

Mr. Lucky Comes To Grief.

CHAPTER TWELVE.

DOWN THE RABBITHOLE AND INTO WONDERLAND.

 In which our hero discovers a home from home, more than what's good for him and falls deeply in lust.

'Together We Are Beautiful'

by Fern Kinney. No.14. April 1980.

'He walked into my life
And now he's taking over
And it's beautiful
Yes it's beautiful….'

We were beautiful! It was 'the chemistry' – or I thought it was……

~ ~ ~

Ah, what a price to pay. Getting here had been a pile of shit, a path littered with broken hearts and bad decisions and I still really had no idea about how to 'be'. I thought it was all going to be so easy:

"COOO-EEEE! EVERYONE!!! I'm gay and everyone is going to like me and not mind and I'll live happily ever after……"

Hadn't quite turned out like that, so far. At least I didn't have syphilis; that's something.

After a (successfully passed) probationary year, I decided to look for promotion and a job in the oh-so-right-on Newham, the borough I was now living in, came up, teaching Traveller's children. It was a Scale Two post, more money, and considerably nearer home. I got the job and the end of term soon came and I left Dotheboys Hall and the fragrant Melody Winehouse and set off for pastures new.

I'd been living with Chris at Wingfield Rd. for a while now and the thought of not having to make the trip to Liverpool St. and then up to Enfield, with all its associated memories, was mightily appealing.

Right-On Newham had constructed a purpose-built unit, for Travellers, on their site in Stratford, the premise being that if they wouldn't go to school, school could go to them and they employed me and A.N. Other to teach them. I can't remember her name – she had really curly hair and sounded like the Queen. Anyway, fully equipped and fully staffed, by we two, we awaited the start of the Summer Term with anticipation. It was all very experimental and Multiculturally Sensitive, and in September we were to have devised a curriculum for the next (and successive) school year, using the experience we were to gain during that first term. Really?

As you can imagine, dear reader, this was doomed from the outset, but money was being chucked at it by the LEA and my new salary was good, plus I had no travel costs. A few pikeys to teach, a quick walk home and freedom to do what I wanted. Cornwall and my family were far away; nobody to spy on me or tell tales, which is just as well as there *were* tales to be told, as you know….

School began that April, and we were ready – lesson planned up to the gills, reading books chosen, story titles decided and we unlocked our door and…..

Nothing. And nobody. 'WHOOOOOOOOOO' went the tumbleweed….

'Ah well,' we thought, 'it's only the first day'….

Same the next, and the next. The site was empty. Everyone was away! Hop picking down in Kent or something. And nobody had thought to tell us! HAHAHAHAAA. We didn't start till the week after schools went back, and the Travellers returned from…erm….travelling. So we sat. Chris dropped in with a couple of beers (which was nice) and we bunked off early – there was gin to be had and beans to cook….

Anyway, the next week, after another weekend of debauchery, too many names and faces to recount, I went back to Pikey School as we affectionately called it and there they were – all home. Or back. And all staring at the Unit and us in with what can only be called a slightly puzzled look but with an undertone of menace and maybe even the murder of the two gorgers that had suddenly appeared on their site.

"Erm. Hi! Hello! I'm, er…er…." Shit. Too gay. Lower your tone, Fotherington – Thomas. Butch up a bit…

"Um. Hi. Erm, how do you do? So pleased to meet you. My name is......" Shit. Too posh.

"Um....Oright? Ah's it goin?..." Cockney! Brilliant! That'll warm their cockles....

"Who the fooking hell are YEW TEW?" Belfast!!! IRA probly......we're going to be petrol bombed any second! Tarred and feathered!!

"What are youse doin on our saight? Nobody told us, so they did." (I think he must've meant 'so they DIDN'T', but I thought it best not to argue grammar at that point.)

"Well....we're teachers and erm...we're here to help your children erm...learn some....um....stuff...."

I trailed away into silence. This wasn't going too well.

"Is that raight? Wehl...... (Pease try to read this in a Northern Irish accent for a more authentic experience) *....."Can you teach may Mammy to fill in her dole form?"*

"Erm...yes, I suppose so....." (It wasn't on the curriculum, but in those days, you could justify pretty much anything).

"And none of the wee ones can read. Can you teach them that? Eh? Can yew?"

"We'll try. Thank you, Mr. erm.. Traveller (for not slitting our throats and feeding us to your rather abominable looking dogs) *for being so erm...welcoming.."*

"Aye. Wehl."

And that was that. In.

The next few weeks WERE an education, but more for us really. Hardly anyone came for two days running, so all the lesson plans went to shit and anyway everything we had planned was completely irrelevant to their lives. It was no surprise the kids never went to school proper – it was meaningless to them other than as a socialising exercise but as they were all so self-contained, that seemed unnecessary too. I rather admired their community and the way in which they supported each other. It was just a bit difficult when, for instance, all we had for a day was a baby still in nappies, and 3-year-old and an old lady who just sang all day and played with Lego. I am guessing this wasn't what Mark Carlisle had in mind, as a beacon of Progressive Education, or what Horace Cutler, head of the GLC at that time, was supposed to be spending his money on. However, if he ever wants to know how to cook a hedgehog so that all its spines come off in one go, I'm your man.....

The education authority soon caught on however - they had seriously miscalculated, and the *'Traveller's Unit – Bringing Education Home'* was a mahoosive white elephant. We jogged along for the term, teaching the intricacies of scamming the dole, claiming (we discovered) for kids that didn't exist or who were dead – they just wanted to know what the titles of the boxes on the form said and we dutifully read them out and, in many cases, actually filled them in, as nearly everyone was unable to write. Why would they need to, usually? They were on the road, working hard manually for a living – Reedin and Writin were of little value. Being loyal, however, was and we were, after that initial skirmish and they decided we were on their side – or at least, were being paid to help them, not punish or betray – and they were nothing but kind to us and helpful.

And so the term passed. A kind of Clark Kent existence – mild mannered professional by day, gin soaked trollop by night.....I didn't have a drink problem, though I realise it may sound as if I did – it was just that I COULD! No one was telling me what to do and it gave me courage, albeit of the Dutch variety, to be someone else. You see, I wasn't comfortable with Me, so I got pissed and pretended to be someone else! Genius! It was many many years before this situation changed.

There was, at that time, quite daringly, a darling little gay club just up the road. This was both good and bad. Good, because we had somewhere local to go and bad, because we went there every night and all weekend. Every weekend. Home from the Unit, beans on toast (sometimes with those little sausages in), large gin or two, change of clothes, into something gayer and off to Selina's went we! The kitchen window, which faced out to the road, bore witness to this as the empty Gordon's bottles filled the sill as testament to our recklessness.

The club was run by John, an East Ender, a Jew (his mother had been one, and after whom the club was named and with whom he had a very unhealthy relationship – she'd been dead years, and he had a little shrine with a hideous painting that he went and knelt or prostrated himself and wept beneath, when things went wrong, which they did, often).

The club was in the cellar of an ordinary Victorian townhouse; just a brown door leading off the High Road. Opposite the nick! Blimey, you may say, but actually it was very handy – John kept them supplied with crates of lager and they kept an eye on us – turning out time was 11.pm of course but we always felt safe as we knew Lilly Law would be vada-ing from across the road.

It was just a room, windowless, airless and manky, with a little bar at one end and the bogs upstairs. But it was home. A refuge. A place of safety where we could let slip our masks, take off the armour we wore every day for protection. We could breathe, be camp, dance, snog, whatever. It was like our own front room but with more peni.

The Bar, Selina's, E11.

It was mixed, lesbians and fag hags and the occasional straight man or couple who lived near or who knew John. It was a family. We all knew each other and over the passage of time we had all shagged each other so there was no need for pretence. It was home. It was a place that, for me, at last, I didn't feel alone, the only gay in the village. There were LOADS of us! I was beginning to know WHHHOOOOO I was, WHHEERRRRE I was, and that bruising, shameful and nightmarish night in Turnpike Lane began to fade –

being queer didn't HAVE to be like that: frightening, desperate, unquestioning.

We looked forward to going, each night. We were welcome, and welcomed, Chris and me, and we were happy to be part of something. This was 1980, in the East End. Pretty revolutionary really but we never had any bovver. Maybe we were SO 'secret' there – it was more like a Speakeasy at this point – that nobody actually knew of its existence and all the queer bashers were up West, where, I heard tell, there were CLUBS and SAUNAS and FETISH BARS. That all seemed far away from our cosy little Cellar, our haven, our smoke-filled hideaway.

What *also* seemed far away was home. Home, where my family was – I hadn't seen them or contacted them for ages - I was always too busy it seemed: a willy to suck, a lager to drink. It was, of course, deflection activity. THEY would be a reality I didn't want to face. For the first time, I was doing what I wanted, no restrictions, no disapproval, no questions asked, no Golden Ear Whizzes, which I most definitely would have got if my behaviour had been witnessed. But, they were 300 miles away, living in ignorance, and telling neighbours about their son who was "*teaching some gippoes up London. What a marvellous thing 'es doing, educating people like that*"......the notion of racism, of xenophobia was alive and well in the shires of my home land. Had they known how I was spending my 'non-contact time', then another kind of phobia would've been in play. But, as I said, they were happy to think they had a son who was doing good in the world, being a Professional, being a beacon of virtue for the family *('not like they other two, gettin' knocked up every five minutes, puttin' themselves about')* and that's how I preferred to let it lie. I was finding an identity, of sorts. I had a decent job (which didn't last), I had money in my pocket (which didn't last) and I was young! Free! Single!! (which also didn't last).

It was April 18th (my yellowed scrap of A4 wiv a pome on tells me so – and no, you're not reading it) and Chris, once again had something up in town and did I want to meet blah blah blah?.

Remembering my last foray in to the world of drunken, puke laden 'romance', I was somewhat wary. "*Can't we go somewhere else this time? Somewhere a bit less...well, WHOREY?*" I asked Chris. "*Somewhere less......*"

"*Less what? You got your end away, didn't you, last time?*" I hadn't yet, out of shame, told him what had actually happened that night – he thought I'd pulled and should be bloody well grateful When I *did* eventually tell him, he teased me mercilessly, doing pretty accurate Kate Bush impressions. The bastard.)

"Less what?"

I had an idea. *"Less common. Somewhere that does cocktails or something."*

"Oh, fuck off you twat." (He was, by now, getting in to skinheadism and cocktails weren't exactly his scene. The 'cock' bit maybe.) *"This is London, mate, not fuckin Paris or poncey Hong Kong, or wherever they're supposed to serve queeny drinks. No. We're going to the Salisbury again. You liked it last time, didn't you? Got a shag, didn't you? Oh sorry I left, by the way. He said he had a sling..."*.

"A what?"

"A sling. It's a....oh, never mind."

"But....."

"No buts. We could go to the Dog and Trumpet on Great Marlborough Street cos that's near where I'm gonna be all day, but Salisbury after. I'm not going to the Pink Elephant 'cos that's for Poofs. If you get there first, mine's a lager."

DOG and TRUMPET? It sounded like a pub out of Dickens or something, and a bit safer. I looked it up in the A to Z and saw it was just off Oxford Street, easy to find from the Central Line tube. So, I got off work early (mostly because they'd all buggered off for the day, scrap hunting or something), got the tube into town and walked along Oxford Street, out and proud (ish) to the Dog and Trumpet.

It was nice. It was like a proper pub, all hanging baskets and the smell of fags and ale. A couple sitting outside, in business suits (Mmmmmmm yummy) talking and drinking, like erm...normal people. No sense of threat here...I got closer; one looked up and said, *"Alright, mate?"* and turned back to his friend. A woman turned up and sat with them, and they both kissed her Hello.

"You look a bit lost, mate. Want to join us?" one of the men said.

"I...erm...I'm waiting for....."

Then the other one turned round and he'd taken his work tie off, opened his top buttons and his magnificent hairy chest shone in the evening sunlight....

"Yes, I'd love to. Just while I'm waiting...."

Nigel Bray! You TROLLOP!! One glimpse of chest hair and you're anyone's!!

Actually, I wasn't, not that night, because a) the first bloke, introduced me then turned and kissed his mate/boyfriend/lover and b) Chris came hollering up the road, saying something like: *"They're WAAAY out of your league, you slapper! Sorry I'm a bit late. Oooh, I need a slash. Mine's a lager!"*

So we had a couple of pints in there and then suddenly the thought of entering Dante's Inferno seemed a much more attractive idea. So, we walked along Carnaby Street (a shit strewn dump. I'm sorry, but it is.) and wiggled our way through the street of Soho (with no inkling of what they would become.....) along Old Compton Street and out on to Charing Cross road, with its bars rapidly filling up with after - work boozers. Threading through the alleys, we came out on to St Martins Lane and there it was - the stained-glass Deco doors, opening and closing, beery laughter spilling out on to the pavement.

Opposite there was another bar, seeming full of brazen homosexuals too! They were mostly what is now known as 'twinks', and all seemed to be squeaking and hooting at each other.

Brief Encounter, still open, amazingly, but no longer gay.

"Oooh! I never noticed this place before," yelled Chris. *"Let's go in here!"*

"I don't really think it's....." but he was gone, through the ultraviolet lit doors of *'Brief Encounter'.*

I followed him in, squeezing between the jackets and the tied-up vests of all the young queens thronging the entrance. And the bar. And the seating area. Blimey! So many homos in one place! (I was still such an innocent abroad...).

Chris was at the bar when I found him.

"Ah, there you are. Good. It's your round."

He, as per, went off 'for a slash', though I suspected he just went and hid round the corner till I got my wallet out. I looked around. It was really quite nice in here, the sort of place I could feel safe and normal. Admittedly, none of the men were my type - too young, too hairless and too, well, girly (Excuse me??)

By the time he came back, I'd got the drinks in and was looking around and all the twinkly twinks (who actually were not that much younger than me, once you got them in the daylight...) all gossiping and bitching. It was nice it was hummy and positive. We stood side by side, looking round and became gradually aware that we were being looked at, from behind hands, their courtesan fans, and realised it was *us* that were being gossiped and bitched about - Chris in his drainpipe camouflage jeans, DMs and his green Harrington, me in my work Terylene trousers, stripy shirt, bri-nylon jumper, sensible shoes and carrying my briefcase.....this was the first inking I'd had that all poofs were not the same and even within our bruised and battered community, there was rancour and prejudice. I would discover, in my travels, that lesbians were not welcome in 'gay bars' (what?) that bears were not welcome at the twinky vest-tied discos, that Trans people weren't really welcome anywhere. To me, this was astonishing, and that night in the Brief Encounter, we were the turds in the swimming pool.

"Chris. Come on, let's go. We're being stared at."

This was my first experience of 'homophobia', by my own people. How fucked up is that? *'I'm no different to you, you know! Same number of bollocks. Same age, ish. Same struggles, pain and victories. Love a willy, same as you....'*

This, this.... injustice was running through my mind as we stood there, like two bacon sellers at a bar mitzvah.....why are you making these judgements? We're all gay, we all fought the same fight, faced the same demons, took the same brickbats.....why am I unwelcome here? If I put on some tight jeans and a lickle bitty vest thing, would you welcome me then? Same body, same person, different coating.....

I was, of course, being naive. This is how the gay scene was (and still is) - divided into little subgroups, and ne'er the twain shall meet. Bears and their cubs went to Bolts, the girls went to Gateways, the old guys and the rent boys went to the Elephant's graveyard on Bayswater road and the twinks came here. It was a scenario repeated all over London and any other town and city where there was a gay scene.

I, right now though, didn't know this. Didn't know that, actually though it goes against all the solidarity we fought for only a decade or so ago, it is actually OK. It enables you to be who you are, more clearly - I was beginning to figure out exactly who I wanted to shag (or, actually, be shagged by) and I knew it wasn't anyone here, in this neon lit, New Romantic playing hostelry. *'Don't you want me, baby? Oooh oo oo?'*......erm, no, actually, I don't, but there's no need to be quite so pissy about it. Each to their own, I say. But it was quite a sad shock to me at that moment to realise I was being ostracised by my own kind.

"I said, let's go," and I grabbed Chris's arm just as he was draining his pint. The lip of the glass slid off his mouth and a couple of gobfulls of lager cascaded down the back of someone's shiny jacket.

"Nooooooo! My coat. My best jacket. What have you done???"

Then he turned round and saw this 6'2" skinhead staring at him impassively and said,

"It's OK actually. I can get my Mum to wash it. Don't worry."

"Sorry, mate," said Chris. *"It was this fuckwit - he knocked my arm and......OI! Come here...!"*

But I'd fled. I couldn't stand the thought of the twink bitchslapping Chris and Chris giving him a Glasgow Kiss or something. So, I left. I elbowed my nylon clad arms through the crowd, which began to part like the Red Sea to let this,

this...... 'thing', not of us, through and I exited the twinky pinky palace and found myself, somewhat bewildered, out on the street.

"Oi, you twat. What's the matter? I hadn't finished me drink. Did you see his face when he turned round and saw me though? Fuckin shit 'imself!"

I should point out here that Chris, far from being a bovver boy, a troublemaker, a hooligan, was a very well mannered, gentle man. He would never fight when words would do. He was too bright, too intelligent to get embroiled in any violence, though, years later, he did get smacked in the face by a bloke he'd got off with at Selina's. They'd stumbled drunk up the stairs, out in to the street. They'd been all over each other like a rash inside, and then Chris tried to get the bloke's cock out. Opposite the Nick. That didn't go down too well and he got a slap and a split lip. I wonder if Chris ever knew that I had actually got a shag off said bloke, the next night, after he'd got slapped? He was called Aslan. Apparently. Anyway... he seemed to revel in this persona he'd created. Was this something that I would need to do, to be accepted 'on the scene'? I hadn't considered this – I thought you just held our hands up, said, "I'm gay!" and then just tried to get as many manshags as you could. Apart from Mr. Carpetworld and the bloke at Turnpike Lane, I hadn't been hugely successful so far. Was that because I wasn't a 'BEAR'? Or a 'TWINK'? Or a 'LEATHER QUEEN'....? I, admittedly, always seemed to look like Clark Kent, all geeky with me briefcase, but inside I was...I was....

I had absolutely no idea.

I was 24, on a summer's evening in bustling London Town, outside a gay bar, in my work clothes, opposite a pub that had led to the worst experience of my life, with my best mate, and I suddenly realised – I was lost. In no man's land.

"What's the matter with you? Fuckin Friday night, work over, down the pub......fer fuck's sake. Cheer up!"

"I'm lost, Chris. I don't know who or what I'm supposed to be......"

"Oh, shut up, you twat. What you're supposed to be? You're supposed to be pissed, that's what! Come on!" and he dragged me out of my reverie, into the road, and over the Salisbury, with its gaping maw and promise of.....who knew?

I wanted to be loved, right? Basic human requirement. Like bread. Shelter. Beer. But those boyz in that bar weren't going to love me. And I didn't understand why. My rather naïve view was that if you were gay (not that I had much experience – wanking in the bushes at school camp hardly qualified, although I knew I liked it. A lot) and you wanted to have sex with other men, as long as you were willing and he was willing and you both had the right equipment, then what was the problem? Why did you have to be a 'type'? I'd seen the Village People, obviously, but they were just a parody, a joke, surely? There weren't really gay men like that, were there? Why was one wearing a cowboy outfit? Why did that one have a leather cap and spiky wristbands? It was panto, surely? Chris was no fucking help, standing there in his 'uniform', his identity. Though I knew him better; had known him for years, knew this gentle and brilliant man who had crafted the witty and sparkling music for '*The Common Room*', all those years ago, who had eased me gently and wisely through my absolutely appalling breakup with Slobbidbobbidy; though I knew Chris Hartley, this man, my friend, what the people passing by on this pavement outside Brief Encounter saw was someone they would probably rather avoid – a man of potential violence and trouble. So, HE had an identity, something he could shuck off and on as the need / party / trade required. But I, with my Terylene pants and stripy shirt, synthetic pully, and (still clutching my briefcase. I don't know why I had it still, as it goes. The Travellers required few lesson plans and there was never any marking. Maybe it was MY badge, my way of saying "I have an identity! I'm a professional person"?) I didn't know where to fit. I knew who I fancied, the *type*, but I couldn't become one of those, in the way Chris could. He fancied skinheads, so he became one. I couldn't suddenly become hairy and butch. SO, what to do? Were there places for 'my type'? Probably, but they would also be rich and young Turks, and I was neither of those things either.

"You OK? Really? Look, let's go in, and we'll find a seat (on a Friday evening? We'll be lucky!) *and I'll educate you, my dear little pooflet. Come on."*

So, once more, I stepped through those beautiful doors into what could be Heaven or could be Hell.

It was fuggy, it was comforting, it was pubby, it was thrumming with chatter and laughter and the clinking of glasses, all at different pitches depending on the amount of liquid they had in. The bar was packed, it was Friday, after workey-poos and people had been paid.....the night was yet young.

"This'll do. I need a slash. Mine's a lager," said Chris as he disappeared into the throng, which was actually very mixed.

There were no seats, but we found a space by one of the pillars; all carved in a spiral it was, with a little drinks shelf.

I settled in nicely, me glancing fearfully, yet fascinatedly, round the room, looking at all the exotic creatures who populated this place, this place where such horror lurked (before, with Kate Bush) and unknown to me, where such joy, albeit temporary, would soon be found.

Chris, it seemed, was wandering round, casing the joint, looking for a possible shag.

'THAT conversation....'

When he came back and I had torn my eyes away from the chest hair of a man who was dressed in a red silk blouse (I kid you not, dear readers) and a blonde wig, which set off his black beard beautifully, in a very strange kind of way, he said,

"Stop staring, fer fuck's sake. How old are you?"

I felt about 12. So naïve and unknowing. And I thought it was all going to be so straightforward....

"Right. Now listen. On the gay scene, and I know, 'cos I've been on it for a few years and I've done and seen plenty, believe you me, there all sorts of groups,

mostly based on sex and attraction. Like, I would never do one of them twinks over the road – not my type, see. And vice versa – specially that one you spilt my drink over! Hahaaaa. Anyway. Bears fancy bears. Twinks fancy twinks. Leather queens, the same, Muscle Marys, ditto. Now, SOME twinks fancy bears and some chasers fancy cubs as they're sort of the same age. Some chasers fancy skinheads, but skinheads only fancy skinheads. Actually, that not true, cos when I was in Norwich, I shagged a cub.

"What's a cub? What's a chaser? Why has everyone got different names? Why can't we all just like each other?"

I knew I sounded like Julie fucking Andrews, but it just didn't make any sense. I supposed I thought that after the agonies of my parting from my darling Bearsy, it would all fall into place and I'd live happily ever after with a big hairy man in a world of lovely cuddly homosexuals. Apparently, this was not the case.

…."and in some lezzer bars (Political correctness was never one of Chris' strong points), *the women dress up as blokes and their girlfriends are all lovely and girly. 'S true. They have suits and waistcoats and bloke's haircuts and even moustaches. Fuckin scary, some of 'em. PLUS…"…..*he was in full swing now…."*blokes, even if they're poofs aren't allowed in their clubs and bars. You'd just get chucked out, you would, or worse. Imagine bein' duffed up by a big lezzer! Avoid them places if you know what's good for you. Or maybe that's the problem. YOU'RE a lezzer!"* He cackled in to his glass, enjoying his joke immensely.

"Shut up, you knob. I need another drink. It YOUR round. YOURS."

"I know, I know, don't go on. I was just going!" And he went up to the bar. He soon came back with two fresh pints and said, *"You owe the barman £2.80. I couldn't find me wallet. I might've left it at school."*

Priceless. FUCKING PRICELESS!

So, I pay for the drinks (again) and we return to our conversation…..

"What did you mean about all those names for people? Cubs and otters and chasers and Muscle Martys. How do you know who fancies who? Are you allowed to fancy who you like? Like, what if you fancied a twink and you were a erm…..leather queer?

"QUEEN, you twat, not queer. And its MARY not MARTY. Jesus. Well, of course you can fancy whoever you like. Nobody can help who they fancy can they? Trouble is, they got to fancy you back. You'd just have to go the right bar or club. Like Gateway, in your case. Pfffft! Hahahahaaaaaaa!" . (Later, much later in this story, I do actually go and have a few drinks in The Gateway, with said 'lezzers', and very nice it was too. If a little scary.)

"Shut up, I'm being serious. What if I fancied someone and....."

"I could go over and tell him, like at school! Pahahaaa. Like last time we was in here. D'you remember? What happened with him, then? Was it good?"

Moving swiftly on....... *"Chris! Fuckin' LISTEN! What if I fancied someone, in here say, or in a club and I was getting all the right signals, how would I know what he was into?"* (Future proofing, against another Kate Bush moment)

"Well, you could just look at the hanky. That'd tell you."

"What? What hanky?"

Christ! Don't you know ANYTHING?? The hanky in the back pocket. Look, get me a pint, while I go to the bog and I'll tell you."

I went to the bar, again, wondering why, if we both teach, and earn similar salaries, I never have any money left and he seems to have plenty. I'm going to need to be Head of Education with the commensurate salary at this rate.....

"Right, are you sitting comfortably? Well, standing. Bollocks, I wish we could get a seat – me lallies are killing me. Oooooh look! There! By them two girls. We can squeeze in there!...............Hello girls! Room for two little ones?" he yodelled, and with that we left my education, and were looking at two girls, who initially didn't seem too keen, but – remember we'd had about six pints by now, and we were just *HILARIOUS* – after a while, kinda had fun. I never knew their names, but they were a blessed, if temporary relief from being exposed to the terrors of being a gay man. I felt like a child; I felt like Alice, lost in Wonderland where nothing was as I'd expected.

"Mind if we squeeze in? Bin on me feet all day, and they're killin' me..."

"Chris, you can't just....."

"They don't mind, do you girls?" and with that he shoved me and I went sprawling across the laps of the two unfortunate and somewhat alarmed women.

They didn't stay long, not surprisingly....

Our New Best Friends, Salisbury Arms, W1.

"As I was saying, Mary," continued Chris after the girls had gone (escaped), though it did mean we now had a comfy seat, *"you wear a coloured hanky in your back pocket, all different colours to say what you like and whether you give it or take it. It all started in America, in San Francisco. LOADS of poofs there, mate. All kinds."*

"Don't call me Mary, thank you. That's a girl's name". Honestly, talk about naïve. Gay men had been calling each other 'she' since time immemorial and gave each other girl's names. I have since found out that there is a gay 'language' called Polari which was used for secret communication between gay men, when being gay was illegal and punishable by imprisonment. So *that's* what *'Round the Horne'* was about! I had listened to it, along with about nine million others, but really had no clue what it was about. It wasn't even English. No, that's because it was Polari, as I now knew. It was common to call men 'she', and give them girl's names, particularly amongst celebrities Did you know that Elton John is known as 'Sharon, Freddie Mercury was known as 'Melina', Rod Stewart as 'Phyllis', Robert Plant as 'Elsie'...but I digress..

"Go on then, erm.....Doris. Hanky in pocket....."

"Oh yes. Those girls were nice, weren't they? What were they called?"

"I don't know Chris. We were never introduced. You just went over, pushed me and I just landed on her lap."

"Well, YOU squeezed her tits."

"I DID NOT, you lying fucker! So…. HANKIES?

"Oh yes. Well, you wear a coloured hankie in your back pocket and each colour tells people what you like. You know, sex – wise. So, you see the hankie and if it's something you like, you know he does it. And Vicky vercky. Saves time. Like Morse code. Or something. Mine's a lager."

"TELL ME!"

"OK, OK. Don't get your knackers in a knot. Well, f'rinstance, if you see a black one, you know he's into S+M. If you see a…."

"What's S+M?"

"Fuck me backwards. It's gonna be a long night….. SADO MASOCHISM, you knob head. You know, bondage, whips, cock and ball torture…."

Well, actually, I didn't know…..I was entering a parallel universe here, wandering paths that I didn't know were even there.

"You mean, if he's got a black hankie, he wants to S+M you?"

Yes. YES. Jeeeze….

OK. What else?"

Yellow is for water sports."

"Cool! I'd like that! I suppose you'd have to go to Lea Valley, if you were in this area."

"No. Are you being a cunt on purpose? WATERSPORTS. Piss. He wees on you. Or the other way round. Depends which side the hankie is."

"WHAT? Wee? Like ……WEE? EWWWWW…"

Deciding I was a lost cause, he ploughed on, hoping to get this over with so he could get another beer.

"If its red, that means fisting."

He must have seen my jaw drop and my mouth open to speak.

"Don't say another fucking word till I've finished. YOU wanted to know, so I'm telling you. Now pay attention so you don't make a cunt of yourself and end up in the dungeon in The Chain Locker with someone's fist up your arse because you haven't listened. I'm trying to save you from yourself.

So, red's for fisting – that where he puts his fist up your ass. Sometimes right up to the elbow.

If it's green he's a prozzy. A rent boy. Or you are of course, depending on the side.

Dark blue is just ordinary bummin'. You know, anal.

Pink is for toys and dildo play. White is for just masturbation. Y'know, wankin and that. Light blue is for gobblin'. Don't look so fuckin DIM! Oral.Blow jobs. Gobblin...."

I was finding it quite hard to take all this in.....yet I found the whole notion compelling - this was all going on, before my eyes, in the pubs and bars and on the streets and I HAD NO IDEA!! Nor did any of the public passing by...how ingenious! How deliciously secret!

"OK, last one. Brown. Now. What do you think brown might mean?"

He was delighting in my shock / fascination of this underground world and had obviously saved the best till last.

"Erm.....doing it with a black guy? Well, a brown guy......"

"No, that's only if you're a chocolate queen".

"What?"

"Chocolate Queen. You only go with BROWN blokes. Geddit? Usually 'cos they've got massive knobs. Allegedly. Same as Rice Queen."

"Uh?" I was losing my grip on reality.

"What do you think a rice queen is?"

"Someone who likes to have a Chinese takeaway with their boyfriend? You know, like when you go on a date," I ventured hopefully, but knowing I was doomed.

"Oh, fer fuck's sake. Who eats Chinese food with.....Jeeez. No. Only goes with Asians. Next. Bean Queen – only go with Hispanic blokes. You know – refried beans? Mexican grub?"

"Well, yes, but why........."

"Hummus Queen – only shags blokes from the Middle East. Spice Queen – only Pakis 'n that. Dairy Queen – whites only. Size Queen – big cock only."

"You're making this up. How do you know all this?"

"Ah, my little pooflet – so young, so innocent...Nah, it's all true. Can't be arsed with it meself. Don't care what colour or where they come from, if I like it, I'll shag it. Apart from you, obviously. Phahahahaaaaaaa", he cackled. He was clearly enjoying himself, both at being so knowledgeable and witnessing my astonishment.

"Now, where was I? Oh yes. Brown hanky. What do you think THAT might mean? Otherwise, known as scat."

"Oh I know that one – it's like a kind of jazz singing. Cleo Laine does it. What's that got to do with sex?"

"HHAHAAAHAHA" he cackled! "Cleo Fuckin Laine? What is WRONG with you? No! Brown is for scat. That's when you play with shit during sex. You know....butt fudge. You rub it on, or eat it or just have a wank while somebody has a shit. I heard about a famous celebrity who used to lie under a glass coffee table, havin' a wank, while someone shat on the table above him. Can't remember his name now. Never fancied it meself, but each to their own, eh? Would you........"

But I'd gone. I was at the bar, out of earshot, my head reeling. Enough already. Some things I could visualise. Some sounded quite attractive. Some were a bit hard to know why you would want to do it, and each to their own. But eating turds was a step too far and I bottled it.

I returned, pints in hand.

"Here. Here's a beer, so shut up now. Enough. Thanks for the lesson."

"One more thing – make sure it's in the right pocket…..otherwise you might end up somewhere BOTH lying on your backs, both waiting for the other one. Thanks for the beer. Miss Helium Heels."

"Piss off."

It was now getting towards mid-evening and I'd been necking lager since teatime and I was feeling a bit swirly.

"I've had enough. Let's go home now."

"Fuck off! It's early. Get some crisps if you're hungry. Cheese 'n onion fer me. And some Frazzles, if they sell 'em. Ta"

I went to the bar (again) and managed to get some crisps. And as I stepped back from the bar, my arms held high above people's pints, my life changed.

Blam, in that instant.

I trod on his foot as I stepped backwards.

"Oh, sorry, I didn't…."

"No problem…."

As I turned round, he said: *"Well, you're a cracker, and no mistake!"* (Really. He honestly said that!)

My heart stopped. The noise stopped. The room disappeared - no one else was in the room but the man who stood before me. Green eyes, with little flecks. Black hair. White teeth with a little nick out of one of the front ones. Blazing red tie, striped shirt. I took all this in in an instant. OH. My Bloody Fucking. Hell. He was THE most beautiful man I had ever seen, and he thought *I* was 'a cracker'.

"You alright?"

"Nnnnggggg."

"Can I join you?"

You can do whatever you want……even that brown thing. Skip or shat or whatever it's called. You could put your hand up my arse, right up to the elbow. You could….

"Um , yes, of course. Over here."

We crossed over to where Chris was, me with the crisps and this extraordinary man, and Chris with the bang needle, as I'd been so long.

"Hello," said Mr. Gorgeous. *"Steve."*

"Hi," said Chris.

"Frluuuurrrrr nggggg," I said.

We sat, the three of us, not saying much, me not able to speak at all, and Chris resentful as he was no longer in charge of the situation. Steve schmoozed him, kept making little jokes, while RUBBING HIS FOOT AGAINST MY LEG!!! OH MY GOD!!! What to do? What would happen? I knew what I WANTED to happen but…

…years later – well an hour, I suppose - he said, *"Can I give you two a lift home? I've got my car and…"*

"Yeah. That'll be great," said Chris. I could see the signs, he'd had plenty to drink and was getting a bit belligerent, now his bestie had been stolen away.

We stood, me swaying a little by now, and followed Steve out of the pub and into the night. Somehow, on a Friday night, he'd found a parking space right across the road in New Row (My Stevie could do anything….) and so we got in his car, Chris, moaning, folded up in the back and me proprietorially in the passenger seat of the little Ford Fiesta. A Ghia. My man had a Ghia!

Soon we were speeding through the London streets, East along the A11 towards Stratford, blurred orange lights, blurred with beer, along the High Street and up Leytonstone High Road. I must tell you, dear reader, that he had his hand on my thigh all the time, in the darkness of the car and he kept scratching my right bollock with the fingernail of his left hand….I remember this, thirty four years on! It was one of the most thrilling, erotic, forbidden rides, full of fear, anticipation, joy, that I can ever remember (actually, not true – 2007 was a very good year. No! You'll have to wait…..there's a long way to go yet…)

We arrived home. There was no 'do you want to come in for coffee'. We all knew perfectly well there was no coffee on the menu. It was ME on the menu, and Chris wasn't invited to the table.

"I'm off to bed. Thanks for the lift. And don't make too much noise. I'm only in the next room and you're a noisy twat when you're getting shafted. Night." And he lurched off down the corridor to his room.

We stood in the hall. I was uncertain about how to proceed, but trembling with lust. We stood in the hall. His eyes were the most astonishing glittering magnetic....oh, stop! This all sounds like Mills and Boon, but I don't know how else to tell you. I couldn't move – they were tazering me to the spot.

Then he leant in, and with the gentlest of breaths, just ruffling the hairs on my neck, and said: *"Will you let me fuck you?"*

Just like that. No preamble, no build up, but....you know what? I didn't care! It was perfect, and a no-brainer – of course you bloody can!

So, we went to my shabby little room, closed the door, and.....

Now, what to do? Shall I tell you what happened? Shall I write a bonkbuster? Or shall I attempt to describe what this lovemaking was really like?

Votes counted. B.

We moved to the bed, which was by the window and the sodium vapour streetlights cast a honeyed orange glow around the room. We stood close, not yet touching, each just breathing the scent of the other. Slowly, gently as a breeze, he smoothed the skin of my face and neck as if to brush away all the disappointments of the past, the mistakes, the unfortunate times, to make it better, to make me believe that this COULD be real and right and perfect. A tremor shook me to my very core as I answered this call for absolution. This was not Turnpike Lane with its fear and stench of vomit and shame; this was not Blackheath with it duplicity and cheating; this was not Pearcroft Road with its pain of loss, of defeat, of the destruction of hope. This was ......nowhere. This was a perfect cocoon of flesh and pale ochre light and the most beautiful man I had ever seen, just a breath away. I felt safe, I felt home, I felt whole and mended.

We kissed then, slow and bristly and full of urgent breaths. We sped up, in time with our rapid breath and swelling cocks, all time and thought eroded, and concentrated into this single moment.

I undid his blazing red tie. I unbuttoned his business shirt to reveal dark, dark hair, covering his chest, his belly and converging into a dark trail (Ahhhh!) which vanished into the waistband of his trousers. His belt. His button. His zip. All slid open seamlessly to reveal his underwear, clean and white and bulging with promise. The trail led under the waist of his pants and I traced it with my finger, underneath to where it was warm and urgent and, lifting the cloth away, I saw his cock. Large, slightly curved, fat and lost in a riot of dark hair.

I could barely breathe. This was the most perfect moment of my life. This stranger, almost naked, in my room, had come to tell me that everything would be OK, all the hurt and confusion would melt away and we would become one.

He undressed me too then, and we folded to the bed, entwined, urgent, naked, hard, hot and as one.

The sex was perfect. It was mine; it is private. And I shall stop here as I want that moment to remain as it was – secret, perfect and holy.

Mr. Lucky! Lucky Lucky *Lucky*!!

I include this because I think it shows how I felt that next morning. No it's not great poetry, it's a bit pretentious and a bit crap, but in the journey of this young homosexual, 24 years old and now completely in love, I think it tells you something, gentle readers, of the state of mind he was in.

Morning.

Shed light through the chink in the curtain.

Quietly as ghosts, my hands

Trace the swellings of your back.

Shadows. Hills and tiny flecks of whiter skin where once you had chicken pox!

Oh glorious broad back!

Triangle made soft and round with curve.

The light plays across it.

Further down. Further down.

Grey dawn light softly on your beautiful sleeping back.

Faint hairs like kisses spread.

Ass soft and paler,

Beautifully shaped and dark with hair.

So as not to wake you

I trace the finely chiselled line of your spine,

Down and down, with butterfly nails and warm breaths.

Textures changing now,

To softness of hair and ass;

From muscled and sun – browned

To pale swelling curves.

I wish I could draw you

Or keep you beautifully there

To look at 'til I'm old.

April 18, 1980.

OK, a bit naff, but that's how it was. I was full of his semen and full of wonder at the presence of this man in my bed. New. Unique to me.

Eventually he woke, with a morning woody, and a smile. I wanked him off (it would have been rude not to) and he got up to go to shower to head back. Back to….back to? Where? Where was he going, actually? It was Saturday tomorrow….

"Oh I need to get back home for the weekend. Can we meet Monday?"

Monday? MONDAY?? That was years, *aeons* away! MONDAY????

"Well, OK then but….where's 'home'?…."

He put his finger on my lips and held me with those eyes……

"Sshhhh….Monday. Outside Centrepoint. I finish at five. "

A brief kiss, a flash of red tie and he was gone, leaving me standing on the edge of a massive void. What was I going to do until MONDAY??

Chris emerged from his room.

"Smarmy boy gone then? Fuck and go, was it?"

"No, ACTUALLY. We're meeting again on Monday, in the City. ACTUALLY. "

"He's a bad 'un. He won't turn up."

Yes he will. Why are you being so shitty? 'Cos I got a boyfriend, and you haven't? (I can't believe I said that.)

"He's not your boyfriend, you prat. He wanted a bed for the night. And a shag. And he got both. Just smile and say thank you."

"He'll BE there. And so will I."

"Where's he gone now then?"

"He's...erm....I don't know actually. Home. He said he had to go home."

"Huh. Probly got another shag at home. "

"Fuck you. I love him, so stop....."

What I said next was drowned out by the gales of laughter coming from Chris.

"Love him? You've only known him 10 minutes!"

"Yes, but we made love. I gave him my soul......."

"Oh fuck off. 'Gave him your soul'. You gave him your ass-soul. You're a dopey cunt and it'll be ME who'll have to be here to pick up the shit. Again."

And he slammed the door back in to his room.

"OOOOOOh , bitchy......."

But he didn't reappear.

The weekend dragged by. We went up the club. We got pissed (no change there then) and everyone was saying *'what's the matter with you? What are YOU grinning about'* and I'd say: *"Oh nothing. Well, actually, I have a boyfriend. He's gorgeous and I love him and I've only known him a little while, but we're in love and we're meeting on Monday at Centrepoint because he works in the city and he's got green eyes and lovely hairy belly and he thinks I'm a cracker and...."*

Eyes glazing over......and I didn't even notice HA HA!!

We watched the telly.

I watched the clock. I tried to do some lesson plans but they were shit. I decided to do the ones I did last week as nobody was going to turn up anyway. Addin' up. That'll do.

We watched the telly.

We went up the club. We got pissed. I didn't get off with any one as I was now, in my eyes, practically married and only wanted my Steve. My Stevie.

Monday came. I went to the unit. I did...some stuff. I watched the clock. 2 0 clock. 5 past 2. 3.0 clock. 5 past, 10 past. 3.15.

"Yeah, bye! Bye everyone! Byeeee!"

SPEED!

Speed up that hellish road at dawn,

Crash, Icarus, into my weekday waiting arms!

I wait! I want.....

I was out of that classroom before they'd even put their books away. Along Crownfield, up the high road, on the tube, off the tube, at Centrepoint . In a blur.

So. Hartley was wrong. (Thank God)

Here you are,

Brown, and full of careful touches

(more careful than when you left)

(May 13, 1980, scribbled on an envelope, to preserve this moment. Sad, I know!)

"Hi."

"Hi."

Two small words, one contract.

Wee'd a bit.

"Salisbury?"

"OK."

Off we went again, threading through those now familiar streets and alleys, through those now familiar doors.

"Pint?"

"Um, yes please."

"I'll bring it over."

"OK."

Not the most scintillation of conversations but I was pretty much struck dumb. Just his presence, his walk, his solid legs as they splayed as he sat, his scent, his eyes. Oh god! His eyes.

I will move on from this episode soon, I promise. When you started this, I am assuming you weren't expecting a Barbara Cartland scenario. You wanted more shaggin', more swearin'......But this is what it was....pure Mills and Boon.....'Handsome man gets his conquest to swoon a lot'. That was what happened. I felt entirely helpless in his presence. I would have walked hot coals, eaten a new born infant if he had asked. I was utterly, utterly enraptured. I felt sick and dizzy and hot and fearful.

Anyway – I shall move this on towards its conclusion – we had a couple of pints and he said,

"Hungry? I haven't eaten yet."

"Erm Yes."

"Come on then."

We left the pub, into his car, hand resting on my thigh as he drove one handed. So proprietorial! We pulled in to the Angus Steak House on Stratford High Road, where he treated me to dinner, bought wine and began to talk....

I'd never been treated like this. Like a lady. As it were. Considered, complimented, fussed over. Better than beans, I can tell you.

Anyway, in his gentle West Country burr, he began to talk. He was from Dorset, he played the organ (no laughing at the back!), he was 'a bit older than me', he had a house down West, he worked for an electronics video thingy in London.....I was interested – it was good to know about the man I was going to spend the rest of my life with, after all. He liked fine wines, dining out – I suspect the Angus Steak House was NOT where he would have chosen but it was on the way home – and he thought I was a cracker. Actually, he didn't say that then, but he must've thought it, because he was, buying me dinner and taking me home.

We went back to the flat. Chris was in the lounge.

"Sorry I missed tea! Steve took me to The Steak House. It was very nice actually!" I trilled.

"Great."

"Night then!"

We went straight to bed and fucked our brains out. TMI? Sorry, but there it is. None of the gentle caressing of the first time. This was full on, animal fucking. Enough detail right there. And I loved it. And I loved him.

And this continued, every night until Thursday. Friday morning, he said,

"See you Monday, I have to go home for the weekend."

"Can't I come? I'm Cornish you know. It would be nice to go down West."

"No, sorry. See you Monday, same time, same place?"

"Okay. I lov........"

Slam. Door shut. My love gone.

"You're a dopey cunt," said Chris.

"Charming. Bit jaloose, are we?"

"Of him? Nope. Just worried for you. You don't even know him."

"I know he loves me." I was sounding like a petulant child......

"Has he said so?"

"Well. No. but, he acts like he does."

"Oh for fuck's sake. He buys you a burger, shags you and gets a free bed."

"It was STEAK, actually. I know he loves me. I can see it in his eyes."

"You can't see further than the end of his dick. He's USING you."

"Go fuck yourself."

Hurt that my best friend wasn't happy for me, I slammed off into my room, like a hissy queen. How DARE he say these things about my Steve?

Chris, darling Chris. Wise Man. Why didn't I listen?

This went on for a couple of weeks: Centrepoint, pub, meal, fuck.

"Tomorrow. Same time, same place"…

Nothing changed though, or moved forward. On Friday mornings, we would agree to meet on Monday as 'he had to go home for the weekend'.

Now, Chris, and probably all of you, could see what was happening here, but he was right, I *WAS* a dopey cunt, too blinded by semen and body hair, and someone with a few quid to chuck around to even SUPSECT what this all might mean.

The following Monday, I went up West a bit early, and walked down Charing Cross Road from the direction that he always seemed to appear from, and there, a few shops in, was......oh I don't know! This was 35 years ago!....a shop selling video equipment. So I went in.

"Hello. Does Steve..erm…." Fuck! I didn't even know his surname! And it was going to become mine!! I'd better find out!!....*erm...Steve work here?"*

"Yes," said the miserable tart on the desk. *"He's just coming down."*

And he did. There he was, red tie blazing, striding down the stairs like a Colossus! Legs, strong and dependable.

Oh. Hello. Erm...what are you doing here?" Slightly panicky, I thought…

"I thought I'd come and surprise you!"

"Is this him?" said Tracey (let's call her that). *"Not worth losing Ian over, I don't think."*

"Shut the fuck up!" said Steve, and dragged me out of the shop and along the road.

Ian?

      Ian?

            IAN??

                  IAN???

                      IAN????

"Who. Is. Ian?" I asked, although I already knew.

"Oh, he's my friend. Down West."

"Your FRIEND. Define FRIEND……"

"Well. Um, hes……he's….."

"YOU FUCKING FUCKING FUCKING BASTARD CUNT SHIT," I screamed, in the middle of Charing Cross Road.

"He's your fucking boyfriend, isn't he? THAT'S why you go home every weekend. You fuck me Monday to Thursday, and fuck him at the weekends. Very convenient. VERY FUCKING CONVENIENT. YOU FUCKING FUCKING BASTARD!!!"

"Can you be quiet? Everyone's looking!"

"NO I FUCKING WELL CAN'T. I LOVE YOU. YOU CUNT! YOU BLOODY FUCKING BASTARD! I LOVE YOU. HOW COULD YOU? HOW FUCKING COULD YOU?" Hurt beyond words, sobbing, red, and standing, beaten and bleeding, in front of a bookshop that sold novels about this sort of thing.

"No, were not together anymore. I mean, I don't love him or anything. We just live together now. Nothing's going on. Now, please stop yelling and let's go home."

*"FUCK OFF FUCK OFF FUCK OFF FUCK OFF!!!!!"*I bellowed and turned and ran back to the tube and went home.

Sobbing all the way from the tube to home – a good mile or so, ignoring the stares – I arrived back at the flat, opened the door and there was Chris. He took one look, opened his arms and in to them I fell.

"Ah, so soon. So soon. Be still, and I will comfort you".

Mr Lucky had left the building.

How Chris coped with me during the next few days will always remain a mystery, and one for which I remain eternally grateful. The comforting arms, the cajoling, the bollockings – all served to stitch the gaping wounds left by Steve, my Stevie. *HOW* hadn't I seen what was happening? Chris had, *YOU* had….I was so blinded, and blindsided, by my feelings for him, the amazing sex, the beauty of his body and the astonishing power of his eyes that I couldn't see, or even imagine, that there would have been anyone else. He loved *ME*. He must've because he took me out, he made love to me properly with gentle touches and whispering breaths. There couldn't be anyone else. "Would the winner of the 1980 Miss Naivety Award please step forward" …..

I thought back to Chris saying: *"He buys you a burger, shags you and gets a free bed."* and I squirm with embarrassment both from knowing he was so so right and also because of the way I responded to his somewhat clumsy attempts to save me. I know, looking back, that my willingness to be entirely subsumed by Steve's attentive kisses and promises (though he didn't actually *MAKE* any) was an attempt to validate what I'd done to Julie, to prove to myself that all the blood and pain was worth it. I COULD be gay and happy – it wasn't the oxymoron it seemed before. I was bad to him, and I'd assumed he was just pissed off 'cos I had a bloke and he didn't, whereas really he was projecting forward to an event he knew would come and to preparing himself for a massive amount of 'there there-ing', which, as he knew it would, came quite soon and quite suddenly.

Before I round off this 'series of unfortunate events', there is a little postscript…..

A few days later, Steve appeared at the door. There was a knock, and I went, expecting HIM to be the last person I'd see, but, no, there he was, and all the hating and swearing and the collection of pins for my imaginary voodoo doll fell away.

"Oh. Um….Come in."

"Thanks."

"Why are you here?"

"To explain."

"Nothing TO explain. You have someone else. That's it."

"No, that's NOT it. Can I come in?"

"If Chris finds you here….."

He stepped through the door and back into my bedroom and into my heart.

We spent some time talking…all the usual old bollocks about how he'd never meant to hurt me (he did), about how he was going to tell me (he didn't), about how he didn't really love him, he loved me (he didn't), and how he was really really sorry…(he was. I think). I wasn't sure what to say. He kept looking at me, pinning me down, and crying. Yep. Crying. If you'd known him, you'd know what an unlikely event that was, but he was genuinely upset. Why? Who knows? Because I was so hurt? Because he'd lost his weekday shags? Because he would now have to pay for B+B, or find another 'cracker' in a pub? Or, as I really wanted to believe, because he did have real feelings for me, if not Love, and he was sorry it had all ended so badly, right there in the street.

"So, what do you want to explain, Steve?" My heart was thumping, gasping with the thought he might say he'd left HIM, and he wanted to be with me…

"Erm…..I should have told you. It started off as just sex, cos I really fancied you. Still do, actually. But then I started to get feelings I couldn't afford. I have a house, a lover and another life in another place and I can't have both. I tried. For a bit. But you were becoming more and more important and I had to choose. It wasn't meant to come out like it did. That silly bitch on reception…..but….well, it did. Ugly. And you can certainly swear when you want to, eh?"…hand crept on to my knee…..it was quite sexy actually. *"Look, I'm shit at this, but I just thought I owed it to you to say goodbye, properly, not just disappear. So, here I am. Can I stay? Just once more. Last time…?"*

Then, inevitably, like there nothing else ever, we went to bed. The last look at this body I adored; it was SO painful I could barely move but he was already undressed, and hard before me. I had no choice. Literally, I could not choose not to. He was my crack, my heroin, my opiate of choice.

"Will you fuck me?" he said.

Astonished, I stared at him. It had always, always been the other way round. I wasn't even sure I could.

"Please. Don't ask why, because I don't know, but just fuck me. Please!"

So I did, dear reader. My first deflowering. My hankie had moved to the other side! It was a very strange experience – amazing, beautiful, but strange – and I know that I hurt him, as he was obviously erm..*unused* to it, but we continued, I came, he came and we collapsed, exhausted to the rumpled sheets.

"I think it's best if you don't mention this to anyone, OK?" And I haven't. Not till this very day, in these pages, when it doesn't really seem to matter much anymore. It was glorious and blissful and unexpected. I gave him my soul and my seed as parting gifts.

In the morning, he dressed, stood by the bed, and said: *"In a different time, a different place, you would have been mine. I could have adored you. Be lucky next time."*

And bang! Slamming of the door, the flash of red tie and he was gone. For ever. Well, for the next ten years, but that's a different story, for later on. Chris came out of his room – he must have come home sometime during the night.

"Who was that?"

"Oh. Only Steve."

"STEVE???"

"Oh, don't worry about him," I said. *"He's fucked."*

And he was.

CHAPTER THIRTEEN.

THE ONLY WAY IS ILFORD.

<u>In which our hero meets his love, his nemesis and gets adopted.</u>

'Upside Down'.

by Diana Ross. No.3. August, 1980.

'Upside down
Boy, you're turning me
Inside out
And round and round
Upside down
Boy, you're turning me
Inside out
And round and round...'

Absolutely head over heels....upside down, and turning me and every which
way, for sure.

~ ~ ~

Selina's, with its decks blaring *'Caribbean Queen', 'Move Closer'* and *'RELAX!'*
(which is the best single EVER made, incidentally) became my source of
comfort. The massive wound that Steve had left, even after such a brief
encounter, was weeping and not healing too well, in spite of Chris'
administrations of gin and admonitions of *"Stop fuckin mopin' about. I told*
you he was a twat, and so were you for not listening. Let's go up the club.
Mine's a lager" (I know you were trying to be helpful, but...really. You
weren't.). So beer and sex were the order of the day – or rather, evening.
School had to be gone to, kids, grans and all between still had to be tended
to, reports prepared for the LEA....when I felt least like it. My heart was
broken – it was, so don't laugh. It was a searing, unceasing ache which I
sought to calm with Stellas and stiffies, pints and penises. It worked for the
times I had one or other in my hand, or down my throat, but the morning
came, the sun rose again and the pain returned.

The only even remotely amusing interlude from this bleak time was what I will call *'The Night of the False Alarm but a Good Chance to Cop Off'*. We'd been up to the club; it was a busy night, the music too loud, the trade all dressed up, the bar too pushy but I wasn't bothered. I was sitting morosely by the PacMan table, downing pint after pint, as if by filling myself up with liquid, it would flush my sorrow away. I would piss him down the toilet. Which is where my life was...... Who could I shag to ease the pain tonight? I looked blearily round the smoky room. Unfortunately, I'd had most of 'em and the ones I hadn't weren't particularly interested in a mopey queen who was always on the verge of tears. Or suicide. Or something.

"You're a bundle of laughs. Why didn't you stay home? You're putting me off me beer. Fuckin' cheer up. Get a shag. Or shut the fuck up."

"Chris", I tried to say, through lips and a mouth that wasn't functioning too well. *"I'm upset. What he did n everyfing. He a fuckin shit. And a manker."*

"WANKER, not MANKER. You Wanker. Hahhhaaaa.Bit pissed are we? I was going to get a round in, but I think I'll get you home. Boring cunt. Come on, get UP!"

And he pulled me to my feet. The PacMan table was fortunately at the bottom of the back stairs and so I was able to get up and out to the pavement before I threw up several gallons of lager, over my trousers, my shoes and the pavement.

"Nice. Come on. Home." And he escorted / marched me the few hundred yards back to the flat.

When we got back, he began to run a bath. *"You stink of puke. Get in the bath. I'm going to have a fag. I don't suppose we've got any gin left?"* This was a rhetorical question, obviously. I went into the bathroom, had the brilliant idea of getting in fully dressed – I reasoned that, as my trousers had sick all down them as well, I might as well wash them now. So in I got.

I must have fallen asleep, or passed out, but the next thing I heard is a BANG BANG BANG on the door and Chris yelling, *"Just coming!"* I got out of the bath, and in a towel wrapped round me, even though I was fully dressed, and feeling really *REALLY* shit, went out in to the passage. There was Chris, in his really really short dressing gown (what time was it? I must've been in there for hours? Presumably he'd been checking I hadn't drowned?...) opening the front door.....the windows on the street side were lit up with flashes – blue, white, blue, white – and I looked out of the kitchen window and THERE WERE TWO FUCKING GREAT FIRE ENGINES PARKED OUTSIDE!!! Meanwhile, about 15 firemen, in full breathing gear were piling in to our tiny hallway, pushing Chris up against the wall and causing me to retreat into the bathroom. The lounge door was opposite the bathroom door so I could see. They were searching round, flashing torches and yelling at each other: ALL CLEAR! BEDROOM ALL CLEAR! KITCHEN ALL CLEAR! One looked at me, in my soaking clothes and towel, raised his eyes to Heaven, and turned back. BATHROOM ALL CLEAR!

Wingfield Rd.

My room, bottom left. Bottom right – kitchen window, gin bottle shelf.

They began to leave the flat. And I kid you not, Chris was standing in the hall, with a huge erection poking out of his dressing gown (which barely covered his ass cheeks anyway) talking to one of them, who later, *sans* uniform came back, a couple of hours later (when he'd finished his shift, one would hope), and fucked him. Never one to miss a chance, our Chris. Anyway. The final fireman to leave came out of the lounge and doing his best to ignore Chris's stiffy and, holding up the wicker wastepaper basket in one hand and a fag end in the other, said, *"I appreciate you calling us. There was indeed smoke in the room. It would be good if you could ensure you've put your cigarettes out before you throw them away. It caught the paper alight. Thank you, and good evening erm…gentlemen."*

"Oooo, sorry Sir. Silly me. I'll be careful next time. 'Night."

And they left. Chris collapsed laughing. *"That was fuckin funny weren't it?"*

"Well, yes. I suppose so. Although we could have been burnt alive."

"You were alright. You were underwater....." and he cackled and roared and lit another fag.

I wobbled off to bed, but I dimly remember hearing the doorbell again and Pugh, Pugh, Barney McGrew, Cuthbert, Dibble or Grub coming back to put Chris's fire out with what was undoubtedly an enormous hose.

This misery went on for months (WAY too long, Chris said); spring passed, Easter came, term ended, caravans disappeared, never to be seen again......when we reconvened for the Summer term, NO ONE came back. The whole camp was down in Kent picking hops again, set up another camp and there they stayed....nobody told us, but there was no one to teach and no date as to when they might be back. So, my brief sojourn into educational right – on – ness abruptly ended with a transfer down to E13...Prince Albert Dock, the 3rd circle of Hell, from which I promptly resigned – it was one flying jam jar too far, but...more of that later.

New job. Being back on London transport didn't serve to enhance my mood. Eternally gloomy and sad, I sought refuge in *'Sooper Trooperper'* and hoped its lights weren't gonna find me, by not going to *'Funkytown'*, by not *'Standing So Close to'* the Police and by not being *'A Woman In Love'* any more.....it was all shit, tbh. I was SOOO fucking miserable and everyone seemed to be against me – they knew I'd been a twat and gave me little sympathy and it all just seemed so unfair. I'd given up a whole life to live this one and now I'd been shat on, from a great height. I wanted to 'end the heart-ache', and the *'thousand natural shocks that flesh is heir to'*. I just wanted it to stop HURTING. Boo hoo.

So, my master plan seemed to be to drink lager. And lots of it. That doused the pain temporarily, but as we all know, it's still there in the morning, coupled with a banging head and occasionally some love bites of an unknown origin. I realise this may all sound a bit dramatic – as dear Chris said: *'You'd only known him five minutes',* but that was NOT the point. The love I'd had for him was fierce, unquenched and, in addition it had reopened the careful stitching of my separation from Julie, which was still fairly recent, although gin and sex had kind of erased some of that. Given my miserable experiences thus far – viz: a wank in a carpet store, a night with Kate Bush on smack and my heart broken by the most beautiful man I'd ever seen, and who I'd even fucked, all in the space of a few months….maybe this was God's way of telling me NOT to be a homo. Maybe it just wasn't for me. Maybe I could go back to Julie, back to solidity, to familiarity – my family will be happier, my Dad wouldn't have apoplectic fits of homophobic fury when he found out – he need never know!, Julie would welcome me with open arms and all this pain would cease. It was reducing me, lessening my ability to function at work and reducing my perception of what would be wise when I had my beer goggles on. Maybe THAT'S what I should do. Go back. Stop whoring. Stop drinking and it will stop hurting.

I was having these internal dialogues, during the times I was sober enough to think coherently; I began to go to the club a little less often, drink less, eat better – in preparation to begin my new old life. I began to feel better, and began to make plans (I hadn't told Julie about this yet, but she was BOUND to want to. Wasn't she?) And then, on August 8th, 1980, I went to Selina's, bright eyed, bushy tailed, full of focus and light of heart.

And that was the night I met Rod.

'Friday night, just got paid. I'm runnin wit my mans, we got plans of gettin laid' as Johnny Kemp once said, only I wasn't runnin wit my man cos I didn't have one. I'd had Steve, and he'd fucked off and I'd had pretty much everyone currently in the club. (Don't judge. So had everyone else – it was a family thing…) SO it was likely to be a usual Friday: beer, couple of quid in the fruity, some dancing, and not *'Usin' It Up' or 'Wearin' It Out'*, which was No1 that week which usually meant Carlos would play the bastard thing every other record, as he seemed to think he was the world's number one record promoter. Some more beer, some chat with the regulars, seeing who'd had who since last Friday, some beer, moaning about the music, moaning about the weather (which was wonderful early August sunshine, but that wasn't the point), moaning about those people over there for being so noisy and for having such a good time. So far, so normal.

That night however, there was a group of people I'd not seen before – brash, self-confident, loud but somehow a welcome addition to the general melee of tired old queens and bright young things having a few stiffeners (ooh missus) before heading up West for a night of discoing and shagging, and more besides – I'd had 'the Talk', remember……

I was fascinated by these people, and by one in particular. Was he handsome? God, no. Balding, big nose, strange teeth…..a kind of gay Fagin. But he had this kind of….stuff around him, this aura, which made him the centre of the little universe he was in. He looked across the room, and his smile, so wonky and odd, seemed to carry with it all the love of the world. The woman, who seemed to be his sister, clearly adored him as did the little fat chap with them. The room kind of grew quiet, the music seemed to dim and just hover in the background – while I watched them. And watched them.

My Nemesis, my drug.

"Who are they? Over there, by the stairs?" I asked.

"Dunno. Never seen them before," said Ian.

"Dunno, but they were here last week," said Pete.

"They were? I never saw them."

"That's because we went up West, you knob," said Chris in his charming fashion.

Yes, indeed we did. This is what happened. We'd gone to The Pigeons, on Romford Road, a great cavernous place that looked to be an old ballroom. It was manky and smelled of wee and fags. (Cigarettes, I mean, although the reek of aftershave was choking.). It had a licence till 1. a.m., pretty radical for the time, at least for somewhere not Up West. We'd gone after the club, which probably was a mistake because a) we were already pissed and b) we had hardly any money left. Anyway, we paid our £1 entrance fee (I kid you not) – you had to pay to get in because they served 'food' – and I say that loosely - as a part of their licencing agreement, and climbed the sticky stairs to the bar room bit.

"You'll be having lager then Chris, will you?"

"I thought it was MY round, but yeah, OK then. Cheers!"

The Pigeons, Stratford, E15

We stood around a bit, listened to some awful stuff apparently called 'Hi NRG', which seemed to be the only option lately and I wondered what we were doing here. Chris, who'd done his usual disappearing act, suddenly came back and said:

"Come over here. Meet these two blokes I've met."

Oh God......fearing the worst, I followed him and there were, indeed, two 'blokes' smiling at us. I have no recollection of their names but Tarquin and Oliver will suffice.

"This place is a fucking dump, yah? Would you like to come up town with us?"

Why they would have asked *us*, I have no idea, but before I could even open my mouth, Chris said, *"Fuck yeah! Come on!"* and before I knew it, we were outside the pub, standing next to an open topped yellow Porsche. *"Come on chaps, in you pop!"* said Tarquin. Or Oliver.

"Yeah, come on you twat! Don't just stand there..." and the next thing I knew, we were hurtling down Stratford High Street towards God knows where. After a very scary drive through the freezing night air, with everyone screaming, *a la Chic*

> *We're gonna use it up - wear it out*
> *Ain't nothin' left in this whole world I care about*
> *I said one, two, three, shake your body down'*

to the pounding car stereo, and then suddenly we screeched to a halt in Oxford Street,

"Come on chaps, out you pop!" said Oliver. Or Tarquin. *"We're here. Groovy, ya?"* Who the fuck says 'groovy'?? Tarquin, obviously. Or Oliver...

'Here', was 'SPATS', a night club which stayed open until 04.00 and it was only half past twelve! Hurrah! Three and a half hours in a cellar with no money! Brilliant Chris. Am I allowed to use the word CUNT here? You know I don't normally swear, but....Tarquin and Oliver had disappeared inside and so there we were, with no drink, no money and no way of getting home. An excellent end to a night out. Nice one, *HARTLEY*.

In the end, the plan we came up with was as disgusting as it was inevitable: we each started chatting up a bloke, a drunk one, who was in a group of other drunk ones and we persuaded them to let us go to the bar and get a round of drinks with the money they gave us. But, instead of going to the bar, we legged it up the stairs and out in to the night, bought a kebab and got the night bus home. I've done some really horrible things, eh? I'm not a bad man.....it's just that I find myself in extremis sometimes, mostly due to my friend....

Anyway, back to the Club, on this Friday night...

"Oh. Right. So we were. Well, who are they?"

"I don't fuckin KNOW! Shall I go ask them?"

"No. No, its fine."

"OK then. I'll have a lager, I need a wazz," and he went over the stairs, that led up to the bogs. As he passed the group, he leant over to them, said something and went up to the toilet.

When he came back, he said, *"The ugly one's Rodney, the woman's his sister. She's called Kath and the fat ones is Milly or Missy, or something. OK?"*

"Erm, yes. Thanks. I didn't really want you to...." but he'd gone to play Pac Man to see if he could beat my high score (he never did).

Friday night wore on, *creeping in this petty pace, to the last syllable of recorded time*; drinks were drunk (as were people), faces were snogged, crotches were fondled, and lurching dances were attempted, and still, STILL he sat there, with his *coterie,* drinking his lager, smoking his St. Moritz (oh God. Cool. As.), laughing and just occasionally looking over the bench seat that ran along the wall, where I was sitting – having none of the aforementioned options. Apart from the beer.

And then. Then. *'Dap dap.....dabbadabbadabbadabba doo doo. Whenever dark has fallen.....'*

"I fuckin LOVE this song!" yelled Rodney, who suddenly leapt off his barstool and came through the throng, towards me, grabbed my hand and dragged me out on to the tiny, jostling dance floor.

Carlos had turned it up to 11 and I found myself suddenly in the arms of this strange man, who had hips like a snake and a generous bulge in his white jeans. *"George Benson 'Gimme the Night',* he yelled. *"He's my favourite! Well, apart from Alma Cogan. Oh, and Della Reese."*

> *'Cause there's music in the air,*
>
> *And lots of lovin' everywhere*
>
> *So gimme the night! Boop boop.......'*

he bellowed, in my ear. And now, 34 years later I can still hear him, still smell his *'Habit Rouge'*, and feel his heart beating against mine. *'Dababababababaaa Boop Boop!'* sends me back to that dive, that smoky room, and the night I met the man I would love with more passion than I knew I had in my soul.

The music ended. We stood still. I was wearing ridiculous fawn elephant cords and a green open necked t-shirt, and looked like a twat who'd put on whatever'd been lying about, which I had. He looked impossibly cool – white jeans, proper leather jacket. None of yer plastic schmutter.

"Well," he said. *"Do you fuck, or not?"*

Rude.

But. Clearly, I did, because when I woke the next morning, in the usual 'where the bleddy hell am I, bad hair' sort of way, which was quite a common occurrence, sad to report, I looked over and there he was, still asleep, chest rising, falling with his breath. I was captivated by this man – in the cold, club - lightless light of day, he seemed to me to be a child, and boy / man, who needed to be healed from some terrible hurt, though I didn't know what. He had a beautiful thick mat of chest hair – not thick and curly, but striated, like proper hair. It was so magnificent, so masculine, and it converged into a deep dark trail down his belly (Ah! Joy!) and into a riot of dark hair surrounding a generous cock. Not Jewish, then. Captivated. Marvelling. Waiting. Not knowing what to do. I didn't even know where I was, but it didn't matter. I wasn't going to nick cash from his wallet for a cab home; I was going to wait to see who he was, this man who took me to his bed. I have no recollection of the sex we had – too drunk, too tired – but residues proved that we did.

He stirred.

"Morning," he said, opening his eyes and catching me staring.

"Oh, Morning," I said, startled, caught in the act. *"OK?"*

"Yes. You?"

"Yes, I'm. Erm...fine. Thanks."

"Sleep well?"

"Erm, yes. Thanks. You?"

"Yes, very well".

"Looks like another hot one...."

"Yes. Seems so. It's only early too..."

The weather. How terribly British. This was beginning to feel a bit embarrassing - should I just say, *'I'll ring you'*, and leave?

"Great fuck, wasn't it?"

"I.....um......god yes," I stumbled. *"Beautiful"* and then, to my horror, blushed like a girl.

"I hope I didn't hurt you? I was a bit erm...insistent. Just that I really fancied you."

'Fancied'. Past tense. Here we go then. I'll get me coat.

"No. No, it was....great. Really." Actually, I was feeling a bit.....*used*, in the bottom department, but I didn't mind. Didn't mind that it was HIM that had caused it.

Long pause.

"How old are you, Nige?" Nige? NIGE? How did he know my name....that fucking Chris I bet. If I find out he'd said *'My friend over there fancies you'*, again, making me sound like a teenage girl. I'll..... And anyway, I didn't. Then.

"I'm 24."

"WHAT? Oh FUCK FUCK FUCK."

"Why, how old are you?"

"36. This'll never work."

"Why? Why not?"

"Well. Well, because...." But he didn't finish because I kissed him, and he kissed me back as if his heart would break. A pause. A long stare and then:

"KAFF! KAFF! I must be meshugena, KAFF!!! Can Nige stay for breakfast?" Then he said, *"Do you want to move in?"*

Boom. Just like that.

"OK. Yes. Why not?"

And so began four years of joy, pain, heartache and wondrous love.

Rod and me, Selina's. 1980

Theirs was a big family. Bit of Jewish, plenty of Cockney. Dad had died not long before I met Rod, a part of his sadness, I think, but there were still Mum – Big Kit, a darling matriarch if ever there was one, in her sixties with her 42 year old black boyfriend, 4 sisters, another brother and Rod, not to mention numerous uncles and aunts and cousins, all dotted around the East End and always in and out of the house, in Ilford. All Jewish, all East End born and bred and bleedin' diamonds, all of 'em. They took me in, without missing a beat, because Rod asked them to, because I was Rod's new partner and so it was OK with them. They loved him and so they loved me. I felt unconditionally loved by every one of them, no judgements made and acceptance in all things. The only proviso was that I shouldn't hurt their brother, but that was, as I was soon deeply in love with him, unlikely. I loved him. His laugh, his madness, his humour, his cock, his way of making everyone feel special. He was unlike anyone I had ever known and I felt blessed and happy for the first time in my life, I think. We drank too much, smoked too much, laughed and fucked, but never too much! There could never be too much of those! It was blissful and hilarious, it was full of laughter and cum and validation, of trips to Brighton, of big Sunday roasts with any number of people who might turn up, or who might have been invited by Rod, with his beer goggles on and his way of making people agree, "*Kaff won't mind!*", down the Royal Oak on Sunday lunchtime. Down the club in the evenings at the weekend, maybe on to The Pigeons on the Romford Road. Then home, sex or not depending how pissed we were....on and on through the fag end of summer 1980, Brighton for my birthday, '*Ashes to Ashes*', '*The Winner Takes it All*', '*Oops Upside Your Head*' and over and over, '*Give Me The Night*' – these were the soundtrack of my love. Della Reese,

Alma Cogan, Mel Tormé…new voices, new sounds, slow dancing in the lounge in the dark; hiding out in the attic with bottles of gin and making love in silence to see if we could. A whole spinning, swirling world of feeling and emotions that I had never known and I knew this would last for ever. And in a funny way it has – I am still wearing a ring he bought me in Romford market 35 years ago; we split up after four years, didn't meet again for another twenty-five, when he was dying; dying, but still working the room like a pro.

We met up with him again in Brighton, my new man and me, and Rod was nothing but generous and warm and welcoming to him. It was his 65th birthday and we had been lucky enough to have been in Cornwall and I had arranged to go and see him on the way home. It was wonderful, sad, joyful – it was like the intervening 25 years hadn't happened. He was still the same man I had loved, still love and he resides in my heart. He held me to his hairy chest, to his heart, and in that moment, all was forgiven. *"I'll come to France to see you both,"* he said, but he barely had breath to get to the kitchen – we both knew this would never be, but the pretence was less painful. The last thing he said, mouthed to me, and did with his fingers, as he waved us off, from the balcony on the top floor, was '1.4.3.', 'I', 'LOVE' 'YOU', the little secret gesture we'd had, made with our fingers, exchanged surreptitiously, secretly in our love, at parties, across rooms, in straight pubs, over dinners in restaurants. He made it with the hand not holding the railing, the one keeping him on his feet, and I gestured back; a simple but profound gesture signifying that we loved, we had loved and we always will. He's gone now – he died, took his last painful breath through lungs that no longer worked, on August 8th 2008, 30 years to the day we met, but he is here in this house and in my heart still.

Our love was perfect. I thought so, anyway. We lived in Audley Gardens, Ilford, near Seven Sisters tube – me, Rod, Kath, Keith (then Neil), Kath's two boys, Troy who rented the attic and various dossers and waifs and strays. A small digression here, but a tale worth telling…

Troy was a PROPER gay boy, all skin tight jeans and blonde streaked hair. He wore blouses and always drank Bloody Marys, large, with an olive. He lived up in the attic and we rarely saw him (although Rod had shagged him one night – or tried to but they apparently just laughed themselves to sleep instead) and he was always so sweet and gentle. BUT, if you crossed him, or hurt one of his 'chickens', (us) he was fierce, Mama, FIERCE! Anyway, this particular night, we were in a cab, heading for the club, and we saw Troy walking along Leytonstone High Road, Selina's bound too. At the crossroads at the Thatched House, a car pulled up at the red lights, just as Troy minced up to the junction.

"OY!" said a yoof, hanging out of the open back window. "ARE YOU A POOF?"

Without missing a beat, Troy turned on his Cuban heel and marched straight over to the car. We watched, in fascinated horror. He was a big bloke, Troy was, but there was a car full of THEM. Rod had his hand on the cab door handle ready to pitch in, when we heard:

"I'm sorry, love. Are you addressing moi?"

"Yeah. I said 'ARE YOU A NANCY BOY POOFTER?"

Troy - and I swear this is true – leant over, ignoring the cars that were now beeping, as the lights had changed, and leant into the car and said,

"Are you?"

"Wot, a poofter? No I fucking ain't!"

"Well, then," said Troy, through the open window and right into the face of the driver: "FUCK OFF and stop wasting my time". And just turned away, waved at the cars, swept his hair in a manner insouciant, and minced off up the road.

We roared, and applauded through our open cab window, and he waved, and yelled, "I'll have a double, and don't forget the fucking olive!"

So, that was Troy, all camp, fierce, beautiful and the lodger in the loft. And the rest of the house was just as exciting to a boy like me, hurting still, needing companions, friends and a lover. All of which I seemed to have. All at once

How Kath managed to cater for us all remains a mystery to me but, with such a large family and a constant stream of impromptu guests, I guess she was just used to it, but the house ran on chaos and love. And I was happier than I could have thought possible.

Lucky Mr. Lucky!

After the debacle of the Traveller's Unit, I'd been shunted off down into the depths of the docks. Like it was MY fucking fault! Shoulda done your research

Mr. L.E.A. Man….. Anyway, the school was an old Victorian edifice, interior walls painted green with tiled dado rails – more like an asylum than a school, and so it proved to be. Again, I was introduced to my class , and so I faced what is now known as Y4, sitting stony faced and sullen at the prospect of yet another teacher. The Head said,

"This is your new teacher, class. It will be nice to have a permanent teacher after so many supply teachers, won't it?"

Grunts.

"Wossis name?"

This is Mr….Erm….. I don't know actually. Nobody's actually told me…"

And so began a very short residency at Prince Edward Primary. The head had his office tucked away out of reach of anything that might be threatening, such as a child, but at break I went to find him and to ask: *"Can you tell me a little about the class, please? They seem rather ….disengaged…"* (I didn't actually say 'disengaged' as I only recently learned this word, but I said something similar).

"Oh, yes. They are. Fed up of a constant train of supply teachers. Doesn't give much stability, do you see? You're in charge of Art. Jolly good."

"I am? No one said." In fact, nobody had said ANYTHING, other than the address and a start date. I looked around the school, in the corridors, in the hall – nothing. Just blank walls. No wonder the kids were so blank. I was on a mission to get Art work up, justify my post this time. But I hadn't reckoned on Class 4 and their complete unwillingness to do any work whatsoever, nor answer questions, write anything down or listen. It was like shoving shit uphill.

No one listened, to me or each other. It was like being in a zoo, or a bad movie which had no end. The days passed in a maelstrom of noise and hurled objects that I was powerless to stop. I didn't have the tools in my tool box for this – I'd had one year's experience in a classroom to date and clearly my training at Balls Park (BALLS PARK!!! HAHAHAAA) didn't cover this bit: what to do when faced with a room full of fucking morons whose only *raison d'etre* was to be each noisier, more destructive and more vile than everyone else. I look back on this episode in my professional life with a kind of wonder….how could such a class of children ever have been allowed to deteriorate to that level of disinterest and fury? Looking back, those kids weren't to blame - it sounded like, that for whatever reason, they'd been abandoned, one supply teacher after another, no consistency, no discipline that was ongoing....they were lost. If it had been later in my career, I know I could have rescued them – I developed the skills and could have brought them back. This was 1981 – they would be in their early 40s now – what kind of lives did they have? How did they fare in the world of Thatcherism and greed – getting 'decent jobs, for decent people'? They probably were decent people, had they been schooled well, and I would have been the man to do it, I'd like to think. But, this was '81, I was 25 – and shit scared of them, if I'm being honest. They were like the baying mob in the Coliseum or something. So, coming from a place of fear, I was an easy target, both figuratively and literally. No one listened. The lesson plans I had assiduously prepared, to 'engage' them, to 'stimulate' them, to 'include' them all went to shit. Never got off the ground. Much like my plans to turn the school into a wonderland of art and creativity. Nobody, and that includes the other staff, was in the least interested. There was no paper, no materials, no equipment and no interest. I suppose the bleakness of the school suited the bleakness of their ambition and they produced NOTHING, or nothing that I would consider worth displaying. It was very dispiriting, day after day, getting nowhere.

It didn't go on for long, however. It was on a Friday, date unknown, that the camel's back got broken. It was an art lesson (I was nothing if not optimistic) and suddenly a boy pulled out a penknife and started yelling about who he was going to stab first. I wasn't really prepared for this – this wasn't in the College curriculum – so I asked him to give me the knife. He called me a 'Nancy Cunt' (what a strange insult!) and got under a desk. Nothing would persuade him to come out, so I gave up trying. And as I returned to my desk, from behind me, a jam jar that we'd been using for water for painting, came flying through the air, past my head and smashed against the tiled wall surrounding the blackboard. I didn't turn, didn't ask. I just collected my jacket from the chair, shook off the shards of broken jam jar, and gobs of painty water, picked up my briefcase, and turned to leave the room, with its smashed glass and boy with a knife, who said, from under his desk, "Where you goin'?"

"Somewhere I'll hopefully never have to see YOU again. You little...er..CUNT."

I then went along the bleak green corridors to the head's office, and said:

"I'm leaving. Now. Goodbye."

"You can't do that! What about the children? What about your contract? You can't just LEAVE....!"

"I didn't sign one - I was just dumped here. And as for the children – your problem. Good luck and watch out for the little shit with the knife."

And I walked out, walked away and left Education, with its ignorant rules and massive failings, behind.

Coo! How brave! How militant! How.....unemployed....

As ever, the family was supportive, with Rod threatening to go and find the little bastard and give "'im a good 'idin'", but I said that wasn't necessary. What WAS necessary was finding some work so I could pay my way in the house. I wasn't good at much else, when you came down to it. Want me to express myself in modern dance, maybe in a blue sack, anybody? No, I thought not, so I was going to have to get out into the real world.

So, I got a job selling insurance, which was commission only and really really shit. I was rubbish at it anyway:

"Oh good evening Madam, I'm from....."

"Fuck off".

"Oh, OK, then. Sorry to have bothered you"

That was pretty much how it went. I even, (shame on me; I can't believe the depths I sank to at times) went round to Julie's, who had got herself a new flat, and after I'd rung to say *'Oh! Hi! How ARE you?"* she invited me round for tea. Oh, alright.. dinner.....

Anyway, she made no mention of me turning up with my briefcase, and we had a nice, if a little awkward, meal and then I said, *"Would you be interested in buying any life insurance?"*

Scumbag, honestly. I really don't blame her for chucking me out. Actually, that was the last time I saw her for a few years, the next time being in less pleasant circumstances.

Well, that didn't last long. I'd walked about a billion miles and sold....nothing. Nante.

So.....

A milk round! Yes. Brilliant. Except the excitement of chugging across Hackney Marshes at 04.00 a.m. in a milk float with no doors, at 4 mph, in the winter, pretty soon wore off. As did finding none of the bastard lifts working in the tower blocks; after traipsing up 15 floors with two pints of milk – **Leyton Dairies! We pride ourselves on that personal touch! Milk with a smile!** – only to find Gladys wanted an extra pint / a yoghurt / some orange juice today. Down 15 floors. Up 15 floors. *"Oh, could I have two bottles of Juice. I forgot my Maisie's coming today and she's a bit partial. Thanks, love."* It was very hard not to stick the yoghurt up her arse, but...Milk with a smile! This happened so often, in the end there was nearly fights to see who would 'do the flats'. Not me, obvs. as I was much too genteel. I just waited politely until breakfast and the awesome smoked salmon and cream cheese bagels in Ridley Road market, which signalled the end of the round. Then back to base to count the thousands of coins that all the old girls had paid with. We did, quite often, plan to stage a robbery where one of us would get beaten up and the money bag nicked, but as it always seemed to be me that got chosen to be duffed up, I refused.

Anyway, this career didn't last long. Too cold, too tiring, too butch.

My next wheeze to was to join a security firm, partly because it was just down the road and I could walk to work, but also because I assumed all you had to do was sit in a van all day. I went along, took a 'test', basically to determine that I could spell my own name and address, got hired the same day, start on Monday...

Well, I hadn't seen the men who worked for PPR, and if I had, I might not have applied. How gorillas and Piltdown men had learned to drive was a marvellous thing, and I soon found myself amongst a company of men that I thought only existed in Dickens or in Hogarth's paintings. I had led a sheltered life, as you know, and my only experience of adult men had been the fey sort, or at least those who'd been to RADA or had jazz hands. These men seemed to be an entirely different species altogether. Nobody talked, they all shouted, and if you would read this next part in, say a Bob Hoskins, or a Danny Dyer voice, it will help you to get a better understanding of how I, this homosexual of a tender disposition, who liked to 'sa '*Hulls sky, hullo clouds*' and skip about like a gurl', found himself marooned on the Planet of the Apes.

Monday. 08.30.

"Ere's yer uniform. Get it on and get dahn the mess room."

"Erm...yes...er..Sir."

"Dahnt call me fackin, Sir, it aint the fackin army."

"Erm, no Sir. I mean, Mr.. erm Mr. Boss, thankyou. Erm, where is the mess room?"

"Dahn the back. Go on, get a fackin move on. You're out on Van 651 at 9.00."

"But I haven't had any training, or anything. What do I do?"

"Oh fer FACK'S sake. ASK, ask the uvva blokes. Train on the job. Now, fack off. I'm busy."

And that, dear reader, was my 'induction'.

I opened the brown paper sack, and there lay......my uniform. Nylon. Zip up jacket, nylon trousers. And it was cerise. I kid you not. FUCKING CERISE! How could I go out in THAT? What if anyone saw me? I would just DIE! But, sensing they weren't going to let me chose my own colour scheme, I began to put on the uniform, which actually still smelled of its former occupant. Ewwww. All stale sweat and fags. I was beginning to regret my snap decision and not to have gone a wee bit further afield in my job search.....

Anyway, suited and booted, I went back through the building and found the Mess Room. 'Mess' describes it perfectly. Full of tatty old chairs, empty take away cartons, overflowing ashtrays, empty sweet wrappers, coke cans and half-drunk cups of tea and coffee with fag ends in, littered the tables and windowsills. It smelled of fags and farts and well, BLOKES.

"Aye Aye! Ooze this then?" somebody said, as I appeared in the doorway. *"A new one!"*

"Oh, hello". (Lower your voice, you pratt). *"Oh Hello. I'm"*.....and in the beat before I said it, I knew I would be committing social suicide, right there on the steps of the Mess Room, if I admitted to being called Nigel. I might as well have said 'Tarquin' or 'Oliver'....."*Steve. Yeah. Steve. Erm...Oright?"*

"Yeah, oright. Wotcher Steve. Come in. Acshally, don't. We ain't got time for a cuppa, cos we're aht at nine an iss five to nah. Fack me, we'll be late"

And he grabbed my arm and led me towards the van, opened the door and flung me in and set the locks. I had no idea what to do! I just sat there in the semi darkness, and waited for the next thing to happen, which was the radio crackled into life, a voice said 'Copy 651', and we were off. Fuck knows where or why. But we were off. And, oh God, it was BOILING!

Not much to report on this really. Lots of sweating, lots of misogyny and lots of swearing. I thought I was bad until I heard one of the blokes (for blokes they are, not chaps, nor fellows) describing a car accident he'd seen on the way to work:

"FACK ME! YOU SHOULDA FACKIN SEEN THA FACKIN MOTA! FACK! IT WAS FACKIN FACKED TA FACK".

10/10 for completely destroying the language. Well done, that man! I mean, Bloke.

My work days consisted of either driving the van (cool), being the 'runner' (not so cool) or 'back man' (shit). The driver part is self-explanatory – the firm covered all of greater London, and I got to know the city and outskirts extremely well. PLUS, if we were late for base, or sometimes for lunch, we could call up the old Bill and they'd 'see us in'. This meant they'd turn up, stick their blue lights on and we could follow them down the bus lanes, thus saving valuable sandwich time. Whilst driving, it gave my 'runner' ample opportunity to ogle and all the passing women, go PHWOAR a lot, ask me *'if I fancied a bit of that'* and *'what I thought of her tits'*. When he got out to collect or deliver bags (cash, cheques, wages, coin) there was ample opportunity to find out, from passing females, whether if he *"met her at the Pawnbrokers, would she kiss me under the balls?"* Invariably they said *'no'*, or *'fuck off you pervy bastard'*, which usually served to inflame his ardour further, so he could do more PHWOARing, a bit of whistling, and inform her that she must be gagging for it. This went on *ad nauseam*, and was one of the downsides of driving – you couldn't get away from it. He'd do the bag dump, get back in, say *"OK, Sarf Ken next, Cahncil Offices"* (like I didn't know). *"Did you see the tits on that? Bet she's got a fanny like the Blackwall Tahnnel."* I hadn't actually seen the 'tits on that'; well, I HAD, but only as an observation. But I HAD seen the rather marvellous bulge in the trousers of the man leaning up against the wall of the bank. But I was guessing he didn't want to compare notes, so....I drove on. To Sarf Ken.

Being in the midst of all this macho shit was really really wearing. I was clearly the only gay in the village (though I reckon there was one, if pushed......) and I really didn't fit it. I couldn't stand the mess, the fucking and cunting, the farting and the noise. Was this Class 4, projected into the future? And most offensive was the way they spoke to, and of, women. I'm not naive – I know this goes on, and was far worse back in the '80s and I supposed I was living in a microcosm swirling with testosterone, but, please.....boys.....nobody want to kiss your balls, or suck you off (well, I might, but that's in another universe) or want to let you *take them up the alley*. Really, they don't. You all stink of fags and sweat, and the uniform...well, cerise doesn't really do it for the laydees. So shut the fuck up and get on with your work.

Sarf Ken done, lunch, the rest of the West End (witnessed a crash on Marble Arch roundabout between a white van and a mini. The mini contained, FIVE NUNS, who all got out and started shouting at the white van man. Sadly, the lights changed and I had to drive on, so I never witnessed the end....I hope they were gentle with him) then back to base, coin check, bag count, then home. That was my day. Then into the furry arms of my Rod, who smelled of sawdust and love.

If you were a 'runner', you were in and out of the van all day, taking bags put into the safe by the 'back man' into banks, shops, offices and chucking full ones into the safe if it was a collection. It gave me a bit of ogling time of my own, but I didn't share it with my driver, for obvious reasons.

Being the 'back man' was the worst of the three – long shifts locked in the back, hot and itchy, chuckin' bags out, pullin' bags in. At least there was a chance to read a bit between drops and if it rained, you stayed dry, but claustrophobics need not apply. I still have a damaged first finger on my left (chord playing) hand from where it got it trapped in the safe one day as I slammed it shut, and once, someone left a Post-It inside the window of the van, with 'IS BRAY GAY?' on it. But other than that, being the 'back man' was dry, hot and dark – the small thickly reinforced windows didn't let in much light and there is steel partition between the cab and the back, in case anyone got in, which rendered any conversation impossible.

And so the days passed....I DID get interviewed by the police about the Brinks-Matt robbery, which happened in November '83 but nothing much else to say really. Except – if you haven't eaten your sandwiches, on Christmas Eve, sitting in a van, sitting, *literally* sitting, on half a million pounds of gold bullion, as it races through London, flanked by police cars, with their blue light flashing, then you have missed out on a rare thrill.

For some reason, in about '82, Rod and Kath decided to sell Audley Gardens and to go their separate ways, house wise. She had a new chap, Rod had me, and all seemed to be stable and maybe sharing a house was now a bit wrong. A bit Famous Five – nobody could really shag when they wanted, and had to be careful of the noise etc. We'd had some FABLIUS times there – Gill, to whom I had come out long since, came up one Christmas and she, a leather queen called Phil (who frankly couldn't really pull it off; think Pinocchio in chaps) and I found some poppers (Mr. Google is your friend) and went...wait for it.... behind the Christmas Tree to have a sniff, and then all fell out on the floor, pushing over the tree and fusing the lights as we fell. Well, WE thought it was funny....I still laugh at the time there was a bees nest in the wall and Keith went up onto the conservatory roof and Rod took the ladder away; the bees attacked Keith and he fell through the roof. Mick (it was MILLSY, Chris, not Milly!) who was painting in the lounge, kicked over a large tin of white gloss paint on the brown shag pile rug and fell in it himself trying to scrape it up.....My how we laughed! Neil poured a large tin of spaghetti hoops over the top of the shower on to Kath and then hid all the towels.....jolly japes. Many more in my head and memories made. But, it became time to move on and so the house was sold; Kath and Neil went one way, Rod and I, another, and so endeth a chapter. One for which I will always be grateful to have shared the happiest time of my life to date.

23 Audley Gardens, Seven Kings, Ilford/

Utterly impossible to resist!

CHAPTER FOURTEEN.

FOUR BOYFRIENDS AND A FUNERAL.

In which our hero gets 'tempest tossed and sore afflicted' and the lights go out.

'Ghosts'.

by Japan. No5. April 4ᵗʰ. 1982.

'Just when I think I'm winning
When I've broken every door
The ghosts of my life blow wilder than before....'

Just when I think I'm winning – haunted by ghosts of failure.

~ ~ ~

Kath and Neil only moved down the road, the other side of the station – a bijou little maisonette. They must've made a packet on the house as the new gaff was about a quarter of the size of Audley Gardens, notwithstanding sharing the profit with Rod.

We, on the other hand, were waiting for a flat on Cranbrook road to be finished – a very des.res. And now worth a mint. Whilst we waited, we had a little flat in Seymour Gardens, still just off Cranbrook, so still a *bit* posh, and that is when things began to go wrong. Not that I acknowledged this – this was my Forever Love and so I would not allow any cracks to appear, any enemies breach the ramparts. There HAD been an incident while we were still at Audley Gardens, somehow all ending up in bed, but I thought once we'd moved, I could say it was just a blip, an experiment, and it would have no impact on our lives. Oh, you silly silly boy.

Somehow, I had regained contact with Tony; I have no memory of how – I MUST have contacted him or some reason, as he wouldn't have had my number, so ......anyway, he had invited us to a party, a house warming at his new pad in Whitechapel and very beautiful it was, paid for no doubt by the luxuriant garden of marijuana, and his drugs trade. It was just as the area was up and coming and he'd been a clever boy and bought in.

The party was very good, I think. Plenty of food, plenty of people, plenty of drink. After the crowds had gone, we all settled down in the snug, big plumptious settees and pouffes, (both kinds) and as we talked and drank, I noticed that Rod's stockinged foot was rubbing Tony's groin, as he sat there, legs spread wide, drinking wine. I only dimly registered this, as I was seriously pissed by then. So much so, that I was sick. Not on Tony's new cream carpets luckily, but Rod said, *"Probably best if you go to bed, eh? You'll be better if you sleep."* (I am, of course, paraphrasing – this was over 30 years ago and I was very drunk; falling over drunk). So, he helped me up the quaint old staircase to the quaint little bedroom and to the quaint little bed, where I fell instantly into a quaint little drunken stupor.

The next bit I have made up, but the bare bones are true, as he told me, after. Rod, with me out of the way, went downstairs and fucked Tony. Had sex with him. Shagged him. Let him touch his beautiful chest. Tony spread his fucking slutty legs and persuaded my Rod to fuck him. Actually, it was not as bad, and worse at the same time. What actually had happened was that the 4 or 5 people who were left, had sex, so it 'wasn't personal'. Apparently. "It was just sex, it didn't mean anything, babe". And they were drunk. It just happened. And you know what? I accepted it. Because I adored this man, and his funny smile and his knobbly knees and his Jewish patois. That's why. I hated him and I loved him, the first of those feelings being a bit alien and alarming and unwelcome so I pretended I didn't feel it. So, how we ended up in OUR bed, with Tony, in our house, not his, I have no idea. I have this photo, so I didn't imagine it and I do remember that the sex was amazing. (I hope you Googled 'poppers', when I told you to...) but HOW? And more to the point...WHY?

Tony and Me.

The phone rang one day, in the fag end of the moving process, and it was Tony.

"Oh hi. It's Tony. Wondered if you fancied coming over?"

"No. We don't. Thankyou."

"Why? What's happened? What about the other night?"

"That was a mistake. It won't be happening again." And with Tony, it didn't.

"Oh, so YOU'RE the nigger in the woodpile, are you?" (I've never been called that before or since!) *"What does Rod think?"*

"The same, of course."

We both knew it to be a blatant lie, but I was NOT having this man's hands, or bits, anywhere near my man again.

Rod knew nothing of this call; I never told him how I had put the kibosh on this..this...thing. Mama lion protecting her own.

"Oh. Well. Shame. He was a good fuck. See you around." OUCH, bastard. But I never did. See him again, I mean. A bit of a sad ending; I actually owed him a debt, he was a player in my story, back in Blackheath when I was but a fledgling, AND he'd taken my virginity you will recall, but...too close, way too close. And I was far too insecure.

So, post Tony, we were moving to our temporary little love nest, while waiting for our proper Forever Home to be finished.

One of the gang, Eddie, a tailor of ecclesiastical robes on Saville Row, known of course as Edie, would often come and stay over at Audley Gardens, (we had 5 bedrooms there – usually full of drunken waifs and strays) and was always around. A good mate. Singularly unattractive - I mean, just like a sister and never in the sexual orbit – and never a threat. Until.......the flat in Seymour gardens was a one bedroomed flat, so one drunken night, Rod decided it would be a good idea if we all slept on the floor in the lounge. What the hell...?? But, I always, always wanted to please him, to soothe this hurt in him, so I agreed.

The next thing I know, we're having sex. Me, Rod and Edie. It was the last thing I expected to be honest. Edie? EDIE? It was like shagging your sister.....a bit weird, I can tell you, yet.....always led by my groin and the heat of the moment. I'll spare you the details....

After, Rod said it didn't matter – he was a friend, it was just a bit of harmless fun, and anyway, Edie didn't get much so it was like a nice thing to do. What? I'm a charity now? But as always, I acquiesced and tried not to let it matter, as he said.

You can see where this is going can't you? I began to as well, as more and more often when we went out, I would get the *'He's nice. Him over there. Do you want to bring him home?'* routine and as often as not, we did. Hugh, who we picked up in The London Apprentice (and who Rod sucked off in the back seat whilst I drove drunkenly home, my heart pounding from the amyl nitrate filling the car) became a regular, although that fizzled out when I accidently did a poo on his carpet. I won't go into details – I'm sure your imaginations are fertile enough to make a good guess why. He cleaned it up graciously, but we were never asked back. There were others – friends from the club, strangers from toilets, often from the cottage on the corner of Dames Road in Wanstead. I'd sit and wait in the car while Rod would disappear into the inky depths of the toilet and emerge with some random stranger, who could have been anyone in the dark and, like some deranged getaway driver, I'd drive us home, while they noshed each other's faces and sucked each other off in the back seat.

I hated it. I hated it with every fibre of my being. So why, you dozy twat, did you do it? Is that the question forming on your lips? 'Because I loved him', comes the pathetic reply. Because I was scared that if I refused, he would leave me. That if I didn't offer myself up, that he would find someone who would. You know: the usual cry of the abused spouse.

Looking back down the years, given what I had (have) always wanted from my life, i.e. a man who would love ME, and only ME, FOR me, and exclusively ME, a break up with Rod was inevitable. I have still not come to understand what drove him, what made him desire others, at the expense of his lovers, and I was by no means the first – I met several at his funeral - and even when witness to the pain it brought. Was he a sex addict (a real one I mean) or did he just like cock? He clearly wasn't satisfied with mine and as this situation progressed, and I granted more and more permission, it became clear that our definitions of 'love' were somewhat different. It became painful. It became humiliating – I hated to see the man I adored with his dick (MY dick!) up someone else's arse, to see some stranger's mouth around it, on his chest, on his mouth. *"For fuck's sake! It's only sex!"* was becoming an argument that was less and less acceptable. Every time it happened, a little piece of me broke off and those pieces, over time, floated away and coalesced into another person, an observer, someone who watched proceedings as if it were a porn film. Certainly I was physically involved – my cock was sucked, I had a cock, his and the Stranger's, in my mouth but it was like I was just in the room, in the corner, watching someone else's heaving buttocks, hearing someone else's panting and groaning as we all came, one after the other. I, the real me, the man who thought his travels were done and was to rest in the encircling arms of this funny, gentle man for ever, was diminishing, was becoming smaller, disappointed, lost again. This was NOT in the script. This was NOT supposed to happen. AGAIN.

Talking about it proved fruitless. He'd either say (resentfully, angrily) *'OK, I won't do it again'* or we'd have the conversation based around; *"but I DO love you. I fuck you, don't I?"* (That bit was meant to be a joke, but in the light of things, not a very good one). *"I don't want anyone else. We've bought a house together….it's just that…you know…."* And then the argument about open relationships and how, if I REALLY loved him, I would *know* it didn't matter, that it was 'only sex'. And, maybe for him, that was the truth. I know, knew of then, people whose relationships thrived on such an arrangement (and many which did not – jealousies, insecurities, one – upmanship, all played out in the embers of the dying light, which was always ignored, justified, until it was too late, leaving the two people to be as 'open' as they liked, as they were now single again). But it didn't work for me. Not then and not years later, as I bravely tried to save the remnants of my imploding marriage. But that's a later story.

Right now, in the summer of 1984, with Frankie, Moyet, Somerville and Wham! marking the going down of my sun, I was finding my position unbearable, painful beyond words. What was wrong with *ME*? A question always answered with *'nothing, babe. Honest'*, but it never served. I felt ugly, unsexy, unimportant and…well, scared. How can I keep doing this? Answer: I can't. How can I leave him? Answer: I can't. I DID need a *'Love Resurrection'* but I didn't know how. I did *'Let the sun go down on me'*, in my heart, as it shrank, just as I let some random stranger go down on me in my bed, trying to please, and failing to feel.

The end came quite suddenly, in the same year. On the surface all was well. Meeting after work, in the Jolly Sailor in Barking, Rod and his brother Tony smelling of sawdust, me smelling of failure; dinner, bit of telly; getting ready to go to Selina's (which was much safer as we'd had everyone there, between us) and then the dread of, *"Shall we go via Dames Road? Fancy it?"* What was I supposed to say? Not agreeing led to sullen argumentative days; agreeing led to a quick fuck and my sunny Rod, back to normal. It was, looking back at the pattern, like a fix for him. And I was aiding and abetting his addiction. Buying his drug.

Amongst all of this sorrow / joy, there was one other very important, pivotal event that occurred and changed forever the dynamics of the relationship with my family. We had a brand-new home, a mezuzah on our door (which belonged to the wonderful old Jewish couple upstairs, but they didn't mind if we rubbed it) to bless our home. I know I didn't technically own it – the mortgage was in Rod's name, he had put down the deposit – but as far as I was concerned, it was MY first ever nest, and I intended to feather it beautifully. We did it up, and the first months were as good as they could possibly have been, him fucking other men aside....

I'd not heard much from down West lately. Gill had been up at Christmas and she'd kept in regular touch but as far as Ma and Pa knew, I had moved and was sharing a nice new house in a 'respectable part' of London, as indeed I was, except for the omission of the fact that my flatmate shagged me, and was my lover. As in BOYFRIEND. This status quo seemed to suit everyone, on a need-to-know basis. Chris had by now, met the love of his life, and he and Vince were getting a place together. He seemed calmer and happier and by default, we didn't see so much of each other and my life (apart from the hated aforementioned moments of sharing) was even, and even ...fun!

One evening, November 1983, the phone rang.

"It's me."

"Hi, Gill! OK!?"

"Erm....no......." and she burst in to tears. I finally manage to get that the shit had hit the fan – like, elephant sized turds.....Dad and she had gone for a walk in to town. So far so normal. Then, *a propos* of nothing, staring straight ahead (I had all the minutiae from a very shocked sister) he said:

"Is Nigel a homosexual?"

She said the blood just drained from her heart and in response all she could answer was,

"You'd better ask HIM."

"That's what I thought," was all he replied.

What happened next, and over the next few days is unknown to me other than what has been reported.

The usual silence (aka. Didn't get my own way; wasn't considered first; sulk) followed until a few days later, by all accounts he and Mum having a stand-up row, right there, in the middle of Newquay High Street. Well, when I say 'row', I mean he yelled and screamed and ranted at her (Odd, given he wanted to keep this monstrous fact a secret) saying it was all her fault for bringing me up 'like a girl' Did he have a point? I was effeminate, at least in HIS eyes; I DID 'sa *hullo clouds, hullo sky*", a lot and skip about '*like a gurl*', not only at school, which he hadn't seen, but also at home, which he did. I did, latterly swan about in a fur coat – but that was just teenagerism, hippiness....

Nobody makes you queer, Dad, no matter what you think. There IS no blame here. Mum, of course, (foolishly, but I imagine, in her fury, brought out by this public shaming) said that she had known for years; Gill knew, Sandra knew; we had had one to stay in our house! At which point, he went nuclear.

Now, at the point (in my naive imagination) where I thought that now, maybe as it was 'official', when I wanted, needed, reassurance and support, he would take me to one side, man to man and say something along the lines of: *"Well, Son. I respect you for not telling me as you knew I might be upset, but I am not. I am proud of you, proud of what you have achieved – a teacher! A teacher in the family! Someone who went to College and was even asked to go to Cambridge! Thank you for considering my feelings and not wanting to cause me dismay – but how could I? You are a wonderful son and a good human being who will do good things in the world"*

I wrote to them, my parents, expressing my gratitude for their understanding, acceptance and to thank them for giving me the life I had. What he actually did, was to write me a letter in return, from which I quote, and the power of which causes me such sorrow, such hurt, even nearly 30 years after he wrote it:

'Yours to hand, I would imagine that it must be the standard letter as supplied in text form by The Shit Shovers Union to placate parents who have just discovered that their son is a fully paid up member, and having made all the appropriate platitudes to explain away the bestial, disgusting depravity of abusing your body and mind, that all will be forgiven and the whole thing will be swept under the carpet and we all go on with our normal lives as if nothing had happened.

Well, it is not like that for us (I doubt Mum had anything to do with this, and he was NOT speaking for her at all). *We are going to make you bear some of the weight of the cross you have made us carry, what you have done to your parents. You have DESTROYED the two people who gave you life and have loved you fiercely all the years and now all this love has gone......after much soul searching I have decided to leave this house, to leave her here. I CURSE you for what you are doing to yourself and what you have done to your parents and I hope this letter will stop you from engaging in these bestial acts, and that you may hear our cry of anguish and might say to yourself ' I once had a mother and father'. I know we shall ask ourselves: 'not did where we go wrong, but how could you do this to us'*

Do not phone.

Yours in blood only.

Dad.'

I have left out the more unpleasant parts.

This dear reader was, as you can imagine, NOT what I wanted to hear. Shock. Dismay. Hurt. Anger. You're my DAD, my FATHER, and here you are, AGAIN, giving me no support, no love, no feelings that it will all be OK. How many more times will you do this to me?

As you were dying, I came to you and told you I understood, that I forgave you. But I think I was lying. I could forgive you for what you did to me, but never for what you did to Gill, to Sandra, to my Mother. All of us, damaged due to your intransigence, your petty spite and grudges. What your letter did, in fact, after I'd laughed it off, bravado flying like rain, was to set up, deep inside me a feeling of shame – not for being gay, exactly but for the fact of my very *being* so was causing so much pain and upset, sadness and hurt.

I AM GAY.

I AM A GAY MAN.

I AM A GOOD PERSON.

I HAVE WORTH.

I HAVE LOVE AND GIVE IT FREELY.

I AM A GAY MAN.

It took me years, years, to be able to say this, to recover from the poisoning administered to me by my Father, who not only actively poured hatred and disgust upon me, but also didn't stand by me, when I was telling my truth, when I most needed love and support and acceptance. I DIDN'T smash those windows, and when I needed you again, here, at this most pivotal moment of my life, you weren't there again.

I had been in London for years, as you know, fucking and shopping, as the play said, (only without those coy asterisks) - for love, had found love, had lived a happy life, lived a sad life, just like everyone else, I have had a 'normal' life. Successful in parts, tragic in others. I've been Mr. Lucky more often than not, but had some grim intervals. I have worked to keep food on the tables in the various places I have found myself. I have contributed, as a person, as a lover and as a friend, as an educator and supporter. So you dare. You fucking DARE judge me as a bad person, someone you hardly know, as you had never bothered to ask, simply because of who I share a bed with.

Ach, enough. This rant, this interminable rant we poofters have against our parents! Enough already. He's made up his mind (in a rather melodramatic fashion in my view!) and **that**, as we all know, was **that**.

What happened next, as I have heard from the other, more rational members of the family strays in to Farce. He instantly revoked his memberships of all his clubs at the Legion – including his beloved Euchre team, because apparently *"everyone would know"*. Sorry? How exactly? You wouldn't breathe a word and I'm in London..! *("Trevor,"* said my hopeful Mother, *"Joe and Brian are both gay! If you can't tell, then I can. They're not leaving the team, are they? It's private.")*. Maybe THAT'S why he left – in case he caught it from *them*...

He screamed and raved at my poor mother for 'making me a queer bastard', for not bringing me up properly, for treating me like a girl, for, for....for EVERYTHING. None of it, obviously, was *his* fault – not that there WAS any 'fault' to be had.

He shut all the curtains, wouldn't go out, refused to answer the phone or the door, refused to eat. In the end, worried about what was going on in the house, my brother and Gill got the priest from St. Mary's (the one who absolved Mary from her shagging sins) but, after shouting through the letter box (please, try to get a mental picture of this!), the door opened and Dad, whiskered, unshaven and filthy, opened the door, stared at the three of them, shouted *"I'd rather he was a spastic in a wheelchair, than one of THEM,"* and then BLAM! Slammed the door in the priest's face. There wasn't really much to add to that really, so they all went home.

My indomitable Auntie Gwen, who'd I'd known all me life, had come down to try to help with the crisis – I am assuming Mum must've phoned and told her. When he announced: *"I'd rather he was a spastic in a wheelchair, than one of THEM,"* she gave him SUCH a bollocking, I think he lost the power of speech. At any rate, he never spoke a word for days, just drifted from room to room, crying and wailing.

One GOOD thing that came from this lunacy was that my Mother had a 'FUCK YOU!' moment and announced that she was going up to London – that I was still her son and she wanted to see me. So she did! Excellent! Rod fell in love with her, she was instantly adopted, a feeling she found quite confusing – hugging? Touching? All a bit alien, but you could tell she loved it. Everyone was kind to her, and with her – they knew of the terrible, punishing time she'd had and she blossomed, flowered in the warmth of these people.

We took her to Brighton - there was a huge party, and we booked her in to a hotel, all posh like and she was treated like a queen. By all the queens. We took her the Rose and Hand, to Legends, to a drag show. She sat, wide eyed and startled, with her Dubonnet and lemonade, but bit by bit, discarded the slights and barbs, the prejudices and disgust that had been fed to her for so long; saw these people, saw us, saw ME, in the clear light of love and joy and acceptance, and I like to think that, in those few heady days, she was in some way healed. At least, when she returned, she would have a whole other world she could escape to in her mind, to offest the barage of hatred that would inevitably be unleashed upon her.

My Mum, with Billy and Jan.

Billy and Jan loved her; the total acceptance of her, and her son by all of these people, some of whom she had met only hours before, was puzzling to her, but was a clue that there could be a different kind of life, peopled with kindness and joy. People welcomed her in, understood her reluctance about being treated well, as it wasn't something she was used to. But I could tell she loved it; she drank it in and we were as close as we'd ever been during those times.

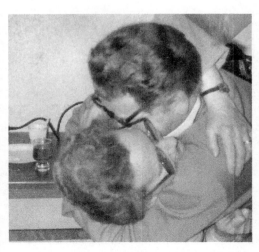

My Mother with Uncle Billy, in Brighton!

She came up to see me several times over this period, the one during which I was *persona non gratis*. On one occasion, and this dates it to Spring, '83, I made her sit and listen to the whole of Pink Floyd's '*The Final Cut*', really loud....I think it was to do with sharing something important to ME with HER. Anyway, after her ears had stopped bleeding, she just said: *"That was nice, dear"*. I felt warm.

It was a strange set up really – he would, wordlessly drive her to the station, when she was taking a trip to 'That Den of Vice', and then meet her from the train on her return. He never once asked her anything – did she have nice time, who did she meet, and, worst and unkindest cut of all, how I was. I had simply ceased to exist. I think SHE saw it as a blessed release.....away from the oppressive silence of her life, her small world. She came to a place of laughter, of fun, of 'being allowed' to spend time with people who asked her questions, showed an interest and made her smile. And I am certain, though deep down I'm sure she would have wished it otherwise, it gave her peace to see that I was safe, I was happy and was loved.

Unfortunately, things were not what they seemed...

As far as the famerly was concerned, all was well. Our new flat was ready, we'd moved in in early March, I think. We bought furniture and lamps, beds and cutlery. But my joy was lost – I knew my new home would be spoiled soon enough. And it was.

My fault in a kind of way. It was a Saturday, we went to the club and there was some fresh meat in! Look chaps....someone you haven't had! Kenny. Wee Kenny from Belfast, with his spiky hair and £300 jacket. Like flies round shit, they were. Most oddly, but Rod had ordered a cab. Kenny was the belle of the ball and at 11, someone said there was party back at somebody's flat. But strangely, Rod had decided he wanted to go home early so Kenny asked *me* to go with him. It was only up the High Road, so I thought I'd tag along, have a bevvy and then head off. To home. Where my Rod would be, alone. Waiting for me. Just me. For once.

Somehow, however, I ended copping off with Kenny. What alchemy was this? He was a twink! A twinky twink, ten years my junior and hairless apart from his Limahl hairdo. What was I thinking? To this day, I don't know. Anyway, we went. Back. To. My. Flat. The one with Rod in it. The demon drink I suppose – but there were far more shaggable people at the party so WHY him, and why, oh WHY did I decide to take him back to my place? Was I bringing a pressy home to Daddy? Like the mouse or headless vole, the cat lays at your feet? Or – GASP! -had some unknown signal passed between him and Rod, so that Kenny was *ENGINEERING* this? To be brought back to the place where the one he REALLY fancied was, all naked and in bed....Did I WANT to get caught and bring it all to a head? I don't know. What I DO know is that we got back to Cranbrook Road, I opened the front door and got half way down the hall and I chickened out; the jury is out here, as years later, when I asked Rod WHY he did what he then after this night, his version of what he heard is different from mine and from my motives that night – which is why his actions were so utterly utterly devastating later, as I believed I HAD done the right thing.... Sort of.

I remember (as far as anyone can, years later and pissed then) saying: *"No, look, we can't do this. My boyfriend is here. You'll have to go."* Rod insists the pronoun was *"we'll"*. It doesn't alter the fact that *apparently,* I WAS going to have sex with Kenny, though God knows why, but I didn't. Rod says I went off with him and came back later in the night. I say I saw him out and went to bed. They're both dead now, so....

The next morning, hung-over and tired, the day started out OK. Rod asked how the party had been, (*"OK, bit boring really."*), who was there (*"Oh the usual crowd. You know."*), did I get home OK, (*"Yeah, I got a cab."*) – all true. Except for the sin of omission. And I didn't know that he'd been awake and heard us come in. And that, dear reader, set him on a path for revenge.

No more was said of it. I thought – hoped – that Kenny was just passing through and he and his silly hair would just have disappeared as suddenly as he'd come and it was done with. Unfortunately, it wasn't and he hadn't.

I need to go backwards a little here, to put all of this into context.

I had travelled down to Plymouth where Gill was living at that time, with the express purpose of telling her about myself. This was long before Rod, but I guess it must have been in the space between leaving Julie and meeting Steve. Eager to validate all the pain I had been the architect of, I decided I needed to tell someone, someone meaningful, someone in the family. I was, as most people reading this will either have felt or can guess at how difficult such a thing can be, pretty terrified. The words got stuck somewhere behind my teeth, and it took several beers to prise them open. I don't remember exactly what I said now, but I DO remember we were in her kitchen and she was holding a cucumber. After the words had tumbled out, whatever they were, we both looked at the vegetable and burst out laughing, which on my part eventually turned to sobbing, from relief, an overload of adrenaline and tension – who knows, but there we were, my beloved sister and I, sitting on the kitchen floor, tear – stained, with her making improper suggestions as to what she could do with the salad component.

After this, she became my ally, the one person I could confide in, rest my weary closeted bones. It's likely she suspected, if not knew – the loons and fur coat were a bit of a giveaway – but had been happy not to say anything. Besides, it's not that an easy question to ask, really. It was great though, because once my closet door was officially opened, she too could walk through it and meet the creatures that dwelt therein. Of course, Rod adored her, and she him, and she was welcomed in to the family as she were one of their own – an amazing and wondrous thing for her, as she hadn't been exactly supported by her own.

Years before this, poor and living in a hovel with her daughter, she had been forced to make 'Sophie's Choice' and give up her daughter, to her father, Ian – my Dad's Nemesis and Arch Enemy, Spawn of Satan. She simply couldn't afford to feed or clothe her; the house was cold and wet and the choices were few. My parents – well, *him,* and she just did what she was told – were less than supportive of this decision of course, branding Gill as a failure (as if she didn't feel that already, to the pit of her soul) as someone who a) couldn't feed her child and b) as someone who would give her child up. Make up your fucking mind! Which do you want? For me, it was the bravest thing, the most loving thing she could have done for her daughter and one, so it proved, which to be the best outcome for them all – agonising enough and made a thousand times worse by your judgement. (Your sins pile ever higher, you awful man. And with each hurt you pile upon us, the chances of me ever forgiving you drip away, drip, drip…*"Daddy, daddy, you bastard, I'm through!"* I'm with you, Sylvia Plath.)

So, years later, when Rod's family, in all their multi coloured hues of love, opened their collective arms, I could see her healing with every visit, each gaping wound being tenderly closed, with love and laughter and beer. She came fairly often during those few golden years, playing pranks, with Irene, being obscene with Rod, dancing drunk down the club with Millsy, and recovering from those years in the wilderness, and it was of comfort for me too, and the one person who understood the depth and width of my grief when Rod and I parted. She didn't know exactly why, but was wise enough to know it wasn't a decision taken lightly or welcomed in. And of course, it was her loss too.

But, for a time, it was as good as it had ever been – my Gill, my Rod and my overflowing heart all in the room at the same time. I had broken off all contact with my Canadian mistress (though I knew she'd be there if I needed her) and all the bad shit was forgotten.

But then.

But then......Kenny, little twinky Ken, became Rod's trophy – half his age, and full of spunk, literally and figuratively and a perfect way to demonstrate his, Rod's, virility. I'm not sure what it demonstrated to me, after I'd made it (disastrously) clear that it was to be 'ME OR HIM!!!!' and found myself sleeping in the other room, listening to them fucking their brains out, next door, in MY bed, using MY poppers, other than maybe this was going to end badly after all. But what to do? I owned the flat, or half of it, and his family was my family – how could I give them up? I couldn't, I FUCKING WOULDN'T you baldy fucking CUNT. Screw Kenny, screw you. It's MY flat, MY CD player, MY telly and I'm STAYING. That, it seems, was cool with them – they liked me!! LIKED ME! HAHAHAHAHA!!! Rod even told me he still loved me. "FUCK YOU!" was my response, and the fork I'd been carrying stayed quivering, where I had buried its tines in the bedroom wall.

This period in the story has become a bit blurred with time; long years past and such a muddle of blood and tears, of hurt and loss, of displacement, of substitution and desperation. But no matter how many beers I drank, or dicks I sucked, how many bars and parties I went to or sexual encounters I had to dull the pain, the ragged tearing hole left by his presence, his funny snaggle tooth and laughter when he was drunk, his hairy belly, his perfect dick, his attentive lovemaking where I felt we were the only two living souls there were, his generosity of spirit, his kindness, was always there, gaping wide, and my guts spilling. All of those things, so familiar, so expected – pulled away from me and all because I had taken Kenny back to the flat. Ahh, but maybe not. History tells me, and ex-lovers at his funeral told me, that it was going to happen – it happened to them, the pattern was the same, history repeating. What if I hadn't? Well, I don't need to ask do I? If it hadn't been Kenny, it would surely have been someone else, next week, next month, the next bar, the next party – too much cock, too much temptation for a man like him. The grass was always greener. Sadly, he had failed to water the grass on *this* side of the fence and it became yellow, then brown, then withered away.

Rod was NOT a bad man; he was a wonderful loving spirit whom everyone he ever came into contact with adored and wanted to be his friend, confidante, lover. But he was also a serial philanderer, and being 'cheeky' wasn't enough.

When what was going on became public knowledge, 3 things happened.

1. Kath gave Rod the biggest bollocking he'd ever had in his life, and a massive slap. (Thanks Kath.)

2. Rod and Kenny stopped going to the club, to make it easier for me, apparently! How was that EASIER, exactly? You were just snoggin' him in a DIFFERENT club. You'd still be in my bed when I got back, or come in, all giggly and pissed when I was already home, in bed. HOW, exactly was that easier? NOTHING, EVER, would make it easier, you arse. Easier on your conscience, more like.

And....

3. I met someone else.

No1 – Excellent.

No2. – Agony.

No3. – Some light relief from the endless grey, and beer soaked, one-night stands.

ONE.

Richard was his name. A real nice man. Rod, on one of his nights off, asked me out for a drink – WHAT? Maybe….maybe…he'd realised his mistake and wanted me back…all the pain, betrayal, despair evaporated in a big shiny cloud of hope….Apparently, he said, there was a new gay pub open in Stratford. Having little better to do, and leaping like a sad whore at the chance of spending some time with him, I agreed and off we went. It was shit. New, and shit. All horrid neon and poncey décor, with the atmosphere of an abandoned asylum. Anyway, we'd made the effort to go, and maybe I was right! After a few drinks, Rod would see sense, see that that Kenny was no good for him and that he wanted me all the time (this did not happen, dear reader, as you may have guessed. That did not happen, in fact, until I was with someone else….), so we kind of hung around, avoiding the drafts and staring around disconsolately, when…..a group, noisy, young, possibly interesting, folk tumbled in through the door. One of whom was Richard, who had taught with me, back in the Traveller's days, when I took the few travellers that were there at any one time to make it worth the bother, into the 'main school'. He was *there*….that's MY gaydar fucked then! How did I not notice him? Too busy stopping little snots nicking stuff and causing mayhem in the class to notice much else really. Anyway, it seemed to be an after school do……in a gay bar? Maybe Rod'd got it wrong? Actually, he had, the twat. The pub was over the road. No wonder there didn't seem to be many homosexualists hanging around! Pahahahaaa. It was full of 'types', if you know what I mean. The pub was making a valiant attempt at 80s chic and failing miserably. I don't think it stayed open long, not surprisingly. Anyway. I clocked floppy haired Richard, he clocked me and we both went on with our separate activities: he laughing uproariously with his colleagues, and me being glum and sad and wishing I was dead.

Richard.

"I don't like it in here, Nige," said Rod. *"It's full of dry lunch cunts. Shall we go somewhere else?"*

"Um, yeah. OK." ('To bed' was whispering around in my head). *"Where?"*

"I saw another pub just down the road. Let's try that one, now we're out. May as well, eh?"

As we passed Richard's group, he looked up, smiled and turned back to his (half) pint. We went out in to the Stratford night.

"What about the Pigeons? Oh bollocks. It don't open till 10. Look, over there..." and we crossed the road and went into....the gay pub! Ta DAH!

"Fuck ME!" said Rod. *"I knew it was round here somewhere! What do you want, babe? Pint?"*

"Yes. Thankyou." STOP BEING SO FUCKING NORMAL. AND NICE. AND STOP CALLING ME 'BABE'.

It was pretty busy, and Rod was at the bar for ages. I was just standing looking round, when the door swung open and in walked.......no prizes for guessing....Richard.

"I thought I'd find you in here. You went to the wrong pub..."

"Well, yes, we did."

"Is that your boyfriend?" he asked as he spotted Rod coming over with the drinks.

"Erm.....no. no it isn't. Not anymore." (OUCHY HURT HURT). *"We split up, but we still live together."*

"Ah, well, that's good."

What was? That we'd split up? Or that we were two civilised, grown-ups who could behave sensibly in a difficult situation? (HA! If only he knew...)

"Hello, babe," said Rod. *"I'm Rod."* (STOP CALLING PEOPLE BABE!! Unless it's me. No, don't call me babe either, actually.)

"Richard."

"You know each other?"

"A bit. We used to teach together."

"Gaw, fuck me! Not another one! I had enough to put up with from THIS one, when we was together, didn't I Nige?" Guffaw.

What the….? I didn't understand all this subtext. I know what you're doing, RODNEY CARR, why don't you just FUCK OFF and leave me with my friend, someone you don't know, that you haven't shagged and someone that, actually, I quite fancy. AND I don't need your permission.

"Richard. Rich", I said, proprietorially, *"Do you want a bevvy?"*

"Aw, you should've said. I'll get it."

"NO, it's FINE, thank you. I will. Rich?"

"Half of lager, please. Any sort."

"Sure. Won't be a minute."

Actually, looking at the crush at the bar, I'd probably be five and Rod'd be there with Richard…unattended.

"Oh actually, Rod", I said, *"We were just going. Weren't we? Rich. Richard. WEREN'T WE?"*

"Oh. Um…yes", he replied, looking a bit confused. *"But I will have that drink first. No worries. I'll go!"* and he disappeared into the crowd. I turned to Rod.

"What are you doing?"

"Who?"

"You."

"Nothing. Why?"

"Yes you were. 'BABE'…you don't even know him."

"Oh, fer fucks sake. How long have you known me? I call EVERYONE babe."

"Well……you were looking at him."

"And……"

"In THAT way."

"I was not!"

"Yes. You were!"

"Oh fer fuck's sake. Grow up. I've had enough of this. This was supposed to be a nice friendly drink, have a bit of fun, and you're just being a prat."

How could it EVER just be a 'nice friendly drink', you stupid man. My heart hurts, I can't get twinky boy Kenny out of my mind, everything you do or says belongs to ME, and my vision of my life, so snatched away…how could it EVER be just that? You are SUCH a fool. And I love you so much I can barely breathe. And I don't want to be here. And I don't want this pint. And I don't want to smell your 'Habit Rouge'. And I don't want to 'have fun'. I want…. I want….but my thoughts were interrupted by Richard's return.

"I've given up. Can't get to the bar. Shall we go?" and he looked straight at me. Not Rod. Me.

"Yes," I said. *"Let's."*

And off went we! Not looking back! HA HA HA HAAAAA.

The last time I saw Richard was Stratford, 1982, all romantics meet the same fate someday….actually, this bit of plagiarism is a lie – we met again years later. Different time, different place….

Any hoo…..off we went back to his lickle love nest in the sky, a flat in a nearby tower block. I was pretty pissed by now (no change there then) and I was now a smoker of St. Moritz (sad, eh?) and the only really clear memory of that night I have was burning his coffee table with a fag. We DID have sex; I remember, vaguely, a size issue and a failure of that particular attempt, but we did both reach a satisfactory conclusion. It must've been okay enough to agree to meet up again, and thus began a really decent, healing affair. Nothing desperate, nothing long term, and I believe it was the same on his part too (unless he could see that, really, he and we didn't stand a chance) but for quite a few weeks we met up – he'd pick me up in his 2CV (yes. Really) and we'd drive around London and for the first time in some time, I felt peaceful….not ripped, not screaming in silent fury at God/Buddha/Allah/whoever about how unfair and totally shit my life is, and not, in that moment, in that little car, or in Richard's gentle arms, wishing I was elsewhere.

He was a decent man, a considerate lover and he could, I'm sure see the depth of my hurt and did his best to mend it. And, sadly, in the end, he failed. He simply couldn't compete. We made love, we had beer, we laughed, but all too briefly the dam got washed away and I was once more swept away in the flood of both not being able to be with Rod, at the same time not wanting to be with him cos he was a *CUNT* and gasping for air in all the mixed swirling waters in between. Rich and I just saw each other less, then less and less; I kept making excuses for not meeting and I think a mate of his put him straight, who, being outside could see the blade of doom swinging overhead, like in *'The Pit and the Pendulum'*, coming ever lower to slice us apart. We parted amicably, if a little sadly, both thinking 'in another time, another place', but *mea culpa*. We didn't stand a chance. I didn't ALLOW it to be. He went back to his City Farm and school, and I continued to play charades at PPL in my lickle purple number.

How had I gone from Mr. Lucky, to Mr. Miserable Bastard in such a short time? I had few friends during this time, as all I did was moan about stuff. People were bored but I was so far up my own miserable arse to notice and so of course it was all THEIR fault. Why can't you see I'm sad? That I need a hug? That I need you to be nice to me and LISTEN? The fact that that the few remaining 'mates' had had their fill of listening passed me by. Apart from Chris. Dear old Chris, who like a big ole rescuing type thing erm.....rescued me. He'd seen me plummeting down, waited patiently until it was clear I wasn't going do anything but get pissed and moan a lot, then rang me and said: *"Right. Get dressed. Tube, 8 o clock. If you're not there, I'll come and get you and drag you out by your big girly hair."*

Remembering previous nights out with Chris, I wasn't desperately keen. Here are a couple of examples:

He decided one time, it would be good to go to *'Heaven'*, under the Arches at Charing Cross. I unwillingly agreed, but went. After paying a HUGE amount of money to get in (about eight quid, I think, but this did entitle you to go through to the Eagle, a side bar, where you get could get tied up and fucked for free; there's another tale to tell here, folks. But not for *your* ears, gentle reader.) We went in and, Lordy Lordy....men. Thousands of men. Mostly stripped to the waist, mostly dancing to that there 'Hi-NRG' nonsense.... (you can take the boy out of Cornwall....) but many snoggin', staring, drinking.....it was like...like... I don't know what it was like, to be honest. Anyway, we stood around like twats, well, I did. Chris had disappeared. Boom. Just like that.

Cheers matey. So I stood. Got another beer, with a 2nd mortgage, and stood around some more. Chris reappeared, slightly sweaty and a bit goggle eyed (I didn't ask, and don't know to this day) and said:

"You dancing'?"

"You askin'?" (Bad Scouse accent).

"No, not really. Mine's a lager. Back in a minute!" and he disappeared into the crowd again.

I went to the bar. I wandered about a bit, trying not to stare. I looked into the Eagle (OH MY GOODNESS!!!), and went back to the original spot, waiting for my 'friend'. Who never reappeared. So, I drank his drink too, gave it another ten minutes and said to the bloke who was eyeing me up (I was a looker in them days you know. Amongst all those buff, cropped shirtless men, I was 'interesting' with me bouffant mullet and bri-nylon), *"I'm off. If my mate arrives tell him I've fucked off home. Oh. And that he's a bastard. Cheers."*

And I left. Lovely. Thanks for that.

Another time he decided it would be a good idea to try to blag our way into Napoleons, in Bond Street, a members only club for 'the older gentleman' with LOADSA MAHNEY......quite HOW we would manage this was never made clear, but off we went, me in tow, on our latest ridiculous adventure which was bound to end in disaster. Which it did.

So, there it was, all lit, subtle – like, with a few lads (that I now know, of course, were rent boys) and Mercs and Bentleys pulling up outside.

"You ARE joking, aren't you?"

No, come on. It'll be fun."

"Exactly HOW will it be fun? And, what happens if we DO get inside?"

"Stop fuckin moanin', and enjoy yourself for once. If we get in, they'll buy us drinks. You can get a shag if you want. Mine's a lager if anyone asks."

So, we stood around outside the club, with the milling hordes of whores and young men looking for love, sex, alcohol or money, or any combination of those. It was both fascinating and sad, worrying and thrilling. After a while this man, really old, about 45, came over and said: *"Do YOU want to come in?"* ME!! Out of all those young twinks.

"Not unless my mate comes too," I said firmly. So he gestured to Chris, who was looking both annoyed and hopeful and took us both inside, waving at the doorman as we passed.

"FUCK. ING. HELL!!" said Chris, staring round. This was opulence indeed. Mr. Bloke came over and asked what we'd like to drink – *"Have anything you like, boys! Anything!"*

I was rather thinking of a fabulous cocktail with a sparkler or something but...

"I'll have a lager," said Chris.

"Oh. Me too then."

I supposed he was up for a threesome with a couple of rough types – we weren't exactly dressed up *marché* – but he was shit out of luck (as my sainted Lady Mother used to say) if he thought I was going to shag Chris. Ewwwww! He was my SISTER!! Maybe he wanted to watch? Make a video? This was getting weirder by the minute.

He came back with the drinks. *"Hi,"* he drawled. *"I'm Peregrine."* (It probably wasn't, but he was very posh, and this WAS 30 odd years ago!)

"Hello!" I said. *"I'm Mike and this is erm...Mark."* (false names. Seemed safer.) *"Thank you for the drinks."*

"A pleasure, to be sure. I have some friends I'd like you to meet. They like boys your age, your type. A bit rough, a bit thick looking."

Excuse me? Thick looking? Fucking cheek! I have a Cert. Ed, you know. What? Was I being purloined here, for sex by a gang of old blokes? Maybe I'd be whisked off and sold into sex slavery? Actually, that one with the salt n pepper hair isn't too....WHOA! Hang on.....

Erm, maybe a bit later? Mark and me, well, we're a bit shy...."

"OK, then er...MIKE." (He knew! HE KNEW!!) *"Come over when you're ready.....don't leave it too long though; there are lots of others who would jump at the chance. Come over when you feel like a little Veuve Clicquot....."*

Ooooh, I like champagne, me I do. *"Pssst Chris......"* whispering, far too loudly...."*CHRIS...... Shall we go over? Look, they got champagne!"*

"No, you fucking idiot. They'll think you're rent and you'd have to 'cough up' so to speak, in return."

"Just because you don't like older men (WOW!! That's the first time I'd articulated my 'preference'.) *doesn't mean we shouldn't go over. We can always just say NO."*

"How can you be so fuckin NAÏVE? How old are YOU? TEN? You can't say NO. That's the point. YOU drink their champagne; they get to fuck you. That's the rules. All of 'em probably. At the same time."

Chris has always been my torment and my saviour. I hated him and I loved him and once again he was right, but I had my beer goggles on and it DID seem like an attractive proposition – well, THAT one did and maybe the others wouldn't mind if their friend and me had an affair and eventually got a house together and everything?

"I'll just have one glass."

"No. No, you fucking WON'T. Stay here with me."

Something in his tone brought me out of my (ridiculous) fantasy and back to the present.

"Look," he said, *"Let's just have another drink. I need a wazz. Mine's a lager."*

So I went up to the bar and ordered two pints.

"That's three hundred pounds please," said the barman. It wasn't obviously, but it might as well have been.

"But I've only got a fiver..."

"Well then maybe you shouldn't be in here," he said. *"Who are you with? Where is your admitting member?"*

"Um..... he's...he's......" But Mr. Peregrine was nowhere to be seen. *"Um...I don't know actually."*

"Well, then you need to leave."

"Yes, but, my friend is........"

"NOW."

As if summoned by some supernatural force or a wave of a wand and a spell, for conjuring up fucking HUGE blokes, two bouncers appeared and picked me up, literally, feet –off – the – floor 239tyle, and levitated – it must have been *Wingardium Leviosa,* that makes you float maybe – me out of the door and dumped me on the pavement. I HAD JUST BEEN THROWN OUT OF NAPOLEON'S! How fucking cool is that? Moments later, Chris appeared, shouting *"You can stick your poncey club up yer fuckin arse!!"*….and there was Peregrine. With two other young fellow – me – lads. As they walked past, he said, *"You should've had the champagne when you had the chance. Now fuck off, you losers."*

"NO, YOU FUCK OFF, YOU SLIMY OLD CUNT!" bellowed Chris. *"That was good, eh? Come on! Where shall we go now?"*

"Home, please. Just home."

"Lightweight."

But he took me home. A saviour.

As I said, nights out with Chris were nothing if not 'interesting'.

So, back to this night…

I DID get dressed, mostly because I KNEW he WOULD come round and drag me out by my girly hair, and met him at the Tube, at 8.00.

"We're going somewhere new now. It's called 'The London Apprentice'. You'll like it."

I wasn't sure I would but, I didn't have much choice. He was on a mission, a mission to save his best friend. And get a few beers for free, of course. I don't think in all the years I knew him, he'd EVER got a round in. Respect. I loved him, the old bastard. What he HADN'T told me was that this was a leather bar, or at least, full of proper hard blokes, in their lumberjack shirts, torn jeans and a rainbow of coloured hankies in their back pockets. Once again, I looked like a prize twat.

"Not as good as the Colherne, but nearer," he said.

"Is yours a lager?"

"HAHAHAHAAAA. Fuck off." He said as he disappeared to the bogs.

Actually, it was quite nice. Nice beer, nice 'eye candy' (See? I was learning!), nice music, if you liked Divine and Evelyn Thomas....perhaps he was right. This WAS what I needed, instead of moping around at home. We had more beer, the scenery improved. People seemed friendly enough. Very friendly, actually, as Chris was at the bar with his tongue down the throat of some skinhead type. So. That's me then. Twatty gooseberry or whatever the expression is for someone who is always left alone in clubs when their best friend and person who brought them cops off with someone. Again. Wallflower. Yeah, that's it.

The L.A., Old Street, long since closed.

TWO.

"You look a bit fed up," said someone, in my ear, above Hazell Dean moaning that she was 'searchin, and lookin' for love', at 130 beats per minute. *"You been deserted?"*

"Erm, not exactly. My friend," – I nodded to Chris, who was having the top of his head licked – *"brought me, and now he's…. otherwise engaged. It's alright. It happens all the time."*

"Ah. So, I see. That's a bit weird, eh? Licking someone's head?"

"You haven't seen anything," I replied. *"That's nothing…."* And we laughed. Together.

We were standing at one of those funny little shelf things attached to pillars, and I had my elbows on it and my hands dangling and the next thing, I felt something in my palm; a finger circling, gently, circling, circling.

"Hi. I'm Ken," said the man and I looked at him then and my heart kind of juddered. He looked to be the kindest man, with the gentlest and bluest eyes I had ever seen. *"Hello,"* I said.

Ken…..much more beautiful than in this crappy photo….
but all that remains…

We chatted a while and I realised he was South African – he had a marvellous burr to his voice; musical, lilting.

"Shall we go somewhere quieter?" he said. *"Like, Jim's Phone Bar. Bit camp, but its close and at least we can hear each other."*

"Yes, sure OK. Let me just tell…."

"He wouldn't be interested, I don't think."

I turned to look where Chris had been standing, by the bar and all I could see now was his new squeeze gazing at the ceiling and just the top of Chris's head as it went backwards and forwards. Oh, Chris…..

"You're probably right. Let's go." And he took me by the hand and he took me by the heart and we left the L.A., and I struck out into waters new.

We went to the phone bar – a cute little place with phones on the tables so you could ring someone up, across the room and…..I don't know. Say: "You want a drink?" "My friend fancies you". "Wanna shag?" "Talk about the meaning of Life"? What a weird concept – why don't you just go ACROSS the room and ask? Anyway, I wouldn't like the risk that everyone'd be on the phone, except me. It was quiet; (well – that's a relative term, and at least I didn't have to watch my best mate giving someone he'd only just met a blow job. These were still my days of innocence, dear reader. I was only about 4, in gay years), we found a table, and I went to the bar.

"Beer? A short?"

"No. Orange juice. Thank you." (What a polite young man!)

"You're not driving, are you?"

"No, I'm a recovering alcoholic." BLAM. Just like that. I wasn't quite sure how to follow that up.

"Oh. Um. Right. Maybe I'll have juice too."

"No, silly. You go ahead. I'm used to it."

(It will help you enormously, to get into the spirit of things if you read any conversations between us in an Afrikaans accent. His bits, obvs.)

We sat and we talked. Just that. And we smiled. REALLY smiled, with pleasure, with amusement. And we laughed. Man, what a strange sensation in my face! All my smiling muscles seemed to have atrophied, and it felt strange, but wonderful, to be back in the real world, where most folks smiled and laughed all the time. And we talked some more and had an evening of joyous, uncomplicated pleasure, the coming together of two brand new people, sharing those first intimacies, those first secrets.

We finished our drinks – it seemed a little insensitive to have another – and we stood up, in to that thousand-year silence. Now what? Shake hands, and say, *"Well, it was lovely to meet you"?* A peck on the cheek, before going our separate ways? No. Here's what happened. Ken took my hand and again drew little circles on my palm, something secret and quiet he would do all through our time together, which would I'm sure have been long and happy if I hadn't been such an utter fucking twat. However....he drew gently on my palm, like some arcane mating symbol and with that it, was decided. We would be together this night, and many after that.

We made the decision to go back to Cranbrook Road. Mostly because Ken had someone called Nicky living in his flat and she was seeing her (married) boyfriend this evening – he was a fireman and worked weird shifts, and they didn't get much 'fokking time' so it would be good to go somewhere else. I was unsure of Rod's whereabouts. It was a Friday night and he was probably down the club, licking his wounds, left by Kenny who didn't love him QUITE that much after all; ha! serves him right.....he'd stopped coming round to the flat, and they didn't meet up much anymore. I still don't know who did what to whom. Or who DIDN'T do what to who, or who did what to somebody else....anyway, they'd 'split up', from whatever the relationship was; something flimsy, something made of air. Rod had disappeared down to Brighton for a few days, to be nursed and Bovrilled by his Auntie Jan, and when he came back, he was all tail between leggy and way too nice. TOO. FUCKING. LATE. MATE.

Anyway, that night, Ken and I went back to Ilford and there began a time of sweet surrender, of gentleness and loving arms. He was a genuine and honest man, whose penis was unfortunately too large for most things (we managed to find alternatives) and who's troubled past put mine well and truly into perspective.

He was in his flat, in fact in this LIFE, because he had been too drunk to even commit suicide. The black cab he had tried to throw himself in front of was actually further away and going slower than he had thought and he ended up just throwing himself onto the road, and cracking his head. In A+E they told him that he didn't need a taxi – booze would kill him soon enough, but more slowly and infinitely more unpleasantly. From that moment he admitted he was a drunk, enrolled on the 12 Steps, got a flat and sorted himself out. All this he told me that night in the Phone Bar, (or some of it – most of that glowing evening we spent laughing and gently, unwittingly falling into each other's hearts. Not too much nasty stuff please, not yet, not now) but it all came out as he gave me his trust and his heart and his soul. Ah, poor Ken. Such a mistake for you. And I am truly, truly sorry.

He had, back home, been a committed Jehovah's Witness, with a wife and two beautiful children - a photograph, creased, repeatedly viewed - blonde, like him, smiling across continents at a father whose heart would never heal. He had done all the things that he had been taught and told, behaved properly and loved his family, the fellowship and God. Unfortunately, he also he loved men. What torment of conscience and soul searching he must have endured, knowing the punishment he would suffer in the fires of hell? And it seems, his faith kept him on the path. For a while. He delivered The Watchtower, went to the Kingdom Hall for lessons, loved his wife and children and was generally loved by God for his good works. But, he loved cock too. And, while there was nothing, NOTHING, to be done about that fact, his love of his life and his faith kept him from the pit. Until, until, one day, on a Sunday, on a family outing with his best friend and their families, Ken was spotted, on the lake, in a boat, sucking his best friend's cock, by another Witness, who was in another boat. Blissfully unaware on the shore, the wives chattered and the children all played, unaware of the catastrophe that was about to befall them.

Ken didn't KNOW he'd been seen, and carried on as normal, until he was summoned by a congregation of elders. He must have known, then, somehow, that he was doomed. He was *Disfellowshipped*, the 'expelling and subsequent shunning of such an unrepentant wrongdoer'. It is the strongest form of discipline, administered to an offender deemed unrepentant. He wasn't unrepentant but in truth there was nothing he could do. Promising never to do it again would have been pointless. He was too emotionally intelligent to know that for the lie it would be and that it would only be a matter of time, a matter of opportunity, before anther erection presented itself and he would fall once more, into that pit, into those fires of Hell. I cannot imagine what this must have been like for him – for *anyone*, let alone for this man of sorrows, this gentlest of men, the one sat weeping before me, and it must have been the end of the world. It was the end of HIS world, that's for sure. He was considered to be past 'shepherding', and received no visits, no counselling, no help, no support or love from the Elders, the church or his friends. His wife then disowned him, forbade him contact with his children and effectively he was alone and cut adrift in a world he barely understood, filled with longings that brought him pain and shame. Coming out is fucking hard enough, but with the weight of Satan and eternal damnation to deal with too…. it's no surprise he sought to numb the pain and turned to alcohol. He left the land of his birth, shunned and alone and came to London where he somehow, in the way only a dedicated drunk can, proceeded to hold down a job, get a flat – the one we were sat in, as I listened in horror to this tale – and got paralytically drunk in the way only an alcoholic can. Every day, and every night he drank, until the time came when the pain of his missing wife and girls became too much and he stepped out, in Oxford Street, in to the path of a black cab which, due to his drunken eyes, was further away than he thought, to make it stop. Just to make it stop. And in a way, it did. Here he was. Brave, handsome and sober, and about to fall deeply in love with me – like the 'Steve' moment had been for me, a vindication that maybe, somehow, all the pain had been worth it. I was now his drug; I kept him upright. My guilt is absolute.

It is not my job to criticise anybody's religion or belief system, but where, WHERE was the humanity in the way Ken was treated by his so-called Christian brethren? Where was the compassion, the empathy, the support for him? Yes, he was different. Yes, he did not conform to your ideals, but surely Christ taught love for all people? It was you, you and your intransigent Jehovah, that threw him in front of that cab, and for that I say, thirty years on, shame, SHAME on you. I don't normally rant like that, but I have clear memories of the evening Ken opened his heart, and his wounds, to me – the loss of his wife, his children, his country, his Nationhood, all unbearable to him. Until he met me. I, according to letters I STILL have, and I quote (Ken, if you ever read this, forgive me; it is a part of our narrative and it is nothing but true)

"Our ability to communicate and the realisation that you actually offered to perceive and understand my wretchedness was as big a bonus as our mutual love. Hence, the inconsiderate and gathering momentum of my need for you…."

Ken was nothing if emotionally articulate and we deepened our passion at a giddy rate. Lionel Ritchie was the soundtrack of our love,

'Well, my friends, the time has come

To raise the roof and have some fun

Throw away the work to be done

Let the music play on..."

'Karamu, fiesta, forever'...that's what it felt like. All flicker and full of light. We went to the Indian and I roared with loving laughter when he said he would *"try the gulab, but could he have them without jam on"*...(true!!). We, or rather, I, drank beer for pleasure not need or loneliness and he said he didn't mind; he went to his meetings and returned, refreshed and powerful; we went to Selina's, my BOYFRIEND and me, and we rubbed our crotches together to Irene Cara and *"What a Feeling!"* and suddenly found ourselves alone on the dance floor, bumping and grinding while the watching crowd whooped and cheered (until we had to stop because, as I mentioned, Ken was rather large in the penis department and he became 'embarrassed' , if you get my drift); we went to Brighton for the weekend with his friends and got a hotel and we only went out once, the rest of the time was spent fucking in our room; we sat on the shingle shore revelling in our luck while the waves crashed and ssshhhhh-ed in front of us; we drove home in silence with his hand down the back of my jeans and his fingers up my bum, giggling with our secret and hard and impatient for the journey to end; we laughed and farted (initially, much to his horror and ESPECIALLY at that particular moment) and we healed each other, stitched back up the wounds our respective pasts had inflicted upon us, in our wars and lives, and found solace and peace in each other's arms and the silence where there was no roaring of failure.

I was still living – or rather, *rooming* – at Cranbrook road, and saw Rod less and less. He seemed to like Ken, or at least, made no play for him, or tried to spoil things. We split the time between there and the majestically named John Drinkwater Tower, where Ken's flat was. The Eleventh Floor balcony was where I stood and heard the news of Torville and Dean getting nine perfect sixes in Sarajevo, watching people celebrating at the bus stop down below, as they read their Evening Standards. The eleventh floor and the lift actually worked – although it was never quite the same after I farted in it, almost melting the aluminium and stripping the posters from the walls. It was a Monday morning and I had had a sleepover after a few beers and a curry and was all in cerise and on my way to work. The doors opened. I got in. I farted, and I mean FARTED. A miasma of green fumes filled the lift and then on floor five the doors opened and an Asian family got in. I died a death. I'm not sure if I was relieved that they walked in, turned round and made a dash for the doors before they closed, trapping them in this box of foul fumes. I didn't know quite what to do.....I just got to the ground floor, and scuttled off to the bus stop. The memory of that small event, burned into my memory, and probable the fabric of the lift...

Anyway, I digress .....I was still worked for PPR, still putting up with all the tit and cunt jokes all day, but hey, it paid the bills and it was reasonable money. The end came quite suddenly though when it did. I was due to be Runner for the day. But when I woke that morning, I had a really *really* bad back. I don't know why – Ken hadn't been there the night before so it wasn't THAT; it just hurt. I rang in and tried to throw a sickie. Unfortunately, and typically, they were short staffed and persuaded me to go in on the condition that I could change vans, and be the Back Man. As that meant sitting on me arse all day, and not losing any pay, I agreed, got dressed and struggled in, in a martyrly sort of way.

"Oy, Bray. You're in van fackin 651. 'Urry up, you cahnt, you're already late".

Charming. I could barely walk but got up in to the van and off we went. I don't remember the run, but we were over the river when a call came in over the radio that there had been an 'incident' at Belsize Park and that all vehicles were to return to base immediately. We turned round and headed back to Ilford, alarmed and at great speed.

We were all assembled in the Mosh Pit, as I now called it, and the Guv'nor came in with the news that the Runner, Peter Clarke, on the North London run, whilst carrying the cash bags back to the van, at Belsize Park Tube, had been shot dead. It seems that, despite the rule we all knew – LET THE FUCKING BAG GO!!!! – the strap had caught on his wrist and he hadn't been able to – and the kid shot him. Gone. Just like that.

Apart from the shock of this, of losing a colleague, who was in fact one of the nicer ones, a bit higher up the food chain than the others here, there came an even bigger realisation - I hope you're keeping up, you lot. Yep. MY run that day. MY job that day. Fuck. FUCKFUCKFUCKFUCK. That would have been me. Maybe the bag wouldn't have snagged, who knows, but there would still have been a crazy little fuckwit with a gun.

I left the next day. Don't say *"Oooh, it was only a one off. It wouldn't happen again"*. You don't know that, and I certainly wasn't going to risk it. We were all dismissed; all the vans locked down and we all went home. Sitting in the bus, with my back pain worse, I thanked every conceivable god for sciatica and never went back. I left my darling purple garb, neatly folded, boots lined up, on their doorstep and went down the pub on Ilford High Street. Karma Chameleon was on the Jukebox.

Mr. Lucky. Mr. V. Bloody Lucky.

I have often wondered what the outcome of that was and have discovered in the course of writing this that the 'young man' was tried by no other than Richard Ferguson QC, who went on to defend the Brighton Bombers and Rosemary West (which was unusual in that it was the first case to be tried in defence of the accused who was already dead!). The boy was found guilty of manslaughter....he 'didn't mean to kill' my friend, apparently. You still did though. And you might have killed me.

'In May 1984, within weeks of his arrival in England, the Ulster barrister Richard Ferguson, who has died aged 73, received his first brief, when he was invited to defend a young man accused of the murder of a security guard killed at point-blank range in a robbery at Belsize Park tube station in north London.' This is from his obituary, in the Guardian, dated August 11th, 2009, when he died. I wonder if HE remembered that boy, from 25 years before. The family shattered that day? I do.

So I was unemployed again (but alive, and no longer having to answer being asked if I thought *'she'd let me fuck her if I showed her my cock'*, and making comments on the size of her tits and taking bets on whether she *'shaved her fanny or not'*. There were advantages in all things) and, whatever, there were still bills to pay. I realised the best way to minimize my outgoings was to move out! Easy peasy!

So, that's what I did. I moved over to Leytonstone in to Ken's flat. He of course was overjoyed. Poor Nicky was not – it was her little love nest where she could have her illicit tryst in peace (Ken was nothing if not obliging. I guess having been so harshly judged himself, he rather erred on the side of generosity). It was OK for a while, but we were sleeping on a crappy sofa bed in the lounge, while they had his big proper bed for shagging a couple of times a week. Eventually, he asked to swap (much to my relief) and not long after that Nicky moved out – I don't know where she went but it was amicable, I think. Anyway, that left us to pursue our carnal interests more freely. We discovered, eventually, after much perseverance, (and it turned out, alcoholism has nothing to do with Amyl Nitrate) a way to fit a quart into a pint pot and thereafter we were happy as sand boys.

Christmas '83 and at last – Mr. Lucky was happy and safe. My sister came up to stay, and she brought Sam, her daughter (Get her used to the gay boys early!) and we had the best of times. The North Star, disastrously close to the Tower was where we went, Gill and I, 'just for a quick pint before dinner', got completely legless and were still in the pub, full of Christmas cheer/beer and Ken arrived about two hours later, with a 'where the fucking hell have you been' kinda glower. We persuaded him we'd just have one more, "for the M11", then two and finally realised that we really SHOULD stop now and *"OOOH! Fuck where's me daughter?"* Ken had locked her in the flat to come and fetch us, but that didn't go exactly according to plan. By the time we fell in through the door, full of giggle shame, Sam was pissed. She had found a bottle of vodka under the sink (Nicky's?) and had drunk half of it. We found her throwing up in the bathroom. Please do not ring Social Services. We, or actually Ken, put her to bed, where she threw up some more little haystacks on the duvet. Gill and I meanwhile tried to get in the cupboard under the sink, for a laugh.

Later, we decided to go down the club – I have no recollection of any food; I am hoping, in a retrospectively guilty kind of way that Ken had not actually got round to doing it. Sam washed her hair, and still drunk, tried to dry it with a hair dryer she'd found.

"Can anyone smell burning?" said Gill.

"MUUUUUUM!" yelled Sam and there she was, smoke coming off her head where she had put the hair dryer directly onto her scalp.

"My hair's on fire."

We rushed her back to the bathroom and dunked her under the tap.

Later, after a bit of a nap, in the process of getting ready, Ken decided he needed to bath before we went out, and was doing just that when Sam decided she 'needed a poo. Right now!' So we had to let her into the bathroom, where Ken sat in the bath, vainly trying to hide his genitals from this small, female child with a flannel that didn't fit, for reasons I have already explained. She didn't, fortunately, have a poo right then as it wasn't really 'convenient'. Ken cut short his bath time and went to get dressed. Gill and I were sitting in lounge, waiting for Sam to finish her hair and in walked

Ken in the underpants that Gill had bought him for Christmas. Modesty had forbidden me to explain fully to her his erm…endowment to her, with the result that there he stood, in his new red pants, with the end of his knob poking up over the waistband, and one bollock hanging out of the leg. My, how we laughed.

"They're a but tyny, but thenks!" he said, and disappeared, fortunately not meeting Sam in the corridor.

We did go to Selina's that night, but I really have nothing to tell you; my only memory is of my niece, sitting on a bar stool, in a throbbing gay bar, surrounded by a mass of whooping homos, with a stack of party hats on yelling, above the din: *"GOT ANY WHAAAAAM! AVE EE?"* in a broad Cornish accent. Happy Christmas everyone!

I look back, marvelling at Ken's patience that day, and many days more, when I behaved abominably and he just allowed it, the inconvenience or embarrassment or annoyance always outweighed by the joy he had found in my company and the deep abiding love he had for me.

Islands in the stream

That is what we are

sang Kenny and Dolly, in the chart that week. And we were, buffeted by the waters that had somehow brought us together, full of astonishment to have reached dry land, at last.

Me and Ken, in happier times.

The North Star. Sitting in the shadow of the Tower, long since demolished. Far too close, too convenient. Tiny, smoky, meety-uppy; I usually met my darling Ken in there after work, he with his juice, if he was there first, and me with me beer if it was me. We would be happy, so happy to see each other - really, like puppies. We would have a drink together, then leave for the flat, have a quick snog in the lift on the way up and then tumble in – to the sofa, to the bed, to the floor, hard, raging, eager – the early days of lust were all consuming – good for me, as it got Rod out of my head for that flame-filled time and good for Ken as it was a luxury, a gift, allowed, really properly allowed, with no shame, no retribution and no sense of looming disaster. We fucked, we laughed, and we (I) drank. We did the things that lovers do, like Billy Ocean said. But that wasn't the whole picture – storm clouds were gathering.

The North Star, Leytonstone. The Scene of Many Joys and Sorrows.

We continued going to Selina's, as we felt comfortable there and it was also a short walk (and stagger back, in my case) down the High Road. It was full of people we knew, and who enfolded us. Rod was there occasionally and it was easier, and easier. He'd buy Ken a drink, like there were no hard feelings and we'd have a chat, but NOT, I repeat, NOT reminisce.....any conversation that included the lines: *"Do you remember when we..."* was quickly shut down or glided over. Of course, Ken was aware of what had happened and was gentle and understanding, as he was in all things. He loved me; therefore, all was well. My references to members of Rod's family were taken as just that – memories, recollections, and my "Bad Rod Days", as he referred to them, seemed to be less frequent.

But, of course, they weren't......my mind was always half with Ken, half with my Jewish Nemesis. I tried I swear, I tried, but as Kylie once said *"Can't get you outa my head"*. Disaster loomed and I was unable to stop it. It was a train, coming down the track, its big cowcatcher poised to scoop me up and bear me away to the land of Pain. Well, both of us really. Ken, I did my best. You were the gentlest of men and the most undeserving of what happened.

It was New Year.'83. Rod's brother Tony was having a 'do'. They were always massive – Tony had a few quid and loved to share it, throw it around – and we had no other plans. Well, actually we did – we were invited to the Club, and another party but no! I said, this one'll be FAB! And it was. For me, at least. All the family was there and I felt at home and loved and cocooned in the heart of these people. And, I had really really missed them. They all treated Ken with kindness and made him welcome in the way that they always did and we partied and partied until I had crossed the Rubicon....I drank, Ken obviously didn't and as the evening wore on, my beer goggles were focusing in only one direction. That fucking baldy bastard over there, the one with the vodka and cokes, the one with the crooked smile, the bit of belly hair showing, the ready open laugh and mis-timed dance moves.

BAP BAP! BADADADADDA BAP BAP went George Benson. And there it was.

The End.

"Come on Nige! I love this one!" he yelled, and he grabbed me and held me up close and did that thing with his hips – a kind of double hitch step; very clever and very sexy – and I was gone. He knew it, I knew it and Ken knew it. Nothing was said, we just danced and everyone was singing *"When there's music in the air an' lovin' everywhere, gimme the night!"* their heads back and their drunken mouths agape, and trying to dance like black guys and failing miserably, and Ken stood over by the bar with Cousin Doreen, who had her hand on his shoulder, comfortingly, like she knew and was trying to rub away the pain, watching. Just watching and trying to prepare himself.

The night wore on drunkenly, and Ken the only sober one in the room, battled on. A room full of people he had never met, all pissed, all one, all united, all one unit, one universe with him orbiting far out, in the cold space of not belonging. Eventually it was over, I was pissed as a fart and was sick on the pavement outside the flats. *"Lucky it wasn't in the lift, eh?"* said Ken as he helped me up to bed.

Ken, Doreen and me, New Year's Eve, 1983

The next day, a brand-new year, began with me and the hangover from hell. *"Did you have a good time?"* I asked somewhat naively. *"I don't remember much after about 12. We did 'Auld Lang Syne' didn't we? God, that Tony, he always puts on a party, eh? Did I behave? Well, would've had to, with all the family there, eh?"*

At this point I was back, in the absence of anything else, trying to sell insurance (unsuccessfully) and doing a bit of bar work at the club. The insurance thing took me around the Ilford area – they were warm leads and had to be followed up by, in this case, a completely useless salesman who just went *"Oh, OK, then Bye"* as soon as the customer said *"We got / don't want / fuck off with your insurance."* I still didn't manage to sell a single policy (or earn a single penny – good job for the bar and Ken's decent wage) but what I DID get was the chance to go a-visiting, as my time was my own, so I went to see Kath most afternoons (who had always been an ally over the breakup with her "fuckin stupid cunt" of a brother) and so I could go round there, have a wee gin and slag him off. Then, I could go across the road. And suck him off.

NO, wait! Let me try to explain! Justify this monstrous situation! Actually, I can't - it was just bad, bad, bad and really unfair to everyone.

Rod had had to sell the flat in Cranbrook Road; he probably couldn't afford it after I'd left (TOUGH SHIT I SAY) and he'd got a little one-bedroom flat, right opposite his sister.

So. Ken is at work and looking forward to coming home to the man he had given his heart and soul to, earning money to keep us both going; Kath is one side of the road sitting with me agreeing with her rant about what a shit her brother was and how he should've kept it in his pants and he was going to end a lonely old man and serves him fuckin well right; Rod is at home, by arrangement, waiting for me to 'pop in' to say Hello. We had sex. Every time. And it was glorious and sweaty and as beautiful, in those moments, as it had ever been. On one occasion, I rang Ken to say I was going to be late home – a difficult client, you know – and I was on the phone and Rod is standing on the bed, poking his erection in to my face and rubbing it along the back of my neck, while I tried to keep my breathing rate as normal as I could. I MUST'VE smelled of sex, of sweat when I got home on those occasions, but if I did, he never said. A gallant loser.

So, as I say – how can I explain? How can I justify this behaviour? I can't. It was what it was. I was utterly addicted to this man and there was nothing I could do. I was a junkie, a smack head, an addict and would have let nothing stand in the way of my next fix. Ken maybe understanding the nature of addiction, knew that I would only get better from mine when I admitted I wanted to. But, you see. I didn't. Aye, there's the rub.

Clearly this was untenable. Ken knew, saw, felt things were different. His attempts to make love were rebuffed – *"Will you get off? I'm trying to watch 'The Thorn Birds.'* I was lying on the floor in front of the telly; he started kissing my neck and then tried to bum me....Cast off in favour of Richard Chamberlain. It went from *'I'm not really in the mood,'* to *'I really don't want to do that,'* and eventually to *'Look, it really hurts and I don't want to, ok?'* Cruel things, hurtful things, but I didn't want Ken's cock now, as beautiful as it was because, though he didn't know it, I had Rod's again. I was often late back, I was earning no money, mostly because I wasn't visiting any clients, I was at Rod's. Maybe he thought I was having an extended 'Bad Rod' time, brought on by the New Year party, clinging vainly to the wreckage as our ship broke up around us.

Then Rod asked me to move back in.

So I did.

I know, gentle reader, exactly what you're thinking. It is one of these three things:

1. You fucking IDIOT! You've got a man who loves you with his heart and soul and you're DUMPING him???

2. Don't do it! Ee ain't wurf it.

Or

3. Poor Ken. Why didn't he see this coming? Oh, btw, you're a heartless cunt.

Any one, or all three of these are valid.

It ended quickly. There wasn't much else to say. Ken said he knew things were all wrong, that at the party he was drowning, but expected maybe I would throw him a life line. I really didn't know just how sad he was; too wrapped up in my own joy at 'going home', I didn't see the overwhelming grief I had caused.

I received a letter from him, shortly after this time, in his strange and original handwriting, that I am looking at now, as I write and I am still, 30 years on, moved to tears, and filled with shame.

"I gave you my soul and you took it. You basked in the warmth of it and healed. To me, you gave the most wonderful sense of security, constancy. I redeveloped a purpose in my love of life. ...

...I have salvaged no fond memories or warm sensations from us. All my recollections and moments are a source of pain so overwhelming, I am unable to function. I will endeavour to blot them out. I will no doubt survive. One unfortunate aspect that I now hate my flat as much as I once loved it. It is a memorial to my misery. Better, I suppose that it is the flat and not you that is the object of my detestation.

Forgive me for indulging in this letter. Of everyone, I imagine you perceive most, the length and depth of my grief, having been the recipient of my love. I assure you that after our next awkward but inevitable meeting, I will exert supreme effort to conduct myself in the polite and civilised manner of a grown man.

I wish you well, and I adore you. Ken"

The most crucifying thing is his politeness, his civility amidst the now chaos of his life. I weep for him even now, even knowing as I do, he is well and happy and in a wonderful relationship. I broke his heart, the heart that amidst all his own pain, he gave me. Yet, and here is the MOST shameful thing of all, in the whole sorry episode, I went, and didn't even look back. So focussed was I on the man I loved, truly loved, despite all the shit we'd been through, in spite of all the shitty things he'd done, I just packed my backs and left. Back to Rod's, leaving Ken standing amidst his shattered dreams.

Fortunately, he had a good friend, from work I think, Paul, who I saw him with, at that 'next, inevitable meeting'. I was back in E11, and decided to drop in to the North Star, I dunno – for old time's sake, and there they both were, in OUR seats, at the end of the bar, both with pints. BOTH with pints. I couldn't pretend not to have seen them and, as he had said, it WAS extremely awkward.

"Hi," said Ken.

"Hi," I said.

"This is Paul."

"Hi Paul."

Silence. No proffered hand.

"Erm.....drink, anyone?"

"No thanks," said Ken, *"We're off soon. Just dropped by to get something from upstairs."*

I wonder to this day whether he may have been hoping to see me there, but I had gone, leaving only traces of my Aramis. However...

"Oh, OK. Um........well, it was nice to...." I didn't quite know how to proceed, but the situation was resolved when Paul stood up and threw his pint in my

face. *"Why don't you just FUCK OFF, you heartless bastard?"* Sotto voce, so no one would know what was happening, other than I was completely soaked with his pint of Murphy's.

They brushed by me, through the silent pub, and as Ken passed, he even had the grace to apologise.

"Look, sorry mate. He's just angry….. Sorry about your shirt. And everything." Standing there, dripping in beer, I just wanted to hold him, smooth him, rub away the scars I had left, but they just kept walking and it was some months before I saw him again, strangely enough, back in the L.A., where it had all begun, a Universe away. I often wonder, as you do, how my life would have turned out if I had been stronger / braver / less stupid / kinder / less blinkered / more growed up. Ken was a lovely man and I was happy that Paul was there. It quickly turned to love, by all accounts, and he found peace again and I felt less of a cunt. Result all round.

So, I was back in the bed where I belonged. It was all very honeymooney, and extremely cramped. But we were together again, all loved up and that was all that mattered. Wasn't it? Wasn't it? Well actually no it wasn't.

After a week Rod decided it wasn't working and said it was probably better that I moved out! Hurrah! A perfect end.

So, there I was, back in the flat, with Nicky, who had had a similar meltdown, but like Ken, I now hated the flat. It smelled of death and sorrow and so I thought I'd look around, ask around for somewhere else. Rod, Richard, Ken, Rod….now what? I didn't really know anything else, and here I was – 38 and YFS. Didn't like it much – I know! I'll get another BF!! Honestly, Bray – you haven't got the sense you were born with.

I began going back to the Club on a regular basis – I got more bar work and a room share in a house opposite Wanstead Park with Tony and two lesbians. One of them was a club singer and 'Bruna and the Boys' used to gig at the club quite often. Tony, a lovely little gay boy, all bouffant and hairsprayed, mentioned there was a room at his place, going so I accepted. And so began another chapter – back on the bevvy, staying up too late, having too much sex (Big chops cos I was the barman, and therefore v. desirable. Not sure how that worked but anyway – who cared? Upped my shag rate no end!). Tony and I, we became really close, even sharing clothes - he was much younger than me and I probably looked a twat, but I was sore, hurting and anything that cheered me up was welcome. Even his twinky cast offs….

The Flats, across which I had to walk, as well as being the location of the aforementioned Dames Road Cottage, was a pretty busy cruising spot – a bit like Hampstead Heath but not so posh and with less trees. Several times I had a quickie on the way home from work – once I got followed by a very nice cub on a bike; we had a quick wank in the bushes and then I arranged to go round to his later for a proper bit of rumpy pumpy in the warm. Which I did. We had some couscous, some wine and a very nice bit of How's Your Father before I headed off back to work at the club.

Another time, drunk, I was lured (well.....) into the bushes by a young man who suddenly appeared out of the foliage, naked – he had a big ole stiffy, so I was lost. I could have been murdered, right there, in the bushes, in the dark, in the open air. But I wasn't. I ended up fucking him up against a tree. Or was it the other way round? Lost in the mists of time and beer haze now, but it was up against a tree. Deffo.

Round about this time, while I was still Y(ish)F+S, we discovered 'Stallions', much to the dismay of my liver and my pay packet. This was located – long gone now, along with all these other places I have shared with you, so pivotal in creating this boy/man/homo – in an alley, Falconberg Court, behind the Astoria on Charing Cross Road, formerly known as BANGS! (Opposite Centre Point, where I used to wait, trembling for my Stevie....). It was open on Sunday afternoons, long before the licensing laws allowed alcohol so it was a 'Tea Dance'......hahhaaaaa. Was it buggery! Well, actually, for two hours it was – *actual* sandwiches and *actual* tea, from 5 –7 but then, happy four hours began, two drinks for the price of one. Well, it was carnage, let me tell you.

During the sandwich hours, there would be played old tea-dance favourites and oddities like Eartha Kitt - *Old Fashioned Girl, Time Warp, Sweet Transvestite*, Liza, singing *New York, New York,* etc. it was so camp, and full of the weirdest people (we turned up on Fetish night once – we were up West and near, and just decided to pop in.....people being dragged around on their hands and knees, wearing jockstraps, or nothing, bollocks dangling, being slapped and spanked by the customers, as they stood idly drinking and chatting. People tied up to the pillars, facing inwards and having things inserted in to their arses, or forwards, cocks out for anyone who fancied it to have a go. I'm telling you – even I, after all I'd seen and done, was somewhat alarmed, mostly I think because it was straight and I felt really uncomfortable with straight sex, although it wasn't really sex per se. I don't really like having it rammed down my throat, you know. We stayed well out of the way, at the far end of the bar and ogled.) and it was the most unusual place – the pillars were like trees and they had fish tanks inserted in them. Truth.

BOGOF!! Everyone got terribly, terribly drunk and made some bad decisions because of it. One night, in the toilets (which were always very busy, if you get me drift) I got...what's the word......waggled at, by the bloke next to me. Beer goggles askew, I smiled at him and the next thing I knew, he had pushed me backwards in to the cubicle. He followed in my, kicked the door shut and pushed me down on to my knees, from where I had just managed to stand up, piss and all sorts on my best going- out trousers, so there I suddenly was, kneeling amongst the condoms, used tissue and cum, sucking him off. You know, when the moment just takes you? Something you would never imagine in the daylit world, but filled to the brim with pints of Stella, it suddenly seemed an OK thing to be doing. Until someone else, pissed or because the floor was a bit er.....slippy, fell against the door of the cubicle. Mr. Waggle hadn't locked it and, just as he'd shot his load over my shirt (I never swallow on the first date), the door flew open, knocked him against me just as I was cleaning him off, I did a bit of impromptu sword swallowing and was knocked backwards and I smacked my head against the toilet. It seems I was knocked out momentarily. Mr. Waggle just legged it and the next thing I remember was someone saying *"Its oright, e's breevin"*, and walking away again. Charming. A hand up would have been nice. Not very dignified, I sat up, covered in spunk and bits of tissue from the floor. Why was it always a debacle? Why did it always happen to me? I cleaned myself off as best I could, and, still pissed and unaware of my disgusting appearance, went back out in to the bar.

"Where've you been?" asked Tony, staring at me and now draped around a city type. *"I thought you only went for a wee."*

"I did, but .....I got.. er...side-tracked."

"Look at the STATE of you! You're SUCH a Trollop!" he squealed. *'You don't know the half of it,'* I thought but didn't elaborate. And so the evening passed.

I ended up – on a different Sunday – in someone's bed, miles and miles away, I had no idea where – nice man, nice shag – and then being dumped at some suburban railway early the next morning – it wasn't even light! - as he, it being Monday, had to go to work. I got the bus home, stinking of fags, and stale beer, wondering my life had gone.

It certainly wasn't supposed to be like this….

Falconberg Court W1, the entrance to what used to be Stallions.

THREE.

Then, one Sunday, I met Edward. We were all shiny and clean, hair all Andrew Ridgelyed up, ironed tee-shirts, in fact I think this was the night I was wearing a vest – I could fit into one in those days – and we were all up for a bit of...well, Tea Dancing. Juice and sandwiches first, then drinky – poohs. Nicky was on the Bacardi and cokes, Tony on the – God knows, pink gin probably, and I hit the Stella. Two for the price of one? It would've been rude not to.

Tony, Nicky and me, Stallions Tea Dance. Bit of a looker, eh?

Dancing ensued. Twizzling round the tiny floor, sweating like a pig, wafting Aramis as I went, when BOOF! I smacked right in to a middle aged, blondish, non-descript bloke.....who had the hairiest chest I had ever seen.

Beer spilt, down both our tops – well, his shirt, my vest – expecting some kind of *"OI! You CAHNT! Watch where you're FACKIN going"* kind of thing, but what I got, over Jimmy wailing about sitting on the platform with everything he owned in a little black case, and the wind and the rain on his sad and lonely face, was:

"Sorry. Not looking where I was going. Crowded tonight, eh?"

"Erm..Yes," I yelled in response. *"Sorry about your shirt."*

"It's just a shirt. It'll dry. Sorry about your vest...Shall we just take them off?"

And there we were, dear reader, topless in a gay bar! Just like Heaven, only with more fat and less ego. He was sweaty and all his chest hair was plastered to his skin, and he smelled...smelled, well, proper manly.

Should've known better than to cheat a friend

And waste the chance that I've been given

So I'm never gonna dance again

The way I danced with yoooooooo'

...... wailed George, and Edward and I, for that was he, smooched and swayed, and slithered and snogged our way through the song that was to become 'OUR TOON' during our brief courtship. I loved the way he felt – he was stolid. That's a good word. STOLID. Not fat, not a 'chub', but solid and hairy and a very pleasant man, a sweetie, a kind man with a nice cock and a gentle way of making love to me. And, as it turned out, a tendency for stalking.

Amazingly, we didn't do IT that first night, but arranged to meet up the following Sunday, which we did. Same packed floor, same heat, smell of fags (as in cigarettes, obvs) and beer, and gay boys wearing (a lot of) aftershave, me included. And there he was, smiling at the bar. He saw me and waved.

"Hello, hun," he said. *"I wasn't sure you'd come. I'm so pleased you did."*

He smiled his lopsided, gentle smile, and, threading my way through the boys already dancing to Eartha, I moved towards my next adventure.

Awwww. That's nice eh?

"I said I would, and here I am." I think I was alone that week – Tony was IN LURRVE with his banker by this time and had no time for such lowly haunts, such hovels...

"I know, but people often say they will. And then they don't. They lie. To me, anyway," and he looked so lonely for that moment and I was pleased I was not one of the ones who had let him down.

"Drink? I noticed you were on the Stella. At least, that's what you threw all over me last week!"

"Oh yes please. Lovely."

So we found a space to squeeze into and just talked; nothing heavy – work, hobbies, ex-boyfriends, what food we liked.....chat, a bit of touchy feely when the moment arose – a hand on the leg with a laugh, a touch of the hair to emphasise a point.....he was a very pleasant man, hairy and generous and mature and I liked him. So, when he said the immortal line: *'Do you want to come back to mine?'* it wasn't sleazy or cheap; it was a genuine invitation to make love with him and I accepted.

He didn't tell me he lived in St. Albans, mind you, so it was a bit of a late night, a whizzy – headed drive out of London, away from the city to the countryside. I was a bit pissed, but not drunk, and I was really looking forward to what lay ahead. We arrived – a neat semi, in suburbia, nets, Everest Windows, conservatory - exactly what one would have expected. A place where Ted (contractions, already!) lived his single life, wishing it otherwise and hopeful that tonight would change it.

We had a gin and tonic; he'd not been drinking due to the drive home but we sat, I drank, had a St Moritz, the last legacy of You Know Who, and it all felt fine. *"Come on then,"* he said and took my hand and led me gently to the bedroom, leaving my gin and my cigarette, which rolled on to his Ercol coffee table and burned a hole before it went out. Seemed to be a habit...

We didn't just fuck, cum, and go to sleep. He was very gentle, undressing me slowly, slowly, so my excitement increased. He was expert – how did he learn these skills? – and once naked, he undressed too. He was very sexy; as I said, solid, well built, a little bit of a belly, but beautifully hairy and a nice fat cock, which was more than ready for the event. We moved on to the bed, and kissed and caressed each other, passed slowly through the stages and finally he fucked me, but oh! So gently, considerately, asking if it was OK, taking his time, taking care.

After we'd finished, he took me to the bathroom and gently washed me clean in the shower, then himself, and returned to the bed, and there we slept till dawn.

In the morning, he offered to drive me home, all the way back to Wanstead. Not really very keen on forking out whatever in bus and train fares, I agreed, and off we went. Big mistake.

'When two tribes go to war...'

blaring from the car radio, Ted's hand resting gently on my knee, occasionally moving up to affectionately rub the back of my neck, we drove south. We arrived back at the Flats and we parked up and, checking there was no one around, he pulled me to him and kissed me. In public! I nearly died! It was a bit exciting, rebellious though and I didn't pull away.

"OK, week's work coming up. Next Sunday, Stallions?"

"Yeah, sure. Thanks for a nice time. Really."

It had done me good, as it goes – after the trauma and grief of the parting with Ken and nothing else other than casual, drunken sex, mostly with strangers and always without joy. The pleasure of that lasted as long as the ejaculation, then just emptiness again. So Ted was nice, it was loving love making, caring and comforting.

He drove away.

Tony, who was at home, went *"OOOOOOOOH Nigel's got a boyfriend..."* or something equally wanky and I told him to fuck off, but smiling in that secret way that new lovers have.

"He's quite nice, ACTUALLY. He takes care of me."

"Loaded, is he? Nice car...."

"I don't fucking know! We shagged. I didn't ask him how big his bank balance is! Anyway, YOU can talk. How is Quentin or Rafferty or Tristram, or whatever his name is? Got into his wallet as well as has pants, have we?"

"No need to be such a bitchy queen. I was only 'avin a giraffe."

"Tony, you are the LAST person who should be using rhyming slang. You sound like Katie Boyle. Polari, maybe, but not slang. It doesn't become you."

"It's Barry, actually. But it isn't going anywhere. I think I might go to Amsterdam." As you do. Which, in fact, some while later, he did. But I'd moved by then (again) so there was nothing binding us together.

Back to now:

"Ted. He's called Ted. Well, Edward actually. Teddy. Teddy Edward. Ha!" and that's what we called him from then on. *"We're meeting again next week, down Stallions. Fancy it?"*

"Maybe. See how it goes. I didn't vader his jolly old eek. Has he got a bona cory?"

"Actually, don't do Polari either. You sound like a knob. Leave it to Julian and Sandy."

"Who?"

"Never mind. And yes. Quite bona. Not that it's any of your business."

"Are you in luuuurve?"

Oh FUCK OFF Tony!! No, I'm not. I've only known him 5 minutes." There was a glow, however, that little tickly thing that hatches in your belly and flutters and wimbles about when you think of them. And yet.....yet....there was something not quite right.....

Great in bed, nice body, fun to have around, kind, generous......and yet.....

Anyway, the week passed. More shifts at the Club, drinking too much, ignoring Rod when he came in - that way madness lies – or, more specifically, as I was also part time DJ (well, the bloke who just put the records on the crappy old deck that was balanced precariously over the sink), playing Michael Jackson's *'One Day In Your Life'*:

'One day in your life

You'll remember the love you found here

You'll remember me somehow

Though you don't need me now

I will stay in your heart

And when things fall apart

You'll remember one day......'

....yeah you BASTARD!! HAHAHAH. See? Serves you right.....I don't know if he heard the song, listened to what it said, heard what I was saying, or even gave a flying fuck. All I know is that it gave ME great satisfaction, in a petty, jilted sort of way. You see, dear reader....I STILL wasn't cured....

The week passed, the club full of the usual crowd.....

......Les, known as *'The Duchess'* who, after a few pints, would always excuse himself, climbing elegantly down from his stool to *"go and spread me tired old cunt lips over the lavvie."*

.......and Ian, as usual, discovering last night's (or last week's, it had been known) uneaten kebab still all wrapped up in his Parka pocket, or not wrapped and his pocket full of chilli sauce and shredded lettuce. He's chuck it in the bin, then replace it that night with another, pissed, with the munchies, thinking *'Oooh I could go a kebab now'* and then deciding to have it when he got home. Or not.

......and Jean and Lola, the tallest and smallest lesbian pair you ever saw; Lola, 5 foot nothing and Spanish, with a Latin temper to match and Jean, about 6 foot 4, but devoted to each other. Lola loved Jean even more than the slot machine, into which she would feed a week's wages at a time, swearing and kicking it when it didn't pay out. When it did, she bought drinks, when it didn't, she turned into Angry Woamn -*Mujer Enojada!* Gill, who happened to be up staying one week, happened to be passing the machine Lola had just left, and dropped a random 10p in and won the £100 jackpot. Senorita Lola was *muy muy enojado*, fucking FURIOUS, judging by the looks of pure hatred directed at my hapless sister, and the string of Catalan expletives that poured from her mouth.

.......And Rita. Glamorous Rita, who in all the time I knew her, never ever bought herself a drink, but was always supplied with copious amounts of brandy and soda; once, she was so pissed, we went next door to Paki Jim's (don't gasp – it was the 80s) and attempting to get something from the freezer, she just overbalanced and slid, gracefully – always gracefully – head first in to the freezer, and lay nestled amongst the peas and broccoli florets, legs and feet, clad in her Minnie Mouse shoes sticking out, until we had stopped laughing enough to pull her out. Another time, at a party, I watched her tip, in slow motion, sideways into a fishpond. When she was dragged out, dripping slime and water from her astrakhan coat, they asked if she was OK.

"Of course, Darling, But I need a brandy."

"Of course! What do you want with it?"

"Oh, I'll have another brandy." Ah Rita. Rita, you were a star, one of the old school, fag hag extraordinaire, and dead now. But not really, not really dead because here she is, on these pages, and in my heart.

......John and Carlos, the most mismatched lovers I have ever met. Carlos, he from Barthelona, and John from Befnal Green – I have never seen two people who should never have met. As barman, I would be left alone whilst a war broke out above our heads. Before the 'top bar' and restaurant, (in which I wined and dined Miss Diana Dors; oh yes, people – I mixed with the stars! Lynne Perry came to do cabaret once too (God, what a filthy mouth SHE had!) and 'that Olive from *'On The Buses'*, as John proudly referred to Anna Karen, came to do cabaret), was opened, and it was still being used as a storeroom, they used to go and fight up there. I mean PROPER fight – there would be ice buckets hurled, glasses smashed, stacks of table overturned – I would go up to fetch something and there they'd be, shirts ripped, bloody....then they'd reappear and carry on as normal. It became SO normal, punters took no notice of the thunder above their heads; I just turned the music up.

And so.The week passed. We didn't open Sundays then so I was free to go and meet Teddy Edward. And there he'd be, all clean, and tidy, freshly pressed shirt, and open smile.

"Hello darling!" he'd say. *"Stella?"*

"Don't call me Stella!" I'd say, and we'd both laugh. Eerie.

It certainly made a change from buying Chris beer all night. I hardly saw him much now - he and Vince were on a completely different merry go round these days – off to the bondage bars, the dark rooms, the S+M scene.

"Hi, Yes please," and the evening would begin – pleasant, nice, easy and somehow, *'Careless Whisper'* would always be played, as if they knew, and there we'd be, chest to chest, slippery, slick and randy. Back to St. Albans, hand in my pants now, caressing me, making me hard, as we raced along Edgeware Rd and out of the city, back to suburbia and to sex behind the nets.

The next day we went to the city. I was sitting on a large stone, just outside the abbey, when he came up and leant in really close. *"I love you,"* he said. *"I really love you. You have to move in."*

And at that moment, something clicked in my head. Something just wasn't right......I saw he was a bit...creepy, a bit axe murderery......

"Well, I don't think we should rush, Eddie. We haven't known each other long and...."

"No, no, you must move in. We should be together. We are meant to be."

"Well, maybe in a bit. What about my job?"

"I have a job. A good job. I can look after you."

"But you'll be at work all day. What will I do?" (stuck out here in lace curtain land, with no friends or anyone I knew...)

" You can stay home and wait for me and then we can fuck all evening if you like. I know how you like it..."

Suddenly I didn't. I looked up at the abbey, *'There's no comfort in the truth, Pain is all you'll find'* ran through my head (cheers, George!) and realised I was quite a long way from home here, and totally reliant on Teddy Edward to get me there.

"Ted, can we go? Umm.....Only its Tony's birthday and he's off to Amsterdam soon, so I would quite like to spend the evening at the house. Sorry, I forgot about it....."

"But I want you to stay here. It's Sunday. It's what we do...."

"Yes, but......"

"No buts, Darling. We stay here. Let's go home now. I'll make you a big gin and tonic."

I looked up at St. Alban, asking him for some guidance, but he just stared off into the middle distance, as he had for the last thousand years, and was no bleddy help at all. So we left the now quite welcome safety of the crowds and went back to what had instantly in my head become The Bates Motel. After a couple of gins, which ironed out some of the anxieties, things felt a bit better. He kept coming over and cuddling me, reassuring me that we would be very happy here and going back to the kitchen to do the dinner. We ate, I drank gin, smoked a few fags (for me nerves) and everything appeared as normal. Except……except…I couldn't UN hear his voice back at the Abbey, the calm certainty of his plans. I drank gin. Then he was beside me.

"I love you. I have never felt like this before. Sex is just out of this world, and you do fancy me, don't you. My hairy chest, my fat penis. (Penis? Who says 'penis'?) Don't you? We can be together, here or anywhere you want. We can move. We can go abroad. Spain! France! Anywhere you choose. Just don't leave me."

"But Ted, I have a job and I like it and…. and anyway, I have paid Bruna for this month so really, I have to ……"

"You don't love me, do you? I'm not good enough. I thought you fancied me…."

"I DO. I do, but it's all a bit fast." (I hadn't told him about Rod or Ken, all still a bit raw, to be honest) *"Can we just slow down a bit?"*

"Sorry. Yes. Sorry. It's just that I have never met anyone like you and I want to spend my life with you."

And he started to cry. Big fat tears rolled down his face, off his chin and on to his chest, as he'd opened his shirt. Bait….

Oh fuck. Now what?

"Let's go to bed shall we?" The gin had numbed the pain and I could work out what to do tomorrow.

Sniffling mournfully, he said, *"Yes, darling, come on, you'll feel better then and we can make plans…."* and we went to the bedroom where once more, he undressed me, gentle as you like and then fucked me senseless. No, wait…that was the gin.

The next morning was work for him (you know, I NEVER did know what he did or where he did it) so up we got, and back to Wanstead, where he dropped me, after a kiss.

I went indoors, and raced upstairs, to Tony's room.

"Tone! TONY! We have a problem. I think he's a fuckin NUTTER. Nice and everything, but a bit meshugena."

"Why? What's happened?"

"Well.....nothing. But.......I think he might be a serial killer. Or something."

"YOU'RE the fucking nutter....he's a lovely bloke."

"Hmmm. Well......."

"Come on, let's go out. Let's go to the Royal Oak for a change. They're open."

So we did, and a few beers took away the panic.

The next morning, I got up, to go the club for the morning's bottling up and.....there was his fucking car! Parked in Ingatestone Road, the cheeky fucker. Round the corner. Just sat there. Then he drove off. OH MY GOD!! He's stalking me!!

"TONY TONY !! QUICK!!! TEDDY EDWARD. HE WAS THERE. IN HIS CAR. ON INGATSTONE ROAD. RIGHT OPPOSITE!"

"Fer fuck's sake. There's no one there."

"THERE!! IT WAS HIM. I KNOW THE CAR. HE'S SHAGGED ME IN IT!" (I haven't gone into detail about that, in case you thought I was trollop. But he had).

"God, you're a trollop," said Tony. *"What was it like?"*

"IT DOESN'T MATTER WHAT IT WAS LIKE! WHAT MATTERS IS THAT HE WAS HERE. OUTSIDE. JUST.....JUST...STARING!"

"Oh well, he's gone now. What time is it? Let's go down the pub. Holly Tree's open."

Busman's holiday. Nice one. But we went and it was fun. If you like drinking in a pub where everybody stares at you, like in *'An American Werewolf In London'*.

"What did we come in here for? Remind me?"

"To stop you freaking out. Anyway, I'm off to Amsterdam. LEKKER!"

"When?"

"Weekend."

Oh, Tone. Gonna miss you, you tart." And if we hadn't been in The Holly Tree, I would have kissed him. But we were. So I just gave him a slap on the back.

"Oooh! Butch! Come on, let's get out of here!"

A couple of days later, we were sitting down to tea. Bruna had just emptied the pepper pot on to her meal – I have never seen anything like it. A layer, an inch deep, of ground black pepper on whatever we were eating – and I'd gone to the kitchen to refill it, when the phone rang.

"It's for you," said Tony. He put his hand over the mouthpiece and said, *"It's him. Teddy Edward."*

"Tell him I'm not here, you idiot!"

"He says he's not here. I mean, he's not here," said Tony. He turned to me. *"He says he wants to meet you for a drink. What shall I say?"*

"Tell him I'll call him. When I get in."

"He says he'll call you when he gets in. ....Ok, bye."

"I don't fucking believe you. You just...oh never mind. How did he get this number?"

"Oh I gave it to him. He was outside in his car yesterday, and he looked so sad and he asked if you were here but you weren't so I gave him the number."

"WHAAAAAAT? YOU DID WHAT? YOU FUCKING FUCKING IDIOTIC FUCK!" (There WAS some advantage of having worked at PPL) *"Brilliant. Just fucking BRILLIANT."*

The phone rang.

Tony picked it up again. *"Oh hello again. Hmmm. Yes. Hmmm. Mmm. Ok. Bye."*

"That was him. He's in the phone box on the corner of Dames Road, and he says there's a little club on the High Road and he'll wait for you there."

"Well, I obviously can't go can I?"

"Why not?"

"Fer fuck's sake Tony. What do you mean why not? How can I? And anyway, it's Selina's and I can't meet him there...!"

"Why not?"

"Because...well, because.....just BECAUSE."

"I'll come with you."

"I. AM. NOT. GOING".

"Poof."

I ignored that, and went to my room. I couldn't go THERE, of all places. I didn't want him to know I knew everyone there, and it was my local. I decided to ignore it.

But, every night – must be after work? Maybe he WORKED nearby? I don't know – I never did find out – but every night, there he was, parked up in his car, in Ingatestone Road, opposite the house, so he could see the front door. I took to sneaking in the back, down the little ginnel that ran between the houses. Why I didn't just go over and speak to the man I don't know, just say Hi and ask why he was there?

"Tony. TONY! YOU go out and talk to him. Go on. PLEEEESE?"

"Erm...OK. What do I say?"

"Well, just say......Nigel thinks you're a really nice guy but he doesn't want a relationship now because he's really really upset about his last boyfriend. Or something. Use your imagination!"

"Right."

A few minutes later he came back.

"Well? What did he say? What did you say?"

"He says he'll meet you in The Holly Tree in ten minutes."

"WHAT?? You fucking idiot! What did you go and say that for?"

"He looked sad. And he was nice. Oh, and he's got his shirt open a bit. Just in case. You know what you're like and so does he, obviously. HAHAHAHAAAA!"

Dilemma. What to do, what to do? If I DON'T go, he'll keep stalking me, or worse, but if I DO go it might give the wrong signal.....

Well at least the Holly Tree is a public space........so, I got my coat and off I went, across the Flats, not feeling very confident, past the tree where I got shagged (or did the shagging – I STILL can't remember) and up to the pub door.

Just as I was about to push it open, a hand fell on my shoulder......OHMIGOD OHMIOD I'm being murdered or raped or dismembered or worse, right outside the pub. I turned, and it was Tony!

"YOU CUNT!! YOU FUCKING SCARED THE SHIT OUT OF ME, YOU FUCKIN FUCK!" (thanks, again, PPL)

"Oh I thought you could do with some moral support. Did I make you jump?"

"Yes you fucking DID!" but I was secretly pleased to see him.

We pushed open the door, and there was Teddy Edward, sitting at the bar. With my pint. Of Stella. Hunnnnggggggggg.....

"Hello darling," he said. *"I got your favourite."* This was getting seriously weird now, and I was glad of Tony's support.

"Oh, thanks. You remember Tony, don't you? From Stallions?"

"Oh yes. Why is he here? I thought I was just meeting you so we could decide what to do. Where we're going to live. We didn't get a chance the other night. I've missed you."

We sat, I picked up my pint and, downing in almost in one, beer cascading down my chin and coat, and I said, *"Look, The thing is Ted. Er, Edward...I....."*

"OK, look, Tedward. He doesn't want to be with you. He loves your hairy chest, a lot and you've got a beautiful cock, - he told me all about it – (Actually I hadn't but I let that pass in the splendour of the moment*) - but that just ain't enough. He thinks you're a weird stalker and he wants you to leave him alone or he will call the police and tell them you raped him. Or something. Oh, and not that you asked, you dry lunch cunt, I don't want a drink. Come on."* And he took the pint glass from my hand, closed my astonished mouth and led me out the pub.

"OH, and don't try following ME, because I'm going to Amsterdam."

Outside, after I'd managed to regain my composure, from the shock of what just happened, I said,

"'Dry lunch cunt'? Where did you pick that up? That was brilliant!"

"Oh, something Rod says. He said it one night when we were out".

"Out? OUT?? You out with Rod???? You fucking....."

"Calm down! No, don't worry, I didn't! He's old enough to be my Dad!"

"I didn't think you did. Anyway, it's nothing to do with me, who you shag. (Please, not him...) Anyway - that was brilliant! Do you think it worked?"

"Hope so 'cos I won't be here to look after you..."

"TONE! I love you!!" And I gave him a great big kiss, right there, outside the Holly Tree, Wanstead, E11!

I never saw Teddy Edward again. And, Ted, if you're reading this, as unlikely as that may be, sorry I burnt your coffee table, your chest IS beautiful, as is your todger, but....you were just too much. Too weird. So, sorry. And thanks.

Round about this time, John, at the club, decided to open an antiques shop, a couple of doors down from Selina's, in an empty shop. He filled it with junk, put outrageous prices on everything and then sat amongst the clutter like Miss. Havisham. Only with a moustache. He didn't sell anything, as I recall, but it was a diversion as he and Carlos were finally parting, before either of them was indicted for murder. John was having to divide his time now between the club and the shop, as Carlos kept disappearing off back to Spain. As I was single (again) and free to choose, I accepted the job he offered me and so become Sales Manager of *'JOHN JACK'S SHIT EMPORIUM'*. I didn't sell anything either, though it was quite a sociable thing, people in and out, saying *"HOW much? Fuck off...."* and *'This is load of old crap"* and other compliments, but not buying. And so the days passed, while I, like Albert Steptoe, sat amongst the de-feathered stuffed birds, old candlesticks with chips on the rims, blackened saucepans and sideboards with knobs missing. There was a tiny toilet, where I used to hide when Carlos came in to have rant about something he couldn't find in the flat or he needed some money, and a small back room where I could go and have my lunch, on the old musty bed that was there, behind the curtain.

In the evenings I still worked the bar, even the new upstairs one, on the street level. Selina's had come out, she was out and proud, even with the doors open on to the street so people could hurl abuse without having the trouble of going down the back stairs to the cellar. We even had a doorman, gentle Ben, whose wife must have been very understanding about why her husband wanted to spend every evening with a load of lairy poofs, who made us all feel safe and protected from the big bad world outside. There was also a swanky new restaurant attached, at the back, through the bar, so we had a chef and at some point, Nicky had reappeared and she was waiting tables. Somehow, John managed to get Diana Dors to come and eat there, and I was invited – a more down to earth lady you couldn't wish to meet. John was in full gear, full of pride, full of shit, but very proud. He'd built this club (as he would drunkenly tell us every fucking night, downstairs…."*Boys and gels…*" he'd go, and everyone would raise their eyes to heaven, saying *'here we go again'*, *'yes we know'* and *'shut the fuck up'*, while he droned on about how proud he was to have the club and wot 'e 'ad done for us etc etc….), he'd got two bars AND a restaurant running and he had, although he was a total knob, *'done a good fing for us'* and I for one am grateful – it was the place that gave ME the courage to face who I was, to be welcomed in to a tribe and get proper shags, at last. I felt a part of a family, a group 'like me' who also *liked* me, and that was a comforting thing. I realised just HOW alone I had been, spiritually and emotionally, with my background, my family and my neighbourhood. All of that was designed to make me conform to its heteronormative rules and quite clearly, I never would've been able to. I would have been one of those bitter, unfulfilled married men, fucking other men in secrecy and shame, never knowing the sense of freedom that being able to say (even if we didn't know the right words for how we felt) "I am gay, queer, a homo, a poof, a nancy boy!" – whatever appellation suits – brought and I got that here, slowly, *piece by piece, putting it together, bit by bit* as Sondheim said, all those furtive college gropes, all those awful events involving cock and sorrow, all the pain caused by taunts and letters from those who were supposed to love me, led to this, this little haven, with Ben protecting me at the door and my friends and buddies all around.

Peace in my heart.

FOUR

I don't know how it happened really. John and I became 'an item'. Yes, dear reader. ANOTHER boyfriend! Number four in this saga, this catalogue of disaster. La! So free with my favours......

As I say, I don't really know how. What started off as a bit of a shag turned into BF and BF, and Runner of the Club to boot!

There I was, in *John Jack's,* selling jack shit, when John Jack came in to *John Jack's* and said, *"Sold anything?"*

"No," I said. *"A couple of asks, but the prices are too high for this erm..material."* It was junk, but he believed with all the acumen of Harold Steptoe, that it was all undiscovered treasure, invaluable if only the people who came in weren't so thick that they didn't know quality when they saw it.....

"Oh well. Lunch time. Did you bring anything? I can get the restaurant to rustle something up if you want?"

"Nah, its fine, I got sandwiches. I'll go and eat them out the back."

"Oooh, I could do with a sit down. Mind if I come?"

"Er..no. Its your shop..."

So we went out the back, and sat in the only place that didn't have piles of crap on it – the rickety old double bed. And, yes, we did. He suddenly leant in and kissed my ear (how quaint!), my cheek, my neck and then took my hand and placed it on his crotch.

How, you may say, do you remember events of nearly 30 years ago with such clarity? And my answer is that these 'incidents', recounted throughout this book, were IMPORTANT, formative, made me who I became finally; they were moments, some tiny and detailed and some momentous in their effect on me, that stuck in my head, like lyrics – I can recall whole songs that were current at those moments. When I hear them NOW, I can see where I was, what I was doing, who I was with, what I felt, what happened around that song in its time. I remember what people were wearing, what the weather was like......

Anyway, back to the shop……the next thing, my tuna roll was on the floor, cucumber awry, and I was on my back, with John on top.

"I've always fancied you, you know, but you was always with someone. Rod, and that Ben, and Tony, and that Chris….."

"Hang on. Stop….. It was KEN, not Ben, I've never 'been with Tony', and certainly not Chris; he's my friend. Anyway, I didn't know you fancied me."

"That's cos I never said nuffin. But I did. And now you ain't wiv anyone so is it OK if I fuck you?" Who said romance was dead?

By now he was seriously up for it, straining in his jeans and to be honest, having caught sight of the hairs on his chest, so was I.

"Well, could we just……"

"Just what? You know you want to. You like it. Rod told me."

WHAT?? Fucking *Hell*, Rodney………

"Well, I do, but, can't we just….have a wank or something this time? Maybe next time, when we know each other a bit better, we can…."

He'd undone his jeans by know and I could see John Jack's John Thomas, and it was fucking ENORMOUS. Deffo attractive but enormous.

"I don't think that'll fit, John. It's rather…."

"Hnnnnnggggggggggg" groaned John as he shot his load all over the bed and my jeans.

"Sorry. Bit quick, couldn't help it. Here, let me finish you off." (Who was it? Remind me. *Who said romance was dead?*)

"OK, just let me get my jeans…."

Just then: *John? JOHN? You in there? I need to get into the flat. Are you there? I want the keys. Dios. Esta tienda está llena de mierda. Tú también lo estás..Madre de dios! Mother of God! This shop is full of shit and so are you."*

"Oh CHRIST!! It's Carlos. Quick, in to the toilet!" and he shoved me, jeans down, pants half off and erection flagging, across the little room in to the cubicle, skidding on tuna and squishing cucumber as I went, pulled the door to.

"I'm in the back, just coming...... (no pun intended. Actually, John never did puns. Actually, he didn't do anything very funny I was to discover). *"I thought you were in Spain. You weren't due back till next week."*

"I know, but I ...needed something. Can I have the keys please? Why are you looking so red?"

"No reason. They're behind the bar. I'll come and get them."

And they went out. I could see through the crack on the door; John WAS looking rather flushed, as it happens. I waited for the 'Jing a ling a ling' of the little bell over the door to sound before I emerged, drying semen on jeans which were still at half-mast and I hadn't been able to move for fear of kicking the bucket. The mop bucket, I mean. And I smelled of fish.

I didn't know, and neither did John at this point, that Carlos had cleared out all the business accounts, and had all the money transferred to Spain (*allegedly*; that was the goss) and had just come back to get some paperwork to do with the transfer. We also didn't know this was the last time anyone would see him for months. Rumour has it, he was seen last sitting on the wall of The Bell, opposite, staring at 'Dirty Nellie's', which was what Selina's had become, when it was forced to close, not long after he'd gone. Mostly thanks to him.

John, in full flight.....

But, for now, all was well. Peace reigned in the Club as the warring factions had gone their separate ways, or, at least Carlos had buggered off. No more fights, no more broken chairs and ripped tee shirts. John was happier, although upset – they'd been together for some time; in fact, just after the Club first opened…..but he was back to his big larger than life self – laughing too much, drinking too hard. We didn't mention the aborted shag; I just thought it was a one off, an attempt at a quick bit of some of the other, but I DID notice that John kept looking at me, being extra nice to me, giving me a drink *'on the ahse'*, in fact, several *'on the ahse'*, though not when anyone else was around. I do believe, dear reader, I was being WOOED! Or he was just trying to get me pissed all the time. Which worked, I should mention.

One night, we were all up in the top bar, chatting and being nice to each other, and someone handed John the newest edition Gay Times saying, *"Whoar! Look at him. Bit bona eh? There's an article about him. Have a look. WOT A KNOB! He is, I mean. Look what 'ee's done!"* John took the mag, went 'WHOAR' and proceeded to read the article, went *'WHOAR'* again and gave it back.

"What do you think about THAT? Fuckin' twat, eh?"

"Yeah, yeah. What a twat!" said John, who then bent down to busy himself behind the bar, fetching up some refill fruit juice. Whoa……something wrong here…..not quite sure what…..

"Show us the mag? I haven't seen this month's." (Actually, I'd never seen any month's. I think the last porn mag I'd seen was at ATC camp all those years back – I can still see those weird crevasses and folds…….).

I looked at the article in question - something about two 'lads' snogging on Oxford Street, outside Spats (oh the memories!) and then calling the copper a 'Fat Wanker' – and asked John, *"Have you been there, John?"*

"Where?"

"The club, in this article."

"Oh. No. I don't think so."

Do you know where it is?" I persisted.

"Oh, erm, yes…..no. I'm busy." And he left the bar and went off downstairs. Nope. Definitely, something not right here.

A couple of nights later, same scene. There was a paper on the bar ('EENIN STANNIT') and I passed it to him, pointing at an article. He took it and appeared to study it. Only, the paper was upside down. Fuck me! He couldn't read it. He had no idea.......Oh my god. HE CAN'T READ! Suddenly, many things, anomalies became clear – hesitations, excuses when I'd asked him to deal with an order, to read me something on a list, anger at being asked his opinions on something being talked about which he would have needed to have read to be able to give an opinion....the poor bastard was illiterate. My heart was suddenly filled with pity – no, not pity, sorrow. He'd endured this all his life and never once spoke of it.

It made sense now, all the bluster, all those *"Boys and gels, I made this club from nuffing. I came up froo the East End wivaht a pot ta piss in, an' I made this club what it is...."* speeches he would make and be endlessly mocked for, were actually the only thing he had, the only proof that was, in his eyes, validation of himself as a person; he'd made a difference in spite of being so severely disabled in the world in which he found himself.

After this realisation, this brash, loud, foolish man seemed to me to be something brave, something powerful and I found myself defending him when other members were being less than kind *('Oh shut the fuck up, you old cunt. It's ONLY a gay bar'*, when in fact, I realised no, it was *far* more than that.) and found myself drawn to him, wanted to help him, wanted to make it better. He seemed to me, now, someone who'd faced massive prejudice all his life, all 55 years of it – he was illiterate, queer and Jewish (though not completely, if you get my drift.... Ha ha) and had had to hide all of those things, and still, in spite of all of that, he'd opened this little bar, this Saving Grace, and had, I believed now, every right to be so proud of it. Yes, he WAS annoying, yes, he was a twat, but still – I was drawn to this man and slowly, slowly, we became 'an item', though one that was to be kept secret, for some reason.

John and me, just before it all went wrong...

I now worked full time behind the bar, became 'manager' (for what it was worth. Nothing, actually) and my popularity suddenly both soared and plummeted – soared because, in my largesse, I was able to give people one *'on the ahse'* whenever I felt like it. Lady Bountiful, me, and everyone suddenly seemed to be my best friend (I knew it wasn't real, but it felt nice) I was able to play what music I liked too, as Carlos was no longer DJ (if ever there was a misnomer, a crappy old record deck, balanced over the glass washer and a pile of out of date records, was it. DJ, indeed!) Anyway, OUT went The Ovaltineys:

'We're happy girls and boys!'

and in came Feargal Sharkey, Level 42 and Talking Heads. I had the 'budget' for the records and I was in control!! HAHAHAHAAAA! A touch of *'Big Yellow Taxi'* here, (she was still my companion in times good and bad), a smidge of Marc Bolan and *'Ballroom of Mars'* there.....I learned too that if they didn't like the music, they came off the floor and back to the bar, to drink and eat the 'free' peanuts which made them thirstier. A little track from Bowie's *'Lodger'* – nothing *like 'African Night Flight'* to get 'em flocking to the pumps! – or a soupcon of Sade's *'Your Love is King'* to kill the night stone dead....I was, let's face it, shite at the job – I played exactly what I liked (and usually no-one else did, ignoring the calls of *"WHAT THE FUCK IS THIS???"*, *"PLAY*

SOMETHING DECENT, YOU POOF" and "CAN WE HAVE SOMETHING WE KNOW, PLEASE?" etc etc) and gave drinks away like they were going out of fashion (which of course, they never would). It was Chris – remember him? The Wise Man. The Saviour – who, one night said,

"You're going to ruin this club. Play music people actually LIKE, so they want to come here! They don't want to hear fuckin Moany Joni or fuckin wanky Mark Bowler..."

"It's BOLAN, actually..."

"I don't care who he is! Play something we can dance to. Fill the floor, make us hot and thirsty, and make us have FUN! It's like a fuckin morgue in here. AND STOP GIVING AWAY FREE DRINKS!! They don't really like you (ouch) *they just know you're good for a bevvy. Use your fuckin nut. It's a business, not a charity."*

I knew he was right. Again.

"OK no need to shout. I got a bit carried away."

"Alright. Good. Put on that Bowie thing – Fa Fa Fa Fa FASHION – we like that. Mine's a lager. Cheers. OH, and I know you're shagging John."

"How? It's a secret..."

Maybe if you stopped playing that...that Laura Brannigan song and making eyes at each other....'Silent Partners'. REALLY?? Pffft. Make it a bit more obvious, why don't you?"

He didn't miss a trick. And neither, it seemed, had anyone else.

"Shagging John then? Carlos has only been gone five minutes," said Gloria. *"Mind you, I never liked him, smarmy dago cunt. Mines a Bacardi..."*

"Gotta charge for drinks now, Glor. It's a business you know."

"Yeah, well, start after me."

That night, after downstairs had closed, and we were seeing off the stragglers out of the top bar, we sat down and I said:

"Look, John, I've been a bit of a knob. Sorry about the music. And the free bevvies. I just got a bit carried away."

"It's alright. I just love having you around. I didn't want to spoil your fun. Yeah, night Ben. Thanks. See you tomorrow."

And then it was just we two. Without going into too much detail, I will say only this: Red banquette, large gin and a re-enactment of 'Last Tango in Paris', as the restaurant kitchen was just along the corridor and there was no time to go upstairs.....

At this point, mostly because of the 'mistake' I'd made one night at Bruna's, I was about to be made homeless. Honestly....you'd think I'm murdered a baby or something. *Honestly!* All that had happened was we'd all gone to Stallions and got wazzed and got kebabs and got the night bus home but Nicky had lost her keys or something so I said she could sleep in my bed and I would share with Tony. Poor Tony, who hadn't come with us that night, was fast asleep and awoke to find his friend stinking of fags and beer climbing into bed with him.

"What the FUCK....???"

"SHHHHHH NICKY HAS LOST HER KEY. SHE CAME WITH ME. SHE DID A WEEE... THAT RHYMES....HAHAHAHHAHA."

"Shut up, you idiot. You'll wake the girls."

"OH. OK. SORRY. SSSHHHHH.....SHE DIDN'T DO A WEE. WE HAD A KEBAB. IT WAS NICE. I DON'T WANT TO SHAG YOU IN CASE YOU'RE WONDERING....!"

"Stop shouting. STOP. Go to sleep."

So I did.

In the morning there was a shriek. *"WHO ARE YOU????"*

Bruna had gone to my room, alarm call as usual, to find a complete stranger in my bed. With a cold kebab.

"Oh, sorry. Nigel said it's be OK. I lost my key...."

"Right. That's fine. You'd better go now though. And take your kebab. Thankyou."

I looked at Tony. The icy calm of Bruna's voice hadn't sounded normal and I feared the worst.

At tea, there was a thunderous silence at the table. No conversation, no sound other than that of Bruna smothering her food in pepper. A thousand years passed.

"We're thinking of decorating your room and using it for a storeroom for my stage outfits," said Bruna, in to the void.

"Oh. That's me fucked then."

"I'm afraid so...you can stay till the end of the week if you like."

Like, six days? Brilliant. Now what.

I know! I'll get Gill to move to London and we can share a flat!

And so it came to pass.

We had to borrow the money for a deposit off my Dad, who was only too willing to lend it (though he never *EVER* let us forget it) because, I am assuming, he thought that living with Gill would get me away from all those predatory homos, out of the Den of Vice and it would give her a chance to entice me to leave the SSU and his son would be normal and acceptable again. He would be able to hold his head high as I would have been delivered from the Devil.

It didn't, as you can imagine, quite work out like that.

I travelled down to Cornwall and helped her pack her stuff into a rented van, up to the roof and in to the remaining space we squeezed the drugged and very resistant cat and set off.....away, away back to London, to the smoke and the lights – to a new chapter for me, a new life for Gill and my parents waving us off, with different agendas – my Father full of hope that his son would now be saved and my Mother wishing it was her.

It was the journey from hell. It rained. And it rained. Then it rained some more. It was dark, the night only illuminated by the oncoming headlights of massive lorries, as we hurtled north through the night. We just drove, and drove, eager to get there, aware of how far we had to go. At one point the cat started yowling and seemed to need a pee so we pulled over onto the hard shoulder, somewhere along the M4, and tried to get the lead attached to the cat which by this time was no longer drugged and was having none of it. We pulled the poor little fucker out of his box, from whence he had lain for, what – five hours now, and attaching some string to his collar, put him on the roadside, on the hard shoulder.

 "WEE! Go on, WEE!" said Gill. The cat, traumatised, drugged, wet and with his fur blown in the opposite direction by the draft of the massive lorries screaming by, not three feet away, covering us all in spray, was not really in an ablutionary mode, it seemed.

"WEEEEE! FER FUCK'S SAKE CAT…WEEEEE. I'M GETTING DROWNED HERE!" But, no. Nothing. Just a plaintive whine, which probably translated something like: *"I'm not going to wee. PUT ME BACK IN THE VAN OUT OF THE RAIN AWAY FROM THOSE FUCKING HUGE LORRIES THAT MAKE MY EARS BLEED. I DON'T KNOW WHERE I AM, WHERE I AM GOING, BUT BY BASTET AND ALL THE GODS OF EGYPT, WHERE I WAS CONSIDERED IMPORTANT, I WILL GET YOU FOR THIS. I WILL FIND THE RIGHT TIME AND RIP OUT YOUR THROATS. YOU BASTARDS."* Or something.

"He's not going to is he?" I said. *"Can we go now?"*

"OK. Please himself," and Gill picked him up and put him back in his basket. We had no inkling of his plans.

We drove on, mile after mile. I knew East London, where Forest Gate is, and was none too pleased that the poxy landlord wouldn't meet us there, but insisted we had to go to his place. North of Edgware. The complete opposite direction. It was late, it was dark and still it rained and this would add at least another two hours to the trip. We eventually arrived at his address, and refused, out of pique, to rub his mezuzah. For those of you who believe in Divine retribution, this turned out to be a mistake.

He was an odious little man, with an equally horrid wife. He was short and fat and he smelled, sour, cigarry and with halitosis that could've stunned a horse. We went into their Parlour - his word, not mine – and said,

"This is my wife. She annoyed that you're so late. All the shops are shut. Never mind, bubbeleh," he said to his equally monstrous wife, all fur coat and no knickers, *"and you all dressed up and farpitzs."*

"We couldn't help it, you know. We've driven about 400 miles as it is and if you'd met us in Forest Gate, it would've been two hours earlier and the shops would have still been open!"

I wasn't, as you know, prone to outbursts, but I was tired and this little fat fuck was just about the end......

"FEH!" said Mrs. Fagin. *"I'm not one to kvetch, but Harrods is at LEAST an hour's drive and I've been waiting FOR EVER. I was hoping for a little metsiah, a little bargain, but it's probably too late now."*

I couldn't believe my ears!! We'd driven all this way, in the worst of conditions and all this.. this ...*SHLUB,* this nagging, irritating old bag can do is dare to moan because she can't go to fucking HARRODS to spend OUR money???? Well KISS MY TOCHES!!!

"Just hand over the money, so we can go," said Gill. And we watched him count it out. Ten by ten, all the way up to £600. Deposit and a month's rent on our new life. And so SHE could go to Harrods the next day for a bargain. Mazel Tov. You arse.

When we got there, over to East London, eventually, with the cat now howling pitifully from the rear, probably with a bladder the size of Kent, we walked in, using the key that Fagin had so generously handed us, to find the flat damp, musty and with all the furniture in the 'furnished flat' all stacked up against the walls – beds included. We could've cried, and probably did.

We spent our first night, huddled up on a mattress on the floor. And the cat did a shit in the hall.

It took us some while to get the place straight. The gas boiler was faulty – we know this because Gill found me almost unconscious in the bath the first day we used it. This meant we had to call Fagin over to see to it and....it was a strict NO PETS policy. So, the poor cat was unceremoniously flung out the back door whilst he was there, with both Gill and me ignoring the wailing coming from outside.

That fixed, the furniture, such as it was (the lying bastard) all in place, we alternated between Selina's and the flat as I was still working, and still shagging John of course. We landlords take our work very seriously you know. Within a few days, Gill was offered a job as in the restaurant as Chef, as the other one had left the same time as Carlos did because she'd not been paid for weeks. Unfortunately, there were no customers, so she only cooked a meal or two, and mighty fine they were too being that she is actually a trained chef. John still paid her though, which was nice of him since it was becoming increasingly clear that we were in trouble financially.

One day I volunteered to give him a hand with the books, so with

'In a West End town, a dead-end world

The East End boys and West End girls

tootling on in the background, I sat in the restaurant 'in an East End Town' and opened the books for 'Selina's Inc.' Jesus H. Christ, on a bike! What hieroglyph was this?

It wasn't this obviously, but it might as well have been. Nothing, and I mean, NOTHING, had been accounted for; nothing had a date, the figures didn't tally.....I am no book keeper but even I, dopey 8% in Maths C.S.E. me, could see things weren't erm....quite right.....

"Ummm. John? Can I speak to you for a minute?"

"Sure. Is it about the books?"

"Ummm..yeeeeessss. I don't think they're in a very good state..."

"Probably not. Carlos dealt with all that side of things....."

I knew WHY, of course, as John couldn't read at all or write particularly well either, but...for fuck's sake! This was utter chaos.

"Well, where's the bit that says how much money there is in the bank?"

"Dunno."

"Well, where's the bit where it says what we have to pay out and what we're getting in from the bars and the restaurant?"

"Dunno. There?" and he poked a finger hopefully at some random column and it was at that point that I realised WHY Bassy the chef hadn't been paid for weeks, WHY the brewery wasn't going to deliver at the weekend, WHY John was taking money straight out of the till to pay random tradesmen who came aggressively in the bar, and WHY, most of all, WHY Carlos had gone. Carlos had had gone and SO HAD ALL THE FUCKING MONEY!!!

He KNEW John would have no clue as to what was going on in the books, with the paperwork, the wages, with the credit and debit...and he stole the fucking lot, probably transferring it to a bank in Spain, gradually, so nobody would notice. The bastard. The conniving thieving greasy arsed BASTARD. Was this the reason for all the rows? Did John know? Surely not, as he didn't seem to understand why his suppliers weren't.....supplying. I knew. I knew it was because they hadn't been paid. Because that fucking dago had been syphoning all the money to Espana. What to do? If I tell him, there'll be a 'Kicking in' chairs and some knocking down tables, in a restaurant, in an East End town' for sure.......

....Shut *UP* Neil Tennant, let me think. And my decision has been my secret to keep all these years. I told him that we, the club that is, just wasn't making enough money any more. Not that his lover had knicked everything, stolen all that he'd worked to achieve (*"Boys and gels...."*) and was now the architect of his demise and despair. Probably best – I'd seen him when he was angry and I didn't like it.....

"You know what it's like, John. New bar opens, all the queens go WHOOOOO and run off there. No loyalty, just the chance of some better lighting, newer music and someone they might not have shagged yet. They'll be back, when they're bored of Benjy's, Harpoon Louis, The Playpen, the Pink Panther...they're all poncey. And expensive. And people have to travel.....It'll be OK. You've got REGULARS......"

Actually, they were no longer quite so regular, and they became even less regular when we found ourselves without any beer. In a bar. We had resorted to me going up the road to the Offie, to buy cans of lager, with my tartan wheelie shopping trolley (oh the SHAME!) and flogging 'em for a quid a go – we had to raise enough cash to buy the same again for the next day plus to try to save a bit to pay the looming bills and, in my case, being very keen not to have my kneecaps shot off by one of the blokes John had 'dunn a bit 'o business wiv'. Gradually, and I don't blame them, for I would have done the same, loyalty or not, people began to question why they would pay a quid for a can of lager they could get next door in Paki Jim's for 26p. Chris was first to complain (no change there then) and he caught the mood of the people (all 4 or 5 of them) when he said:

"A quid. A QUID? For a can of lager? I ain't paying that! Fuckin ridiculous. Come on Vince, let's go somewhere we can get a proper pint." And they left. And sadly so did everyone else, over the next few days and weeks until we had no customers at all, and no way to keep the wolves from the door, and the kind of wolves John 'ad dunn a bit 'o business wiv' should be kept from one's door at all costs.

As all this was going on, Gill and I were still living in Forest gate, chucking the poor cat out every time Fagin, as we now liked to call him, came round for his rent or to fix the huge number of things that were shit and didn't work….. *"Yes ACTUALLY, you DO need to have boiler fixed or get done for manslaughter"*….

….*"Ooooh! Look! There's that really annoying stray cat again Gill. I wish it would stop coming into our garden all the time. It's very annoying. It poos in our garden. Honestly, the neighbours should keep it in or something"*…..

…and generally realising that, though we loved each other dearly, and she was working at the club (I say 'working', but really just sitting round with us, and getting paid for nothing) but she'd met someone back in Cornwall just before we'd decided to set up home together, and of course, I was now getting a regular dose of John's appendage (we'd sorted out the issue of 'accommodation'. All along, it was just practice!) which was quite a powerful draw; Gill had been home a couple of times to see him and it was becoming clear she wanted to be with HIM, not here, with a leaky boiler and the cat pissing all over the cover of my 'ALF' LP.

So, after not very long, it was decided that we'd admit that we both needed shagging on a more permanent basis and to hand in our notice.

Once it was decided, it was obvious that after I would move into the flat upstairs with John. It was a bit sad, after all the trouble we'd gone to, not to mention the bound – to- be never ending comments from Pater about how generous he'd been (check), how he'd hoped it would work out but once again his kids had let him down (check); about how we'd never repay him but that was OK because he loved us and would never mention it again which as you can imagine was absolutely not the case. He mentioned it constantly. And of course, Gill hadn't managed to save me from damnation. Hey ho.

Anyway, just before she was due to leave, John decided to treat us to a night out at the theatre and got tickets for 'Evita' at The Prince Edward Theatre, UP WEST!! Oooooh went the two Cornish peasants, and not without reason; though I'd been in London for some years now, I'd not been to the theatre very often.....

...one notable exception to that was one night when I was still at Pearcroft Road, and Chris and I had gone to the Salisbury (like some junkie, unable to resist) and he, of course had copped off and left me. Again. HOWEVER, this night, I was schmoozed by a very nice gentleman:

"Hello there. Erm..Hi!" he said. Oh myyyyy – A Southern Irish accent. I was done for...Yes, YES!! I'll do whatever you want.....

"Hi," I said. Here we go again. Two 'Hi's' and the deal is done.

"Alone you are? I tought I saw you wit someone?"

"I was. Now I'm not."

"OK. That's good news, so it is." (*He probably didn't say that, but I'm just trying to build up the picture. Please read all his lines like Paddy O'Flaherty). *"Well, I would like to buy you a drink,* (Mine's a lager!.., something I would later regret as I had to push past a whole row of tutting people as I needed a piss and couldn't make it to the interval. Should've had a half.) *and then go home with you, so I would, but, I have two tickets for 'Romeo and Juliet' at the Aldwych for tonight if you'd like to go. First. Then I'll follow you home on me bike, so I will.* (Really? I could live in Reading, for all you know!)

But, the voice unmanned me, the Shakespeare enthralled me and the chance of a shag after decided me.

"Yes! And Yes!" I said.

So that's what we did:

Had a drink, saw a play and then shagged. A very nice night thankyou, Christopher Hartley – if you hadn't buggered off, Seamus (*not really) wouldn't have come over and.....

I digress....

So we borrowed John's vegetable van (Used for delivering them, not MADE of them. Honestly.....) which had two front sliding doors neither of which worked unfortunately and were jammed open, and it blew PLUMES of black exhaust, leaving both of us doubtful we'd get from Leytonstone to Forest Gate and back at all.

However, it didn't let us down, so there we were, all glammed up, Gill wearing a FABULOUS black evening gown and me in a suit, tightly belted in in order not to fall out of the cab of the van through the open doors as it went round corners and we farted and belched our way across Wanstead Flats, like a scene from 'The Grapes of Wrath' only with Ma Joad slightly better attired. And no alfalfa sprouts.

There was a cab waiting and off we swished, heading up West. The show was stunning, but even better and more memorable was the end of the evening when Gill made THE most spectacular entrance you could wish for, to lock away in my box of 'The Funniest Things Ever'.

John and I were down in the foyer, with all the luvvies, going "Mahvellous Dahling. Mwah mwah" and "That Laney, you know, Laney Paige. Mahvellous….." when all of a sudden, my sister came into sight, careering, nay, HURTLING down the curved stairs from the Circle, people flying for their lives, or getting knocked out of the way as she careered past. Apparently, she'd caught her heel in the hem of her dress and stumbled forward from the top step and hurtled like an Exocet missile down the stairs, furiously flapping her black dress as she went, unable to regain her balance or stop, gathering speed and squealing like a squealing thing as she went, down in to the foyer, people scattering and leaping out of her way until she glided, ladylike, to a halt in front of John and me.

"Ah!" she said, not missing a beat. "There you are." Cool as. Utterly brilliant.

Fagin was less than pleased when he came round to return our deposit as we weren't going to stay on the extra month but threatened instead to tell the council about his British Gas Death Trap.

"Shnorrers, both of you, Spongers! Thieves!" he said. "Bubeleh was right about you. And YOU!" he said, pointing at me - "Faigelah! HOMO PERSON!! And YOU!" pointing at a very bewildered Gill, who had not had the benefit of living with Rod and having heard all this Yiddish before, "YOU – are probably a nafka!! ("He's calling you a whore," I whispered) "MOMZERS!! ("Now he's calling us bastards! Good job I listened to Rod, eh?" I said.)

"OY YOY YOY!! Out of my house!!"

This was rapidly turning into a scene from *'Fiddler on the Roof'* – any minute he was going to break into *'If I Was A Rich Man'* and start 'Deedle deedle deedle deedle dum' –ing all over the place until, that is, the cat arrived, pissed on Alison Moyet, again, strolled around the room and then nonchalantly swaggered out of the open front door, with a 'FUCK YOU' look, that only cats can do.

At this point, we thought we were dead, well and truly busted and deposit-less but instead, he yelled something unintelligible both in fury and in Yiddish and *THREW* £300 at us, up in to the air, notes flying around and falling through the air like in one of those gangster movies, only we didn't get riddled with bullets at the end.

"MEESA MASHEENA AF DEER! I WISH YOU A HORRIBLE DEATH!!" he bellowed and just turned around and stormed out. Result! Money and still alive!

"Well," I said. *"That went well".*

So, Gill went home, and I moved into the Club, now a shadow of its former self. No money, no punters and an increasingly drunken Landlord.

To cut a long story short, in which nothing much happened, we had to sell up to the first buyers, and as the club was in so much debt, we came away with....nothing. Selina's became 'Dirty Nellie's' and an era came sadly to an end. All those faces; all those loves, tears, fights, hopes, laughs.....where did we all scatter? Who survived the War? Who married as soon as we were allowed to? Who died? Who went to foreign shores? That parade of shared hearts and minds and genitals, all passing through this little world created here, here among the brickbats and arrows of the East End when we thought that none of us were even deserving of such a thing.

It all happened very quickly. The two guard dogs, Sebastian (too savage) and Bruno (too old) had to be destroyed and we suddenly found ourselves in the Housing Office for Waltham Forest, with 2 suitcases, 3 cats in boxes, 2 Shih Tzus, a Mynah Bird and a Great Dane pup (don't ask.....John was offered it, 'cheap like', and he thought I'd like it. In another life, it might have been a good idea....), refusing to leave until they found us somewhere to live. Probably due to the fact that Lena and Prince wouldn't stop barking and trying to bite anyone who came near, they found us somewhere pretty quickly – a one bedroom flat, in Walthamstow, in a block right next to the pub, which according to Google Maps, has ceased to exist, so I can't give you the name....

And so we moved. All of us. Plus the furniture from the club. Freddy, who CONSTANTLY yelled, *"QUITE NICE!!!!"* was on the kitchen window sill, the dogs were wherever they could fit in, and then Lena had pups. The place stank of ammonia and birdshit, dog farts and cat piss, and we weaved amongst the huge antique (fake) buffets, climbed over clothes, tripped over animals and each other...it was fucking CHAOS!.

John decided to 'go back to his roops', as he put it (never having seen the word) and got himself a pitch on Walfumstow Market, selling pet food. He got a little van and off he went, early each morning to set up, to yell *"NOT FREE PAHND! NOT TWO PAHND! WHO WILL GIVE ME A PAHND FOR THESE LAHVELY CUTTLEFISH? YER BAHDGIE WILL LAV YOU FOR EVVA! FREE PAHND OF BONIO FOR A PAHND. YER DOG WILL LAV YOU FOR EVVA..."* etc etc, on and on, all day, wind or shine, until packing up time when he'd load it all back in the van, his life measured out not in coffee spoons, but in packets of Trill and hide pig's ears, come home and more and more frequently, go straight out the back in to the pub, from where he'd emerge, red and angry and on the verge of doing me harm. Luckily, he had the oil painting of his Muvva on the wall so he would sink to his knees in front of it and sob and sob until I gently, like he was a child or a wounded bird, led him to bed, where he would fall into healing sleep, to begin again the following day. *"ONLY A PAHND, MISSIS. YER CAT WILL LAHV YOU FOR EVVA....."*

I meanwhile, also unable to stay in the menagerie we called home, with its stink and hairs and puppy shit, decided to go back to teaching. Yes, dear reader, the very thing I said I would never do, in ANY circumstance, for ANY reason, having HAD IT with education and shitty jam jar hurling kids, I was desperate to return to as it was my only skillset and means of escape from that flat. John came home at lunchtime to see to poor Sam, the Dane, who was growing still (but who by now I absolutely adored), to let him out in to the tiny garden and I signed on with the Supply Pool and ventured back into the classroom.

Dear Sam, way too big for this life....

I struck gold, as it happens. My first job was in Chingford, for a week. Someone had gone off sick, and it turned into two weeks then three and then I was offered, subject to interview, the job full time. Hmmmm.... what to do? Sit at home with Freddy shrieking *'QUITE NICE'* without a break and stepping on dog turds? Go and stand at 'John Jack's' and sell millet sprays for budgies, OR......get the fuck out of there, earn a decent salary and have some social interaction with people who knew stuff about STUFF. John's range of interests, and therefore conversation, was quite limited, to say the least. I had begun to wonder why I was there at all – or had been, in the first place. Was it because I'd felt sorry for him? Because I would be running 'my own' club? Because he had a gorgeous todger and was always keen to use it? Probably all of those things, in the beginning – great sex, a bit of glamour and free beer. But it would not sustain.

So, I took the job. Mr Lucky's back in da house!

John was not so thrilled. In fact, he was livid.

"Who would look after the animals?" Erm...YOUR animals, actually. *"Who would cook tea?"*

"Well, YOU. Or we can share it........OK, I'll cook tea (you fucking BLOKE) *but it will have to wait until I get home and sometimes, I'll be late. Rehearsals, or staff meetings and stuff."* (I didn't elaborate on the 'stuff' but, dear reader, if you promise not to let it go any further, I will tell you: I was having an affair. With a LAYDEE! Tell you more in a bit.....)

"Well, I can go to the pub until you get home."

This turned out to be a singularly BAD idea, and often I'd have to go in and get him, and he'd be slumped in a corner, pissed and sad, or all revved up. On those occasions, he'd go on and on, pint waiting for me when I arrived, to make me stay (regardless of any food I'd been preparing) I'd have a drink with him and then he'd think it was OK to take me home, all 10 yards of it, across the car park, past the cockle and whelk van – classy eh? - and in through the back gate of the flats and try to shag me. I say 'try'. It usually ended up with him either losing his stiffy or his temper, neither of which was conducive to shagging. I preferred the first of those two scenaria; at least he'd then fall off me and then asleep, rather than the other option which usually involved him in screaming at me about the Club folding (like it was MY fault!), about Carlos leaving him (like it was MY fault!), about not being able to read (like it was MY fault!), about everybody treating him like a cunt (like it was MY fault!) and he wished his Muvva was still alive….the abuse would turn to tears and then we'd have a session of him kneeling in front of her portrait, now hanging in the hall, sobbing and wishing he was dead.

His Yiddische Mamma…

I would watch this scene with conflicting emotions: on one hand, I would feel desperately sad for him, all his dreams in tatters and his celebrity gone or, on the other, I wished he WOULD SHUT THE FUCK UP AND GO TO BED. And, no Freddie, it is NOT *"QUITE NICE"* so you can shut the feck up as well.

So, this was my world. Full of cat hair, dog shit and vitriol.

Or, half of it was. The other half, almost like some kind of secret life or a parallel universe, was full of creativity, and inventiveness (this was before the National Curriculum and the carnage that Kenneth Baker wrought) and interesting people. I was staying on late at school, partly due to planning and marking (funny how you get back on the bike, seamlessly) but also the less time I spent with Mad John in the Crazy House the better. I was growing again, the kids watering me, and nourishing my spirit.

And there was Miss....and, you know what, I really CAN'T remember her name – that's awful, eh? ....Hughes? I think that was it, Hughes! But let's just call her Sue. She was very beautiful, with the most amazing hair and open ready smile, and a wonderful lilting Welsh accent. And fabulous tits.

Now, dear reader, I haven't been able to explain this to myself, and as nobody (except, now, you) has ever known about this, I have had no one to talk to about it, to rationalise it. But. It happened. We had a fling, a 'do', an affair, a tryst. We crept out of school into the pub, The County Arms, on the corner, where we would hold hands under the table, or sit side by side and I would stroke her neck whilst pressing our hips together. It was the behaviour of teenagers, but utterly transporting. I was aching for her, and the fact I was a poof never came into the equation. We would write each other notes, staple them closed and send them next door with a child; *"Could you just pop this next door to Miss, Jason?"* Jason, the least likely to open it, and unable to read it even if he had, would go next door and in a few moments would return with a reply, agreeing that she'd quite like it if I had a wank over her tits, but only if she could suck me off on a bus. Triple staples.

I don't know if the other staff knew; probably they did, as we behaved irrationally and giggled together like fools, brushing against each other in corridors easily wide enough to pass in; I would use her to 'demonstrate' dance positions, holding her waist, her arms, her legs, drinking in the scent of her, as the kids looked on in rehearsals for a re-enactment of the Blue Bag thing I'd done back at Balls Park (BALLS PARK!! BALLS!! SIR, YOU SWEARED!!). We went together to lunch, went together to get anything needed for school, took any chance to be in each other's company. Was it love? It was certainly lust, but, I hear you say – she has all the wrong bits for you. We've all read what you get up to, what you like, so.....? All I know is that back at her flat, with hubby late home, we snogged and I fondled her boobs like a good 'un and eventually, pressed for time, shot my load in my jeans as I humped between her open legs as she sprawled backwards on the stairs, leaving a wet patch on her crotch. Now, YOU explain this. I can't. It was utterly wonderful though and yet somehow, I must have justified it by saying it can't be real because I am in the SSU, and my history, laid out in these pages, would suggest otherwise. So was it OK? No, of course not. She was married and torn by her behaviour. I was with someone too (whatever that meant) and we were both unavailable and from different species. Maybe SHE too justified it to herself by saying that I was a homosexual and so no real threat to her marriage. Erm…You have a wet patch in your crotch, made by my semen – I think that's quite a weird one to explain to hubby though: *'Oh it's OK, he's a poof!'* I don't think that's gonna go, somehow. That though, was the apogee of our…our….whatever it was. I think we were quite frightened by the red intensity of that encounter; aware that maybe, had there been more time, I would actually have fucked her, crossed the Rubicon, from where there would have been no going back; I couldn't have unfucked her and the consequences of that moment became clear to us both. So, somehow, we sort of smiled ruefully and walked away; she began looking for other jobs and we behaved like normal people around each other. I can still feel the bones of her pelvis, though, as she ground against me. How strange, after all these years.

Hughes. That was it….

Then, one day, a normal day, a day of Maffs n Spellin, a day of packed lunch and Banda machining, the secretary came to me and said, *"You had a phone call. Can you meet your friend in The County Arms for a drink at lunch time?"* Really? It was a Thursday; we only went down to the pub on a Friday… What friend? Well, that wasn't too hard to guess as since leaving Selina's. I hadn't seen anyone apart from Chris and Vince – I wasn't allowed out much you see – so it must be them. Odd. *"OK. Thanks. Right, you lot - Number 10. DEFINITE. And be careful with that ending…"*

One day. A normal day.

12.00 came, the kids went out, I managed to get someone to swap canteen duty and headed off down the road.

One day. A normal day and there they were, the only customers, three fresh pints on the table. Quiet. Something in the air…

"Fuck me! Don't tell me you bought your own? Wonders'll never…..

"Hello," said Chris. *"I've got AIDS".*

The County Arms, Chingford; the place of such joy and such sorrow....

....and a FUNERAL.

I felt like I'd been kicked in the chest, like I was doubled over, no air, unable to catch my breath. The blood was banging in my ears, I was spinning, falling, over and over, down to some alternate Wonderland where what he'd just said would make sense.

There was a silence of a thousand years, and into the silence I said: *"What do you mean? What kind of AIDS?"*

"Don't be a cunt all your life. AIDS. **AIDS**. *There's only one sort of AIDS. Well, there's hearing aids but they don't have capital letters and they don't kill you. AIDS. AIDS. AIDS, as in: I'm dying. I wanted you to be the first to know."*

An honour, a bitter bitter gift.

"How do you know? Are you sure? They might be wrong. They might've...."

"Look," he said, and knelt in front of me, there in The County Arms, in the bar where so much joy had been had. Gently taking my hand, he said, *"They're not wrong. I've had several tests and it's quite advanced so I don't know how much more time I have. I came here to tell you, my oldest, my loyalist, my oldest and twattiest best friend, so that maybe we could spend some time together. Not seen much of you lately what with that old cunt you're living with and me being in bed quite a lot. You reckon you can spare me some time? Now that I don't have much of it left? Eh?"*

I looked at him now and could see the grey pallor, the gauntness of his features; I hadn't noticed it before, but then, I hadn't seen him for weeks. I felt shame, self-loathing and utter utter desolation. Not my Chris. Not my angel, the man who'd guided me away from disaster after disaster. Who would guide me now? Not my Chris, who'd got me into the most awful trouble, who'd made me so furious I could've stabbed him, who'd made me laugh so hard I thought I would choke. How would I manage?

I looked across at Vince, a man I didn't know too well, and he was sitting there, as still as stone, agony etched into his features, giving his beloved man this moment of reconciliation, the first stage in a long long farewell, preparing his friend for an inevitable tragedy, one that was being played out all over London and beyond, but knowing that this, this was the only one that mattered.

"Yes. OK," was all I could manage.

"Drink up then!" and he downed his lager in the time-honoured way, as if he hadn't just said what he had, as if time had rewound itself and there we were, down the pub.

"I need a wazz," he said and stood up to go to the loo. *"Mine's a lager."* THAT hadn't changed, then.....

A little unsteady, a little light, the beginnings of his wasting away.

"He's pretty sick, Nige," said Vince. *"I don't know why he's not contacted you before now, but it was his decision to make. I guess he just wanted to be sure there was no exit. He's been on this new thing, AZT, but it hasn't worked, so he will die, sooner rather than later now. He's getting sicker. He's been to hospital twice with PCP and his CD4 count is nearing zero. You read the news; you know what's what. All you can do is give him some of your time, and love him. He's always calling you a twat but I know there's no one he loves more. I'm really sorry it has come to this, but you must know how hard this was for him today. He's being his usual gobby self, but he's terrified. Not of dying but of the manner of – it can be pretty grim. So please. Please just be there for him and see if you can.....*

"Christ, Vince, how long have you known? Why didn't he say anything before? Why didn't he....

"I don't know. He probably wanted to be certain, that there was no hope before he said anything. He's been having test after test, but he didn't want anyone to know. It's been hard, so hard to see him deteriorating, every test coming back positive, and worse and worse. You remember when we went up town ages ago? Last time we saw you? We'd come straight from Bart's and..

"Oh fuck, mate....I didn't know. Surely, there must be some....way....some...

"No, no, there isn't. He....

"What are you two fucking talking about? Got yer knitting out have you? Les tricoteuses who haven't even got the bevvies in. I hope it was about me. As Oscar Wilde once notably said: 'If there's one thing worse than being talked about, it's...

".....NOT being talked about," we chorused dismally.

I went to the bar.

When I came back, I realised that forty-five minutes had passed and I was feeling a bit pissed (being Chris, the first pint was Stella, and I'd had no lunch. Hurrrrrrr.) And you know what? The art lesson I had planned for that afternoon now seemed a teensy bit irrelevant. How could I go back, smile at the kiddies, smelling of beer and on the edge of tears and talk about Seurat in order to facilitate a lesson on pointillism? I couldn't. My friend, my dear terrified friend, was dying, before my eyes, and whatever consequence of my next action would be was not as important as that. I went back to the bar, borrowed the phone, rang school, told them I'd received some terrible news and I wouldn't be back that afternoon. I hung up before I was asked any questions, ordered three more pints of Stella and returned to the table.

"Come on then you fucking lightweights. Beer." And I drank to drown my sorrows and all those that were to come.

That evening, when I eventually got back, John was already asleep in the lounge, drunk and sad. I had nothing to say but went to bed, where he joined me at some point later and woke me. We lay there in the dark. I searched for his hand and said,

"Chris is dying."

Sleepily he replied, *"Never mind. We'll talk about it tomorrow."*

"I want to talk about it NOW please. He's dying. He's got AIDS."

John sat up and put on the light.

"How do you know?"

"Because he TOLD me. How do you think I fucking know?"

"Oh well. He was always shaggin' around. Not surprised really. Pity though, eh, him being your friend and all that. You haven't shagged him, have you?"

"NO, I FUCKING HAVEN'T!! DON'T WORRY YOURSELF."

Selfish bastard, but actually I knew he was right to ask. The demon was in our midst. The war was coming to our door, and striking us down. I suddenly was aware that it wasn't that surprising that Chris had become infected – he was, indeed, 'always shagging around', and his 'proclivities' were somewhat extreme. He and Vince regularly went to the The Chain Locker, The Colherne, and the Mineshaft where the hankies were most definitely on show, and Chris had a veritable rainbow in his list of preferences - dark blue, light blue, grey and red. He'd also gone to Amsterdam for a *'Beer, Bondage and Buggery'* weekend, with an American serviceman he'd been having sex with. You can imagine what went on; at least, he came back with a smile, and a sore arse. And, he believed, HIV.

I DID begin to make time for him, to make up for lost days, lost hours. I went to Leytonstone Tube rather than Blackhorse Lane; went to Burghley Road instead of to home. John got more and more angry; I got more and more determined to be the best man I could for my friend, and John could go fuck himself if he neither liked it nor understood. We argued, I stood steady, whilst not neglecting my 'wifely duties'. He would never come with me, would never involve himself in what was happening in that house – Chris was someone he'd known for years and I found it hard to understand or forgive him for his disinterest and pettiness about stuff – having to clean the flat more, having to cook after selling *'dahn the market all bleedin' day'*. And I could understand that, I could, but I needed HIM to understand that I needed to be with my friend, whilst I still could be. John had no knowledge of our history, our long years together, of the deep and abiding love we had and so failed to grasp the significance of what was happening, and happening for ME as well, with the day of loss speeding closer.

Then, one day I went and the agony had deepened.

I went round, knocked. No answer. I pushed the door, and it opened. I went in.

"Hello? It's only me. I let myself in.....Vince gave me a key. Why is the living room upstairs? All the furniture is different. Why is it so dark in here?"

"Dunno", said Vince as he met me on the landing, *"That's the way he wants it."*

"Bit fuckin' depressing..... I''ll let come light in, shall I?"

Out of the gloom, I heard Chris' voice, from the armchair in the corner

"Leave 'em!" he yelled. *"It's not your fucking house. What do you want anyway?"*

"Chris, you said I....I came to see you like you said. You said you wanted me to..."

"Well, I don't. Why don't you just fuck off home again?"

Vince tried to placate him.

"Hey, Chris. Go easy…you're pretty angry these days."

"DAYS? Days might be all I have left."

We didn't know how to respond, so we said nothing.

"Sorry. Sorry, ok? Vince, put on that Bowie thing we used to like".

As the music started to play, with all its joy and memories of when things weren't all fucked up, Chris pushed himself out of his chair and began that gangly dance of his. I wondered, again, how, for such a gifted composer and musician, he could have absolutely no sense of rhythm. He reminded me of myself, so long ago at Laban…

"Turn to the left! Turn to the right! Remember? Fa fa fa fa fashion! Like it was down the club! That fuckin' dago cunt, Carlos, used to play it for me .. "Fa fa fa fa…..!

As we watched, in jubilation and horror, he began to kind of 'run down' like a clockwork toy, until he suddenly pitched forward and fell to the floor. The sound of bones meeting wood.

"It's not 'cos I'm pissed.", he said, embarrassed, furious. *"Just can't seem to stand for long these days. Fuckin' lallies aren't workin' too well.."*

"Come on mate", said Vince, tenderly, helping him up, again, as if this had become a regular thing, which, during my short absence, it had.

"Thanks Vince. Right. Now put that other thing on…".

"Which other…..?"

"The other fucking thing!! The train thing. You're a useless cunt. And you…" and he pointed at me, *"You're a useless cunt as well… "*

"What? I haven't done anything!"

His bolts of fury ricocheted around the room, hitting us both, one after the other.

He was becoming incoherent with rage, his arms flailing, conducting the requiem for his own death…

"Exactly. I don't know why you bother coming round here. Why don't you just stay at home with that fat cunt you live with? "

"It's OK. Nige", said Vince. *He gets like this. It's not personal. The music will calm him. It's just fear. Fear and rage. What was that poem? 'Rage, rage against the dying of the light'? That's how he is now....*

The sound of Steve Reich's 'Different Trains' fills the room. We listened in silence. I quietly wept, in the darkness of the room, impotent and full of sorrow...

Those few brief months passed too soon. I met John Adams and Steve Reich, Terry Riley and Michael Nyman, Gavin Bryars and Philip Glass – they would fill the lounge with their insistent throbbing tones, while Chris would sit motionless, listening with his musician's sensibilities and would visit places in his mind only we could guess at. Even now, *'Different Trains'* takes me back to that room, that driving rhythm, *'one of the fastest trains'*, *'The crack train from New York'*.......maybe he was wishing he was on that train, *'From Chicago to New York'*, taking him away from here, from this room, from this speeding death.

We smoked, we drank copiously – the answer for us, for that time, WAS to be found in the bottom of the bottle; it made things funnier, blurred, unreal for those few precious hours. But as those days passed, so did the time we had remaining to us. There were constant phone calls from sobbing lovers who had lost their dear ones to this war, this enemy we were fighting but with no weapons; Tony, Mike, Harry – all gone, all wiped away, wasted to nothing, rotted, sometimes blind, dementing as the virus attacked the very thing that made them who they were; these calls from these screaming, wailing men made us all too aware that Chris was soon to be added to the list of the lost. As he comforted his grieving friends with words that could not soothe, he heard his own death rattle down the telephone line.

We went down to 'Dirty Nellie's', once and once only – too painful to return – but mostly we stayed in. His only other outings were to Barts, only to have the boxes of his demise ticked off, one by one. Another bout of PCP, a throat infection, peripheral neuropathy – the troops were mustering, calling him home, and his flares of anger – at us, at his sickness, at the world, began to subside to resignation and he spent more and more time in bed and I was going less often, partly as there was little I could do, partly because I felt it was important for he and Vince to have some time alone, together, such little time, but mostly because it was so agonising to see this man, that I had loved dearly, sworn at, adored, bought endless pints for, my Wilfred Weed, wither and become nothing. No life left. Smaller and smaller he became, and more ready to leave.

One Sunday, I was at home listening to John moaning about something as usual and the phone rang.

"Nige, its Vince. Chris is back in Barts, the PCP has come back. Could you come?"

"Of course. Half an hour, tube depending."

"You can't go out, dinner's nearly ready," said John.

"I'll see you later. I have to go."

"You spend too much time with those two."

"SHUT UP YOU SELFISH OLD CUNT. SHOVE YOUR DINNER UP YOUR ASS."

And I left.

At the hospital, Vince was waiting outside the room.

"Thanks for coming".

"Of course. Why wouldn't I?"

"It's bad this time."

"Can I go in?"

"Yes, but I think he's asleep."

There lay my friend. Thin and grey and small, tubes everywhere like some monstrous anemone and machines whirring and beeping. My friend, who, I could see, was not long for this world.

Suddenly he opened his eyes and looked straight at me and said, in barely a whisper,

"Oh, it's you. You're a cunt." And then laughed, but it ended up as a fit of coughing and gasping, so bad the nurse had to come and do something; I don't know what, as I'd been shooed out and was standing next to Vince.

"Really. Thanks for coming. He asked for you." And then he just crumpled, slid down the wall and lay in a sobbing heap on the floor of the corridor.

"It's OK, mate. Well, it's not OK, but you know what I mean."

"I won't have a life without him. Who will look after ME?" and he sobbed and sobbed, like he had lost everything in his world. Which, soon, he will have.

I realised what he'd said.

"Oh fuck, no. Not you too?"

He just nodded dumbly.

Just then the nurse came out.

"He wants to see you again. You can go back in. And DON'T wind him up."

I went in. He was breathing normally again.

"No," I said. *"You're a cunt. A cunt for doing this. A cunt for getting sick. And a CUNT for leaving us."*

"Stop swearing. I find it offensive. And don't fuckin cunt me, you cunt. I need a wazz," and he started to get up. He got to one elbow, paused, turned to me, held out his skinny, tube-laden arms and said,

"I'm so sorry, about all this.".

He continued in a reedy voice, pushing through the effort it was costing him, simply to breathe...

"Funny y'know – lying here in bed all time, you get to thinking. About life – 'specially when you don't have much left. You appear quite in it a lot, as it goes. Fuckin' typical- can't even have me last moments without you fuckin' in it! I was remembering stuff you know, when things were happier, not so fucked up and horrible. Stuff we did. Do you remember that night I took you to the Salisbury and told you about the hankies? You should've seen your face! Hell of a funny....! And then you got off with that smarmy twat – what was his name....? Oh yeah – Steve. Cunt he was, an all...broke your virgin heart, I remember. I warned you, but you were just a dopey cunt, as usual....I wonder what happened to him?

It was nice, if painful, to reminisce...:

I said, *"We had some laughs though eh? What about the time you thought it was a good idea to go to The Pigeons, after the club? We were already pissed and had no money left but...."*

Chris seemed to find energy with the joy of remembering.

"Oh yeah! Christ, I'd forgotten about that. Those two blokes we met... What were they called?

"Dunno. Anyway, YOU met them, not me. I just got dragged along, as usual. We never found out. You called them Rupert and Tarquin or something. They had a big fuck-off car..."

"Yellow! It was yellow!"

"That's it! A Porsche. A fucking yellow Porsche, with the top down. And they said "Let's go up West!" And you said. "FUCK YEAH!" and you just jumped in. I really should have stayed behind....."

"But you didn't though, did you? "

"We didn't even know where we going...I remember we were all singing and the roof was open. What was it again...that Chic thing...'Use it up, wear it out'! That was it! Remember?"

He paused, searching his memory, a memory ravaged by his virus...

"SPATS. That was it! That little club on...um....Oxford Street. Middle of the fuckin' night it was!"

"Yeah, and we had no money and Tarquin and Roops...no! Oliver! It was Oliver!.. had buggered off...Brilliant".

"Yeah, but my plan worked though..."

"What happened? We obviously got home...."

"Yeah well, both of us offered to get the drinks for a drunk bloke who was getting a round in for his pissed mates only we legged it up the stairs with the money, and got the night bus home! Fuckin' brilliant!"

"I'm not a bad man, but you made me do terrible things....my Mum would've given you a Golden Ear Whizz..."

"Fuckin' hilarious that was..."

Just then, the nurse came in, because Chris fell into another bout of coughing, deep, ravaging his lungs.

"I told you not to wind him up," she said crossly.

"Sorry", I said. *"We were just remembering. Laughing about when the world wasn't so fucked up and our lives lay ahead of us. Now, here we are, only six years later...."*

"Yeah, sorry about that, Nurse Rached", Chris said.

"Cheeky little sod you are!", she said and patted his arm.

"Lungs get clogged up. Bastard, innit?"

"Fuckin' attention seeking, if you ask me..."

I suddenly had another thought, some distant stirring of the good times we'd had together.

"I've remembered something else. ANOTHER brilliant wheeze you had. Napoleon's. Remember that?

This just made him laugh, and choke again. Maybe we should stop this, but the memories seem to enliven him,

"Trying to kill me, are you? Yeah, I remember. You nearly got shagged by a group of millionaires. Beer goggles."

"How did we get in? Members only, wasn't it?"

"Yeah, but the doorman thought we were rent...."

" Oh yeah, that's right...he let us in, and there was this group of blokes in the VIP area. We were going to get champagne and...and then I was going to go over and sit with them and..."

"Yeah, and in return for the poncey drink, they got to shag you. Gang banged, you woulda bin. Good job I was there, to save you. As usual."

"Save me? We wouldn't have BEEN there if it wasn't for you! Anyway, we got chucked out. Thanks to you."

"Me? What did I do?"

"Made me order two pints – for a change – and I tried to pay with a fiver. It came to about fifteen quid, we got sussed and the security came over and threw me out on the street. You called the doorman a slimy old cunt, and we ran away. Into the night. With no money. Again. I don't remember how it ended..."

"But you actually got thrown out of 'Napoleon's'. How fuckin' cool was that? When I'm gone, you'll be telling people about it for years. You could write a memoir and put all this stuff in it. That's something else you can thank me for.

"Oh, Chris, you have NO idea how much have to thank you for..."

"Oh don't start getting' all fuckin' mopey. It is what it is. I'm just glad I got to see you. For the last time, I expect.

Suddenly, in to the quiet space that had opened, he said,

"You won't forget me, will you?"

I had no answer.

And I hugged him, so thin, so light, ephemeral, a man of no substance at all.

What could I say? Not much, really, as by this time, the lump in my throat was the size of the world.

"Help me to the bog?"

And he struggled to standing and shuffled towards the door, a man of 110 years old. *"And get me fags out of the drawer. I think Vince smuggled some in."*

"FAGS? You're not supposed to smoke! You've got PCP for Chrissakes!"

"Oh shut up you twat. What difference is it going to make? Come on! Don't just stand there, strarin' like a knob. I need a wazz. Help me to the bog. You can get me a pint while I'm in there......" Telling stories, even now...

We shuffled across the corridor, his drip stand swaying, to the toilet, where he disappeared. Next, we heard what would have been a shout if he'd had the breath:

I CAN'T GET UP! I'M STUCK ON THE BOG! You fuckin' pair of…I cant' get up, me drips caught..oh, fer FUCK'S SAKE!! he wheezed through lungs full of his own body fluids.

We went into the toilets and there he was, door open as he hadn't been able to manoeuvre the drip stand in as well, pyjamas round his ankles, unable to find the strength to rise. In another world, a world full of light and joy, it would have been hilarious. But it wasn't. It was sad and heart breaking and just another indignity.

We squeezed in, Vince and I, and pulled him upright.

"And you Felicia, don't be looking at my cock. We're not at Balls Park now, you tart."

Gallows humour of the blackest hue. And memory laden, with love and courage and making the best of a situation worse than any I could have imagined.

We got him back in to the corridor and he croaked,

"Vince, get me a chair? I want to sit out here for a bit."

It was the end of visiting, almost and my heart could stand no more for this session.

"Look," I said. *"I'm fucking off now. I'll try to get back tomorrow."*

"Fuckin good job. You were getting on me tits," he croaked. *"And if you're going to the pub when you get home, say hello to that old cunt you live with and thank him 'for all he dun for us boys and gels'. And have one on me. Mine's a lager. Don't start fuckin moanin. It's the last one. Think of the money you'll save. You always were a tight – arsed cunt".*

And of course, he was right. The last time I'd buy him a lager, and he wouldn't be there to drink it and then piss off to the bog when it was his round.

"John says to say….."

"No, he didn't but thanks for the thought. Now fuck off. You twat. Twatty cunt. Hahahaa, he gurgled, and then he lit a fag. Right there, where he sat.

"PUT THAT OUT!!!" shouted the Nurse. So he just threw in the bin hanging on the wall beside him. It caught light and as I watched, he became wreathed in smoke from the paper that was in the bin.

Another memory swam up through the sorrow.

"Chris, do you remember that time you dropped a fag in the waste paper bin, and nearly set the flat alight? No firemen this time though....

"Yeah", he wheezed, *"that was fuckin' funny too. I think I shagged one of 'em, didn't I?*

Yes, Chris. You did. Would've been rude not to, after all the trouble they'd gone to.."

I then realised what he had done. He had orchestrated this, from the start. You wily old rogue...

"A final gift, eh? Thank you, my friend. Thank you".

We all waited, the three of us, for some clue as to what to do next. I leant into him and said quietly, into his ear:

"Do you remember our song? You said we were going to sit a on park bench together. You said that, by then, we'd be too old to give blow jobs. We'd have to take our teeth out. Seems like that won't happen ow, eh? I am sorry. Chris. I am so sorry...."

I began walking away down the slope of the corridor and when I got to the door, I turned back, like Lot, and I could see him, sitting in his chair, and by then, billowing out of the bin were plumes of black smoke just as he'd set the bin on fire in Wakefield Road, in our teacher's flat, so many centuries ago, back when the world was kind and funny and not fucked up, but without the firemen this time, and he was looking at me, looking at me and laughing, through the glue in his lungs that was consuming his very life. Laughing, laughing.

That image is what stays with me. Not the shrunken hollow man he'd become but the laughing rebel, wreathed in smoke from the burning waste bin. Class.

I rang from home; a couple of pints later and he'd gone. Just like that. He'd gone back to bed and with Vince lying on the bed, entwined, beside him, he breathed his last breath and was no more. So that had been my last sight.

Oh! Clever Chris – his last gift was one of comedy and irreverence not a dreadful bedside gurgling departure. He'd seen me and had given himself permission to go. That thought sustained me in all the bleak months and years to come, when I could really REALLY have done with him to stop me fucking up, which I did with ineffable style in the future that was mine to come. Without him in it.

In 'Old Friends', by Paul Simon, there's a line about being old and sharing a park bench and saying how strange it would be to be 70. We liked that song; it was ours.

'Old friends. Old friends.

Can you imagine us, Years from today,

Sharing a park bench quietly?

How terribly strange,To be seventy.

Old friends,

Memory brushes the same years,

Silently sharing the same fear...'

(Paul Simon, 'Old Friends')

The last photo I have of him. Dying, but smiling.....

The funeral took place on the 16th October, 1987. We'd had massive problems with all the local undertakers as their pall – bearing staff all refused to carry Chris's coffin unless they could wear rubber gloves and masks. Yes, dear reader, this is the truth. All the ones in the area made the same stipulation and in all of those offices, Vince, like a smoter of vermin, said: *'WELL YOU CAN ALL GO AND FUCK YOURSELVES. I WILL BE WRITING TO THE PRESS ABOUT THIS, YOU BUNCH OF IGNORANT CUNTS'*, before going around the corner and sobbing in my arms.

In the end we reached an agreement with one firm that they would supply the cars for free (funny how the threat of a bit of bad publicity changes people's minds) and we would carry the coffin. Vince, me and four of their friends who were still fit enough, did the honours. As we brought the coffin out of the house, they took great delight in telling the Director, in his black hat and tails, and his *cronies 'LOOK OUT!! WE'VE ALL GOT AIDS, YOU KNOW!! ALL OF US!!'* and watching the ignorant terror in their faces. Anyway, Chris was stowed in the back, mourners were in the cars and off we went and oh! What sweet revenge! It was the day after the Great Storm, October 17th '87 and the road all the way across the Flats was strewn with broken branches, all of which the Mute, the arrogant cunt, had to stop, bend, and pick up and move as we proceeded. HA HA HAAAAA!! This meant it took AGES, and he would have been late for his next job. What was that quaking? Oh, yes – that would have been Chris, laughing his bollocks off in the back.

The funeral passed in a blur. Julie was there, but there was little to say – this was the man who'd stolen her life away, and yet here she was. We didn't speak; there wasn't much to say. We just smiled small sad smiles at each other, of understanding, of recognition, of knowing this was OUR parting too, as we both said goodbye to the man that had changed both our lives forever. All I remember is that on the flowers that John and I (who had also deigned to attend) had brought was attached a label, with our (my) message of condolence. And in inside the little bag were some coins: three 10s, a 5p, and 2p and a 1/2p. You bastard!!!! When we lived together, aeons ago, one of us has spilt beer on the electric fire and the element had blown. The new one cost 75p and he'd paid for it, and forever after, drunk, as a joke, or in anger, he would say, *"You owe me 37 1/2p for the element."* I'd always promised I'd pay but never did and it became our standing joke. So, I thought as a final and irrevocable joke, I'd put in in the envelope and it would be burned with him as the coffin was burned. But no. The ushers had collected all the bouquets and there it was – the money, NOT paid back after all, so he could tell all the angels what a tight arsed cunt I was. As I say – class,

I've had this, all these years, to remind me what an arse he was!

We went sadly back to Burghley Road, to a house less full, a house stripped of its power, for the 'do', which, given the circumstances went from sombre (most of the guests were facing the same future) to euphoric (from a sense of relief that all the pain was done, the event went off smoothly and there was no more to be done.) There was one table of food, and about eight tables of drink, probably on Chris' instructions. We all stood around, awkwardly for a while until the alcohol hit our bloodstream and forced the sadness out, at least for now.

"Shall we go?" said John. *"I've had enough and I have to drive."*

"Go on then," I replied, gin fuelled and manic, *"I'm staying. I promised I'd look after Vince."*

Without argument, for once, maybe recognising both the importance of the event and the fact that he'd be wasting his breath, he left. No goodbyes, no words of thanks or comfort. Fuck off then. And I returned to the bar.

In the front room, Vince was surrounded by his friends, a group I was no part of. A special, select group who all shared something so intimate, so indivisible, that it was 'members only'. The one thing that bound them, made them close, made them stronger was the one thing that would kill them all. And, to offset this fact, they drank, and drank and shouted LIFE! to the skies above; raised their paper cups to each other and to an enemy they could not vanquish. 'L'CHAIM' to their shrinking world.

Seeing that Vince was (for now) OK, I returned to the kitchen for more alcohol.

"Hi," he said. *"I'm Bill. A friend of Vince."* Middle aged, cropped hair, firm body, nice packet etc etc....all taken in in an instant.

"Oh, hi. I'm a friend of Chris. Was a.....".

Two 'Hi's'. Contract made.

"Must've been popular. Good turnout..."

"Yes, he was. I will miss him; he was a very special man" I said, but I wasn't really listening as, gin addled, my attention was now fully on the hair that was poking out of the neck of his shirt. There was that silence where the things that needed to be thought were thought, and then we looked at each other and Bill said, *"OK. Shall we go upstairs? I don't suppose anyone will miss us..."*

"OK", I replied. *"Come on."*

O and **K.** Two small letters that have defined my life.

So we did. We went upstairs, and he fucked me. On Chris' bed. A Funeral Fuck. A Fuck for the Fallen. It was beautiful, it was sweaty and hard, he was as beautiful undressed as clothed, and it was redemptive. Covered in sweat and cum, we lay gasping, and smiling, with Chris looking down and saying: *"Nice one!"* I felt no guilt, no shame, only that somehow it was the only thing that would have made this shitty shitty day right. Gin and cock. It worked.

We returned to the party. Many people had left, others were unconscious, and there sat Vince, drunk and alone, more alone that he even knew yet. He saw me, saw Bill, nodded, smiled a small smile and raised a thumb. A benediction and a recognition that life goes on – people will still fuck, drink, cook and toil, and somehow, so would he.

He did. I know he found another soul to love; comforting and a solace but never a replacement for Christopher Hartley, drink blagger extraordinaire and all-round wonder. Vince lived for some years more, doing good work, buddying the infected, nursing the dying until he too succumbed in April 1992. Five years of living, but only half living, as his reason for being had gone. The piano silent and unplayed now, gathering to it, the motes of dust in the sun coming through the unopened curtains.

Chris' mug, made some 45 years ago now, holding pens and memories.

Did you know, *kintsukori* is Japanese art the of repairing broken pottery by mending the areas of breakage with lacquer, dusted or mixed with powdered gold; it treats the breakage and repair as part of the history of an object, rather than something to disguise? Broken many long years and repaired (with Superglue, not gold!) making it more beautiful, to me that is, and all the memories it holds more precious.

Where did they go, those lovers, each at their separate hour? Where is the sheet music, marked and scored in pencil as he composed? Where are the Steve Reich LPs, the great grey steel pistons they proudly used as ash trays? Where are the Doc Martins (18 lacers), the camouflage trousers, the love letters, the handcuffs? Who has them? Who has kept these doomed boys alive? Me. Chris lives on in this story and in the mug he made standing on my desk holding my pens. In the photos of Wilfred Weed and the drunken poems he wrote and I keep in my trunk and my heart. And Vince lives on in the letters he wrote to me after Chris left us and his heart was so broken the pages are stained with his tears. And in this poem he wrote when he thought he'd never rise again.

'Soft, For the Music Dies.'

Soft, for the music dies within this room
Where once the bridge that Heaven sings
to man, returning him to grace,
is an empty space.
Soft, for music never silenced never can return
and we the living must, its passing mourn
sighing in the gloom.

Soft, still within the silence lives the love
he crafted here upon an earthly stave;
the song, moon slivered nights and sunscaped days.
Soft, threading memory stakes the muted claim
which we, the living, tearful, bear the blame
denial of our grave.

Soft. Dying music's timbre strikes the note
discordant; chaos brings the age of truth
to him; returns all harmony and places times innocence.
Soft, here lies the living ache, seek the dawn of melodies.
Each day his love reborn sustains undying hopes.

Vince Lively, January 1988.

I wish I had written this, this elegy, which conveys the desolation and sorrow in the lack of music and love which had sustained them both. But I didn't. Poor desolate wandering Vince did, and I include it as a tribute to him and to my dear dear friend who had left us both.

Chris was gone. Bill drove me home, asked if we could meet again because the sex was awesome and I was a really nice man…. but of course I said no. I had John, I had my job, the animals, the flat….it was a tempting but completely unreal thought – yes! Run away with this sexy man and not have to think about any of that stuff! Go! GO!!. But of course, the reality was that no matter how gorgeous he was, how beautiful were his cock and chest and eyes, that fuck was just medicine and a final goodbye to my best friend in a weird kind of homage – life goes on in the face of death and it was necessary to prove it to myself.

I thanked him, kissed him gently goodbye, knowing somehow it was a goodbye pretty much to everything. He drove away, and left me standing on the corner of Pretoria Avenue, full of gratitude, and some hope for the rest of my life.

It became crystal clear, in an instant. As the car drove away, with it went the last thing connecting me to this place.

What did I know? What did I know that I didn't know 12 years before, when all bright eyed and bushy tailed, full of testosterone and hope, with my gal on mah arm, I arrived in London?

I know that the streets are not paved with gold. They are strewn with shit; broken hearts, rubbish boyfriends, (well, not rubbish boyfriends – it was just ME that was rubbish at HAVING one. Or four.), failed employment, dying young men, and a dead friend, for a start. I thought the years had been kind but when I kaleidoscoped them all together, it had all been pretty fucked up. And now, with the last thread cut, and turned to ash, there was nothing to keep me here. I didn't care what John wanted to do – he could come or stay. I wasn't even sure why we were together – feeling sorry for him because he couldn't read and his dago boyfriend had chawed all his money wasn't really a very good basis for a relationship. We had no financial ties; I had a decent salary and was therefore independent, so……and yet, and yet….as I stood on that corner, wreathed in exhaust fumes and grief, my arse full of semen and my heart full of sorrow, I felt…..I felt….obliged to look after the old fart somehow. A decision that would bite me on the arse, as it turned out, but then, at that moment, my heart softening, I felt that I couldn't really leave him behind. And darling Sam, a big boy now, was firmly lodged in my heart too, and so...so we all had to go. As a family.

I went in, sober now.

"John," I said. *"I'm moving back to Cornwall. You can come with me if you want. With the pets. But I AM going. I can't be here now."*

"Fuck me!" he said. *"That's come out of nowhere. What brought that on? Did something happen at the funeral?"* If only you knew, I thought, but chose not to enlighten him.

'If you have to ASK........' I thought, but said: *"I just think it's time for a change of scene. It will be nice* (for me) *to be nearer my parents and Gill's back there. You like her, don't you. It will be nice. Back near the sea, the high cliffs...."*

And as I spoke, I knew how right I was. It was like a flower reopening, as I thought about returning to the place I truly belonged.

"So, I'll start looking for jobs, when I get back on Monday. Fancy a pint? Time for last orders..."

We went in to the pub and I got a couple of beers.

"Sorry, I left early. But. You know. What with the pets an' all........!"

I knew he wasn't very good round death and dead people or even dying ones and I was glad he HAD gone. If he had stayed, Bill wouldn't have fucked me and there would not have been that seminal moment (no pun intent ended) where I knew that it was all done. Over. That paradigm shift from sorrow to strength of purpose. Here's Chris saying: *'Stop fuckin mopin about, you miserable cunt. Get on with it, do something new.'* And with his permission, I was about to.

"Another pint?" I said, sure that even HE wouldn't have a hissy fit, tonight of all nights.

"Go on then. One for the M11......"

"Stay there, I'll get them," I said, and went to the bar.

Then, some *BASTARD* put on Level 42, singing *'It's Over'*; that, coupled with John inadvertently quoting Rod, undid me. The strong beer I was drinking had reactivated the gallons of gin I'd consumed and I fell to pieces, right there, in my local, in front of Alan, the butch barman, in front of the quiz team, in front of John. In front of the WHOLE FUCKING BASTARD WORLD.

MY BEST FRIEND WAS DEAD. DEAD. DEAD. DEAD. DEAD.

All these hours and weeks and months of knowing he was dying, watching him turn from man to ghost, watching him choking on his own body fluids as he STILL sought to reassure me, and even apologise, became all too much. I just shattered, broke in to shards of grief. And I wept. And sobbed. And wailed like a lost soul.

I just clung to the bar rail, while everyone stared.

"It's OK. His friend just died."

"Oh, I'm sorry," said Alan. *"Was he young?"*

"'Bout 45."

"Oooh, that's young. What was it?"

"Oh, erm," said John, *"Pneumonia, I think."* and he prised my fingers off the bar rail and began to drag me out of the pub, before, presumably, I could mention THE 'A' WORD, which would, by association, mark *him* out as a poof, a homo, a queer.....like no-one knew, with his Village People moustache, his flappy hands and the fact we lived together in a one bedroom flat right next to the pub......

"It wasn't poomomia. Noomomia. It was...."

"Never mind, come on. Sorry, Alan, he's just a bit upset..." he said,

......and dragged me away, sobbing, snotty, gasping for air, crying in the way only a drunk man can cry. In act of gentleness, uncharacteristic, as it would've involved showing feelings, he lay me gently on the bed, and stayed with me until I fell asleep.

I didn't eat for days, went to school, and rehashed old lesson plans as I seemed to be unable to think properly. How could he be dead? He'd ALWAYS been there, guiding, swearing, loving me. Dead? No, not him. Yet he was, and I knew that I was on my own – John was about as much use as a chocolate fireguard, and I seemed to be working on autopilot, running on empty.

"I'm really sorry about your friend," said Sue, resting her hand gently on mine. "You seem very upset…..maybe….maybe you should get away from here, and all the things that remind you?"

Before this small act of kindness could undo me, I forced down the lump that was threatening to block my vocal cords and voiced my decision. As Kate Bush once said: 'Even saying it can really make it happen' – I said: "I am. I have already decided. I'm going home."

"No, I meant away away………."

"That's what I meant too. Not home to the flat; home to HOME. Cornwall. Back home. Where I should never had left and then none of this would have happened. I wouldn't have gone to College, never have met Chris. He would still have died but it wouldn't have mattered because I wouldn't have even known him. I can't stay here now, I just can't…" and burst, once more into a spate of uncontrollable weeping.

"For fuck's sake, stop crying, you tart. No wonder you haven't got any friends. You're such a miserable cunt that's why. It's not all about you, you know. And you're FORTY FUCKIN TWO! Grow a pair, get another job and do something useful. Anyway, think how much beer money you'll be saving…"

I heard his voice, and my tears turned to smiles and then to resolve.

I went to staff room and picked up the Times Ed. Supp. and began to search. And, as if he was guiding me, there it was: a job, in a school, in North Cornwall, not far from Truro where Ma and Pa were now living. It was like Fate or Providence, or maybe just Mr Lucky had returned – and the interviews were still two weeks away.

So.

Phone call; speak to nice lady with Proper Accent, you.

Interview invite.

Train to Cornwall.

Stay at Mum and Dad's. (No mention of anything remotely homosexual or connected to me or my life).

Interview. In purple suit.

Hand shaken and 'welcomed aboard'.

Train back to London.

Resignation from Handsworth.

 Leaving party.

Get away with dry humping Sue and fiddling with her lummies. (God, I KNOW!! I have NO idea...)

Start packing......

This was easier said than done. John had to sell his little van and all his Trill and cuttlefish (*LAHVELY! AN ONLY A PAHND!*) about which he was not happy, but I reasoned we'd have little use for it at the other end so the money would be more useful. And NOT for going to the pub every bloody day, while still working. Pack, man. PACK! Pack up all your horrible tatt, and cheap print of the *'Crying Boy', 'The Blue Russian'* bint and *'The Wings of Love'* with the two naked people enfolded in giant swan's wings. Jeez. Am I REALLY gay? I want O'Keefe and Klimt, John Lewis and Libertys, not this old shit! But, it was *quid pro quo*, and I was taking the boy out of Lahndahn.....only fair he should have his stuff I suppose....

Anyway, I worked up till the end of the Spring term, of '88 and, leaving John amidst the chaos of boxes and cat hair, went back to Cornwall and to my Mum and Dad' as my house (£28,000! Bargain!) had still to be finalised. So I moved in with them for what seemed like eternity, though it was in fact only six weeks. In the spare room, me and Sade,

> *"I still, really love you, love is stronger than pride......"*

Over and over, Sade crooned, but unsure who I was playing it for......

...struggling to have any conversation that didn't include ANY details of the last twelve years of my life. Mum DID ask about Chris; she knew he'd been ill but had never asked what with, probably guessing and therefore that too was out of bounds. I had taken Chris down to Newquay once during a school holiday, long long ago, and I remember my Mum saying, in a hurried whispered conversation (in the very same bedroom my Dad had caught me sucking Peter off! Lol what delicious irony*!*), *"He's a very nice boy, you know....for one of those. I hope you're being careful?"* (Mother, what ARE you implying??). *"There's this awful new disease going round. I saw it on the telly.*

It had the nice John Hurt, and it had lilies and everything". I just told her he'd died and left it at that. Another anonymous passing, cloaked in shame.

Julie was of more interest, (naturally) but I didn't have much news.

Ummmm…..no, I really am NOT going to get back together with her.

Ummmmm……no there really aren't any nice girls (they're not girls, they're *women*) at my new school. Well, there are, but they're married and / or straight. And anyway, what difference would it make?

Ummmmmm…….hope you won't be lonely in your new house on your own. Who will do the cooking for you? FFS! This is 1988 not 1833. I WILL! ME! USELESS LI'L ME……

I should add that at this point they didn't know about John – and probably just as well. For now. The six weeks passed agonisingly slowly, with Dad ringing the solicitor about eight times a day, implying that he was useless and what was he paying him for…? Yes, dear reader – my Father had agreed to loan me the money for the house purchase – yet something else he would hurl at me for the rest of his life when I did something he didn't agree with. Which was pretty much all the time. And THIS is why I'd decided not to mention John – another Spawn of Satan who went around sodomising everyone, no doubt! Another fully paid-up member of the SSU! He certainly wouldn't have agreed to 'promote the homosexual lifestyle' by lending me the money. That's why he thought I was coming on my own. Leaving London and its perversions; leaving the sins of the flesh and returning to Cornwall where, as if by magic, there would be no men's peni to tempt me! His boy – no longer a Union member, and now an upstanding pillar of the community and all-round good egg. Well, *'two outa three ain't bad'*, as Meatloaf once said.

There was cock aplenty, as I was to discover, but for now, I had my own supply waiting for me back up north of the Tamar; I'm afraid to admit that, really, that was ALL he was – so why may you ask, was I bringing him with me. 'Cuz I luv im' wasn't really true. I suppose it was some kind of security – new Job, new house, new social circle…maybe a bit too scary on my own. I don't know, but whatever….

…the house came through, I got the keys, moved out of Uplands Crescent and in to my own house. Mine. The first thing I had ever owned. Well, Barclays bank owned it, but you know what I mean. All it needed now, as I walked through the echoing council house rooms (Cheers Maggie! 'Right To Buy'! Right for me!) was furniture, and my dog. Oh, and John. So, off I went, back to London, back to Walthamstow, back to the tiny flat caked in dog hair and smelling of cat piss, stacked in every corner with John's furniture and I knew that I had made the right decision.

We hired a van, and set off, axles scraping the tarmac, everything we owned, plus the cats, the dogs, all drugged up to the eyeballs, squashed in to every available space and, given that Sam was now the size of a small horse, this was no mean feat. Even Freddie had decided it wasn't *'quite nice'* after all and had withdrawn under his wing, fortunately – given the van weighed about 400 tons and therefore our speed was likely to be about 30mph, him shouting *QUITE NICE!* For the next 36 hours was not an appealing thought.

However, we were on our way. All regrets packed up along with the boxes of shit I had determined I would gradually lose/break/sell over time until it (and its accompanying smell of animal faeces and bad memories) had gone and been replaced with new, to go with my New Life.

M4.....

M5.....

A30.....

Home.

Sorted! I was free! A proper homosexualist, with a BF, a house, a job and a future. I wasn't going to die 'old and lonely', thank you very much. I had shagged my way round the East End, drunk the barrels dry. I had 'found myself'! I'd gone looking – from Newquay to Hertford, through Blackheath and Deptford, to Leyton, Leytonstone and Walthamstow – not a particularly salubrious journey, but just as surely as other explorers, as surely as Mungo Park had found the Niger and Dr. Livingstone, the Victoria Falls, I had, knowingly or not, found my goal. True, I was currently lumbered with an oaf and several malodorous animals, but I DID have the aforementioned material things AND, more importantly, I had ME and the sense that being a big old poof wasn't a death sentence, an affliction, or something not to be seen or heard in Polite Society. I liked me. I liked my life. I liked men and their willies and was no longer afraid of such a notion.

I thought back to that long-ago pavement, outside *'Brief Encounter'*, with dear Chris, Chris the Skinhead, lost and not knowing where I belonged exactly. Which hanky should I have? Which side should I wear it? And I realise, now, that none of that matters. I YAM WHAT I YAM, and if you don't like it, you can go fuck yourself. I'm not in a group, I'm not a 'type' (though I most definitely HAD a type, so it was just as well there WERE types, or I wouldn't have a type to like), I don't wear any identifiable uniform.....was THIS what is was all about? Blending in? Being Normal? I bloody well hope not! After all the blood, sweat and tears (actually, not blood; substitute that for 'cum') that I'd been through, all the heartache and betrayals and betrayings – I hadn't waded through this amount of shit to come out the other end NORMAL.

Although......

......what was about to happen? I had a wife (read: John), 2.4 kids (read: dogs and cats), a house, a 9-5 (well, 8 – 7.30) job and a mortgage....you don't get much more normal than that. Bugger.

I wanted it to be......I don't know...GLORIOUS! SPARKLY! NOISY AND RAINBOW COLOURED!!! Instead, I was in a van, heading for suburban oblivion, with a load of shit furniture, 5 crapping machines and a man I knew I didn't love.

M4.....

M5.....

A30.....

Roads to Cornwall, the land of my birth, the place my heart resides. And the place that would eventually see me shrink, waste away and become SO small, you wouldn't even know I was there.....

I couldn't decide if I was lucky or not. Probably not, on balance.

We parked up.

There it is, in the middle. The white one.

Now what? Who knew? And if I had known, would I have come…..?

'Fings could only get bettah', said Howard Jones, back in '85. How wrong could he be? Although……in the end, he was right…….but not until they'd got worse.

A whole lot worse.

Part 3.

Mr Lucky Finds His Way Home.

CHAPTER FIFTEEN.

FINGS AIN'T WOT THEY USED TO BE.....

<u>In which our hero returns to the land of the Gods, becomes bamboozled and then finds himself a SGWM (GSOH, DDF) who would like a LTR. (Someone who isn't a tosser would be good).</u>

'Crash'.

By The Primitives. No.15. April 1988.

'So shut, shut your mouth
'Cause I'm not listening anyhow
I've had enough, enough of you
Enough to last a lifetime through...'

"Please...just **SHUT UP**. I've had enough......"

~ ~ ~

M4.

M5

A30....

We arrive at our new house. It was late. SO late. The van barely made it up the incline to the car park, but after what seemed like days of travelling, we were there. Brand new life. Me, John, Snowy, Sooty, Prince, Lena, Sam and Freddie. Everyone pissed off, tired, needing a wee. All of us.

"Ooooh! I need a slash," said John. *"Like, **now**. The animals will too,"* and with that he opened the door and the dogs, startled awake, all jumped out and started weeing like it was the finals of The Great Weeing Competition. Up against car tyres and in people's front gardens.

There was a gap in the hedge so we two went through it and wee'd, in the only way you can when you've been sitting for hours and hours then you stand and gravity takes over and there is nothing you can do to prevent the weight of liquid seeking its escape. So we wee'd, and wee'd, John me, while the dogs ran round like things possessed, and when we'd finished, we went back to the open van and found the cats had gone. Fer fuck's SAKE!!! We'd only been here five minutes......

"SNOOOOOOWY! SOOOOOOOTY!!!" bellowed John, who had gone from blissful to ballistic in the blink of a zip. *"WHERE ARE YOOOOOO?"*

"SHHHHHH! Shut up! You'll have the neighbours on at us. It's nearly midnight."

"I DON'T FUCKING CARE. I'VE LOST ME CATS!!!!. THE NEIGHBOURS CAN GO AND FUCK THEMSELVES. SNOOOOOOOOWY!! SOOOOOOOTY!!! COME ON!! WHERE ARE YOOOOOO?" and with that he took off, over the hedge, through the trees in the pitch black. All I could hear was snapping of branches and OW! and OUCH! FUCK! and OW! MY FUCKIN FACE! as he plunged like a madman through the trees.

Lights began appearing at windows, in our little *cul – de – sac*. Not a propitious start for the two poofs and their menagerie.....

"Can I help?" said someone.

"Oh, no, its OK. We've just arrived and lost the cats. My...er friend is trying to find them."

"FUCKING CUNTING CATS!" bellowed John as he appeared over the hedge, bloodied and scratched in the dim lights from people's windows.

"Ah, John. This is one of our new neighbours. Mrs.....?"

"Val. You can call me Val." (Fag hag. That's a good sign).

"Ok, er..Val, Sorry to have disturbed you. John's just worried about his two...."

...cats, which were sitting by the front wheels of the van, looking completely unperturbed by all the noise.

"They're there, John. Look. By the van..."

John ran down the grass to the van, yelling SNOOOOWY!!! SOOOOTY! and the cats, understandably alarmed, legged it. Oh god no....

"COME BACK!!!! COME BACK!!! SNOOOOOWY PUSS PUSS PUSS!!! SOOOOOOTY!! COME ON HERE!! HERE!!! PUSSS PUSS..

"They're not going to come back with you yelling at them. Just leave them they'll be back. Shut up fer Chrisssakes. Its past midnight........Val, I'm so sorry..."

"No, Really. It's fine. It's been......interesting" ....as in: it'll be all round the neighbourhood before dawn that two poofs are moving to no.64....

We'd had the foresight to put a mattress and some sheets on the van last. So, after pacifying John, who was by now practically sobbing, we dragged the mattress out and across the grass, possibly smearing it in dogshit, but I was past caring, and in to the house. No64. My very own house.

We dragged the shit-smeared mattress in to the lounge and then John disappeared and came back with the dogs, who were bounding around like mad things and Freddy, who by this time had decided it was *'QUITE NICE!'* again and kept saying so.

Freddy shouting, John snoring, the dogs pacing and whining – engulfed by the tang of canine excrement, I think I just cried myself to sleep.

Dear reader, as you can probably guess, this was doomed to failure and it wasn't long until the cracks became far too wide for any roll of wallpaper ever made to cover; they became fissures that were never going to close. It was OK for the rest of the Easter holidays, before I started my new job (EEEEEK!) as we had domestic 'challenges' to overcome, such as how to stop the cats pissing off every time we managed to cajole them in to coming into the house. They were probably quite happy – liberated from the concrete suburbs that was Walfamstowe into the stretches of Arcadia that was The Beacon. Why WOULD they come in? They were out! They were doing cat stuff, and were not about to regress….we rarely saw them over those following three months until in the end, they never came back at all. John had moved by then so they had probably found a more peaceful solution. Decisions to be made over where to put the furniture, where the dogs were going to sleep ("NOT IN THE FUCKING BEDROOM!! NO NO NO!!!"), what John was going to do with himself now – not much chance of a job really, given his 'problem', although he did actually, after he'd moved out, get a little job in a Nursery (plants, not 4-year-olds. Thank goodness), doing God knows what, or even how. He hated it of course, and began to stop off in the pub on the way home – they had lent him a little van to transport the plants and stuff around, and so luckily we both had transport but it did mean I couldn't keep my eye on him - and I only say this from the point of view that it was ME who got the shitty end of the stick if he'd been to the pub on the way home as I'd get in to find him either asleep and the hall swimming in dog wee because he hadn't taken them out, OR just shouty and aggressive, full of blame and spite because I had *MADE* him come to this fucking place where there aren't any fucking street lights (of course there are, you silly man) and where, apparently *'nobody fucking talks properly'*….. Out of the two, I preferred the first, dog wee notwithstanding – that was moppable - I could get out in the clear air with the dogs and he'd leave me alone.

A very weird thing happened, dear reader, which I want to include as it just demonstrates what it was like dealing with my Dad. Cast your mind back a few chapters, to 'ARGHHHHHMYSONSAFUCKINHOMOGATE'. Cast out, abused by letter, shunned, and rejected….not a good time for me. Then six weeks of obsequious gratitude and living in his house with conversation restricted like we were in Stalinist Russia or something. In the end, after I'd moved, I had, of course to tell them about John. I rang one day and whilst on the phone, John yelled at one of the dogs or something, and Mum said, *"Who's that?"* and I grabbing the bull by its bollocks, decided to confide in her.

"Oh. That's john. He, um, lives here. He's erm....my...my friend. I mean boyfriend..." (he was 20 years my senior – 'boyfriend' seemed a bit stupid. 'Sugar Daddy' wasn't appropriate, as he had no sugar. Daddy then? OMG. A pattern emerging and I didn't even see it!!)

Anyway, to the phone call.

"Yes, my new...erm partner. Well, not that new actually. We've been together for a while. He's......"

"Freddy, shut the FUCK UP!! I'll shove your beak up your fucking arse if you don't stop yelling....!! came John's dulcet tones from the kitchen.

"Oh. He sounds quite um...loud," said Mum.

"He's a Londoner," was all I could think of to say.

After a few strained pleasantries, during which time we didn't speak of the huge John shaped elephant in the room, we hung up.

Half an hour later, - and I have absolutely NO IDEA what went on in their house after our call – the phone rang again.

"It's your Mother. Your Father says to bring your Friend over for tea and biscuits this afternoon. Bye." Hung up.

To say I felt surprised, is somewhat of an understatement. Head fuck! WHAT game was he playing now? But I decided we'd go. Why? Don't know. Because my Dad said so, and so I had to do it? Because I was too shocked to refuse? Because I wanted to see what would unfold? Or was it because I'd hoped there was forgiveness, reconciliation between a homophobic Father and his son? The last seemed the least likely, the most bizarre, but the option I preferred.

"John. We're going to Truro this afternoon. OK?"

"'Spose so. What for?"

"Because my Father has invited us for tea and biscuits." Even as I said it, it sounded completely unreal – I had long since given up such imaginings.

"Oh. OK," was the reply.

O. and **K**. Those two small letters, again. We all know where that leads. Usually to trouble.

So off we went, John – I kid you not – in a suit and tie, despite my protestations – to towards Truro and who knew what.

The IDEA of it, as it turned out, was nowhere NEAR as surreal as the actual event.....

We rang the bell, John and I, and waited on the doorstep – the Devil Spawned son and his equally perverted fudge-packing friend – and my terrified Mother opened the door – grey faced, impassive apart from the eyes which darted wildly to the person behind me, checking he wasn't in drag or wearing slap (this, from the woman who gave it some welly in the gay bars of Brighton...), decided it was relatively safe, remembered to say hello to me, and stood aside.

We walked in.

There he sat, my old man. In his chair, King of all he surveyed.

"Em..this is John. My....uh.......well, John. John, this is my Dad."

"Hello, Sir", said John. (Brownie point, x10). *"Pleasure to meet you. Nigel talks a lot about you."* (Nothing you'd want to hear however). And they shook hands.

"Get the teapot, Darl," he said. Teapot? TEAPOT?? *"Sit down, please."* This was getting to be a like a meeting of civil servants, in the 40s. Mr. Chalmondley-Warner. Totally doing my head in....

Mum went out to the kitchen. I followed...

"What the f...... heck is going ON????"

"I don't know. He just said to ring you. Now you're here and I really really don't know what to do...."

"Well, it seems to be OK. What the hell is he playing at?"

"I have no idea". She looked beaten. Scared.

"Look, it'll be OK. Listen...."

And there they were, homo and homophobe, the abomination and the perfect, yakking away like old mates, like they'd known each other for years.

"Trevor", called my Mother, from the safety of the kitchen, *"We need some more sugar. We'll just nip down Spar, OK?"*

No answer. Too busy talking.

We went out, glad to be out of the tension. We were AGES! Dawdling, going back to the shop to get biscuits we didn't need, stopping to introduce me to a neighbour *("He's a teacher, you know..")* When we got back, they weren't there, but we could hear voices. Looking out of the French doors, we could see down into the garden and they were, tea and fags, guffawing and hooting with glee. This was just too much. It was like a parallel universe where my Dad was a nice guy and didn't want me dead after all! There he was, talking to my lover like he was his best buddy. Super weird. The only explanation I came up with was that because John was an older man, he had somehow disassociated himself from his obsession with our bedroom activities, forgot that this man whose fags he was nicking was NOT the same person who, in his fevered imagination stuck his cock up his son's arse. Whatever the reason and however this insane meeting came about, I couldn't fathom but, as we watched them, I couldn't shake the feeling that something ghastly was going to happen. My Mum rested her hand on mine on the railing, both looking for and giving comfort.

"Oh there you are! Where's the bleddy tea? We're CHACKIN 'ere!"

"Sorry, yes. Just coming!" said my Mother / slave and hurried off to make a fresh pot which we drank in the garden, eating custard creams in the sun at Uplands Crescent. The afternoon passed in a haze of tension and well, confusion and when all the tea was drunk and the biscuits eaten, he just stood up and said,

"Well, nice to meet you. Bye"

..and went back into the house leaving us just sitting there. I was anxious not to leave Mum with whatever aftermath there may be but even more anxious for this whole charade to be over, so I stood too, said, *"Right, we'll be off too then, bye Mum. I'll ring you,"* and dragged a confused John out of the back gate, shouting *"BYE DAD!"* but not looking back.

That was the first, and last, time they met.

One of the weirdest days of my life.

So, we returned home where he immediately reverted to who was becoming an increasingly aggressive and angry man. And hit the bottle, several door frames and the bed.

As you can imagine, this whole edifice was ripe for collapse. He didn't like Cornwall, or the house, or the job, or the accent, or probably even me by now. I didn't like him, him being in my house, him getting pissed and screaming at me, chucking things around, ripping the leg off the bureau (*"Its MINE"" I'll do what I fuckin want wiv it….."*), breaking the glass in the cupboard in the sideboard…….not really conducive to harmony in the home, eh?

We used to fuck still but it was cold, mechanical, passionless, and usually only on Sundays after a session down at the Borough; he'd be pissed and 'manly' and insist on his 'congergals', as he called it, never having seen the word. So off we'd traipse up to the bedroom, he'd strip off, make himself hard, not noticing for one second that I was somewhat reluctant, as evidenced by the lack of interest in the nether regions....still, I'd lie down, put up with the perfunctory fiddling, try to make him come, to get it over with so he'd then sleep it off. But, this day, he decided he wanted a fuck. A proper fuck.

"But, John I don't really want to. I'm not in the mood...."

"You're never in the fuckin mood. My cock not good enough for you? Too big is it?"

"No, John, of course not. It's just you're a bit drunk and you always get a bit rough and you hurt me when you...."

"Well, I'll do it gentle then. You used to like it rough. What about that night back in Selina's, with the butter?" (I fancied you then, you moron).

"I know but it isn't really very....."

"OH WELL, JUST FUCK OFF THEN! YOU ONLY WANT SEX ON SUNDAYS WHEN YOU'RE PISSED (Which part of that are you not surprised about, John?). *JUST FUCKIN FORGET IT. I'LL HAVE A WANK. AS USUAL".*

"Stop yelling at me! Look I'll do that if you'd like me to...."

And I went to get hold of his erection, still really hard, fuelled by his anger no doubt and started to wank him off, but he just knocked my hand away and stormed out of the room.

"I'm going to have a drink," and he went, stark bollock naked down the stairs, his cock bobbing, leading the way, spluttering with temper. This was not looking good.

I gave him a few minutes, hoping he might just go to sleep. I went down shortly after to find him in the lounge, sprawled naked in the chair, masturbating furiously.

"SEE? I DON'T FUCKIN NEED YOU…." And he shot his load on the settee, and his legs. *"HA!. THERE!! I'M STILL A FUCKING MAN. I CAN MAKE SPUNK. NOT LIKE YOU, YOU FUCKING QUEER. ALL YOU DO IS..IS…..WHERE'S THE BRANDY? WHERE FUCKING IS IT?"*

Brandy and John were a spectacularly incendiary combination; it was what fuelled the violence between him and Carlos, and I did my best to keep him and it apart. But, not today. Naked, cock wilting and covered in his own semen, he lurched in to the kitchen, and got the (full) bottle from the cupboard. I *was* fucked, but not in a good way.

"I DON'T FUCKIN NEED YOU. I CAN HAVE SEX WITH ANYBODY. ANYBODY. EVEN ME!!" and he started pulling on his dick again….

*"ANYBODY WOULD WANT THIS. MY COCK IS MY PASSPORT TO EVERYWHERE. EVERYONE WANTS IT. 'CEPT YOU. YOU'RE A FUCKING MISERALE CUNT AND I DON'T KNOW WHY I'M HERE. TOMORROW I'M MOVING OUT. WIV ALL ME ANIMALS. OK? **OK?**"*

He looked so pathetic, naked, cock now soft and floppy, leaning on the door jamb or else he'd fall over (how the hell did he get so pissed? We'd only been to the pub and I was with him…) but although he was slowing and slurring, I was still in jeopardy.

"AND YOU. YOU FUCKIN LITTLE POOF. I'M NOT QUEER. NOT LIKE YOU. YOU PANSY. FUCKIN POOFTER….."

What? I was being abused for being gay, by a man who had just tried to stick his cock up my arse? This was now getting insane…

"John, listen…."

"I'M HAVIN A FUCKIN DRINK. YOU CAN PISS OFF IF YOU DON'T LIKE IT." And he started drinking brandy. From the bottle. This was not going to end well.

"John, look. I know this has been difficult for you. This transition. But it will get...", I started, pointlessly to say but was cut short as he hurled the bottle of brandy at me. It was a very poor aim, missed by miles, but it hit the reinforced glass window that Council houses all had at the time, the sort with a wire mesh in, and smashed. Shards of flying glass, animals bolting for cover, brandy splattering everywhere, over the furniture, the walls, the carpets and me. And *that*, dear John, was the Rubicon and you just crossed it. He lurched to his feet and went to the hall where he slithered down the wall, beneath the portrait of his Mother, and started his usual routine of *"WAHAHAAAA I'm sorry Mum. I wish I was dead. Why did you leave me blah blah....* He was slumped now naked and sad in the hallway and I, fearing for another assault, though in reality, he was done, stepped over him and headed for the door.

The End.

The next morning, as usual, he was *'really really sorry'*, and it *'wasn't really his fault'* (I thought I'd let that one pass) and *'it won't happen again'* (that one too) but I too had made a decision, so, sitting on the chair nearest the (open) back door, I said,

"Look I thought about what you said, and I agree. I think it would be a good thing to do."

"What?"

"You know, what you suggested. Yesterday......"

"What? What did I say?"

"About, you...er...you know...moving out....?"

"Oh, I was a drunk. You know. I didn't mean it."

"Oh."

"What did I say?"

"I just said. The bit about moving out. With the animals."

"I never. Did I? Well, if I did, I never meant it."

"Well, the thing is. John. I think it'd be a good idea. So, I was thinking, if we went to look for a bigger place, for you to rent for a bit – you'd get your rent paid cos you're on the dole – and then when you're settled, I could come and live there and we could rent this house out and make some money ….so let's go down town and have a look in the window. What do you think?"

I'd made this last part up. No fucking way.

"Hmmm. Yeah, ok. Sounds good. I hate this fuckin' gaff anyway. And that nosy old bitch over the other side. Come on then…"

So that's what we did, and, as if by some miracle, there was a house, sent by the Housing Angels, way WAAAY on the other side of town (in Love Lane, ironically), vacant, available, willing to take pets and ready. RIGHT NOW. Fan-fuckin-tastic.

Within two days, he was gone, all the animals and their stink, Freddie and his incessant yelling, poor Sam (who I would miss terribly but it was a good trade, if you ask me), all the ghastly furniture and the threat of violence. All gone. And…..breathe. Breathe in the clean and empty air.

I did used to go and see him (and, my bad, make him have sex – his cock and hairy chest were still a pull, even though *HE* was a wanker, but I could go home after. Shameless. Don't care!) and to take my darling boy out for long walks – he of course, along with poor old Prince and Lena were left all day as he was still working at the nursery. The cats (which miraculously had returned) were OK, because he had cut a hole in the back door….

I don't know how long this went on for – a few weeks, I think, but he suddenly announced he was going back to London, to live with Joe. Joe, his ex, with whom he had a relationship even more violent than the one he had with Carlos. To his small flat. Where they got streetlights. And they spoke propah. So he did. Packed up. Drove off. Gone. I only saw him once more.....

.....months later, I had a call from him (still alive then and not dismembered and stuffed in a freezer? Didn't know about Joe...) asking if I would be willing to take Sam back. The flat (DUH) was too small for him and he was working (as a hearse driver!! Just perfect!) and had no time to exercise him plus Joe didn't want him there and he smelled (Sam that is) and he was too big and it was Joe's flat etc etc....Yes, John, alright already! I will. End of.

So we (new chap. More later....) drove up to Gordano Services on the M5 near Bristol and he drove down from London with Sam. The poor dog got out the van, and he could barely walk. I was horrified. He was about twice as fat as when he'd left, and his nails were so long he couldn't walk properly. He saw me and hobbled over and just stood, silently, head down, before me, in recognition but also fear – fear maybe that I wouldn't take him. All anthropomorphising, I know, but there was no question. I walked over to John, this man, the man I allowed to make love to me, to do the most intimate things and I looked at him and all I felt was......nothing. Just nothing.

"Thankyou. He'll be fine now."

Sam got into the back of the car (much to Lisa's chagrin) and we drove off, back down the motorway...M4, A30, Home. Sam was home too.

CHAPTER SIXTEEN.

BACK ON THE BIKE.

<u>In which our hero finds himself lost, found and lost again. Then found again.</u>

'The Only Way Is Up.'

by Yazz. No.10, July 24, 1988.

'We've been broken down
To the lowest turn
Bein' on the bottom line
Sure ain't no fun...'

It just HAD to get better, surely? The only way is UP now.

~ ~ ~

Fuck, fuck, fucketty fuck.

It was all very well, but I was now living on my own. For the first time. EVER. And I hated it. John had (thankfully) taken most of the furniture, but his presence still lingered, like a particularly malodourous fart; the kind he used to do in fact. What I needed was a Good Spring Clean. And some more furniture, obviously. I was working of course, and earning, so for once I had a proper amount of money which was not allocated for Beer Money, as it had been in the past: do some work, buy beer. Do some work, go up the pub. Do some work, go Up West, with Chris and get involved in some hare-brained and properly unfortunate set of circumstances. No I was a House Owner. I was a Pillar of Society. I would buy.....a Settee! Who'd have thought, eh? Anyway, in the event, I bought two pale green velour Chesterfields. (It WAS the mid-80s!) and very nice they looked too.

Went to work, watched telly, went to bed, went to work, went to the pub, went to bed.....this wasn't how it was supposed to be. Need a man. Need some how's yer father....this was long before YouTube and Xtube. Masturbation, whilst OK for the time it took, is a solitary pursuit. I was sorely lacking in the real thing. So I decided, weekend, I'd go to town and...er..see. 'The Hole in the Wall'. That's where I'll go. No, not what you're thinking, although given that happened later and the fact they're practically adjoining, they could just make a hole, in *their* wall to next door....save time, see?

The Hole In The Wall.

It's an old debtor's prison, now a lovely pub and this is where I headed. Why? No idea. It was very nice, very noisy, very drinky, but I felt...well, alone. Nobody knew me, nobody spoke more than *'Right?"* and *'Right, are ee?"* and then went back to their beer. I had a couple of pints, couldn't find the loo (it was actually outside.) so I decided to head off back up through town to another pub, to see what was what. I don't know what I expected to find, really - a friendly face would be nice. I got half way across the car park and realised I hadn't done a wee. There was a public toilet in the corner and that's where I went. The two urinals were flooded so I went into a cubicle. I sat down. I was a bit pissed and a more than a bit pissed off. Fed up. Tired.

Cornish Country Cottage....

Then. The foot appeared under the wall. Yes, dear reader, I had apparently chosen the local cottage for a wee and was being *cottaged*. For the second time in my life. Not quite as posh as Harrods, but nevertheless, the chance of a bit of cock was undeniable. Any gay man reading this will know, will understand the pull of such an opportunity. And I took it. I nudged his foot back. His hand appeared then, waving in the air, presumably expecting me to put my cock in it. As I was still sitting, fully clothed in the toilet, this wasn't really a practical proposition. Remember, I was quite unused to this (honestly) and there appeared to be a whole set of rules and codes that I knew nothing about. So, I kind of tickled his palm. I *know*. But I didn't know what else to do. It was a bit *'round and round the garden'* which, unknown to me, was a signal for the next stage. Or maybe he was just making it up, but the next thing, his lower half – his legs (no trousers or pants), and his cock and balls appeared on MY SIDE OF THE WALL! Two things went through my mind, completely unconnected to each other and the possible danger of this situation. One was......Mmmmm what a beautiful cock, fat and lovely hairy balls and wanting to touch it and do what any gay man would do, presented with such a treat, and two.....fuck! This is really dangerous.....what if we're caught? How would he get out in time? He was naked and had half his body stuck under the cubicle wall. And certainly I was party to such shenanigans..... *"Oooh, no guv. I was just having a rest and these legs and genitals just APPEARED! I had no idea what was happening..."*. I'd heard a story once about a bloke sticking his todger through a glory hole and the bloke the other side STUCK A HAT PIN RIGHT THROUGH IT! Think about that for a minute.....Really. Just think that through....

Then, as if on cue, diminishing any chance of the erection I had begun to develop, some people came in. Well.., men. Hopefully they'd see the piss-filled urinals and leave. But, what if *THEY* were here to do a bit of cottaging and found the two cubicles locked, and decided to look under the door?

"This is where poofs come for shagging, you know," said a voice.

I froze.

"What, in 'ere? Why?"

"I dunno. There id'n nowhere else in town to go I 'spose."

"Never knew that, Bri. What do they do?"

"Oh just give each other blow jobs. They stick their dicks through a hole in the toilet walls."

"Really? How do you know that, Bri?"

"Oh. I just do, tha's all. Bleddy disgustin', if you ask me. 'Tid'n right. Blokes together. Queers, 'n that....."

Silently as a panther, a very scared panther, I had taken the only course of action I could think of and was crouched up on the toilet, so my feet weren't showing. Meanwhile, matey was still under the wall, cock wilted, bollocks shrunk up in fear, no longer so attractive, actually. Frozen, not moving a muscle, presumably able to see the feet of the people who were possibly going to murder him....don't look under the door, boys. Please. Just go.....

"Bleddy hell I need a piss. C'mon. Fuck, look at that. The bogs're blocked. Fuckin disgustin'.

Then someone, presumably 'Bri,' rattled the door of the cubicle.

"Bollocks. Engaged."

Then I heard him rattle next door.

*Bleddy 'ell, tha's engaged too. (pleasegopleasegopleasegodon'tlookunder...)
We'll have to do it outside.*

"Yeah, but Bri. How do you <u>know</u>? About queers 'n that?"

"Just fuckin shut up. C'mon."

And they left, to pee up the wall outside and then on to the next pub. Much relieved, I got down off the toilet and my 'friend' began to extract himself from under the wall. I was just waiting, trying to still my racing heart, when a note came under the wall, written on bog roll, in biro (it must be a Thing – Bodmin, Harrods – all the same, in the search for cock) which said: 'TOILIT, LANIVET CAR PARK.TEN MINITS'. (it must be a thing, to misspell, too). The toilet flushed, the door unlocked, and he was gone. Obviously, I didn't go. I was on foot and anyway, no matter how delicious had been that set of genitals, I was really shaken up by what had just happened, and aware to the potential danger had been in. Thinking back on what I'd heard, it seemed to me that 'Bri' knew far too much about the 'mechanics' to be that unversed or inexperienced himself. *'The lady doth protest too much, methinks....'*

Anyway, a bit drunk, a bit cold and now, in spite of a near brush with being murdered and dismembered and making all the papers, and now a bit randy (even NOW), I got a cab to the top of town and went in to The Garland Ox, just for 'one for the M11' – Rodney, you will ALWAYS be a bad influence, wherever you are now!

Always been a bit rough, the Ox, but it was on the way home, and I needed something to calm me nerves. Meeting Bri was just a bit too close for comfort.....

So, in I went, and stood at the curve of the bar.....

The Garland Ox, Bodmin.

And bam. Pulled Just like that. Bit skinhead – y, but definitely up for it.
Hurrah for beer goggles! We did the old *'looking, but not looking'* bollocks
(do you ever wonder how much time gets wasted, in the world's bars, by this
petty rigmarole? *You* want to. *I* want to. Why are we doing this? Maybe a
safety device – if you're wrong, you can just pretend you *weren't* ogling, you
just happened to be glancing in that direction. 47 times.), then he came over
and said: *"Wanna drink?"* and I said, *"I'll have a la*ger." (brief flash of Chris's
grinning face, watching me heading for catastrophe, with foresight of angels).
Ah well, at least it was something I would be able to talk about over (select)
dinner tables. He said, *"I ain't seen you in here before."* And I said, *"No, I
haven't' been here before. Just moved here."* And he said, *"Oh. So. Wanna
drink er no?"* and I said, *"I haven't finished this one yet"*, and he said, *"Well,
drink up then"*, and I said, *OK, I'll have a lager"* and he said, *"OK...Hi. Nigel"*

WHAT?? How could he know me??

"Me. My name's Nigel."

"Oh, so's mine".

"Must've meant to meet then. Wanna a drink?"

"No, really. I can't drink that fast, I've still got the other one."

"OK. I'll just have one before we go."

'Before we go'? Excuse me? But then he scratched his crotch and that was that. Fortunately, he only lived down the road, as I was now severely incapacitated – Chris would've been ashamed. Fuckin lightweight! – but, though I'd had about six pints, my beer goggles were well and truly in working order.

We got to his place, went straight up the bedroom, he stripped, started to take my clothes off and.....

This time, gentle reader, I cannot tell you more. Not because I fear for your sensibilities, but because I barely remember any of it. Was probably good, but I can't be sure. I remember he was hairy (tick), nice cock (tick) and he was a good kisser (tick) but what we DID.......well....

I DO remember though he was into being spanked. HARD. I, undressed, but not very able, managed to make him come, eventually. There was some CBT (look it up) I know that and a lot of shouting and him calling me 'Master' and 'Sir', but I have no idea what I actually got out of it. He came, I went. Never met him again, though I lived in the town for another seventeen years. Actually, I *did*, briefly, but in a very different set of circumstances....

The following morning, with a banging headache, I decided that being a SGWM (GSOH, DDF) was a bit rubbish. I hated being on my own and then as if the angels were listening, I had a call from Gill. She and the Hairdresser (that she'd left London for) had split up. *"Never mind!"* I said, sympathetically. *"Come and live with me!"*

And so it came to pass. Again.

SO, here we were, the blackest sheeps you could imagine, back together. I suspect this was thought to be a very good idea by Pater as Gill was bound to keep me on the straight (no pun intended) and narrow, but as you can imagine it was anything but. Gill copped off fairly soon after with a bloke from the pub. It was bottoms up! In a 2CV. Use your imaginations, people. It was fairly successful until one morning, after I had negotiated the pants hanging from the antlers of the large stuffed stag's head that John hadn't taken and was still over the stairs, reminding me daily, I went to the front window upstairs to find the said 2CV had rolled down the car park, over the embankment, across the road and down the embankment the other side and was now resting, nose first, against the wall of the flats opposite. With all its lights smashed. Oh dear….I yelled up:

"TOM!!!! (Let's call him that, for privacy's sake, if you get my meaning). *"Your car's rolled away. It's across the road…"*

"OH FUCK! FUCKKITY FUCK!! How the hell will I explain this?? What happened?"

"I'm guessing you left the brake off?"

"What can I do? Gill. GILL!!! What can I do?"

I have no memory of what the solution actually was. The result was we saw Tom a little less often…

Sis and I were often down the pub. We were both working, and we had (for the first time in my life) quite a good disposable income and we had fun for those few months, through that summer. My GSOH returned and it felt good to be able to make it up a bit to her after the debacle of Forest Gate. How would it have been if the thing with John wasn't happening at the same time? Would she have stayed, or gone regardless? I think it was just jolly bad timing…

…but now, it was like we were making up for it. We were kind to each other and were enjoying each other's company. She, of course, was entirely *au fait* with my past – indeed had been a favourite at the Court of Rodney, back in the day, and so we had plenty of shared memories and 'do you remember when...'s to keep us going.

Something worth recounting here as it chimes with a later event, where all harm is undone and I was able to see things more clearly; the longings for and unfinished pathways of pain still being trodden, is an episode when Gill and I decided to go up to London to see Rod (me) and Kath (her. And me). We got on a coach and went back to Ilford, the scene of my burn out, where all my hopes and dreams were tattered and scattered in my bed along with tissues and the semen stains of other men.

Why, you may ask, dear reader, do you want to revisit this...this....agony? Answer: 'Cos I luv 'im'? Um....no. 'Because I **loved** 'im'. Past tense. At least that was what I was telling myself.

Anyway, off we went, back to the big new gaff, up Ilford Lane, where by now (don't ask) Rod was back living with Kath in a bleddy great house, big enough to have converted the cellar into a bar.

We rang the bell, two small people, nervous orphans, returning, hoping for.....what? For Gill, I guess another dollop of the unconditional love they always gave her, and me....some absolution, some resolution for what had happened to my perfect life. And probably a final shag. And as we expected (had hoped), even after an absence of several years, arms and hearts were opened and we were welcomed in.

Much hilarity ensued down in the bar, which after cuddles and whoops of joy, was the first place we went, to drink toasts to the past, to homecomings, to old friends, to family – so many toasts, we were fairly quickly wazzed.

So, we all sat and laughed and remembered, and Rod was sitting on the old settee and I anxiously went to sit with him; he put his arm around my neck and pulled me in, and said, "Nige. Come here. Closer...So lovely to see you, babe", and I was undone. In that moment all was forgiven as I inhaled him and breathed out the hurts of the past we'd shared. Did he know? Was he feeling the same? It was all too late now – we were living in different counties, universes (though probably, if he'd asked, in that moment, I would have crossed them and gone back – to what? Disaster, of course) and too much damage had been done. But for that moment, when he enfolded me, took me home, in his arms, the world was whole and I was filled with perfect grace and light.

Inevitably we went upstairs, and there he was – brown, hairy, erect and willing and we made love so slowly, so tenderly – like the world stopped, we two were the only living souls, in communion. Like those first times, when it was to be him and me, only, for always. How could something so perfect, so sacred have become so sullied, so broken?

After we had come, and lay in the silence, I asked. I asked the question that I'd held for the longest poisonous time.

"Rod?"

"Hmmm. Yes babe?"

"Why did you, you know…. do it?"

"What?"

"The thing with Kenny. Why did you choose to be with him, like you did, with me in our house, having to see, hear, smell the two of you? I'm not asking for apologies – it was what it was, and is long past (Clearly, it wasn't…) *just an explanation"*

"I don't want to talk about it, Nige."

"I do, though"

He sat up, all the evidence of what had just happened glistening in the beautiful trail of belly hair, and said,

"I need a shower".

I followed him in.

"Please Rod. I have to know it wasn't me – that I wasn't inadequate, second best…"

He turned, cupping his balls in a strange attitude, suddenly looking crumpled and vulnerable, somehow resembling St. Sebastien: forlorn, beaten, and said,

"Nige, you were NEVER second best. Never. You were the love of my life. I fucked up."

The whole world hung in the silence that followed that sentence. What? Then….

"I loved you more than I could ever say. You know I'm bad with words 'n that. But you brought Kenny back to the flat and I heard you and it really hurt me and I wanted revenge 'cos I felt betrayed, you going with somebody else (Excuse me??) so I just wanted to hurt you for a bit and then Kenny got serious and I was stuck and then you met Ken and you was gone and it was too late and then Kenny fucked off, but you were happy with Ken..

…..he was sobbing now, years of pent up confession…

…but I thought I could get you back but it wasn't the same when you moved in so I thought you'd be better off with him so I made you leave again. It was all fucked up and I never meant it. You were the love of my life and I fucked it all up. If only you hadn't…..

"Whoa, hang on….you can't blame all that on me. And anyway, I didn't do anything. He left. Oh Rod, what fools we were."

"Yeah, Not many, eh? Still, we're back together now, eh? You could move in. Kaff'd love it and……"

What did he mean? Was he saying…..?

*"It would be the same thing, Rod. Your heart may be mine but your body will never be and I won't settle for less. We'll end up the same. So, no. I can't. But you have no idea how much it means that you asked. You were the love of **my** life too, you baldy ole bastard"* and with that, the world returned to normal and it was done. The reason for this visit had, for me at least, become clear and I knew now we were cleansed. It *WASN'T* me, he *DID* love me and he really *HAD BEEN* sorry. As sorry as I had been, all these years, and that was enough. We had become each other's favourite memory and it was good.

Time passed, the weekend flew and we left, Gill and I, and I didn't see him again for twenty-five years.

Autumn was approaching and in September, I once again met up with Steve.....Why? I hear you ask. Not sure myself really, given how painful it had been at our last meeting seven years earlier had been. But...you know me...

I had decided to try to find him and had tracked him down through his surname and, thinking that as he said he was down in the South West somewhere (and Dorset wasn't that far), and I soon would be, it might be nice to meet and mend our differences, or at the very least have a shag. Y'know, 'Jus' for old time's sake', as it were. As it turned out, we did both. To my surprise, it turned out that he was living only about ten minutes away – with his new boyfriend – well not actually *THAT* new; they'd been together for some time, not that would make any difference – so we arranged to meet up. He was renovating an old stone barn, on his own – no mean feat- and when I drove up, there he was, glistening, muddy, glorious. Was this a good idea or a bad one? I was ONLY meeting up, to catch up, for old time's sake as I said. But, fuck me, he was beautiful. My memory and mind were racing.....could we? Were we alone? Is this a good idea? There are always consequences, you daft old tart....

Steve, many years later, but still enchanting …

"Hi", he said.

"Hi!" I said. "How are you? You look well". (*WELL*? Somewhat of an understatement).

Two 'Hi's' and a half naked man.

"I'm fine. Long time, eh? What – seven, eight years? Are you OK? Where's that fuckin Chris? He's not with you, is he?"

"Yep. Eight years actually. (Eight years since I fucked you, and you fucked off). *I'm fine. And. No, he isn't. He's dead."*

*"Oh, fuck. Really? Look, I'm sorry. I know he was your mate (*you have NO idea). *What happened?"*

"AIDS."

"Oh."

A four-month silence followed. You never were very big on difficult stuff like *Emotions,* were you?

"Yeah, well. Doesn't matter. A year now. Nearly. Miss him though. Anyway. Came to see you, not to moan about stuff. Doing a grand job here...."

"Oh, yes," he said, grateful to be let off the petard he had hoisted himself upon. *It'll be great when it's done. If it ever is....,* he laughed. *"Well. Come on in. His Majesty's at work. He won't be home for hours yet. Plenty of time...."*

'Time'? Time for what? Though I knew perfectly well.....a gin and tonic or four later, my at-risk driving licence far less of a concern than what I knew lay between those thighs, thighs even stronger than when last I saw them...

"I need a shower. Been digging for hours. Hot work..." and he started upstairs. Then looked back, and like a whore, I followed, not being able to stop what was now clearly going to happen; nor did I want to.

He stripped off his work clothes, and there he was. Bronzed, more muscular, as utterly beautiful as I remember. Thick black chest hair, that impossible trail of belly hair, the riot of dark pubes in which nestled his astonishing cock. Hooded, but beginning to stir. I was, once more, helpless and hopeless to resist, not that I could've or would've - only the arrival of His Majesty was going to prevent this.

"Shower?"

"Yes. Oh yes!" and I undressed too, never looking away from that gaze that he'd lazered me with, so long long ago, and walked across the room, in to the wet room and into the arms of the man who had both broken my heart and brought me the fiercest joy of my first love; who had lifted me to ecstasy and brought me to despair; who had shown me the physical joys of who I really was whilst all the time was with another. The agony and the ecstasy. Yet here we were, wet and hard against each other; all that fell away and we moved to the bed, not bothering to dry where we fell into each other's souls and

body. He still fitted me like a perfect skin, no pain, even in our haste, just that long burning headlong slide into bliss.

I recount this, so many years later and see it clearly, but am wise enough now to understand that that was just how *I* was feeling; to him, it may just have been a fuck, a *cinque à sept,* a quickie, when the chance was there. I didn't care then and I don't care now. It DID flicker through my fevered dopamine filled brain at the time, but so fucking what?? For me, it was thrilling, passionate, an *aide memoire,* a reminder of what I had spent so many lost and painful years searching for – a man, not this one of course; too much history, too much pain, but a beautiful man who filled both my spirit and fantasies, making me feel *whole.* Just for a moment.

After (too, too soon), covered in our sweat and semen, we showered again, smiled shyly, dressed and returned to our flat gin and tonics. I had gone before His Majesty returned and we never spoke of it again.

Some weeks later, Steve phoned.

"There's a party on, down west. We're going. Wanna lift?"

"Nah. I think I'll stay here thanks." The last thing I felt like was getting all ponced up, and going to a party with a load of people I didn't know, pretending to be having a good time, a sort of New Year's Eve enforced jollity.

"Please yer fuckin self. Stay there and be miserable then. C'mon. There might be some spare cock."

"Thanks for that". My SGWM status had become particularly boring now; the GSOH had evaporated. Vicious circle really. Who wants to be around a misery ass like me?

Then, as if on cue, I heard his voice: *"Fucking hell, you're a miserable cunt. No wonder you haven't got a boyfriend......"* and he was right. Again. Chris, I love you and hate you, both at the same time.

"No, actually, Steve. I will. Give me half an hour I'll drive over to yours, OK?

"Well I wasn't thinking of picking you up, you twat. You're 30 miles in the wrong direction. And back, and then again if you don't pull. See you in a bit."

I raced upstairs, chucked on what was lying around (no time for prettifying these days), got in the car and drove to Steve's.

"You going dressed like that? Bloody Hell. Not like when I knew you before. Quite the dandy gay boy then, with your big gay hair….."

"Yeah, well that was the 80s. It was allowed." (Embarrassing memories……moving on….). Anyway, it's only a party. It'll do. What's wrong with jeans and T- shirt?"

"It's **OCTOBER**…….never mind. Come on, let's go I have to set up before it starts."

To my relief, as it would have been a tad embarrassing, having shagged the last time I saw him, to have His Majesty with us. He wasn't coming, so it was just me and Steve. Also embarrassing, given the noise and wailing of our last encounter. However, it wasn't mentioned and we drove down in companionable silence, only talking when fond memories arose – and there were *some*, amid the rubble and the bruises, to be resurrected from that bloody time.

The Barn, Treglisson Farm

We arrived, and it was in a barn, an ex-cow shed, the party, full of hay bales like a hoe-down and the smell of cow shit. And lesbians. Loads of lesbians. It turns out that the hosts of said party are brothers, both gay, with a gay sister. Ooof. Well done, Mum and Dad. She had obviously invited every lesbian in Cornwall and far too early...Steve hadn't set up his 'Diamond Vision' screen yet; that's why we had to be there early. I wandered around the loft, with a beer, like a turd in a swimming pool. My mind went back to that night, long ago, in 'Brief Encounter' and my experience of being 'in the wrong tribe'. Obviously, I wasn't going to fit in to the lesbian's 'division'.

I thought back to my night, with Rod in The Gateway, on the King's Road in London, the notorious LESBIAN ONLY club in the West End, and the longest running lesbian club in history. They filmed parts of 'The Killing of Sister George' in it you know.

Beryl Reid and Susannah York, 'The Killing of Sister George'.

Begun in the 20s, it survived all through the war and beyond, fiercely protective of its heritage and clientele. How the hell Rod managed to get us in I have no idea but I can quite honestly say it was one of the most terrifying nights of my life.....these women were *seriously* butch: short cropped, slicked back hair, drawn on moustaches and 3 piece suits, with dainty pretty little girls on their arms. I clung to Rod like a frightened limpet, praying that no one would speak to me....he, of course charmed the erm...dungarees off 'em. It didn't make sense to me, but it was no different I guess than the red-hanky wearing, fist fucking leather boys in the Colherne or the L.A., or the tee –

shirt tied twinky boys in Brief Encounter. I think what didn't make sense then, or indeed now, is why we can't all just get on? Why do we all have to be exclusive? Like we don't have enough trouble? Those drag queens didn't get the shit beaten out of them in the Stonewall to create this segregated, gay – within- gay world, surely? I'm just an idealist I suppose – I'm not saying that like doesn't attract like, that the hairy blokes like other hairy blokes and that CDs shouldn't have their own places of sanctuary, but really...this fenced in attitude, not approving of twinks in a bear bar, or a lesbian in the LA. Seemed wrong. Still does. To me, anyway.

These Cornish dykes seemed harmless enough, even if a bit dismissive of a strange (as in 'unknown') homo wandering around the edge of the room with a beer, wishing Steve would fucking hurry up so I would have someone to talk to.....my attempts at conversation had mostly been met by grunts of acknowledgment – not hostile exactly, but not inviting me to have a conversation. I had another beer and waited some more. The room slowly began to fill. Another bloody group! Homos from down West, who all knew each other. I circulated some more, wearing a groove in the straw on the floor. I had another beer as I passed the table. It was going to be a long night. 'Dallas' was on. I should've stayed home and watched Crystal and Alexis bitch slappin' and brawlin' and the 'Golden Girls'.

Unknown to me, whilst I *HAD* been at home, moaning to Steve about how pissed off I was and how I didn't want to go to the stupid party, there was another man who, the weekend before, had been dumped by his lover of ten years (standing, not age, silly) who had come home from work and said '*I'm leaving. Bye!*' leaving a devastated and bewildered man behind. That same man had been bullied into 'getting out', and 'getting over it' by his mates, thrown (literally) in to the bath and practically frog marched to the party, where he Would. Enjoy. Himself.

I heard them come in. Heads turned, appraisals were made, crotches were examined. Three or four of them, I don't remember now, but one was particularly striking He had a sadness clinging to him and my mothering instinct lit up. Awww, bless, he needs cheering up.... Actually, he was quite attractive in a 'beary' kind of way. A little overweight. No, solid. That's more accurate. Very short hair, beard. Quite sexy really, especially with these beer goggles on. He too, was scanning the room, checking out the possibilities. Just habit. He might've had a broken heart but there might still be a cock or two, eh? I was looking at the new group, all of whom knew everyone else – much MWAHing and hugging while looking over shoulders at who else might be around and available – and he, scanning, came to rest on me. Stopped. Our eyes met. And moved on.

The party grew, the noise got louder, the voices shriller, the snogging more ardent, the camping more theatrical and the bitching more exquisite. He was looking over again. So, obviously, was I or I wouldn't have known. By now, I was sitting on a hay bale, having been propositioned by what I thought was going to be a top shag, but in spite of all the leather, turned out to be like Kenneth Williams when he opened his mouth.

"Oooh, hello love! Hiyaaaa! How are you? I've been vardering you all night. I quite liked 'er over there, but 'er riah's all a bit too zshooshed up for me. I like my omis butch. She's a bit omi-polone for me. You gotta a bona eek though. Nice riah too, if you don't mind me saying. I hope you don't mind me saying, do you girl? I always say what's on me mind, and when I saw you trollin' round the gaff, I thought 'Ooooh! She's got a dolly ole eek, I'm going to HAVE to open me screech and say hello. I 'ope you don't think I'm too forward?'

If ever this was a mismatch, this was it – head to toe in black leather, wrist cuffs, peaked cap, speaking fluent Polari and camp as the campest thing in the Campest Thing in the World Contest. I was kind of flattered – but not in any way tempted. It was like being in an episode of *'Round the Horne'*. I briefly tried to imagine what sex with him would be like. Hilarious I imagine. Like trying to shag John Inman.

"No, I don't mind, but......."

"Mike. Piss off, eh?" said a voice, and there was Mr. Bear, coming to my rescue! He moved away again, after Mike had gone off in search of someone more sympathetic, after the kind of glance that said...well you know. Just milliseconds too long, weighted with intent. He went back to his mates and I sat again on a bale. I looked over. He was looking too. Oh myyy.....

He said something to his mates and came and sat on the bales. We spent the next half an hour edging ever closer along the line of bales along the back wall of the barn. Edging. Pause. Edge. Pause. Then we were on adjacent bales, only separated by some orange binder twine. Then a hand laid down on the straw, then mine just next to it. A hair's width between. Heart beating. Waiting. Then. A brush against my little finger, and our hands rested side by side. Another weird cottagey sort of thing, but without the smell of urine. And no misspelt notes written on bog roll. Breathe…. Then his hand on top of mine, holding it loosely, loose enough in case I wanted to pull away. And in that moment began the next nineteen years of my life.

"David."

"Erm… Hi. Nigel."

"We're going to get out of here for a bit now. It's too noisy," and he just led me out. I found this exciting, but was the first of a million times he would control what I did. But of course, I didn't know that then. A bit pissed, magnetically attracted to this older man, signals reaching my groin now. We went to the tractor shed and fell into each other's arms, kissing hard and desperately (he, I guess needing reassurance after what 'that cunt Steve' had done) and me…well, a bit pissed and just wanting sex with this man.

He pushed me down, so that I was kneeling. And stood over me looking down and I could see him hard in his trousers. (Trousers, not jeans! This is relevant.)

"What would you say if I went down on you?" I breathed. Yes, dear reader, I REALLY did say that! How ridiculous!

"Try. Find out," he said. So I did. I got his cock out and sucked him off in the tractor shed. Classy bird, me.

Steve came out and went over to his car, which was parked next to the shed. Banging on the roof, he yelled:

"OI! YOU TWO! If you get spunk on my car seats, I'm sending you the bill." while we watched, giggling, hands over our mouth from the darkness of the shed.

"Can we go back to yours?" he said.

"Not sure".

I didn't know where Gill and her 2CV man were. I ran back into the barn, quickly, to prevent him going off and finding someone else – how different my life would have turned out if he had…but then again, if he had, I wouldn't be here now, writing this. So…

 "Steve. STEVE! Can we come back to yours tonight?"

"No worries. Leave the key out. I'm staying on 'cos I need all my stuff."

So we drove away, away to bed, to beautiful sex with this wonderful hairy man.

This was the first night of the nineteen years I was with him.

 October 22nd. 1988.

CHAPTER SEVENTEEN.

EXIT, PURSUED BY A BEAR.

In which our hero loses his shape, get chipped away and made into a facsimile.

'One Moment In Time'.

by Whitney Houston. No.1 October 1988.

'I want one moment in time
When I'm more than I thought I could be
When all of my dreams are a heartbeat away
And the answers are all up to me....'

You know that moment, everything seems to come together? We did.
Or so I thought.

~ ~ ~

It was going swimmingly. I thought this was IT. I was in LURRRVE with this big hairy man, and he with me. He lived 'down West' with his wonderful black lab, Lisa, in a lovely Cornish stone cottage. I lived in a terraced ex-council house on an Estate, with plasterboard walls and really REALLY weird neighbours. What to do? We just couldn't live apart – I was driving 30 miles after work to his place, and 30 miles back the next morning, all sexed out, books unmarked, lesson plans rehashed....staying down there weekends. Poor Gill – pretty much deserted (Again. Men eh?) though this did mean the house was empty for whatever shenanigans she got up to. Many I hope, though she's never said.....

After a few weeks, travel and time apart became too much and we decided that, as my work was near, he'd move up to mine.

As I said, it was all going well. Apart from the fact that Mr Bear hated Gill. He was at first polite and friendly, and we all got on 'fine'. Me, ever the dork, saw nothing wrong. I was living with the two people I loved most and we had FUN! We went to the pub together, did stuff...but I was unaware of the seething resentment building....nothing specific, nothing overt...

It was New Year, 1988 and we were due to go to the pub with two lesbians we'd got very friendly with, one of whom, coincidentally Gill had once worked with (and was terrified of) years before. We'd been up on the Beacon with Lisa and Sam (who was by now, acclimatised, slim and the most loving creature I have ever known. He was also a TOTAL wuss – afraid of leaves, children, the wind if it made his ears flap) and the two women came towards us and their black standard poodle came running over. Lisa was delighted and showed him her Bally; Sam hid behind my legs, peering out like ScoobieDoo. We passed, nodded, said 'Hello, oooh what a nice dog', etc and went our ways.

The conversation WE had, as we walked away, was apparently identical to the one they had: "Gay". "Yep, deffo." "Tell a mile off." "Yep."

We met them again the next day, in November of '88, stopped, chatted and became the firmest of friends for the next 19 years. Until I left, that is, but that's a story for later.

We were all there, that New Year – the 'Girls' as we called them, though Jean is 20 years my senior and Mary 15 – their kids, and what a swell party it was. At midnight, if you did a conga, they'd give the leader a bottle of Champagne (well, probably Asti Spumanti or similar. Who cared?? It was freeee!) as the conga went past the bar. So we just kept changing leaders until we had a bottle for each of us, about 15 all lined up on the table. Which we drank. Somehow, drunk as the proverbial skunks, we ended up back at someone's house, drinking whisky out of priceless china cups, and I managed to persuade the daughter of whoever's house it was that I was actually, in real life, Miss Budapest, 1956. The fact I was British, male and it was the year I was born all seemed to escape her. She marvelled and insisted on sitting next to me – maybe she thought she was in with a chance, me in me white suit 'n all. Ha! Wrong tree barked up. Anyway, as we proceeded to get even drunker, David decided it was time to go; he was probably right (before I trashed the heirloom) but I, as drunks always do, insisted on one for the road (M11?) and thus began a little friction, as Gill sided with me. I was too pissed to notice the resentment in his face and of course I agreed with HER. The evening ended being poured into a taxi and then.......no idea.

Gill and me, After midnight, New Year's Day, Après Party, 1989.

There were no rows that I remember, just a gradual wearing down of her spirit. Then sadly one day she announced she was moving out, to share with a friend as it was 'nearer work' and so once more, we parted, not happily, but of course, I had mah man, and as usual that was all that mattered. I know she will read this and, in my defence, I will say that I had no choice – he was implacable, immovable and very very cunning. I am sorry, Sis – I should have been bigger, stronger but he was stronger than me. Clearly, he wasn't willing to share my affection or attentions; she apparently 'made me stupid and childish'. I thought she made me laugh and be childlike – there's a difference – but what he said, went. And therefore, so did she. Not too far away and we saw each other often but there was always a massive elephant in the room or the car or the pub and it was wearisome. And sad. She never knew why he disliked her so intensely and neither did I, but......Sorry Gill. Really, I am.

So the next thing, David moved in, got rid of all my furniture, brought his, and so my 'married life' began. I only needed .4 of another child and I would be Nuclear!

And so went the next 19 years.

The Borough Arms, Bodmin, former haunt of John and scene of NYE 1988.

And so it went. Repetitive, barren, endless.....not yet, no! Noy yet! Now, it was all full of light and promise. But if I could have foretold the future, what choices might I have made?

Tomorrow, and tomorrow, and tomorrow,
Creeps in this petty pace from day to day,
To the last syllable of recorded time;

Get a promotion √

Go to parties √

Go out to Dinner √

Go to the theatre √

Go to work √

Go to friends for dinner √

Go to Friends for Christmas √

Have friends over for dinner √

Visit my family* √

Visit David's family √

Go to work √

Walk the dogs √

Go to weddings √

Go to funerals √

Go to Christenings √

Go to Morrisons/ASDA/Tesco √

Get a promotion √

Get more (useless) qualifications √

Go down the pub √

Do the washing/ironing/cleaning. √

Go to work √

How weary, stale, flat, and unprofitable seem to me all the uses of this world!
Where was the man/boy who broke into the bakery and had sex amongst the
flour bags? Who blagged his way into Napoleon's Nightclub? Who ended up
shagging a Kate Bushalike in Turnpike Lane? Who leapt into a yellow sports
car with two strangers and drove off into the London night? Where has he
gone? What has been traded up? Why did what sounded like everything I'd
ever wanted feel like it wasn't, actually?

Look, don't think I'm ungrateful. Don't get me wrong – in terms of security,
stability, solvency, sociability all was good, so why was I feeling so....trapped?
Stop fucking moaning! What else could you want? You're lucky! Mr. Lucky!
Yet...and yet....

Anyway, I put my head down, did what I was told and got on with it. Months
passed, turned into years.....

When John left, I went to tell my parents, of course. My Dad seemed
nonplussed – like he couldn't understand what I was talking about, like he
didn't really believe it WAS a relationship so *ergo* it couldn't be real and so
what was I moaning about....

"OH. I quite liked him. Nice chap." And that was that.

A few weeks later, with Gill apparently keeping me safe from Hell and
damnation, after I'd met David, I again when to see them and said: *"I've got a
new...er..partner. He's really nice. Shall I bring him over next time?"*

"No. You won't."

"Why? He's a really nice chap!" (Did I REALLY say 'chap'?)

"I don't care. I said no."

"But you liked John, didn't you?"

I've met one of them. I won't do it again. That's the end of it."

And it was. That's how he was, the old bastard. Implacable. Intransigent. It was EIGHT YEARS before David and he met. It was the weirdest thing. We were in Truro and I rang my Mum from a call box (remember them?) and asked if she'd like to meet for a coffee. Poor old Mum – back to the clandestine meets, always having to come alone, although I DO think she rather enjoyed getting out for a few hours. I heard her say, *"I'm just going into to town to meet Nigel"*, and then there was a silence. Then she said it.

I emerged from the phone box, ashen faced. Kind of stumbling.

"What's the matter? Has someone died? What's happened?"

"Dad says he wants to meet you. We're to go to the house. Now."

So we went, me crapping myself – it felt like a Church Windows moment, and I couldn't get rid of those demons, now, some 30 years on and I felt like a child.

We arrived. Mum let us in, pale and anxious.

"He's through there," she said motioning us in. And so he was. Standing, hand extended, smiling.

"So, you must be David. Pleased to meet you." WHAT THE FUCK....??? Eight fucking years later, God speaks, we go running and he acts like nothing's happened, or peculiar or wrong about this situation. David, on the outside at least, seemed completely unfazed, smiling back, shaking hands whilst we, Mum and me, watched in astonished, yet horrified, fascination.

After what seemed like three years, but was probably only about an hour, we left, with Dad saying, *"Any time you're passing, pop in! Bye for now. Bye!"* and me saying, *"What the fuck was that.....? "* and David saying, *"I don't know why you say those things about him. He's a nice old boy.."*. We drove home in silence, apart from the '*Best Rock Ballads. Ever*' drowning out the confusion in my head.

My life as a housewife / breadwinner continued apace, ticking all the boxes above, even, now, the one with the asterisk. No more was I driven to family Weddings (we'd drunk champagne while 96 Liverpool fans were crushed to death), to be dropped off at the door and collected, drunk, later on, usually when it was dark. No more being dropped off for Sunday Lunches and collected, full of spuds and sorrow, bloated and sad, a few hours later. No. God had spoken and now all was well in the world. Well, only if I never spoke about my life, where I'd been, what I'd done. School was OK – Pillar of Society an' all -; family was OK, David's family was OK. But nothing to do with love, relationships, 'being together'...it was all bollocks really and I don't know why I played the game other than, I suppose, to be able to operate 'normally' for Mum, although she was constantly on edge in case one of us said anything 'homosexual'. There was always a large pink elephant in the room. I think she was always quite relieved when we left, that nothing had kicked off and she'd only be left behind with the snarling man who would blame her for everything; the better and familiar option.

The weeks, the terms, the holidays, the months, the years; '*life slips by like a field mouse, not shaking the grass*', as Ezra Pound so accurately said. Was I happy? Yes. And no. Was I sad? Yes. And no. I just... WAS. Clouds with occasional sun. Or the other way round. My edges were becoming flatter, my spontaneity was disappearing. The waters were flat and calm.

The one thing that did save me though, made me feel alive though, in spite of the routine nature of the job and its increasingly excessive demands as the years went by, was TEECHIN. I loved being with the kids. Their spirit was young and uncomplicated and life was new and bright and I could be a part of that; *WAS* a part of that.

When I started back in school full time, after leaving London, it was still 1988. Baker hadn't been Ed. Sec. long and hadn't fucked up my universe yet. I continued to 'do the show right there!!' I'd find a coin on the road, take it in and say, *"Look what I found! Whose pocket did it fall from? Where has it been....?"* And I'd do an English lesson on that – original, non-proscribed, free from judgement and tick boxes. Maths? Oh, times tables practice, is it? *"Don't groan – let's go outside and march round the playground – ok – four groups of eights please! Ten groups of four..."* It was fun, it was anticipated, it was effective, it was memorable. I will NOT get into a discussion over the National Curriculum; other than to say it was a monumental fuck up. It fucked the lessons, the spontaneity, the fun and the creativity. It fucked my children's confidence – my painters who would never 'be a 3 in Science'; my poets who would never 'be a 4 in Maths'. And, it fucked a whole generation of brilliant, gifted and dedicated teachers who lost heart and faith in what they were doing and, refusing to become a tick machine, left the profession. A whole generation. Replaced by inexperienced and cheap labour. To all of you, my friends and colleagues, who were beaten, driven out by the new Men, the corporate ethos, the new Heads whose vision you no longer fitted - I weep for you for having your life's work belittled, devalued and made irrelevant in this Brave New World. Enough! I will not mention the TEN folders every teacher in the land was given, in which all our lesson plans were set out, minute by minute, one for each subject, at a cost of SIXTY THREE MILLION POUNDS that, a year or two later were scrapped! And we were given new ones. Over and over as each new Education Minister sought to make their mark: Kenneth Baker, John MacGregor, Kenneth Clarke, John Patten, Gillian Shephard, David Blunkett, Estelle Morris...Buffoons all of them, pandering to politics and toadying to their Masters in Westminster, pretending to know what they were doing, while the morale and performance of the nation's children plummeted. It didn't work then, and is not working still, with a minister, after Michael Gove ('SIR', for his services to Education!!!!), Nicola Morgan who has NO educational background at all! No matter! She'll just do as she's told....

There. See? See what happens? I told you not to get me started! Although, actually it IS relevant to this story. To backtrack....

As all this developed, as it all went from Teaching to EDUCATION, and I climbed the Career Ladder – ending up as Deputy Head before I left, as well as being on numerous Committees and Boards, the only thing that really gave me real joy, any sense of still being able to do what I loved was the Drama productions I did. Every year, Year 6, the oldest class of 10- and 11-

year-olds and I would mount a full-scale musical. I did 12 in all, one each year I was there.

So, this is for you Jonno, who couldn't spell, but could break dance like a boss; this is for you Mary, who couldn't read very well but could sing like Charlotte Church or Beyoncé – you chose which; this is for you Paul, who only got a Level 1 for handwriting because he was left handed and all his work was illegible and therefore considered unworthy, but who could play *'Wonderwall'* on his guitar in front of a hall full of adults; this one's for you Peter, who hated and detested Maths, felt stupid and a failure in the Maths tests which I was obliged to deliver at 09.20 on Monday mornings, apologetically, because it just didn't work for you and I am truly sorry for making you feel like that, Yes, and for *you* Peter, who could rap like 50Cent and knew all the words to *'At the End of the Day'* from 'Les Mis' and for all the others I had the privilege to work with who will never be scientists or statisticians but who loved Drama Club and singing and dancing and saying: "LOOK! I CAN DO THIS!" and seeing Mum and Dad weep with joy to see them happy, for a while, at school. Here's to all 350 of you who went through that process with me; the singers and groaners, the tappers and clodhoppers but the ones who didn't care and found a home where no one judged them, no one gave them marks out of 10, made them do it again because it wasn't spelled right or was too untidy, or stay in a playtime to finish the work that had been too hard to finish in too short a time but that was just tough shit because I have another box to tick after playtime – here's to you all and I should be thanking YOU for keeping me sane in a world that was changing out of all recognition and out of control.

'Not allowed to comfort a crying child'? 'Not allowed to pick up a child who had fallen over'? 'Not allowed to sit and have a boyfriend chat with a confused Y6 girl'? 'Not allowed to mop up the blood from a grazed knee'? For me, this new world was madness – they were children, we were *in loco parentis*. Absolute bollocks. I ignored it anyway – how can you stand by while a 5-year-old howls on the ground, pouring blood, while you wait for the designated First Aid person to come, who had run out of latex gloves because the budget didn't allow any more, so she wasn't allowed to help anyway? I didn't. At the very least I'd get on the floor and comfort them, hug them.

Health and Safety be fucked. Fuck right off and when you get there, fuck off some more.

The world I knew as an enabler, a teacher, a story teller, a weaver of magic, a kindly man who gave my heart and skills to making these kids fit for the world, was vanishing, disappearing under the implacable weight of new legislation, appearing almost weekly: new rules, new curricula, lists of tick boxes, score sheets, assessment files – where was the time to teach? Not to mention marking, planning (which became a labyrinthine exercise in time keeping) and classroom preparation. Oh yes, and trying to have a life. Even Drama club was failing to feed me – it was harder and harder to find four hours a week for rehearsal, upon which I insisted to maintain the quality of the productions. By this time, and God knows why, I was training to get my NPQH (two years of hard slog, for fuck all. Never used, even when I was still in teaching, never helped me get a job, a monumental waste of resources, though I DO have a rather splendid certificate, 'Nigel Bray, awarded the *National Professional Qualification for Headship',* whoopie-fuckin'-do, signed by Estelle Morris, who was Education Minister that week);

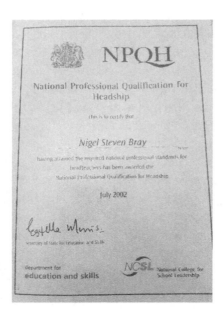

Two wasted years....

I was Deputy Head, Staff Development Officer, ICT Co-ordinator, History Co-Ordinator, Key Stage 2 Team Leader, Manager of G.E.S.T. Budget, (you can look this stuff up, if you can be arsed) Appraisal Team leader, Teacher Governor, Chairman of School Council, Chairman of Curriculum Sub – Committee, Child Protection Officer....oh yes, and doing half the Head's work because he was either out at meetings, building his Empire or decided it was "good for my career development" AND teaching a Y5 class of THIRTY FIVE 9 / 10 year olds, TWELVE of who had special needs statements, and with only ONE teaching assistant. Julie, I bless you for holding back the tide....

Trying to put on massive productions after school, look after my partner, go to rehearsals for Phoenix Drama, which by now was mounting THREE productions a year, was all rather taking its toll. I firmly believe that if I hadn't seen the teeny two-line ad. in the Times Ed that day, I would have had some sort of breakdown. I was in crisis.

Meanwhile, back in la-la land.....

When I was 36, it was a very good year....it was a very good year, for luvvies to ply their trade upon the boards (if you sing along, it really does fit...!)....I joined the local Drama group (a decision that was to cause SOOOO much trouble later) and suddenly, instead of just 'helping out backstage', suddenly found myself with the lead role in 'AN INSPECTOR CALLS', a play WAY beyond the skillset of the group and one that should never have even been considered. Apart from having TWO WEEKS rehearsal and learning a 55-page script (which should've been a warning – how could that have been good enough?), I was 36, 'Arthur Birling' was late middle aged. Hmmm, what can we do? I know! Put some white talc in my hair and draw some wrinkles on in black eyebrow pencil. Oh, and put a cushion up me tux. Yes, dear reader, it was dire. Just the worst am- dram stuff....the stuff I swore I would never get involved in. What it DID do though, was get me an in.....the next thing I know I had been asked to choose the next play, AND direct it. That was more like it.

'Abigail's Party' fitted the bill nicely –one of the things I did was to choose a play which we could actually cast with people of the right(ish) ages and the varying amount of skill and stagecraft. Here began my deep and abiding, often troubling, mostly rewarding, friendship with Ann, who was bloody

marvellous as the horrendous 'Beverly Stern'. Apart from much hilarity
(known only to us, and me tearing out what remaining hair I had, as 'Tony'
got lost in the dungeon of Bodmin Jail, in which we were performing, with
Ann whispering as *sotto voce* as she could whilst not trying to set off the
echoes that would boom through the subterranean tunnels, "TONYYYYY! I
mean PEEEETER....you're ON! NOW Now Now Now Now Now!!!", then returning to
stage, adlibbing like a trooper, saying, *"Hmmm, Tony's a long time, Ange. I'll
just go and see where he is..."* and going offstage again while the rest of the
cast desperately ate stale nibbles and asked how Abigail *really* was...., it was
a great show, well received – in spite of its apparent froth, it's quite a
challenging work. It was reviewed well and enabled me to do pretty much
what I wanted (or, believed to be right). Next, we did a play, *'Bitter
Sanctuary'*, set in a refugee camp next. We'd constructed the ceiling of the
'barracks' out of a sheet of black fertilizer sack plastic. Unfortunately, I hadn't
factored in the heat of the spots above it and as the play progressed, the
ceiling got lower and lower, as the plastic sagged, almost scraping the heads
of the cast. I just pretended it was deliberate and meant as a metaphor for
the world closing in around the refugees, their lives narrowing.....

More plaudits for the acting and directing, with the local press taking notice.
We then decided to do Genet's *'The Maids'*, a 3-hander with my best 2
women. The Committee hated the idea, said Bodmin 'wasn't ready for it',
and so we said: *"Fine, we're leaving and going out on our own"*.

Phoenix Drama was born from the ashes of the old company; all the cast
came with me and we went on to fine things, taking on challenge after
challenge:

I had a trumpet back then and I'm blowing it here, for myself and for the
people with whom I shared the tears and joys of working on these wonderful
plays. Wherever you all are, I thank you for sharing your spirit, dedication
and humour with me on this dramatic journey.

Plays Wot I Have Done.

I was using Phoenix, as I suspect were most of us, as an escape. Two nights a week rehearsal, then three nearer play week, then a whole week, every evening. A week or two off then back to readings and auditions for the next. We kept up this crazy pace for years, not daring to look behind us, not wanting to be ordinary. Off to Summer Schools, where we could be who we wanted. Nobody's wife / husband / mother / boyfriend / colleague. We were just actors, singers and dancers – and the lucky ones were all three. Wedding rings were stashed, names changed, middle names used, nicknames made up...no history, fresh minted where we could indulge our passion, sing, dance, smoke drink, swear, cry, moan....just be free for one glorious, shining week. They were the best of times, the worst of times. Hot- housed, emotions ran much higher without the brake of our normal lives. People shagged, had flings. I did too – nothing serious, just a quickie, cocks that passed in the night, when I was pissed. When he was pissed. When nobody cared and nobody judged. A cocoon which, like summer, was over all too soon and we'd return home to the places we'd come from, promising to write forever and stay in touch (and never did, until the following year when we all met up again) though some real and lasting bonds were made. I have a dear dear friend whom I met through Summer School and if you're reading this – I thank you for your abiding love. Boop boop be doop.

All the while, my relationship with Ann deepened. We were the best in the group. That's not boastfulness, that's just a fact. We also were the most committed and hardest working, which is why we always got the lead roles – because they were the hardest, the longest, required the most learning and commitment. There is a play called *'To'*, where the two actors play all fourteen parts – extremely demanding, extremely complex for the actors and Ann and I did it and did it well. We took it on a mini tour and also performed it on the professional stage at The Drum in Plymouth.

'TO', The Drum Theatre, Plymouth

When I hear

> *My love,*
> *There's only you in my life*
> *The only thing that's right*
>
> *My first love,*
> *You're every breath that I take*
> *You're every step I make....*

anywhere now, any time, I still remember the dry mouthed terror we felt, as the opening music, *'Endless Love'*, played, waiting backstage to go on and start....but we did it and it was wonderful. Ann and I hurtled closer. *'When She Danced'*, a play about Isadora Duncan required me to learn the entire part in Russian, as Sergei Esenin, her lover. It was terrifying -- normally if you dry, you can ad lib, say something approximate, or be prompted by your fellow actor, but this – no one knew it but me, no one was able to get me out the shit if I got lost. And, I am pleased to say, I didn't! Not once! It's a very clever play – read it, if you get a chance. 'Sergei' and 'Isadora' had a fair bit of fondling and snoggin.....our relationship deepened. The last play we did together, before I had to leave, was the massive Arthur Millers *'Broken Glass'* – hugely demanding parts for us both. I had a terrible and inexplicable problem getting my lines down – there were so many of them, in Bronx patois – and so Ann came to help, where that was usually David's 'job'. We spent days and nights together at Summer Schools, rehearsing constantly....and you know what? We fell in love. She was married, I'm a homosexual so it was never going to work, was it? Nevertheless, we had a fierce passion, a burning need to be in each other's presence, justifying it in the name of Drama. And, yes David loathed her. Did the same stuff he did with Gill, tried to freeze her out, but she was made of stronger stuff. It was a stormy sea we sailed; she had her own troubles and demons and the type of plays we took on served only as catalysts, excoriating and flaying us just a little each time, peeling back skin and revealing truths that were hard to bear. We were in the wrong lives. Deep down we knew, but we were both creatures of habit, developed over years, unwilling to face that truth.

Obviously, we couldn't be together, didn't WANT to be together, but our 'other life' showed us the possibilities, the place we could exist in joy. So we continued in this *faux* life, and gradually both our partners began to lose their grip.... eventually, Ann left her husband and her old life and went travelling, found her peace in other lands and eventually alighted in Canada, found the love of her life and is being the person she truly is. I like to think that the time we spent in Phoenix, where Art mirrored Life, and the times we spent acting out alternatives, were a part of the change she became. It was a far from easy time; the only time I was free of the whirlpool of feelings – feelings of passion for Ann, confusion for David, disappointment for teaching – was during rehearsals and play nights. When I was someone else. And THAT, dear reader, is the key. THAT is why, I think that being a Luvvie, if I trace it back over the years, through the school plays, all the stuff at Balls Park (HAHAHAHHAAA BALLS PARK), the Drama Club, and the intense workout of being in a Phoenix production, was so important for me. BECAUSE, FOR A SHORT TIME, I WAS SOMEONE ELSE. BOOM! RIGHT THERE. So what the fuck am I supposed to do with that? And I knew INSTANTLY what and why – it was *him*, his loathing of his son, for being in the SSU, for being mis-created, for being an embarrassment. Not for being a decent man, a good teacher, an accomplished actor, a holder of a Cert. Ed (credit), a recipient of the NPQH...none of those good, wholesome, societally good things that I had to offer. I was a disgusting queer, and nothing more. So, being *'Sergei'*, *'Phillip Gelburg'*, *'Bob Jackson'*, *'The Landlord'* et al - *was* that just me, NOT being that person that my father found so repulsive? Was that all it was? I hope not – it brought such joy, such fulfilment – I want to remember it as something positive, not as a way just NOT to be me. But, the more I examine this idea, the clearer it becomes. I owed him nothing. He did to me what may be regarded as one of the most awful things a parent might do: he rejected me because of what he considered, and did so to his dying day, to be wrong, immoral, (*YOU* talk to *ME* about morals, you child beater), against nature and that, because I CHOSE it, I should suffer the consequences of that rejection (NOT, I should remind you, by my Mother), and disgust. That's pretty hard to handle when a) I didn't choose it (Why would I? Why would any gay person make a choice that inevitably leads to sorrow to some degree, vilification, abuse and often harm?) and b) it was terribly difficult thing and I really really needed his support, his hand upon my shoulder guiding me through the maelstrom of finding my sexuality, telling me it would be OK, and that he'd love me, whatever. This, as you know, was not what happened...

So, I have decided to OWN my luvviness as a badge of honour, *sa 'Hullo Clouds, Hullo Sky' and skip about like a gurl*... It was NOT an escape (well, it was, but from other things); I did not want to be someone else. And he could go fuck himself. It was such a balancing act; he would never and did never, in all the 19 years I lived there, come to 'the queer's house'. He'd drop my Mum off, who came often, and then pick her up at a prearranged time, from the end of the road, and yet – he'd invite us round to HIS house, for tea and biscuits; he and David would get on like bosom buddies or, even more painful to me, like a long-lost son. We never mentioned the **Q** Word, EVER. So, conversation was reduced to the weather and what had been on telly (censored before we discussed it. No allusion to *you know what* in any programmes mentioned. *'Dallas'* was deffo off the list...), with Mum hovering anxiously in the background, making tea that nobody really wanted. So, as I said, he could go fuck himself.

To repeat the mantra, I had created so long long ago, to protect myself,

I AM GAY.

I AM A GAY MAN.

I AM A GOOD PERSON.

I HAVE WORTH.

I HAVE LOVE AND GIVE IT FREELY.

I AM A GAY MAN.

And therefore, if he (or anybody else) didn't like it, well...their loss. I'm a nice bloke; a little effeminate, sometimes acerbic, open hearted and I'm kind to animals and small children. The same as you, you who are reading this. Where I put my willy is none of your business, nor relevant to having a decent relationship with you, if ever we should meet.

Where was I? Oh yes. Stuck. Lost. Bored. Nice house, good job, faithful (I assumed) lover. Stop bleddy moaning. Actually, I wasn't moaning. I just *was*. Day after day, week after month after year. Boom! Up the ladder of success, although that was weighing more and more heavily. I had a better income, but less and less time to enjoy it. David kept the books. We never seemed to have enough money, which was a strange thing (although when I questioned this, I was told I *'could do the fucking accounts myself if I wanted'*, eliciting the reply. *"Ooooh, I wouldn't know what to do. No, you do them"* Right answer.) but we also never had enough time to go anywhere. We went on holiday once. Once. In all that time. Spain it was. Very nice too. I had become 'Mr. Normal'. Wasn't that what I'd always craved? I'd done my thing, spread my seed, boogied my nights away, shagged myself sore – now I had a nice, normal life. Most people would be grateful And I was. But with each play, each Summer School, I went further away from suburbia and towards something…. unattainable. And I didn't even know what it was.

Summer School, Bristol, when times were good, and we were free

CHAPTER EIGHTEEN.

LOST FOR WORDS.

<u>In which our hero's heart breaks once more and he finds solace with the Angels.</u>

'Unchained Melody.'

by Annie Lennox No1. June 14th 1996

'A long, lonely time
And time goes by so slowly
And time can do so much
Are you still mine?
I need your love
I need your love
God speed your love to me...'

My love, my darling, how I hungered for your touch, when it was too late.

~ ~ ~

We went shopping a lot, to buy things we neither wanted nor needed. I became known as 'Imelda Bray' after my collection of shoes that over-ran the porch. Coats. Jumpers, all folded, in colour order. Ornaments. Stuff. Stuff. By now, both Sam and Lisa were gone so we had more free time! Yay! Shopping without having to get back to the car. Poor Sam had eighteen months with us; a happy time he would not have had and he was loved and adored by all who met him. But cancer got him; it got to the point he could no longer swallow the mush I was feeding him with by hand and so we made that endless silent journey to the vet, where he died in my arms. I scattered ashes up on the hill (when it wasn't too windy – he never liked the wind – it made his ears flap in an alarming manner). Poor Mr. Fizzle, with his big feet and his big heart. Gone too soon.

So, to fill the dog shaped holes, we bought things. Stuff. Stuff we didn't need. On June 14th, in 1996, we went to Truro, to get some stuff, probably. We had a meal quite early on, went to the pub, had a couple of pints and headed back home.

Passing Threemilestone, David said,

"Do you want to stop and pop in on Mum and Dad?" Not *'your'* mum and dad. Another bit of me he owned. How strange *he'd* adopted (and been adopted by) my Father, who loathed *me*.....

"No, I don't think so." I couldn't stand the *faux* polite bollocks, the making up interesting things to talk about – David shagging me in the cave on Perranporth Beach was off limits, I suppose, so no, I didn't want to. *"I'd rather just get home."*

"OK, suit yourself."

So we drove on, along the by-pass, past the end of their road, past their house, inside which as we passed, my Mother lay dead on her bed.

"Put the radio on? We've run out of CDs and I don't want to open any of the ones we bought today." Stuff. Stuff.

'Common People' playing. *"I bleddy hate Pulp. Try another station."*

'A Whiter Shade of Pale.'

"Oooh, I like Annie Lennox. D'you remember the Eurythmics were around when we met?"

"Hmm."

"We tripped the light fandango, turned cartwheels cross the floor..." I wailed. Blimey, those beers were a bit strong. *'I was feelin' kinda seasick, but the crowd called out for more... doo doo doo doo dadada......"*

And my Mother lay dead.

"I'm putting pirate.fm on now. Oh YESS! UNCHAINED MELODY!! I LOVE THIS! IT'S NUMBER ONE! I'M NOT SURPRISED MIND. DID WELL THEM SOLDIERS, EH?"

"Can you stop yelling?"

"Sorry. Just love this song. 'Time goes by, so slowly and time can mean so much. Are you still MIIIIIINE?'"

David drove in silence.

Lay dead.

When we got home, I raced upstairs to empty my Stella – filled bladder, and coming back out of the bathroom, noticed the answer machine flashing. Thirteen messages? THIRTEEN? Alarm bells jangled faintly.

I picked up, pressed play: *'It's Rosemary Ring me." "It's Rosemary. Ring me'*, and variations of this. Thirteen times. I rang her.

"Hello? Rose? Sorry, we were…."

"I got some awful bad news. Your mother's dead." She was never very good with grammar, I thought. As you do.

"Eh?"

"Sorry, but your Mother's dead."

Now, I remember very little about the next few hours. I DO remember saying: *"What sort of dead?* And then saying to David *"she says your mother's dead. Do you think we'd better go round there? Poor Ruth…"*

David came up, took the phone from my hand, spoke briefly and then said, *"No, it's YOUR Mother. Rosemary wouldn't be ringing me about MY Mother, would she?"* Ever logical, even then. *"Get in the car."*

And we drove back to Truro, back to the house we'd passed not an hour ago. My memory of that journey was both blurred and crystal clear. My ears were muffled, the road noise was silent.

"STOP! STOP THE CAR." We pulled over. *"I can't her voice. I can't hear her voice. I can't hearhervoiceIcan'thearhervoiceIcan'thearhervoice...."* And then trailed away into silence. We drove. In slow motion towards some horror, I as yet couldn't comprehend.

The house was cloaked in a kind of deadness. Everything was still. People were moving in slow-motion around Dad who was sitting in the corner, looking tiny, tiny and stunned, smashed. Debs was there, Barrie, Rosemary, and Sandra, all busying themselves doing nothing, in silence.

"She's gone, boy. She's gone." That was all he said, his voice reedy and worn. I didn't know what to do, physically. His legs were stretched out on to a pouffé and I just sat on them; they were so thin I could've snapped them in two. Still, I said nothing. I didn't know who this was, this man being emotional with me. All I could do was reach over and lay my hand on his face. It was cold. He said no more.

Mum, according to Rose, who of course knew everything, had been ironing that afternoon and had felt a bit tired. She went to have a lie down and simply died. Dad, a couple of hours later, took her in a tray of tea and found her cold and dead on the bed. According to Debs, who we'd met up with the next day, in the pub, she had arrived at that moment, and heard screaming, went into the bedroom to find Dad kneeling over Mums body, shaking it violently, slapping her in the face, shouting "WAKE UP WAKE UP!!. PAT WAKE UP!!" Her head was flopping violently up and down and her hair, her beautiful always – groomed hair was flying all about. As she approached, Mum's teeth flew out of her gaping mouth onto the bed and she ran. I don't know how the news broke. Maybe Debs rang Rose? Her mother? Maybe Dad did later, I don't know, but in the time between David and I driving past and back, she'd been carried away in a body bag, and I never saw her.

'She'd gone', in all senses of the word – from the house, from our lives and from the world. It's so hard now, almost 20 years on to fully describe how these first hours and days were. I guess, anyone reading this will attest to a similar experience – it was just sort of floating, floating through the days. That evening, we - Gill, Debs and me - found some gin in the cupboard that they'd bought for Queen Victoria's coronation of something and we drank it, right from the bottle, passing it round, like proper seasoned vagrants, necking it straight from the bottle until what was real and what was pissedness all became one surreal, misty family gathering. But still no noise. No drunken whispering, no enquiries about how people were. It was just silent, just that 'gollop' that liquid makes in a bottle as it is gulped from and passed on. We were drunk, and we were numb. Best result all round. Apparently, Barrie then decided it was Gill's 'turn' to look after Dad and we all left. I have no recollection of leaving, only being full of gin and lead, too heavy to move.

The following week was just full of fuzz. I drank a huge amount, as if when I sobered up, she'd be there, moaning at me for being in such a state and it had all been a terrible mistake. But it wasn't. *"She's gone, son"* was the only true thing.

MYOCARDIAL INFARCTION. How grand! How fuck off 'n *die*! Which of course she had. Fucked off and died. According to the autopsy, she'd had an undiagnosed heart problem. There'd been something wrong with her heart and no one knew. Not even her. Now there was something wrong with all of ours – they were all broken. Who was going to fix US, eh? *EH?*

Gill had done her 'shift' and I said I'd do mine. Clearly, I was in zombie mode as I would never have volunteered to go there, back to that house, to the place, the world as I perceived it, the world that my little, sharp tongued, perspicacious mother once inhabited. Dad was no use; no conversation was to be had. Gill and he were talking in the front room and I went to the bedroom. To her dresser, her red, too – big – for- her – face glasses still lying there, one arm open, never to be peered through again, while watching

'Corrie' or *'The News at Ten'* or laughing inside, but silently, as tears ran down her face at *'Morcambe and Wise'*, before being laid on the mantelpiece while she went to make their cocoa. Her powder compact, her brush, a few stray grey hairs bouncing in the bristles, as my breath disturbed them as I pressed it to my face to breath in her scent. Her talc, Max Factor, pink and inert, and now forever to be left unscraped. I kept that compact for years; if I cracked open the lid, she would flood out, borne on a wave of sorrow and regret.....

....regret that I didn't know what her religious beliefs were; what her favourite colour was; what she did during the war; how many boyfriends she'd had; what she thought of Granny Bray; what her Mum was like before she became 'my Nan'; what school she went to; where she'd been on holiday before I was born; was she really religious; why she married my Dad; what she was like at school – was she clever? Was she naughty? What were her favourite subjects? Regret I'd never asked her these things because I was always going to ask her dreckly and now it was too fucking late and now I would never know stuff. Fuckfuckfuckfukfuck. OWWWWWW I hurt.

She was 19. Now gone. How?

The room was so silent. The bed where she lay dying, alone and nobody knew, where nobody came and said goodbye or smiled as she left us, was smoothed out, the storm of sheets created by my incoherent father as he shook her and slapped and knocked the teeth out of her cold mouth had been smoothed out, all evidence of the terrible moments erased. Just the faint smell of 'Tweed' and powder.

She came to me that night. As sure as I am sitting here writing this, I know this to be the truth. Dad had gone to bed, it was 11.11 on the clock, the room suddenly chilled to zero (just like in the movies) and there she was. Well, not in a whooo whoooo sort of way, but just a clear and definite presence. And she said; *"I will never let you fall"*. And you never have. It was joyful and wonderful and peaceful and terrifying and then it was done. The air got warm and an hour had passed.

Because she had been taken away, I wanted to see her. Once more. And again. And again, but time was limited and they were going to take her away, away to a place I would never be able to see her or touch her again. Her body was now in the morgue in the hospital in Truro. Sorry – 'chapel of rest'. I wanted to go. I WOULD go, and nothing my Dad could say would stop me. It was up to me whether I would be upset – I was thirty fucking six years old. I could do what I liked. In the event, Dad Gill and I all went. We sat outside the door – the terrifying door behind which lay my Mother; far more terrifying than those glass doors of the Salisbury which had terrified me so many years ago. Plain, pale brown, giving no clue as to what sorrow lay behind.

"You can go in now," said a kindly voice, a voice made of brown, practiced in making little noise but whose words held all the anxiety in the world.

"Thank you," I said and stood. I turned to the other two. *"I want to go in on my own"*.

"You can't. You'll be too upset".

I almost told him to go and fuck himself, for the thousandth time, in my head, but Gill said: *"Let him go. He'll be OK"*.

I thank her for that little act of kindness at that dark and terrible time.

The door swung open, without a sound. Why is everything so silent? Then the second door stood in front of me, blank, unassuming, not telling of the despair and the lakes of tears that would have been shed in the room behind it.

I opened the door (shwwwsshhhhhhh, hinges moving silently, the door not touching the carpet) and walked through. I was like a puppet man, a little unarticulated spikey thing whose joints didn't work. The impulse NOT to enter was immense, but the knowledge that it was the last, the very last time I would see her, pushed me through and it swung silently shut behind me.

There she lay. A purple velvet cloth up to her collar bones, her hair beautiful, thin (she hated that) and set beautifully upon the pillow. I stood transfixed and realised that this was the first time, or at last the first time in many years, that she wasn't looking beaten, afraid, troubled or tired. Yes, she looked at peace – everyone says that, but I mean it was *deeper*; it was that for the first time in god knows how long, people weren't causing her grief. Me included. I approached (why was I on tiptoe?) and came up to her body. Pale, smooth, still...wait! What was that? Peeping over the edge of the cover were black threads. I reached over and pulled it back a little, then more and then down to where her breastbone was. Stitches. Great black ugly stitches, holding together a great white gash where they'd cut her open. Cut her *OPEN*. CUT MY MOTHER FUCKING *OPEN*!! It was terrifying, shocking, yet somehow it wasn't OF her. It belonged to someone else's body. The doctors would have seen her lummies! She would have been horrified. I replaced the cover quickly – being caught looking at my Mum's boobs was a most embarrassing thought.

After my breathing had slowed, I looked again. There she was. The woman who had suckled me, raised me, fought for me, cried over me, golden ear whizzed me, loved me, defended me, fed me, never gave up on me in the face of the fiercest opposition – dead. Breathless. Hearbeatless. Cold. I took her hand, held it. Cold, from the fridge where they'd kept her, with a label on her toe and a cleft through her body, stitched, neatly overstitched with black shiny thread. How I hated her then, in a flash of red, for leaving me, business unfinished, too much unasked and unsaid. For leaving me with HIM, without an ally, without someone to defend me, to silently say 'it's OK'.

'You haven't finished your job! YOU were supposed to go second! You created me, he thinks I'm an aberration and you just fucking LEAVE ME!!' All that in an instant, in a flash of self-pity, cos my Mummy wasn't there to protect me from the big bad world. And then gone.

"Sorry, Mum." I said. *"Sorry for being gay. Well, not for being gay, but for it causing you so much grief. We should've spoken more about it, should've discussed it more. Uncle Billy loved you, you know and so did Rod. Everyone you met did. Now you've buggered off. What are you like? Ah well. I probably would've too. But thanks for making the effort you did. SO, I'm off into the world, alone now. Well, Gill will look after me, I expect, so that's good...."*

I was crying now, the first real tears, silently (of course) drips on the end of my nose, in the creases of my mouth and a tear fell on her cheek and as I kissed it away, I realised that Gill was now in the room, her concern aided by the silent door.

"Feel her Gill. Take her hand. It's a bit cold, but it's ok", and there we stood, orphans, one each side, lost and in a world with no touchstone or idea of how to proceed with our lives. And there we stood, brother and sister, stunned, helpless, each holding a pale cold hand of our dead mother. Oh! How I wanted it to slap me round the ear. Hold my cheek. But it just flopped back to bed when we lay them back, and arms around each other's neck, we stumbled from the horror that was the death of our mother.

No words were spoken or necessary on the way home. To the pastyless, Corrie – less house, that echoed with her voice and smelled of her hair.

She was taken to the Funeral Directors next and once more we all filed in, all of us just grabbing one more chance.... Dad, then Barrie, then Gill. I followed her in, unknown to her and sat quietly in the corner while she cradled her mother's head and sobbed into her hair. Eventually, sensing some kind of meltdown, I stood and led her gently away. Enough, enough now. It was leading nowhere except into hopeless despair and we needed to be in some kind of shape for the last stage of this ghastly process.

Wednesday, 21st June. 11.00. In loving memory of Patricia Helena Bray, it said on the front. A 'programme' for her funeral. A paper memorial to something I cannot clearly remember. I was asked to be one of the bearers and I just nodded dumbly. It couldn't get any more awful, so I agreed. We all turned up at the church and the hearse opened, and there she was – in her oaken box. What a waste of fucking money! She'd be fucking FURIOUS. The undertakers slid it out and we hoisted it on our shoulders. Man, heavy! Must be the wood, she was only titchy. Smells of wood. Nice. Sandra holding on to the doorframe, like Garfield, having to be prised off and dragged in side; my dear friends, Liz and Ann laying a comforting hand on my shoulder as we passed (an unforgettably kind gesture that meant more than they will ever know), passing down the aisle, resting the coffin on its bier, backing away rubbing my shoulder, sitting with the family (front row seats), singing the WORST hymns ever, trying to comfort dad (Me! How ironic!), David sitting behind me with his hand on my shoulder, (Even more ironic!), Gill sobbing, me seeing *her* sitting in the corner, looking really grumpy in her lime green suit, Dad throwing himself across the coffin and howling, howling howling....all these fractured memories...

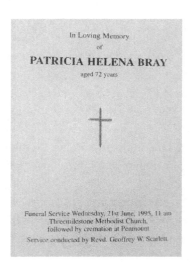

In Loving Memory
of
PATRICIA HELENA BRAY
aged 72 years

Funeral Service Wednesday, 21st June, 1995, 11 am
Threemilestone Methodist Church,
followed by cremation at Penmount
Service conducted by Revd. Geoffrey W. Scarlett

Nothing will ever be as bad again.

...then, in the hearse, filled with fag smoke, a long long journey to the crem. for the final act. Another service, shorter – there were more people waiting; in, orate, burn, out, next – the click of the mechanism as the curtains began to slide along the rail, the clunk of the gears as the ratchets engaged to drag the £500 coffin with my dead mother inside into the flames. Stand, turn, exit into the sun. Go down the pub. See ya.

Actually, we went back to the house, where Rosemary had laid on a 'do'; there was more quiche in that room than there was in whole of France. Cucumber sarnies, *vol au vents*, puff pastry sausage rolls sadly sat on plates, untouched – completely misjudged, though meant well. It was *party* food, fer Chrissakes and we really didn't feel much like partying. Dad had returned, silent and closed, to his chair in the corner and soon people stopped saying *'Sorry for your loss'* and *'She was a wonderful woman'* as it became increasingly clear he wasn't listening or caring. Gradually, the gate crashers (Granny Bray and Lylie would've loved it) and acquaintances left, leaving family – cousins and nephews, aunts and nieces, to sadly pinball around the room, pretending to want to talk, but really wondering when it would be possible to fuck off without appearing too rude. Liz and Ann, bless them, stayed for a while, one each side, propping me up, until they too left. Thank you, thank you both for an immeasurable act of kindness that day. Out came the gin (thoughtfully replenished by the gin fairies) and we – Gill, Sam, Barrie, Rose, Debs, Dad, David and me – went out to the garden to proceed with the business of the day, which was, in my case, to get properly drunk. Gill and Sam went to sit in the car where they held each other and sobbed and sobbed while they listened to a cassette of Mum's favourite, *The Carpenters;* the rest of us rolled fags and drank. Eventually, as we all knew he would, Barrie stood and tapped on his glass – his normal method of beginning his 'speech', the one he always made at 'do's' and parties and weddings (when it was none of his business usually) and that went on and on until everyone had lost the will to live – and began: "We all know why we're here. To honour a great lady who..." What? It's my Mother's funeral you wanker, not a retirement or a 100th birthday. My MOTHER. Who is DEAD!! So I stood too, with the help of Debs and said (though the following had been recounted since as I was too pissed to remember it):

"Shut the fuck up. Barrie. Boy Borrie. We're here because my Mum's dead. Our Mum's dead. Fuckin dead, so **YOU**...*shut the fuck up with your speeches. She's dead and I'm fuckin furious about it and I want it go back the way it was and I don't like it and I'm upset and let's just all have a little drink instead. 'To Mum' and I fucking fucking miss her..."* and by now I was howling and had to be led away into the house. The rest of the day eludes me. I hope I slept and that my speech goes down in family lore.

The days as an orphan passed (dead to my Father, my Mother now ash) and apart from the mournful day we all met again to have her ashes dumped in a £200 hole at the crem, it was all over. Three ghastly weeks that would change me, and the family, forever. I felt more alone than I ever had; I was unkind to my friends, and when I went back to work, having had two weeks off, 'sick, with grief' as my wonderful doctor phrased it on my sick note, I was dull and inert. Everything was an effort. The stories we all took so much joy in at the day's end were now a marker of time to go back home where nothing was. Drama club was an effort, devising ways of delivering an utterly dull prescribed curriculum was an effort. I was lost, truly lost and there was an abyss that I was afeard to look into, for at the bottom lay the answer I didn't want to seek. Ann had looked and gone; it was to be another seven years before I did.

CHAPTER NINETEEN.

MINT EGY PARTRA VETETT HAL. LIKE A FISH OUT OF WATER.

<u>In which our hero finally grows a pair, goes to live on Mars and finally begins to understand where his future lies. (Clue: It wasn't here).</u>

'Castles In The Sky'.

Ivan Van Dahl. No.4 August 2001.

'Do you ever question your life?
Do you ever wonder why?
Do you ever see in your dreams
All the castles in the sky?....'

I was lost; wot's it all about, eh? Dunno. Really. Castles in the air.

~ ~ ~

One of the more influential people I met though my time with David – many people bump in to your ship and send it on a course unexpected – was Anna. She was (still is, of course) a homeopath, a sacral craniologist and channel to spirit. All of which, until I met her, I thought was a load of old bollocks.

This is not the place to go into to the ins and outs of whether you think this is guff or truth; whether it works or if it doesn't. I thought the former, now I know that, for me, it is the latter.

I was a prime candidate at this time to be sucked into a vortex of anything that would give me some hope, some belief that things would be OK again. The family was fractured, Dad was sat in the centre of his web was spinning lies and spitting poison at each of us in his grief and anger at not 'having gone first'. This he continued to do until he died, playing each of us off against the other, lying about each of us to the others, not thinking that of course we all talked to each other and were aware of his games. The family was rudderless now – strange to look back and see just how much power, in her quiet way, my Mother had had – and I particularly was anxious to find something to fill the gaping hole left in my centre. New shoes didn't do it, nor restaurants, nor CDs or stuff of any kind. Though we continued to buy it at an alarming rate, it was an empty, soulless pastime. I could've probably become a Moonie or a Scientologist or anything where someone would have said 'There there, come on, we can make it better...' I didn't want to *pull myself together*, thank you very much. I needed an answer as to why my Mother, without so much as a by your leave, went to bed that afternoon and died. And how I was supposed to recover and get on.

Living in Cornwall provided plenty of 'alternatives' – it was and always has been an intensely spiritual place and, boy, did I need my spirit fixed.... I began, due to Anna's open mind and willingness to talk to me, The Unbeliever, about what SHE believed, to have a think that maybe there *is* something out there for me. I went to see a psychic – whilst not dismissing it, it didn't really do it for me. I went to see someone who talked to angels. No, not there either. Tarot. Nope. Meditation – nice but just made me sleepy. I was just a fiddler, a serial therapy trier, a man on the edges, not really believing anything could help.

Then, I found reiki. Or rather, it found me. The last possible thing I ever thought came to save me. And, the Universe moving in the mysterious ways that it does, planted the seeds for the rest of my life. There it was, in the Cornish Guardian, which I hardly ever read: '*Talk. Reiki. Wadebridge Library*'. It couldn't have been more parochial. Why would I bother with that? It was a Tuesday, EastEnders was on...nah. I'll stay in. And yet.....

I went. Jim Wildman, an unassuming bearded, unkempt and hairy bloke, surrounded by a group of lost souls, who maybe didn't care about Sanjay and his clothes stall that he was trying to run with Gita....and I sat at the back and in that moment my life changed. Forever. He talked about reiki, what it is, what it does, its provenance, but I wasn't really listening. I was trying to understand the feeling that I had in my centre; a kind of insistent throbbing and I knew right there and then that reiki had found me, that reiki would fill the space left by my mother, that reiki would heal me (because it does) and that it would become my life's work. I had met the angels, in secret, on that grey plastic chair in the municipal library that evening. Of *course* I was going to be at that meeting, of *course* I was going to meet Jim, who became my Master and trained me during the next few years. As the talk progressed, I became aware that he was addressing everything he said directly to ME, like he knew, like he recognised his next protégé, and a cord of golden light held us together.

After the meeting, the small crowd dispersed and he lightly tugged on the cord and I crossed to him.

"I knew you would come," he said.

"So did I. I think. It sounds...erm...very interesting. Could we meet again maybe?"

"I have a training class next Saturday and I would like you to attend."

"I will. Yes. I will."

I don't want to labour this...this revelatory moment. You can look up reiki online, there's tons of information, but I didn't need to find out any more, you know? I just KNEW. It was like I had ALWAYS known this man, and I felt, somehow, in a place I couldn't really reach, but knew was there, that Mum dying had made the space for reiki to come in. Anyway, I went to the class the following Saturday and it was just extraordinary. We did the initiation where Jim transferred the healing gift to our hands and we were asked to practise, focus on what we felt, and whatever we did, Jim's eyes never left me. When we got a chance to practise on one of the group on the couch, I didn't need to be shown the 'positions' – I already knew them, placing my hot hands in the correct places without any doubts, and it was wonderful, ecstatic. When the class ended, he said: *"Can you wait behind a moment?"*

When we were alone, he said:

"I have been doing this for many years and I rarely have met someone so untrained that is so deeply connected with spirit. I would be honoured to take you on as a student. If you will have me."

And so, just like that, I became a reiki healer and over the next two years completed my training with Jim and became a Reiki Master. The funny thing is, I never saw him again. It was like he was invented to give me the opportunity to find my true self and carry on the work. I had been given a purpose, a new lease of life and my 'other life' was seeming less and less relevant. It felt now like I had stuff to do, though I didn't quite know what.

I'd really really had enough of school. It bore no resemblance to what I had loved and known. I was desperately tired, and rudderless. I'd left Phoenix, as I could no longer function – something had to give and being a Luvvie didn't pay the bills. Unless you're Ian McKellan or sumfink. I missed it, and Ann (or at least her bright spirit and the fun we had together, which included not being at home). Now, I was there all the time, living with my Dad. Being belittled, controlled, managed. None of which I realised or could articulate; if there was a household job to be done, I was forbidden to attempt it - *"You'll only mess it up. We'll get someone in"* – just like 40 years ago, trying to help to fix the car. Small and wee. Obedient. And bored.

Funny, innit? How you just don't know things? I didn't know just how I had got myself deep into this controlled environment – it seemed the norm. I didn't know what was being done to me and it wasn't till after, after 'What I Did', that anyone told me. It is so clear, looking back, that all my doomed relationships followed the same pattern: older men, surrogate Fathers, who loved me and didn't loathe me for being a homosexualist; who controlled me, told me how to be and what to do, cos that's what Dads do, and that's why I did it.....oh you foolish child! It was NEVER going to work – you can't fuck your Dad! But it was what I was doing – being loved by these father figures. First prize in the 'Most Pathetic Needy Twat Contest'.

Is that all there is?

If that's all there is my friends

Then let's keep dancing

Let's break out the booze and have a ball

If that's all there is….

Yes, Peggy Lee. It seems so. But I couldn't even to do that, without disapproval. How did I get here?......

Spring Term, 2001. Same old, same old. Feeling like I was going to implode…. What's the use of this job if it's killing me? I'm a reiki Master and it seemed to mean nothing, although Jim did say reiki *knows*…..maybe it wasn't my time. Maybe it had to 'cook', harden, and when the time as right, for me, it would burst forth in all its healing glory. Right now, it felt like a waste of time.

Lunchtime. Scotch egg and chips. Comfort food. Pick up the Time Ed Supp. Hundreds of ads, great blaring calls to go and teach, get a promotion, make a difference! I thought I had, once upon a time, now I was overburdened, overworked and listless. No good to me, no good to the kids.

'Have you ever thought of teaching in Eastern Europe', said the teeny-weeny ad, sandwiched between dozens of other teeny-weeny ads. *'Call this number'*. Just leapt out. Boom. Erm..no. not really. Bell rings, Science. Deep joy. Then PE then English then rehearsal. Plod plod plod.

Rehearsal went well, drove home, had tea, splat in front of the telly, dozed off, started awake, marked tomorrow's English books I'd forgotten twice, went to bed, got up, drove to school, made coffee….. *'Have you ever thought of teaching in Eastern Europe'….*

"Hello? Oh yes, I saw your ad in the Times Ed. Can you tell me a bit more, please?"

Bell rings, get kids in, registration, Maths for 20 minutes, pack up, handwriting practice. Etfuckingcetera.

At home that evening, I said, *"David. Have you thought about living abroad for a while? You know, if I got a job somewhere, say…. Hungary?"*

And to my utter astonishment, he said: *"That's an interesting thought. How?"*

So I recounted my conversation of that morning, not really believing a word that I was saying: teach English in a University in Hungary. HAHAHHAAAAA!

"The bloke is based in Barnstaple. He wants to interview me." I was expecting a bollocking for not having asked permission but no, I was told to ring back and arrange it. And that, dear reader, was the start, the first moments of my new life, and of the beginning of the end of my relationship, though I didn't know that then.

To cut a long and rather bizarre story short, I went for an interview (two, actually) and I just knew, KNEW, that this would be the right thing to do, in spite of everyone at school going; *"What??? You're doing WHAAAAAAT??? Are you mad???"* but knowing I absolutely was not. Their main source of their astonishment was based around money. My salary was to drop from around £1800 a month to £200. What was really strange was that this didn't bother me in the least. There was a free flat, with just phone calls to pay for. Work, apparently was just a short walk away, and everyone in the Language Dept spoke excellent English. Which was lucky, as Hungarian is known to be one of the most difficult languages to learn, in the world.

Here's part of a fairy story:

Egyszer egy félkegyelmű ember kiment az erdőbe fát vágni.

Ahogy fát vágott, egyszer csak ásított egy nagyot.

Nagyon megijedt, mert azt hallotta, hogy aki egymás után háromszor

ásít, az meghal.

Dolgozott tovább, de hamarosan másodszor is ásított, sőt harmadszor is.

No, ha háromszor ásított, akkor ő most halott, gondolta a félkegyelmű.

Lefeküdt hát az erdő közepén a földre és nem mozdult.

Otthon várta a felesége a vacsorával, de a félkegyelmű nem jött haza.

Az asszony meg a szomszédok keresni kezdték.

Kimentek az erdőbe, s meg is találták a félkegyelműt.

How on Earth is anyone supposed to pronounce any of it? What do all those funny marks do? I recognised nothing, NOTHING that would tell me how to say this, not any clue whatever as to the meaning of a single word. In French, Spanish, Italian – you can hazard a guess at least as to what it *might* be about, but.....

Just in case you're interested and want to use it in future, here's the bare bones of the story, translated by my Hungarian friend:

Once there was a nitwit (a kind equivalent of an idiot) who went to the forest to cut some wood. As he was cutting the woods he yawned a big one (I'm not quite sure how to translate this...)he got really frightened because he had heard that the person who yawned three times one after the other would die.

He went on working, but soon after that he yawned for the second time and even for the third time. Well, if he had already yawned three times, then he must be dead, thought the nitwit. He laid down in the middle of the forest and did not move.

His wife was waiting for him with his dinner but the nitwit did not go home. She together with their neighbours started to look for him. They went to the forest and finally they found him. To be continued.......

No. I thought not.

I don't feel it has much purpose to write and write about that year in detail, but it's important in the fact that of how it changed me. I went from a lost boy to a hero. I went from a person who had no worth to someone whose worth was recognised. I was valued and respected for what I did; people were grateful for the teaching they received. It felt all very strange! Like the Olden Days...

It was a most unlikely scenario, mind. I had expected to remain in Bodmin, restricted and sad, suppressed and depressed, comfortably off but with no value. Well, for ever, I suppose. The new car, the point on the pay scale, all had come to mean less and less; it was getting to the point where there was no time to actually enjoy the fruits of my labours. So this quantum leap, this paradigm shift in my thoughts was a massive surprise – not least to me! Mostly people were supportive and wished me well, not voicing their opinions on the complete lunacy of it; people were already jostling for position for the space I was leaving; fer fuck's sake, the body wasn't even cold....

We packed up our stuff, rented the house out, found out where this 'ere 'Kecskemét' was on the map and set off, in the middle of one night, on a bus bound for London, barely able to carry the luggage we'd brought as we had no idea how long our stuff would take. We arrived at Ferihegy airport (rather alarmingly, it seemed to be just a field) in the middle of Summer, the day of the Budapest Grand Prix. August 19th, 2001. The day I went to Mars. The plane had been full of stupid English twats, all pissed up, and embarrassing themselves, pinching the stewardesses' arse, bound for the race. We landed in sweltering heat, wearing about six layers of clothes and winter coats, trying to bring as much as we could carry. Including my guitar, which was the very last thing off the plane and I was by now in a state of near panic as I had no clue where to go, what to do or how to ask. Eventually, it appeared, and as we were the only ones left, the man brought it me, said something utterly unintelligible and we set off, south to where we were to be living and I was to be teaching for the next year. I hadn't even completed my TEFL exams. *"Oh, never mind!"* they said....

I couldn't even pronounce it!!

As we travelled down through an utterly alien landscape, I began to realise what a MASSIVELY STUPID thing I had done, really without adequate preparation. I didn't even really know where Hungary WAS, let alone what it was like. I didn't know it was going to be like this....all weird and brown and dusty and miserable looking. As we got out of the city in to the countryside, with storks amazingly nesting on the lampposts the landscape changed – rural is a bit of an understatement; Houses in ruins, fallen walls and roofs, homesteads, dry barren gardens where chickens scratched and disconsolate children played in the dust; laybys, populated with whores servicing the truckers that crisscrossed this vast plain, out from Budapest, South to Serbia, East to Romania and the Ukraine, North to Slovakia and West to Austria; hoardings advertising things that seemed to have come from a galaxy far, far away – until buildings, with strange names began to appear, and before long we were in Kecskemét, and parked up outside of an old, brown, rather forbidding Communist Housing block, in Bosckai Ut, with Sandra, the outgoing teacher and occupant hanging over the balcony, yelling *"Isten hozott Kecskeméten!"*which I assumed meant Welcome.

7, Bosckai ut. My flat, top floor balcony, where Sandra hollered down!

We went up to our little flat on the top floor, at the end of the block, past the window where sat, for the entire year, a child with learning difficulties, whose eyes followed us when we passed the window, never moving, never smiling.... she's probably still there.....and into a flat which probably hadn't altered since the 50s. It was like a movie set – a house in aspic. The furniture was massive, dark and ponderous and arranged in a totally impractical way. Two great single beds in the bedroom; a dreadful dark brown and orange bouclé bed – settee and a telly that had been there since Logie Baird had invented it. Sandra seemed surprised to see *two* of us, even though I had told her on the phone, but she said, *"I'll stay on for a couple of days, as long as you help me move to Pécs. Who's sleeping where?"*

"Oh, you stay in your room; we'll take the put you up for a couple of nights."

"You mean.....? Oh.... I see......."

No more was said.

We went to Pécs with her a few days later, me in the car with her and David by coach, passing a dead horse on the roadside, all four hooves pointing to the sky, which nobody had seemed to notice, helped her move in, stopped over and then returned to our new town, our new flat and our new life.

As it happened, our stuff *was* ages. It was impounded at the Austro – Hungarian border for days and we had to pay to get it back. It was all so very strange. The food, the manners, the customs, the buildings, the language – oh god, the language... It took about 3 weeks to be able to say 'a kilo of mushrooms, please' in the market. (*Egy kiló gombát, kérek*, if you must know!) but it was so liberating – after I'd got over my crippling homesickness and feeling utterly lost in this strange land. And I was, proper homesick. Why else would I pay 4000HUF, about ten quid, for a copy of The Sunday Telegraph which never arrived until the following Thursday, and fall upon it like a man possessed? Toast? I couldn't even have toast!! Bits of bread, held over the gas ring on a fork, charcoal on the outside, hot and raw in the middle, was as close as we got (although we did discover a toaster, a new-fangled foreign artefact, for sale in the supermarket. But, still in its infancy, toaster technology – there was a single strand of wire inside so you ended up with hot bread with a black stripe. And it packed up after a week and you had to get a special form before you could have it repaired and the only repair shop was miles away. We binned it. But it was a start). But, gradually, gradually, as I got used to these wonderful polite and welcoming people, uttering strange things like *Csókolom*! (I kiss your hand!? What??) and *Jó Reggelt Kivánok!* – Good Morning, everyone! (Only around breakfast time though - after that it changed to *Jó napot Kivánok*!. Obviously...) *and Viszonlátásrá*! ("Bye! See you later!") as I passed, and I was loved by my students – an exotic creature, from a strange land, far far West of here – and teaching returned to that place of wonder and joy, where people had a thirst to know and to learn....I remembered. And it was good.

Hungary had been occupied, suppressed, and oppressed since 1956 – all of my lifetime! – and when the Berlin Wall fell in 1989 (a wondrous event, David Hasselhoff, notwithstanding... of ALL the people in the world to choose from….) and the Russians finally packed up and left, the population didn't quite know what to do with itself – it had been told how and what to think for 33 years and still, in 2001, 12 years later, there was an air of disbelief, of not being sure that 'this' was allowed. Of course, the people I was teaching were the new age, they were still in primary school when the Universe shifted, speaking Hungarian and Russian. A tsunami of TEFL teachers swept East, sweeping away the oppression and Russian and bringing welcome English and Kiwi fruits, received with joy and wonder. So, I was in the vanguard, still, of this new age, teaching trainee teachers at the Uni who would qualify and then teach MY skills in the primary schools – a kind of Pyramid Selling for Nouns and Verbs. It was exhilarating, knife edge stuff dealing with students so excited by acquiring a second language, being so proud, in Year one, of constructing *"Hello. My name is Gábi and I am learning to speak English so that I can teach children"* Those tenses! All agreeing! Meaning loud and clear. They loved it and so did I.

Entrance to my College.

It no longer mattered I had to use a crappy old twin tub that flooded the bathroom every time I did the washing. That I couldn't get any English telly. That all the red wine was sweet (yes, really!), that my mobile wouldn't work properly, that I was earning 1/8 of what I was before – I had enough money, plenty in fact compared to the Hungarians, whose economy was severely depressed – I was a millionaire practically, and in more ways than one.

Racing, at dawn, across the Great Hungarian Plain, in a Trabant with 5 Hungarian language teachers shrieking at each other in Martian (this was September, a month after I'd landed, and I was also now working for a Language School in the city – even more money! Really – a meal out for two, with drinks? About a fiver) going to the airbase at Szolnok to teach helicopter pilots how to pass an English exam, I was struck by how utterly surreal the situation was...

.....after being body searched by a fully tooled up soldier, we were allowed in to the base and I was confronted by a classroom full of 20 or so pilots, in full uniform; guys who flew helicopters in war zones, all calling me 'Sir' and looking at me with hope in their eyes that I would help them to pass. How they hated it, this requirement, how unmanned they felt, but without which there could be no promotion, but with great deference, they asked for my help to prepare their 'live talk' (I never want to hear about truffles or the assembly of a model battleship again or his phone card collection. Ever), with good humour at their poor pronunciation and mangled sentences, constructed in such convoluted ways and so different from their Magyarul tongue, but with a fierce determination that was both impressive and humbling.....

......so far away from the life I'd known. I was asked once by one of the teachers why I had come to Hungary – nearly all the young folk were determined to leave, now that they were able – and I replied: *"For an adventure and to teach English; I'm good at it and I needed a change"*. They seemed perplexed and then asked me how much I earned 'back home'. Extrapolating it up, my old salary worked out at about SIXTEEN MIILION FORINTS a year. They were on about 400,000HUF. I worked it backwards – about 900 quid. I felt a flush of shame. And a revelation in myself. WHY did I need that? I didn't – that much is proven.

At what joy I found here! The main town square? That was designed by renowned architect, Farkas Gábor. I taught him *Angolul*. Prof. Dr. Török László, Internationally reknowned cancer specialist? I taught him *Angololul*....I was given a free ticket by a student as a thankyou, to go with her choir to Budapest to see Sir Harry Christopher and The Sixteen perform; the most generous of gifts – and just for talking to people and empowering them in a different language. I was asked to teach a Saturday morning class for adults (who needed yet another paper qualification) and it was wonderful – and at the end of the course, The Saturday Morning Gang, as they dubbed themselves, got up on the main stage and performed a play, In English – from *'Play Ten'*! Still serving me, after all these years! – those people, embarrassed and shy 12 weeks earlier, acting, up there, in front of their peers, all the other Saturday morning students, in English and just bursting with pride. As was I. Mothers, after a long day in the shop came to me, after work, to learn – 'The Leetle Preence' was one woman's favourite story; she sat her exam FIVE TIMES, just to be able to say to her children she had done it, that she had passed, and that she was she was now an 'English Speaker'. Students of all abilities, all improved – not *because* of ME, though I'd like to think I played a part, but because they were able, they were free, they were motivated, they were proud of their new skill and it was wonderful.

It was a strange and wonderful time – snow! Snow, deep and crisp and even, for *months*, a totally new experience – snow duty, to shovel clear the pavement outside our block; the coldest winter in thirty years – on New Year's Eve, in Hösök Tér, Heroes Square, in Budapest, it was -28C – thrilling and other wordly and brilliant for putting the champagne on the ground to make it cold for midnight, after which we left the Square and ran back to the flat, not Heroes, where I was sick behind the radiator in Doug's spare room, and passed out. Too many pints of *sör*! Curse you, *Pálinka,* you spirit distilled by the Devil himself! Damn you, *Unicum,* hell in a black and yet inviting bottle! Sorry Doug...

Pálinka   Unicum

Satan's Liqour....

That Summer was the hottest I had ever known – up to 40C and no beaches for hundreds of miles! It was surreal to see the pavements shimmering with the heat, and people sitting in the fountain, newly built in Szabadság Tér, *'Freedom Square'*, every place name celebrating Liberty and Freedom, and after strong men who fought and died for it. Beer tents sprang up everywhere, I soon learned to order a pint or two *(Egy pohár sört kérek, a barátomnak pedig egy pohár vörösbort legyen kedve!"*....a pint of beer and a small glass of red wine, thank you very much, for my mate! (Diana, from Atlanta, who was studying voice and flute at the School) and there were free concerts in the main square, it was joyous, I was learning to let go of what I knew, and to embrace the new.

There has been much writing about matters serious, and I imagine, dear reader, you may be wondering what had happened to our jolly little homo? Well.....nothing! Nothing doing! Hungarian men, like all races (except I suppose, the Chinese) were lovely and hairy and hnnnggggg to look at but their political freedom apparently wasn't the only thing that had been suppressed.... they were so far back in the closet, they were all in Narnia. There were of course (as there always, always is) those furtive looks, holding eye contact fractionally longer than is necessary, just long enough to telegraph signals but...Well, when I say *nothing*, I meant only *once*, m'lud.

Location of the *Sör kört, Beer Tent, Szabaszád Tér...Freedom Square!*

David was back in the UK – I was working, it was term time – and the usual huge *sör kört* ('beer circle'? Never did work out why….) had been erected in the square, there was a band, of sorts, givin' it some welly, and yours truly, several *pohárs* too many, (why were Hungarian pints so lethal?) was wibbling around the flower beds, pleased to be alone for once, and then... I caught the eye of a lovely hairy bearded man, sitting alone on a bench. So, shamelessly, I went and sat next to him! Trollop! Look, this isn't going to be particularly romantic or even titillating...it was just a cock that passed in the night; or, more accurately, the evening. It wasnt even dark!! Nothing to write home about, and in fact never written about *anywhere,* until here, now. The deal was struck but then the problem of *how* and *where* arose. He had no English at all, so he couldn't ask me anything and my Magyarul was still shite.

"Szia," he said.

"Szia,"

I replied.

Two 'Szia's'. Deal done.

"Házas," he said, pointing to his wedding ring.

"Erm, me too," I said, pointing to mine. I mean. *"Én is."* 'Me too'. Well, as good as.

I said, *"Ház?"* House? I knew that!

"Nem itt lakom. Van esetleg egy ház, ahova mehetnénk?" 'I don't live here. You have a house?' I think that's what he said.

I hazarded a bilingual guess: *"Nem. Erm....f....um...f...felesége. Bocsánat."* 'No. Wife. Sorry'...Boy Bray! You liar! I didn't have a wife and anyway, if I DID, she was in England.

This went on for some time, me racking my addled brains for the simple vocab I had learned around 'Family' – who knew it would come in so useful? Then he said:

"You. Me. Go."

And he sort of pushed me through the crowd, out of the square and down a side street, where I sucked him off in some bushes, behind the Chinese Restaurant, as the *rendőrség* drove by in their patrol cars....

Was it romantic? No. Was it hot? Fairly, I suppose, but my *sör* goggles always made things seem a better idea than they actually were – and, as my Mother used to say *"A cock is a cock. Get it when you can"*. Well actually she didn't. I made that up. I think actually she'd be less than pleased. Still not too big for a Golden Ear Whizz.....but THAT, dear readers, was the total sum of any shenanigans for the whole year. And I didn't even know his name.

I got brand new porcelain fillings, replacing the old mercury ones I'd had as a child – perfectly done, although FUUUUUUCK!!!! THAT HURTS!!!! is the same in any language; Gabriella was very kind and did her best to ignore the weeping and flailing Englishman, bleeding all over her whites. The year passed, teaching all over the city, groups, students, adults, school children, professionals, all keen all respectful and a pleasure to be a part of their lives. Fifteen, twenty trips to Budapest, sometimes for a weekend or a day trip, sometimes with the Language school that had sent me from Barnstaple, who met up three times in the year for the weekend (no shenanigans), doing the sights, claiming the City as my own. Budapest, the Paris of the East, faded, glorious, and beaten but rising will always have a place in my heart. Thank you, *thank you* to all the reiki angels that sent me there, for I know it was they, preparing the way for a new and different life.

The year sped by, its end being marked by the annual ball, put on by the Coventry House staff for...I don't know who they were, but I *DO* have an abiding memory of, after singing a song about a cabbage, in *Hungarian*, no less, and watching a sea of bemused Hungarian faces wondering what the fuck they were hearing - me playing and singing *'Big Yellow Taxi'* was something they'd not *really* heard before.....you couldn't make it up. Priceless.

There was also an end of year concert for the Kodály students to which we were invited, quite an honour; the school is world famous and very prestigious and a bit of a closed shop, so we were lucky to get the chance to listen to the most hideous piano music for two hours, brilliantly, sparklingly played by these young people but, that Bartók – but, jeeez, what a bloody racket, and that Liszt isn't much better.....the flautists were wonderful as was the choir but after all that astonishingly profoundly performed music the highlight, the thing I shall always hold in my memory of that bright shining year was Stefan, from the US, sitting, at the end, on the stool, while we all sobbed –

- sobbed for the friends we'd lose, for the promises we wouldn't keep, but mostly because it was the truth, and the end and playing this song:

Another Turning Point, A fork stuck in the road

Time grabs you by the wrist, directs you where to go

So make the best of this test, and don't ask why

It's not a question, but a lesson learned in time

It's something unpredictable but in the end it's right

I hope you had the time of your life

So take the photographs, and still frames in your mind

Hang them on a shelf, in good health and good time

Tattoos of memories, and dead skin on trial

For what it's worth, it was worth all the while

It's something unpredictable

But in the end it's right

I hope you had the time of your life.

'Time of Your life'. Green Day.

The World Famous Kodály Institute

Yes, I did.

In more ways that I could even know right then, sobbing and sad and grateful in the Concert Hall, Kodály Intézet - Kéttemplom Köz 1, Kesckemét, Hungary.

And on we went. .

Szerencés Mr.Lucky!

CHAPTER TWENTY.

NEARER TO, YET EVEN FARTHER FROM MY HOME.

In which our hero discovers bratwurst, bockwurst and, the very worst – he's in the wrong body.

'The Logical Song'.

by Scooter. No.4. August 1ˢᵗ, 2002

'There are times when all the world's asleep
The questions run too deep
For such a simple man
Won't you please, please tell me what we've learned
I know it sounds absurd
Please tell me who I am….'

It's not a difficult question, but…can someone tell me who I am?

~ ~ ~

The end of my Hungarian adventure came quite suddenly really; retrospectively, I don't know why I made the choice I did – I was settled in this strange land, valued and solvent and I had no reason to return the UK (as long as my supply of videos of EastEnders kept coming, deliciously eked out, one every couple of days, to make them last) so…..

David was away again, and I, browsing the internet for porn and jobs (do they go together?) on TEFL.com (oh, I had completed my course by the way – with honours. I found some teaching materials the other day: I did actually know what the pluperfect was at one point…) and saw they were recruiting for TEFL/TESOL teachers in Germany. Bremen. Never heard of it, but that hadn't stopped me this time, had it? I rang the number, like on autopilot….it was like being back in Enfield, 1979:

"Hello? Is that the English Language Service?"

"Yes. Hello."

"I see you are looking for staff?"

"Yes. Are you TEFL qualified?"

(Swelling a lickle) *"Why, yes. With honours, actually."*

"OK, where are you? In the UK?"

"No, Hungary."

"Oh, OK, when can you start?"

Like, don't you want to know my name, age, experience, shoe size....?

"Term is finishing here in a few weeks – I'm at the University, you know – so, maybe September?"

"OK, see you then then. Bye."

And that was that. When David rang that evening (no doubt to see if I was in) I said,

"Erm....Ive got a new job."

"Oh, where? Was it that new ifjúsági klub they were trying to get on the books?"

(If U SHAGi HAHAHAHAHAAAA Grow up Bray) "No, not the Youth Club." (why do you always have to be so fuckin clever?) *"Its um....in Germany. In a language school. September I start."*

SILENCE. This wasn't going too well.

"Really good money....and a flat. New experience......"

"We'll talk about it when I get back". And he hung up. How rude.

Surprisingly, when he did get back, after the usual huffing and puffing, mostly because HE hadn't made the decision, he acquiesced, admitting that it WOULD be interesting and new. We were both really sad to be leaving, but at least we weren't going back to the UK.....

The time came soon enough. Of course it wasn't only us and it was made easier because our friends were leaving too – the Kodally students (as idiot James would keep calling them) were also graduating and being dispersed back across the globe, solfege-d up to the eyeballs, so, fa, doh-ing to the children of the world (or maybe not – perhaps they all went straight home and into McDonalds..) and so many of the anchors holding us here would be weighed and so maybe it WAS time to go too....pretty hard to leave though. I had grown to love the city.

Before we knew it, all our stuff was back in in the boxes we'd saved and *en route* to Bremen, as were taken to Keleti állomás to catch the big blue train West, through the Czech republic, past Brno, past the spires of Prague, this sprawling land which would soon be under feet of water as the country suffered the worst floods for years, us watching it on the news, thinking "we were there, oh my........", each border being checked by fully armed guards - scary, but delicious, nonetheless - checking our passports, glaring, through Dresden, changing trains with moments to spare and on to Berlin where we'd booked a two week break. Well, I say, 'we' – HE had booked a two-week break, as if to snatch back control of the situation.

It's very strange, this period. I felt disconnected, lost – in Hungary I really felt I knew where I was, who I was but now, suddenly back in the heart of this great throbbing city I felt undone again. This is all retrospective of course and it all unravels as I write and look back on that time. Guess what? We bought some stuff!! Massive CD store, bargain bins, and there I was, frantically buying stuff I would probably never listen to....how quickly we forget....

The city was busy, it was August, we pointed, and oooh-d and ahhh-d at stuff – the Dom (utterly obscene, with homeless people on the steps outside); the Fernsehturm, with its super-duper lifts and revolving restaurant at the top, from which you could view the deprivation and acres of Communist housing from the former GDR; Ka-De-We with its glittering escalators and acres of perfumery and 'fancy goods'; *Der Deutsch Oper* with its velvet and marble and posters of the famous singers who had performed there, where we were lucky enough to get seats to see the Alvin Ailey American Dance Theatre, at €45 a pop; all of this was wonderful and I was grateful for it; the restaurants, the bars, all gratefully received but it somehow felt wrong in my heart. I put it down to 12 months cultural deprivation (In all that time, the Sixteen and Sebestyén Márta were the only cultural events we'd seen.) and it felt a bit weird to have such undiluted emotional responses to wealth and opulence. Even as we strolled down Unter den Linden, I missed my unmade roads and dusty buildings where I had felt the first becomings of what I felt I truly was.

Visiting The Jewish Museum, an apparelled design by Daniel Libeskind, was powerful and more real to me than visiting the Kurfurstemndam with all its glittering shops; the small underground spaces, with empty bookshelves built under the paving stones on Bebelplatz, the *'Night of Shame',* the monument to the Book Burnings that took place there on May 10, 1933 was a very visceral experience.

Bebelplatz, monument to the Book Burning in May 19933

as was the Wall, or what was left of it, painted on by people in pain and fear.

Part of the Berlin Wall, East Side Gallery, dismantled in 1989.

The small crypt holding the statue of the mother holding her dead son while rain cried tears through the hole let in the roof was far more moving and relevant – it was pure spirit, pure grief.

A mother embraces her dead son, turned to stone in silent pain.

Neue Wache Memorial

Checkpoint Charlie with is faded militarism and board where people stood mooning at cameras, trampling on the place where people had died, suffered, were lost.

Checkpoint Charlie, Friedrichstrasse, Berlin.

I came to understand that this place, for all its glitz and glamour, wealth and effort, was barely concealing its past – a place of loss, and mourning, exemplified in the great grey monoliths of the Holocaust memorial, across which students and kids jumped and skittered and shouted, unaware and ignorant and the graves of 8000 Russian soldiers in Treptower Park.

But, I pressed this all down, and sightsaw and shopped, imbibed and ate like nothing was wrong. I was glad to leave. It wasn't a holiday; it was a lesson. It was my reiki helpers saying, '*Open your eyes. Look beneath…..you may not like what you see, but you must look….*'. I was unaware of any of this going on 'below'. I just felt wrong. Our two weeks staying at Willi's B+B was shall we say, adequate.

We left, and went on to Bremen.

Central Station, Bremen.

Another four hours, via Hamburg, to my new home. Hot, hot sun, and Bremen *banhof* was packed, on this bleaching August day. And, the man who was supposed to meet us wasn't there. *Ja*. Great start. He turned up eventually and bundled us ('Us? You never mentioned 'us'?' Ooops.) and our four suitcases and guitar in to his car and then said:

"*Steve. My names Steve. I own the school. You must be….?*"

"*Nigel. We spoke on the phone?*"

This was sounding a bit weird now – it was like we weren't expected....

"Yes, I know. And this is....?"

"I'm David." That was it. No 'friend', boyfriend', 'partner' bum chum', nothing. *"Pleased to meet you."*

"Oh, and your flat's not ready. Sorry. Will be soon, though!" This was the beginning of a kind of Frank Spencer World, where nothing was quite real, ever on time, finished.....

"But, I've got you somewhere else, just temporary, until it is. I'll just have to give her a ring and tell her erm.....well, just tell her....hang on," and he dialled a number and in what appeared to be fluent German spoke to someone to tell her she had two homosexuals moving in to her house. Fortunately she was cool about it, though he wasn't, because it seemed she just increased the rent....I'm *SURE* I told you....how interesting that maybe I didn't and what did THAT mean on a subliminal level?....and so we set off around the quaint city, buzzing with Summer people to our new home.

Quite nice, I suppose. Kitchen, bedroom, lounge. Ghastly décor but.....and after a few days our stuff arrived again. This of course was a pain in the arse because there was nowhere to put it and no point in unpacking it because our proper flat was going to be ready 'soon', which actually turned out to be almost a month. So our stuff, still all boxed was crammed down a stairwell to the basement and everything was unreachable. Frau Schwimmer was very nice though we only bumped into her in the shared lobby; they lived upstairs, but as there were no shenanigans of any kind, having two homosexualists beneath her feet seemed to be no problem for her.

And so began the next phase of my journey and without sounding all whooooooo and poncy about it, I was beginning to realise that this, the travelling, the things I had seen, experienced and felt were planned, as the journey was becoming very much an internal one. Jim had said to me, long long ago, that Reiki will find its way, do what it needs, in its own time and – DUH – I was realising that this was as much a spiritual journey as anything else. I went to the school, met the staff – all itinerant, passing through, earning enough cash to travel on; the turnover was astonishing- the whole staff must have changed 3 or 4 times during the 10 months I was there. Some were nice, some were arses, some single, some couples, some barely able to *SPEAK* English, let alone teach it, with accents so broad even I couldn't understand them so the poor German students didn't stand a *katze* chance, and to my knowledge (and my Gaydar is usually pretty good), nobody gay. How weird is that? I was assigned some classes, often at really shitty times of the day (new boy – hurrah, thought the others) having to be out at Stahlwerke Bremen at EIGHT A.M, and the steelworks were a tram then a bus ride away. I'd expected it be full of rough tough muscly steelworkers, but alas, it was the corporate HQ, full of offices and suits (though I wasn't complaining at THAT bit), professionals who needed better English, so they could climb the corporate ladder....and get a bigger car, and a nicer office, and boss more people around....like a Deputy Head only with grownups. Hmmmmmm. Why was I here, I wonder? Most of my work was like this – a late gig, 6.30 – 8.30, at Kellogg's HQ (which took me through the cruising park. Quelle domage!), same clientele; Kraft Foods – young women striving to make it in the corporate world needing English; the under managers at BMW; the buyers at AirBus who needed to go to Filton in the UK to Do Deals – all these people needing little old me! It was hard work, I have to say and the clients were particularly demanding (Lucky I knew what the pluperfect tensw was, how to identify a gerund and modal verbs and use a past participle when asked, eh?) but, they were paying for it, it was a significant investment for the companies who funded it and Steve was very good at negotiating a good deal. Which meant, too, we were paid decently. Which was just as well as we were now living in a city with all the attendant expenses – a *pohar sör* was no longer €1.20, but about €4.50, (even a pint of Beck's, which was bloody well brewed in Bremen, right across the road from the flat!), eating out was dear, rent was high.....and here I was, back in the 'civilised' world. Karstadt, Kaiser, Kaufmann. H+M, all the big stores, groaning with stuff to buy. Shops, bars, restuarants, banks, commodities all yelling, yelling....It was noisy, lighty, shouty, sparkly...

Dont get me wrong, it was pretty good on the whole – the city is small, manageable with a long cultural history, lots to do and lots to see. There is also a large expat community; there's an American airbase near and the boys were often in the bars, so, unlike Hungary, language was never a problem and most of the Germans spoke, and liked to practise, English. We soon settled back in to the comfortable pattern of being consumers, and for a while after the 'difficulties' of Hungary, it felt nice, it felt deserved – we worked hard, unsociable hours so why SHOULDN'T we have a bit of a spend up.....? And yet, yet.....it didnt feel quite like it used to. Maybe I was just out of practice? Imelda Bray needs more time.....

Why was I ignoring the reiki working away inside? Probably because it would start saying things I didn't want to hear...

...SO I set to. There was a fabulous bar just around the corner from the School, and on our way home. We had, after about 6 weeks moved into our proper flat, on the very top floor of the building in which, at street level, was Burger King which often proved most useful, staggering back form Johnny's after a few Beck's.... It was very modern and airy, with massive rooms, although getting up the78 stairs after a night on the lash was not always welcome. However, we could see the main street through town, there were tram stops right outside the door (handy for that 07.00 stumble out the door for the Steelworks gig), 5 minutes walk from school, 2 minutes from Johnnys....just perfect, except that the landlord had his office in the flat too so if we was shaggin (not that often, sadly) we had to keep the noise down. A small con for a flat with a great many pros.

We found Johnny's almost right away. One lunch, after David had met me from my 10 – 12 session with the unemployed adults, who had to get a certificate to show they were serious about being employed – some resentful, but on the whole, a nice if sometimes unruly bunch, we set off to the tram to get back to Moselstrasse and watch a bit of the Commonwealth Games (and reports on the awful floods in the fields we had sped over just a few weeks earlier) and, a bit peckish when one of us noticed the awnings on what looked to be a busy bar.

'Johnny's'

We went down the alley and got a table outside and the waitress (who turned out to be the owner) came out and spoke to a German couple, in German, but as I pointed out to David, with a strong Dublin accent....Really? Anyway, we were looking at the menu and she came across, said, "*Sind Sie bereit zu bestellen, meine Herren?*"

"*Erm...we nicht sprechen Deutsch very gut*", I said. "*Boscánat...Oooh, sorry, no that's Hungarian. Erm...Spechen sie Englisch?*"

"*Aye, for sure,*" she replied. "*Ai'm Irish, so I am.*"

"*Oh. Um, OK. Well, two um... Johnny Burgers, please.*"

"*OK, now will you be wanting to drink anything at all?*"

"*Ja, I mean, Yes, please. Beer for me and red wine for my...friend.*"

Ok, Oi'll just be a minute..." (Please now go back and read this conversation in a Dublin accent for a more authentic experience).

Not long after, she came barrelling out of the door with a tray bearing the BIGGEST burgers I had ever seen and the drinks, wobbling precariously as she came towards us, nodding to customers – "*Tschüss! "Vielen danke!", "Auf Wiedersehen"! Eine minute, bitte!*" until she got to us when she said,

"*OK, fellahs, what's the craic with yous tew?*"

"*Oh! Well, we've just arrived really. I'm teaching at the language school and er..my friend is just erm....*

"*Oh, glory be! Wisht, will ye? I'll be getting me friend Jan- she just LOVES the gay boys!*" and she scuttled back inside only to re-emerge with Jan, a little Welsh woman, who sat down at our table and, camp as you like, said: "*Welcome. Really. You're very welcome. Ignore her – she just an old tart. I'm the real fag hag!!*" and with that, we became firm friends. The four of us became inseparable (the husbands couldn't get a look in. Joan's, the owner of Johnny's, was just a miserable twat and Jan's couldn't speak a word of English. Fuckin GAWJJJ though. Huge, hairy, muscly – Jan was half his size but he adored her and they were a wonderful couple – he just let her get on with it.) Being mates with the owner certainly had its perks – free beer was the least of it! As 'a pillar of the community', and being fluent in German, she had access to all the 'do's' and quite often we'd be invited too. We ended up at the Landlord's *Fruehschoppen*, which is a kind of breakfast piss up.

Freuschoppen, Bremen

We drank 184 miniatures that morning, before 10.00, supplied by the various pubs around town, as 'tasters'. TASTERS?? Didn't touch the sides. And Becks. Oh, yes. Becks by the stein. I won't include the photo of me wearing the pink bunny ears..... oh, alright then.....

There was something, twice a year called a *rundfahrt* (HAHAHHAAAAA FAHRT!!!.Oh, Grow Up...) which traditionally meant you just loaded up a shopping trolley with as much booze as it would hold and everyone set off round the town, stopping periodically to eat and play a game, with the intention of returning from whence you began. 'Round journey'. Do you see?

As you can imagine, Bremen was littered with pissed landlords and their mates who, even though they did this twice a year and think that they'd know better, didn't quite pace themselves. The road to the *schlachte* was littered with people who, on the last leg, back along the river, on the 'slaughter', so named from where the pigs were run and butchered so the blood could easily be washed into the Weser, never quite got *rund* the *fahrt*. Better luck next year.....but it was carnage.

It went on in such a fashion for the best part of a year. Either the gang from Johnny's, or the crew from the School would hit the town and mayhem ensued. Great for the spirit, bad for the liver. It became clear to me I was 'drinking to forget' – I was ill at ease, out of joint...nothing felt quite right; indefinable yet naggingly present. I wasn't *unhappy*, I just wasn't *right*. So being on the lash, out to dinner with our Argentinian friends, at poetry readings (free bevvy) with our German friends, down the Cellar bar with our Aussie mates all seemed a good distraction. '*Unbehaglich*' is the German – ill at ease, and uncertain as to why. Though I knew. Really, I knew. But I didn't have a clue **WHAT** to do, as that bloke in Sweet once said.

Christmas came, which we, the six of us, spent at Jan's, and we were suddenly halfway through the year. It was a lovely day, other than the fact David fell over on the icy pavement and split his head open, arriving at Jan's with his head, face and clothes covered in blood. It was warm and comforting. We went out in the evening, in to the cold and snowy night, to the Christmas Market, which was every bit as magical as you would expect – *gluhwein* and *schnitzels*, oompah bands and goose – pimpled, lederhosen clad legs, bratwurst and bockwurst, and of course the dreaded *Feuerzangenbowle* – a concoction brewed by Satan himself: a traditional German alcoholic drink for which a rum-soaked sugarloaf is set on fire and drips into mulled wine and makes you really *really* pissed.

Feuerzangenbowle - The Devil's Brew.

At least it did with Joan – falling around like a ragdoll, grinning and singing – and I recognised something then, in her, the same sadness I had – the feeling of being in the wrong place.

Wurlitzer, spinning like our heads.

Later, after we had left and were back in the UK, Jan contacted us and invited us to Joan's 40th birthday – a huge surprise party, with her sisters all flying over from Ireland, and we, if could come, would make it complete. We did, flying back from Bristol, all cloak 'n dagger, hiding out at Jan and Werner's. It was a wonderful, beer stained, tear stained success and Joan had a wonderful time. The next thing we heard was that she had disappeared – had just walked away and gone back home. Just like that, leaving Johnny's, her husband and Germany all behind. That sadness that I glimpsed that night – and the fact she held my hand all the way home in the taxi from the *rundfhart* and I didn't really know why? Maybe she felt it in me too, though I was so happy that night as Gill had flown over and was staying with us and it was party time! – had maybe manifested. We'd gone and we were really very close and perhaps it had been the spur, the means by which she took a good hard look, screwed her courage to the sticking place and walked away, to happiness, to a place where she did feel right. I never heard from her again.

And neither did Jan, her dear best friend who was so lost without her. Darling, generous Jan who was killed, in the end, by those marvellous breasts – her "Fabalus Tits", 'Fi bronnau rhyfeddol', that she'd wobbled in our faces, that she'd hidden her purse between and captivated Werner with, had turned on her and the cancer had killed her within the year.

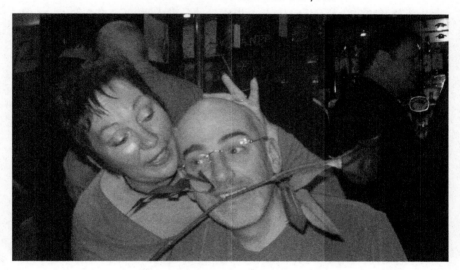

Jan and Me in The Blarney Tavern, April 2003.

They say people drop by for a purpose and I guess, though we knew each other for such a short time, that Joan was one of those; her purpose or at least THE purpose of our meeting was to light that spark of recognition that lay hidden in the dark damp, that was always guttering into light and then being snuffed again and again. Hers burned bright, bright enough for her to be guided out. Mine was barely visible to the naked eye.

We had fun fun fun, though in Bremen! Always having a jolly at Johnny's! Some dear friends came for that New Year and we all watched in amazement when at midnight on New Year's Eve as all the blokes (while we stayed inside shrieking at both the sight and the insanity of it) went outside with the bags of fireworks they'd all brought and let them off. There. In the street. All at the same time. By hand. Rockets were screaming past the windows, exploding against shop fronts, hitting people in the nuts and the knees, holding Roman candles and bangers, jumping out of the way of the Catherine wheels that just took on lives of their own and shrieked along the street while the blokes jumped out of the way. Joan must've seen the 'WTF?????'

look on our faces, as we watched our friends hilariously getting scorched, and just said, *"Oh it's traditional",* and went on her way while her husband risked his eyesight and being burned alive by fireworks that were attaching themselves to their winter coats. It was mayhem, but – it was 'traditional'! We were lucky enough to see Jan Garbarek and his band in concert; plenty of films (saw *'Iris'*, or most of it, through the Afro of the man in front who sat in front of me in an otherwise empty cinema); went the fair with Joan – up on the screamy rides with her, then down into Paddy's Pit, just 'for one', on the way home. This turned out to be the night when David came closer to violence than I'd ever seen him.....

Paddy, almost certainly not his real name, had run his bar for years, in a cellar just by the station. Of course, he and Joan were good mates (in a business warry kind of way) and as we were passing, she suggested we just popped down, as *"He'll be pleased to see us, so he will."* As it turned out, he probably was, as we had 'the one', then another, and another. Their speciality was the 'Irish Flag' a large shot of fuck knows what other that it was orange, green and white (there was also the 'American Flag' that they served in Johnny's, same thing, red white and blue to make the airmen feel at home. And bilious). Anyway, the place was packed and I was having a jolly good time, thank you very much, friend of the owner of Johnnies', who was a friend of the owner of Paddy's and there were a few crafty 'housers', and oh my bleddy goodnight – were we pissed! We must have had 20? With a few Becks in between. The Flags were only €1.00, it would have been rude not to. Finally, it was closing. We'd been in there for hours and we most definitely needed a taxi. We got back to Hutfilterstrasse and I (as I was told the next day, by a gleeful Joan) just fell out of the cab on to the pavement, unable to stand to get out. So I poured. 78 stairs later, giggling and bruised, I arrived at the door of the flat.

"What fucking time do you call this?" I wish I could've said *'You're not the boss of me,'* but a) in fact he was, b) and I was pretty much in capable of speech of any kind.

"IT'S HALF PAST FUCKING ONE! WHERE HAVE YOU BEEN??"

"Joan. Paddy...!" I managed before I started that drunk laugh thing. Which was when he grabbed me by the throat and with his fist raised at the level of my face; hissed,

"Don't you laugh. Don't you ever EVER fucking laugh at me. EVER." and he pulled back his fist but nothing happened I think mostly because he couldn't support my dead weight with one hand and I slumped to the floor, there in the hall where I passed the remainder of the night. We never spoke of this again. The next day, (luckily not 08.00 at Kraft Foods or Stahlwerke!) back to work, as if nothing had happened. Though of course for me it had. 1) I'd been out, on my own, had a laugh, got pissed, didn't care and 2) I'd been threatened with violence and, given my past history with insane Father figures, that was not a good place to have revisited. Such a small moment, such a repercussion, though it would not be felt for some time yet. The flame flickered, flared and.....subsided once more.

The year passed. The trips out to AirBus, and the daily ritual of giggling like a five-year-old when the driver said *'Endfhart, bitte. Endfhart'*, came to an end with the completion of the contract. I was given an extra evening shift at Kellogg's – Calloo Callay – but this did in fact lead to the only bit of shenanigans that happened in all of that year (despite being desperate for Jan's Werner to pick me up, carry me away and give me a good seeing to. Which he never did.) and it all came about quite by chance. Yes, it did, actually.

'Out of interest' we'd looked up 'Cruising grounds in Bremen' because there didn't seem to be any which was rather odd, given a population of some half a million people so, if Kinsey was right, 25,000 of them must be poofs. SO where did they go for their jollies? There were hardly any bars – one, *'Vater und Sohn'*, which surprisingly David seemed to like - Hello!! Wakey wakey...!! -, which was tiny with hardly any fathers, or indeed sons. So where....?

We found a web page, in German, with a google translate which told us that, apparently you could go, in the afternoons to *'the putrid stews, near the shrups and flaps'*. That sounded fun, eh, readers? Anyway, it seemed, later looking back that I had wandered through those very same shrups and flaps the night I decided to walk back home after Kellog's, instead of getting on the tram. And there were men, all ogling each other, in a really dodgy looking fashion. Not like Wanstead Flats at all! The next thing, a (I have to admit) rather beautiful blonde gentleman came up beside me on his bike and said something I didn't understand. Though the meaning was quite clear.

"Sorry.....er....ich spreche kein deutsche."

"OK, all ist good," he said and just took me by the arm and led me to what appeared to be an electricity substation (classy bird, me), pushed me against the wall, and said,

"English man. Ist good!" and got his *schwanz* out, which was already hardening. He began to undo the belt of my trousers (and dear reader, please envisage the splendour of the setting – maybe this was the putrid stews? – me in my shirt and tie and, yes, carrying my brief case which by now had seen its owner in more difficult situations that it could remember).

"Kann ich ihn blasen?" *"?"* he said, fumbling with my flies. *"Suck the dick, bitte?"* he said, pointing at my crotch.

"Well, erm..yes well...ok.....but..." This wasn't going to well, I couldn't get my cock out because it wouldn't cooperate. Tension? Embarrassment? Don't know, but then he gasped.

"Das ist ok. Du bläst MEINEN!"" and he grabbed my head and pushed it down towards what had turned out, by now, to be a most impressive erection.

"No, but, wait, just a min...." but could say no more as I suddenly found myself with a mouthful of fat German dick.

"Ahhhhh", he said, *"Das ist gute....."*

"Grrm mmoom mmm mm" I managed when just then, a voice shouted: ***"JA!! HOMOSEXUELLE!"*** I understood it, as it was a little bit similar to the English.... ***"JA! JA! JA!!!"***

I didn't know what was going to happen. They seemed to be shouting approval – we actually could be plainly seen from the other side of the hut thing; we weren't hidden at all! – but I was taking no chances. With a great slurpy POP! I pulled his dick out of my mouth, grabbed my gaping trousers (and my brief case) and just jumped through the hedge that edged the park, in a blind panic and fell down a bank on to the main railway line. Briefcase skittered one way, I fell on my knees, trousers round my ankles, arse in the air hoping, REALLY hoping that another train wasn't due for a few minutes....I arrived home, not having been killed by a speeding train, with a grass stains on my trousers, a hole where I'd ripped them on the stones on the track and a sprained finger.

"What happened to you?"

"Me? Oh…nothing. I fell over….on the way home. I walked. And I …fell over…."

He just looked, and said no more.

I avoided that little park from then on, although it meant a longer way home. It didn't matter though, as things were drawing to a close there. My contract, such as it was, was coming up for renewal and the question of wanting to be away for another year arose. We decided not, after some discussion, deciding that even a year in Education was a long time, and I'd been out for two now, and that if I wanted to get a job back in the UK, I had better return before things had changed too much and I would be unable to compete in the market place (Just LISTEN to yourself, man! What the hell are you THINKING?? Why did you leave in the first place? Have you forgotten so soon…?). Looking back on this, I am tempted to say that it might not have been entirely *my* decision, if you get my drift…..

Joan had opened a new pub, 'The Blarney Tavern' (nothing if not original), two doors up from Johnny's and had little time for play, as she was very busy running two businesses. After the outrageous opening do, we were able to see less and less of her and our access to events became more limited too – nothing personal, just a moving on. So our social life became somewhat truncated, it was cold, and grey and February….maybe our travelling was done? I began to look online to see what was available back in the UK and quite quickly was invited back to Cornwall, for a Deputy Head interview…so off I went, all prepped, reams of notes on the 'role of ancillary staff', 'tools for learning', 'pyramidal management' (oh fer fuck's sake……you LEFT because of all this ole bollocks!) and flew to Newquay where I was met by Jean and Mary; back to theirs for some gin and reminiscences – but not enquiry……which was odd. Anyway, the interview (Enfield it was not - two days!) came and went, sat anxiously by the gin, waiting for the phone to ring, to hear that they were *'really sorry, but I wasn't quite right for the post'*. Actually, I fucking well was, but there was nothing I could do about that. Even more galling was the fact that one of my ex colleagues from where I was *HER* boss, got the job. Proper stitched up, I was. Ah well, Fuck 'em. More gin, waiter!

As it turned out, within weeks the head had gone off sick on long term leave and the job had suddenly become Acting Head of a Failing School which OFSTED had put into 'Special Measures'. *LUCKY* Mr. Lucky!

It had been arranged that Gill would come to visit again, reluctantly, as she was afeared of flying but...! Have no fear! I had booked myself on the same flight back and crept up on her at the airport. *"BOO!"* I said. She was astonished / thrilled / relieved and we had a jolly ginandtoniced flight back and an even more jolly week, during which David quite clearly remembered why it wasn't a good idea putting us together.....it was nice to have someone to play with, have japes instead of just being...watched. And well behaved.

So, Gill went home, and soon we were going home too. April we left, alone, in the rain, taken to the airport by our landlord (with whom I very nearly had sex with once - a final 'Huzzah'!...we were packed and ready to go, David was at the school and Bruno and I were alone in the flat, side by side looking at a painting on the wall and our little fingers brushed together – insistent, not an accident, and there was that moment of suspension when it could've gone either way. A bit like a cottaging, but without the partition and he didn't pass me a note written in biro. In the end, he bottled it. Shame – nice hairy older man. One that got away) and soon we were in the air, homeward bound, back to Bodmin, unemployed, uncertain as to what would happen next. Tired of travelling, tired of feeling I belonged nowhere.

There was no feeling, for me, of a happy return to the land of my birth, to the Land of the Gods – I was, rather, *Unbehaglich* – uneasy, out of joint and I was increasingly aware that I was going to have soon grow a pair and face up to what was becoming inevitable. My feelings of being in the wrong life were crystallising and it would be the empty space I was now flying back to that would finally allow the reiki, the power so long stored, to come bursting forth annd ensure my real work would begin. There would be no stopping it, and no turning back.

CHAPTER TWENTY ONE.

TREADING WATER.

Where our hero meets Michael (who'd been patiently waiting), faces the truth and finds you really *really* can't go back....

'Beautiful'.

by Christine Aguilera. No.17. April 15th, 2003

''Cause we are beautiful no matter what they say
Yes, words won't bring us down, no, no
We are beautiful in every single way
Yes, words can't bring us down, oh, no
So don't you bring me down today...'

I will not be belittled. I am beautiful. I have worth. Fuck off.

~ ~ ~

So, we walk in and it's like walking into a squat. The last straw really. At least, I thought I'd have my house to go back to, but the family to whom the agency had let it to had fucked off without paying rent and left the place like a, well a squat. It stank of fags and cat piss. It clearly hadn't been cleaned for – well probably hadn't been cleaned at all. There were drifts of animal hair piled up along the skirting boards, black greasy hands prints on the doors and walls. The 'recycling' was just outside the kitchen window and it reeked. It was heart-breaking. The agency, to whom we paid £200 a month to manage the house, to deal with the rent, clearly had been nowhere near the place and we'd been too far away to know. Not a propitious start, I think you'll agree. But *'somebody, somebody, up there likes me'*, as David Bowie once said (not about me obviously).

My Dad – remember him? Two years of not having to see him or deal with his Machiavellian shit; it had been most welcome – he'd decided to sell the house where Mum had died some years back and had moved into Newquay, across the road from Barrie and Rosemary. What they'd thought of this is unrecorded but I imagine Barrie said something like: *"That's fantastic. He IS my Dad."* and she, *"Oh for FUCK'S SAKE. I really don't want to have to put up with the miserable old cunt living next door practically, and being over here all the time, moaning about everything and everyone.*" I'd have been with her on that one. After some time, he then decided to sell – sorry GIFT - that house, split the money between we five (including multi-millionaire brother Michael...) and we ended up with a lump sum each. He eventually ended up in a sheltered flat in Truro, overlooking the Cathedral. The lucky bastard.

So.

Sandra spent all hers on some failing business she and her latest fool had got themselves into.

Gill lent her £15,000 of hers to prop up said business, against everyone's advice. Business went bust. Gill never got a penny back. Massive split in the family, which had never healed to this day.

Barrie probably put his in the bank and Michael probably never even noticed.

And I, I used mine to remodel my house. New kitchen, new furniture, decorated throughout, new this, new that, new Stuff. When what I should have done, while I had the money and the chance, is fucked right off, and when I got there, kept fucking off. But I didn't. We just paid some debts and it, and my chance of escape, was gone.

We now, suddenly had no income, apart from David's benefits, and a mortgage to pay. Welcome to the real world. The world I had fled from......are you just not listening? Although, to be practical, I had to go to work again. In schools, as it was the only toolkit I had.

....Angels flapping their wings in frustration....

And so I applied to be accepted on the supply pool, so I could be back in the classroom! Brilliant. It was the only thing I was good at and we needed food and of course we had to start buying some Stuff again. How quickly we resumed normal service...

I got quite a lot of work actually. Some very good – more permanent, half terms, or a few consecutive weeks which at least gave you a chance to learn the kid's names and for them to learn to stop fucking about because I would be back the next day. And the next. Those were the best gigs. The one-day covers were the worst...nothing was ever achieved, the kids were uninspired and disengaged and often bore a striking resemblance to those kids, so long ago, back in the Dockland School. One class, post – SATs, Summer holidays approaching, school play over (Do it the *last week*. It's not rocket science) were so bored, so difficult, that in the middle of the double Maths lesson I had been left to teach (what was she THINKING??) I slammed shut the text book, packed up my stuff, closed my briefcase and walked out.

"Where you going sir?"

"Home."

"But what about the Maths Sir?"

"I couldn't give a shit, to be honest." (Not very professional I know, but I'm a teacher, not a zookeeper and I had had ENOUGH of the little bastards.) *"Do what you fucking like."*

Passing the reception, I tossed by security badge through the hatch, said, *"You can tell the Head I've gone. Year 6 are alone. I deserve better."* And walked out. Probably never to be employed again. Actually, about a week later I received an envelope containing 36 letters of apology, obviously written under duress and therefore meaningless. I binned them.

But there WERE some great times, one in particular, which was how it USED to be – spontaneous, engaging. The head, a formidable but adored woman had called a meeting for all the staff, 'just during assembly, ten minutes at the most...'

"No worries," I said. *"I can take assembly. I can do a song with them."*

"It's the whole school today, Friday."

"Oh. Well, its OK, it'll be fine."

And it was! Bloody marvellous in fact. The meeting dragged on for almost 40 minutes, but when Jane hurried in, full of apologies, she was met by a wall of sound – her whole school singing a four part round and just loving it. When they'd finished, she said, *"Well children, that was wonderful! Let's all thank Mr Bray!"* and they applauded, with real enthusiasm and it felt great. Then one of the Y6 girls put up her hand and said,

"Miss, can we sing you the others?"

And Jane, seeing this for the perfect moment it was, got a chair, and sat right at the front and listened, astonished, to her school, all of them, singing songs in 4 parts that half an hour ago, they'd never even heard. All of them – the lazy, the naughty, the usually disinterested, loving the feeling that only unison singing can give. That was the highlight of all of that time and I look back on it with fondness.

One other incident of note - have you noticed how few there are? How little to tell you? When you consider the early parts of this book – always stuff going on. Now? Not a lot. What had happened to me? *Meeting David* had, that's what. And I had let it happen - concerns an old Object of Desire….

I had a few days booked in at school on the South Coast and my route to it took me past a newly developed block of apartments; chic des.res. places (in one of the worst places imaginable other than it was near a massive tourist attraction), developed by none other than Steve, my nemesis, my oldest friend and still, burning bright in my memory from 30 years earlier, the most beautiful man I knew. Anyway, one of the times, coming home from school, I saw the front door open and on the spur of (premeditated? - who am I kidding?) the moment, pulled in and knocked. And there he was, all business like, still with those eyes from which there never an escape.

"Oh. Hi!"

"Hi! (There they were again. Tacit agreement.) *I was just passing and saw your car. I thought you could show me round your 'project'? You keep going on about how good it is, so….."*

"Yep, come on in."

I have to say he'd done a fantastic job but then having seen his house, it was always going to be very upmarket – we went in to the lounge of the first flat and sat.

"Well….I have to admit you've done a great job here. Very nice."

A small smile played across his face. *"Yeah, its brilliant, isn't it?"*

Still such an arrogant twat….but he was right. The boy'd done good.

"Let me show you round. Kitchen – sorry about the mess – we had a party here last night; I'm here trying to clear up….Bathroom…..two bedrooms, very well appointed I think you'll agree…Nice size.." What are you, a fuckin Estate agent now? I don't want to buy one, I'm just here for….well, what? What

WAS I here for? We both knew of course and he was just playing me, like he always had.

Back in the lounge, sitting facing each other.

"Well, there you go. They're all the same, so there's no point in going around them. Anything else you want to see?"

And there it was – that great space, that great silence we both knew would come, into which like a junkie, unable not to, I said: *"Your cock, please."* Just like that. Oooft.

Again, that slight shimmer of a smile, like he knew this was going to happen, like he'd just been waiting…*"Bedroom Two, I think,"* and off we went.

It was like being 19 again, trembly and full of guilt and screaming passion. Hand on arm. Hand on face. Pull in to kiss, brush against rough face, hand on belly, fingers on shirt buttons, hair, oh! Sweet Jesus! that belly hair, belt buckles clicking, trousers falling, cocks straining, pulling together feeling the thrust and heat of erections…and a great silence, a stillness that echoed back down the years, a hurricane tunnel of memory, to London, to Chris, to the agony this man had caused me and with that fleeting rush of thought, my ability to perform this ritual was over. My erection wilted and I felt foolish and ashamed.

"Hey. What's up? Don't you fancy me anymore?" He was holding his cock, proudly jutting out from that impossible riot of hair, dark strong legs, full balls, belly hair – like a photograph, like the most beautiful thing, in aspic.

"No. I mean, yes of course…I don't know what happened. Give me a minute…." and standing in the bathroom, looking at my shrivelled dick, I knew this was a huge mistake and I just didn't know why I was even here. …..Actually, yes I did. I did actually. It was to prove that I had a life outside of my tiny room. Being able to make a decision, to do something spontaneous, to do something I wanted, without having to ask….to prove that I still had a life of my own….even if it was to cheat on my lover.

I looked into the bedroom and he was now on the bed, in the falling light, his cock hard and proud and he was still beautiful, still capable of inflaming a rage of lust and with that thought, I responded and joined him on the bed. Running my hand across that glorious spread of hair on his chest, down his belly, down the dark trail to his beautiful cock, cupping his balls tenderly……it

WAS déjà vu, but beautifully so, and, knowing this, I was healed – that sadness, residual in my heart from so long ago, left me with a soft whisper; I didn't even know I was carrying it but there it was, and now it was gone.

"Can I fuck you?" he said.

"No, it's too personal for me. Too symbolic, too.... we're not lovers, so for me it's a bit too much."

"You didn't used to be so fussy..."

*"Ah. But then, I loved you; then, I thought we were lovers; **then**, I thought that we were, we would be.....*"

Oh, OK, well, just suck me off then." Nothing if not pragmatic....

Which with great alacrity and joy, I did, knowing as I took his cock in my mouth and as I tasted the salt of his semen, it was like a benediction and I knew for certain, that this would never happen again. It was done. Just like it had been with my other drug, Rod, back in Ilford – the last hurrah. I didn't know how heavy the burdens of memory, of failure, of grief and pain had been, until they flew away.

So here we were, back in the world I'd left behind. Going out to the curry house – *'there's nothing like an English curry! They're shit in Germany....'* – and the kebab shop. Clothes. CDs. Stuff. Shoes. Stuff. Bigger better telly. Stuff. It all felt so wrong, like I had had an out of body experience. You know, like in those films where the action freezes for ages – days, months, years even – and then starts off again exactly in the same place? Well, that's what it was like. It was like I'd been abducted by aliens for two years and it all went on, same old, same old and then I just reappeared and it seemed nobody had noticed I had gone! I don't recall being asked, not once, about my adventures; not one single *'ooh what was it like in Budapest? 'What did you do in Germany?'*....it was a feeling of dislocation, being back in a world that SEEMED the same, and fact was, very much so, but I was different. I'm not saying I'd *'moved on'*, *'improved'*, become *'better'*; just that I didn't fit anymore, I was on the edges, looking in.

Sure, people were pleased to see us at parties, when we went, but it was the same old thing, the same group, the same conversations, as if I'd just nipped out for a two-year fag break. Don't get me wrong – I loved these people, they were my friends and I had known them many years, but now....and I only know this now as I look back and try to unravel all the events that led me down the path I took later...but now, there seemed to be a....a sheet of glass between me and them; very thin so I could hear everything, see clearly, but not quite be in touch.

So...what was this telling me? Probably that I was the world's worst Reiki Master who couldn't tell his angelic realm from his arse. Why didn't I connect these two things? I was being guided, guided away to a new place, nudged gently by spirit and I just kept buying CDs! Brilliant.

On our return however I have to say that meeting up again with Anna was a significant thing – she was and always has been an old soul, able to see through most of the bullshit of this world, including mine, so when she said, *"Why haven't you started your healing practice yet?"* I was both flummoxed and busted at the same time.

"You were sent away so you could shake off this life, and find a space to begin a new one. Spirit has been yelling, so loud, I could hear it, and you just keep turning up the volume on the CD player drowning it out. What are you so scared of? Of course, you can choose what you want – that's part of the deal, but really, should you be wasting time and NOT beginning? You will be a very powerful healer, if you don't let your ego get in the way. Now go. Make a difference".

I'd been busted and bollocked. All at the same time.

What I was scared of was being shit at it. It was all very well 'doin' yer mates', but asking people to pay for something *SO* intangible was a difficult thing for me to reason. The energy, the chi, the Universal Force was free, so it just didn't feel right to ask for money. David's *"Well, you could get the £450 back that I paid for your training"* aside, there was something about people paying for a service and I guess giving reiki was that, albeit a mighty life changing one. Actually....put that way, it was worth every penny – so, armed with a somewhat shaky reasoning, I bought a couch and began to advertise and...LO! They came. *'Build it and they will come'*, as Kevin Costner once said, and it seemed as if everyone had been waiting for me (or more accurately, someone who could give them reiki) and I soon built up a small, but regular client base. What this also did was to move me further still, away from the life I had had before. As I tuned into spirit more and more, I became reluctant to be buying stuff I didn't need - shopping became something about which I felt increasingly guilty, but conflicted because I still had another life, one which involved parties and restaurants and needing clothes for them, and maybe a different cologne. (I didn't! Of course I didn't, but undoing so many years of habit is not easy, so don't be too hard on me - I was doing my best, with Michael's help.) Oh, let me introduce you – Michael, say hello! These are my lovely readers who have been with me for some time now (about 435 pages and 47 years); Readers, this is Michael. He is an archangel. He is the one to whom I have been assigned for guidance and when healing, he's the one who comes and shows me what to do. Nice wings, eh?

There is a third strand running along in this interlude in my life, where I was between lives, and one that also had an effect on what happened later. When we came back, we had a new neighbour. Well, she'd been there before we left actually, but David thought she was 'hippy' and beneath us, so we never spoke to her (I didn't seem to have much choice – I thought she looked pretty cool, but.....well, you know.) But when we came back, she and I made a real, deep connection, on two levels: she was deeply spiritual and connected with the Earth, its fairies and its plants, and, she was a total pisshead. We got on very well, and by now, somewhat more independent, I began to spend a lot of time with her, next door, laughing, smoking roll ups and sometimes joints (the first drugs I'd had since that heroin I had back in Clapham, in the late 70s, when I was still with Julie but fucking my mate while his sister, a high-class escort was out earning thousands of pounds and being dined (but not fucked) by rich Arab business men......

...I have just realised that I hadn't quite mentioned any of this! OK. My bad. I have thought hard about this episode, quite forgotten, and I cannot remember for the life of me where I met him....it MAY have been Harrods, it might have been.....no wait! I think it was Slobbidybobbidy who met his sister at the Piccadilly Hotel where she then worked and presumably where Fran was also 'working' Anyway, she invited us to their magnificent house on the edge of Clapham Common. That must be it – I cannot think of any other way, or place. Her brother Steve, or Deemo, was there, as he preferred to be called, and he was obviously gay and not my type at all, and anyway, I had a girlfriend blah blah.....thin, hawkish, no body hair (I didn't know yet what hankie he would've worn, as at that point I hadn't been 'educated' by Chris in the Salisbury, but as it turns out, it would have been Navy blue, and worn on both sides. FYI.)

Anyway, dinner was very grand; mostly because Fran worked as a high-class escort and the night before, one of her regulars had given her a ruby ring and two grand. This was the late 70s remember. That was a fucking fortune! So, we had my very first lobster, and good (apparently) champagne. We all got completely pissed, Julie crashed, and I ended up fucking Deems. And the other way round. It was nice. Unexpected, and it didn't mean anything cos I had a girlfriend etc. I KNOW what you're thinking....but the Cock Imperative + Champagne = Inevitable Shagging. Many of you would have done, have done, the same. Thing was though, I kind of had a little thing for this sweet unsuitable man and went to see him quite often – *"Just going over to Clapham, be back late. Love you.."* – how it was ever entertained I don't know; sometimes she came with me and, dear readers (OK, now this *IS* bad) we used to get really pissed and go to bed and then I'd get up when she'd fallen asleep, creep down and shag Deemo, who would always be waiting. Or the other way round. Or one after the other. It was a very odd thing. We'd go to the Two Brewers on the High Street, a notorious gay pub, and somehow it was alright. The more I write this the more I realise what a transition period this was. Before, the 'I have a girlfriend' stuff only applied at Balls Park (BALLS Park HAHAHHAAA!) and we had already been through the Tony debacle and were now in our little love nest in Leyton. Only clearly it wasn't THAT cosy. We had a nice time – it was like *being* gay but not really, because ...yeah, yeah. Fooling nobody, least of all Julie. This was clearly the chrysalis stage; I was pupating in Clapham. Anyway, that set the scene for this bizarre interval of time; it couldn't have gone on for more than a few months because by 1980, I'd moved out, Chris had come to London and it had all gone a bit Pete Tong, as they say. So it must have been May 1979. I know that, because I was at Deemo's and Fran came home, after a night shift, clutching a bag and contained therein was David Bowie's *'Lodger'* album which was just released on May 18th and she had bought it instantly (cash probably, as she'd made about £800 that night – *"He's not one of the generous ones"*, she'd say, waving around a wad of money it'd take me a month to earn. "*Dinner was nice though, and I did get this necklace...*" and put it on the record player and *'Fantastic Voyage'* filled the flat, with Bowie's extraordinary voice soaring through the flat and making her wee a bit. After we'd had some dinner, and as Talking Heads' *'Fear Of Music'* was put on the system in the lounge, this happened:

"I've got some coke, if you want some." said Fran.

"No, I'll stick with the beer thanks," I said.

"No, you tart Coke. COCAINE," said Deemo.

"Oh. Erm….."

"I'll have a line, Fran," he said and cut it on the black and green album cover. I watched in fascination. I KNEW about it of course, but had never seen it. I felt very cool indeed. After two or three more beers, I was feeling rather less inhibited so when Deems said, *"Can I have another line, Fran?"* I said, *"Me too, please!"*

"None left. He only had a bit. Got some heroin though."

And yes, somehow, they persuaded me. I wasn't injecting it in to my eyeballs or anything, before you all gasp. It was tablet form and anyway they and the beer said it would be OK, so, to the sounds of 'I ZIMBRA' I took my first (and only) heroin. I don't know what I was expecting, actually. But, if you try to listen to the lyric of the last track on that album, *'Drugs'*, you may get some idea.

It was fuzzy, it was rushy, it was hot, it was peculiar, it was loving……I've never had it since, although I would've then, in an instant, but they of course refused. Anyway – there you go. May '79 until 2003 – completely clean! I don't know what happened to little Deems. We lost touch gradually – it was one of those strange interludes, strangers colliding, moving through. For me, it was another brick on the tower of homobricks that I was, at that time, valiantly trying to balance, the weight of which was becoming unmanageable.

So, my neighbour. The third of the Three Tall Women, sent to make David's life unbearable…. Gill, which bond he could never break; Ann, who was too wise to be daunted and Gaynor, who really didn't give a shit what he thought. His unholy Trinity. But I loved (and still do) love them all and each brought something to my table: love, courage and joy. Some of each from each of them. They were my saviours and my tormentors, my jokers and my truth tellers, and when things got really really bad, they, each one, carried me along on their unfailing tide of care and love.

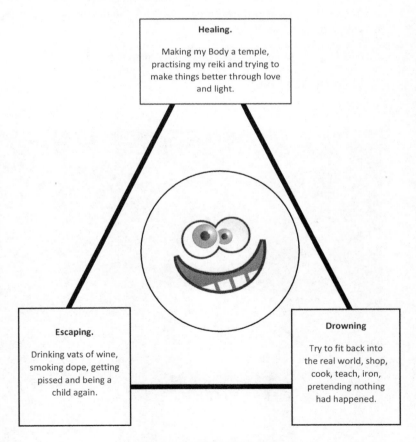

Healing.

Making my Body a temple, practising my reiki and trying to make things better through love and light.

Escaping.

Drinking vats of wine, smoking dope, getting pissed and being a child again.

Drowning

Try to fit back into the real world, shop, cook, teach, iron, pretending nothing had happened.

Mr. Lucky's Triangle Of Confusion.

I had no bloody idea where I was. I careened from corner to corner of this triangle, never settling, at each point feeling that I should be at one of the other two. It was madness and I felt really really lost. In addition to all this – between setting up my practice (ignoring Michael tutting and flapping his wings in impatience), trying to get a Normal Life, like it was, in the Old Days, where nobody had any curiosity, just carried on as normal – same houses, same parties, same shops, same sex, and nipping next door for some wine a bit of weed and a mad half hour / afternoon / all dayer, I also wasn't feeling especially well. Just knackered. Verk, as we say. I put it down to too much excitement! Parties, boozing, going next door too much....I was getting on a bit you know – couldn't do it like I used to.....

How did I go from Kecskemét hero to Bodmin zero so fast?

And so the year passed.

Looking a bit desperate here.....

CHAPTER TWENTY TWO.

MR. LUCKY IS WELL AND TRULY FUCKED.

In which our hero gets somewhat of a shock, gets to pay his dues, forgets what size shoes he takes and find out who his friends really are.

'Comfortably Numb'

The Scissor Sisters. No.94. 11 November 2004.

'There is no pain you are receding
A distant ship smoke on the horizon
You are only coming through in waves
Your lips move but I can't hear what you're saying...'

My world shattered. I was numb and dumb and all apart. Can you show me where it hurts?

~ ~ ~

11.11.11

What does that mean to most of us? Armistice, probably. The end of slaughter. Our boys, the ones that were left, coming home, with varying amounts of limbs but still coming home. The memory of war. Poppies. Everyone in black. Mourning. Loss. One war ended. Laurence Binyon. Last Posts.

Well, for me, apart from that, and it being the old man's birthday (Oh! The irony!), it was the day, in 2004, I was told I was HIV positive.

At exactly 11.11.11., 2004. My war began that day.

Mr. Lucky was, as my sainted lady mother was wont to say, SHIT outa luck.

Let me take you back.....

1980. Met Rod. Faithful (ish). Met Ken. Faithful. Moved back home to Cornwall. Met David. Faithful (apart from a couple of mutual wanks here and there) for 18 years. So. I know, having met Rod since, he was not infected. Ken is alive and well, and although I don't know his status, I DO know, that as a very scared ex- Jehovah's Witness, I was the first person he'd fucked. And David, as it turns out is one of the blessed few that carries the gene which prevents HIV from attaching itself and so he cannot become infected. Therefore, surely this must put the date of my infection somewhere before 1980, those few months of glorious sex when I had left Julie and was putting myself about a bit. It MUST'VE been then, surely? The freedom, you see – I was able to be me, a gay man, a walking erection, a thirst for identity. But oh, what bad luck was mine – AIDS, as it was, all lilies, falling tombstones and BIG CAPITAL LETTERS, was barely in the country then, or at least not amongst the people I knew. Clearly, I was wrong.

Looking back through wiser eyes, I know *now* that I was **POZ** – look at those three letters, standing out from the crowd, with no other meaning! – for TWENTY FOUR years, without knowing, having unprotected sex with David (lucky for CCR5,eh?). POZ when I lived in Leytonstone, POZ when I lived in Walthamstow, POZ when I lived in Bodmin for 17 years, POZ when I was in Hungary, POZ when I was in Germany, POZ while I was teaching….who knew eh? I didn't, that's for sure.

So, you can imagine my horror, gentle reader, that morning on Armistice Day 2004 when the kind nurse said, *"We've got your results…..and I'm afraid to tell you that they're positive…."*

"HA!" I hear you cry! *"What did you expect? We've read about your shenanigans! We know you were shagging in woods/cubicles/cars/junkshops/stranger's beds…..what did you expect? No more than you deserve, I say…."*

But, no. Nobody *deserves* this. Not the sexually active, not the queers or the hetties, not the mainliners, not the whores, not the unwilling wives of African men, not the haemophiliacs, not the trauma victims needing blood. Nobody DESERVES it. Like cancer, it has no heart or soul, no freedom of will. It is just a lickle bitty virus that some folks get – and yes, even straight ones – and their life choices or otherwise are irrelevant. It takes one needle from thousands; one fuck amongst many. You throw your hat in the ring and hope. Could've been a bus. At least you wouldn't have judged me then, eh?

"We are the product of our choices and those choices do not render us more or less deserving of love. Love me because I am human. Love me because I am

flawed and made mistakes. Love me anyway even if you disagree with my choices", says Dr. Rick Coons, an American Clinical Psychologist. Just be nice, eh? It's hard enough as it is without *you* thinking I'm bad.

Anyway…..

There then followed a thousand year silence….funny that…not much earlier I'd been planning to have a minute's silence for my fallen ancestors…. I don't remember much about it actually, other than saying, *"But that's impossible. You must be wrong."* in a very tiny voice, but knowing, judging by the looks of concern from the ring of nurses looking down on me, that they weren't. But how? HOW? I hadn't had sex with anyone else for seventeen years, and yet, and yet….I'd been feeling pretty shitty on and off for quite a while. Nothing definable, just a bit verk. Looking back at my old passport photo, which I'd had to have for Hungary, I can see, now, a ghostly pallor, a kind of sickness….nothing obvious, just…well, as I said, verk. Unknown to me of course, the virus was multiplying and killing me softly, with its deadly song. Apparently, as I found out later, I was a 'long term progressor', which means I had been infected long ago but the virus had been dormant for years and years. Why it begins its march toward victory and death is not known, but for me it was my salvation. Had I 'converted' earlier, joined the church of the dying and the damned, I would have been given AZT which would have killed me sooner. As it was 2004 by now, the treatment and medication was exponentially improved and so, I was saved from the horror of cancers, blindness, dementia and death. For now, anyway.

Thinking about it now, I had had a peculiar incident the April before this, which went unresolved. I was sitting in bed at home one morning, naked, as always and David said. *"What's that?"* *"What? Where?"* I answered. *"There. On your chest. Oooh. And on your arms…."* Fuck! What the hell…..? As I watched, this rash appeared, as if someone was flicking pink paint. It just spread and spread, like a speeded-up film until, within a few minutes I looked like Leopard Man, only pink. What the….?

David rang our doctor who, clearly puzzled and concerned, rang for an ambulance and before I knew it, I was in hospital, being stared at and prodded with a biro. No one seemed to have any idea of what it could be and stranger, I felt perfectly well - no fever, nothing. They went away, obviously puzzled having asked me the statutory list of questions. They hadn't come across the

Amazing Leopard Man before and clearly weren't too clear on being anywhere near me. Maybe THEY'D catch it.....

I know now that I was 'seroconverting'; that is, that after nearly two decades of lying dormant within, something had caused the virus to break out. Having no other answer, the consultant said "HAVE AN HIV TEST". Yes, in that voice, in those capital letters, but clearly, as I couldn't possibly have HIV, I told her to fuck off. Well, not quite, but obviously such a thing would have been pointless, wouldn't it?

From that time though, I began contracting odd illnesses; nothing serious but frequent. I kept going to see my doctor (for whom grateful thanks – when the ghastly truth came out, she was nothing but gentle and kind, and in the world of terror and disease I now suddenly found myself, her gentle voice and her helpful manner was of incalculable value) who kept coming up with no answer.

That day, that dreadful day, when I heard the nurse say, "YOU'VE GOT AIDS AND YOU'RE GOING TO DIE!!!!!" was a life – changer, in more ways than one. Snippets, little pieces of fragmented memories, come back when I recall that day. The consultant to whom I had been assigned (and again, whose manner and skill were to be the saving of me. Literally.) said, I remember: *"I know this must be a shock, but we can get you on the right drugs and soon you'll be saying to yourself - I have hazel eyes, I have size 8 feet. Oh and I have HIV. It will become that normal"*. I just stared at her. How could it EVER become normal? I was diseased, full of worms and death. How would it be NORMAL??? I didn't reply; I was just battered into silence by the voices in my head. *How did I have this ...this **THING**? What will I tell my family? Who will ever speak to me again once they know? How much longer do I have to live? DON'T fucking lie to me!! I've seen it. I've been at the bedsides of the blind, the cancerous, the dementing ones as the virus dissolved their brains. I watched my soulmate choke to death. I KNOW. I KNOW. Just tell me. ......*

11 / 11. At 11 a.m. as well. Ha! That's funny, eh? My world spun away from me that day. I don't recall what David said or did. He was probably horrified too, both for me and what the implications were for him, unknowing then about his charmed life.

I was then whisked off in to the innards of the building, following the white coats dumbly. They sat me down and smiled and took some more blood and smiled and took my blood pressure, smiling, smiling, smiling as if that would make all better. Nothing, NOTHING was going to make this better. My sense of horror and my sense of fear and my sense of shock and my sense of bewilderment alternated, phased in and out while I just sat, motionless, speechless and tearless. How did she know I had size 8 feet? Maybe it was just a metaphor.....or an analogy. The walls were a pleasant colour. Her hands were a bit cold, the cuff a bit tight, the vein blue and pulsing, my bladder full (just as well as they wanted my piss as well as my blood and my soul).

And so it went.

We went home, numb, voiceless, to a future I was certain would be short, full of fear as to which of the sicknesses would do for me....Karposi's Sarcoma? Dementia? PCP? That's what killed my best friend, I saw it. (Oh I knew all the names from my buddying days, days when it was nothing to do with me and I could hold hands in safety). Who would be there to hold MY hand as I drowned in despair and disease? No one must know. Maybe my Dad was right? This is my punishment for joining the Shit Shover's Union.

I don't really remember the next few weeks linearly; they just consisted of countless trips backwards and forward to the clinic, where I just sat and listened, sure that it was all a waste of time. I KNEW the score, both figuratively and literally. I knew all about CD4s and CD8s, viral loads and HDL. I had been on the internet all through the nights when I was unable to sleep, trying to find answers to how long I could expect to live and how to limit the horrors of what was surely to come, neither of which, of course was possible. 25 miles one way, 25 the other, over and over.

This memoir was supposed to be a light hearted romp through my life, but gentle reader, for now, you will find no laughter here, no anecdotes, no joy. Fear, and shame. Nothing more.

I KNEW that there were drugs available to me and I also knew the side effects – constant diarrhoea, vomiting, nausea, weight (and cholesterol) gain, lipodystrophy, Buffalo Humps, 'Sculptra' to fill in the pits in your face and your arse, 'The AIDS Face', which would mean be being pointed at in the street, spat at like my dear dead friends were and beaten up. Lots to look forward to...

....but as my CD4 count was THIRTY ONE, and yours is probably 700, 800 and it is recommended that therapy should start when your count has fallen to 350, I was right up shit street.....the only variable really was *when* to begin the drugs. My consultant gave me good advice, but somehow, I was scared, more scared of the drugs than what would inevitably happen if I DIDN'T take them. The final process was that she would prescribe them and I could take them "when I was ready". When was that going to be? Now? Next month when I was even sicker? Sometime in the future when I had summoned up the courage to face the awful consequences of putting these massively toxic chemicals into my body? Once a day. For ever – however long THAT might be.

OK, so here's the thing. On November 10th, I was OK. Not very well, but OK. 24 hours later, I knew I had AIDS. Not just HIV, but AIDS. That kills you. Well, the stuff you can no longer fight *kills* you. Just capital letters – same shit.

 What a difference a day makes; 24 little hours…..it was, I don't know now, maybe a week before I began my HAART. And having AIDS brought far more with it than a compromised immune system. It brought fear and shame and stigma and shunning and loneliness and eventually a descent into a possible pain filled and messy death. And I HAD IT! Whoop whoop! What a turn up! Oh, *LUCKY* Mr. Lucky. Everyone I had befriended and nursed and comforted when I worked at the respite centre had died, more or less, as the years went by, so it seemed fairly likely that I would do. Bollocks. Bollocks **BOLLOCKS**. This was NOT in the plan.

So. I sat on the edge of the bed, holding the pills in my hand – 3 for the HIV (only one now. Ain't science amazing?), 1 to combat the sickness I would feel, 1 to combat the diarrhoea I would get and one for the little boy who lives down the lane. They were all lovely different colours too – that would make it all much easier, much more fun. I sat on the bed. And I sat on the bed some more, knowing that from the moment those three tablets passed through my throat, that there would be no going back – I didn't know what side effects I would suffer, but I finally saw I had no choice – the virus would continue to devour me, with less and less to defend myself and eventually – quite soon, if the subliminal messages from my consultant were being correctly read – it would overrun me and I would die. Simples.

But. BUT!! And here IS some joy in this dark chapter – I had NO side effects! None whatsoever! Well, except, and I remember this clearly, much to the amusement of Nicki, that the one psychoactive episode I DID have from the Tenofovir, was that I dreamed I married Beyoncé. Really. That's all. No nausea, no squits, no humps or wasting of fat. I knew these things, if they WERE to happen, would not be immediate, but I was relieved enough just to wake up the next day.

After a week I had my next appointment (someone was sitting in MY seat, cheeky bastard. I should've had a plaque put there), I had blood results and my viral load, which had been immeasurable as the detector only went up to 1 million, had dropped to 2,038 and my CD4 had 'leapt' up to 115! In a week. In a FUCKING WEEK!!! Oh *YES*! Maybe I wouldn't die? The drugs DO work, Verve! They fucking well DO!!!! Euphoria! We all had a little dance, and a group hug, the blood nurse and me, with Nicki happy as it seemed I was responding and she wasn't going to lose me after all. We grew very fond of each other actually and it was quite hard to say goodbye when eventually I left her care.

I was so chuffed (the understatement of the century) that momentarily I forgot the reality of my situation, which was although these Wonder Drugs (they certainly WERE Highly Active!) would probably reverse my AIDS, I would still have HIV, and would ALWAYS have HIV. Dealing with that, at this point wasn't a priority. Manana. Dreckly. For now, I was going to live.

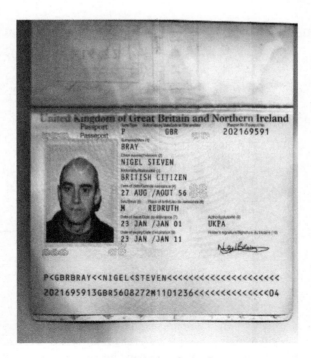

How did I not know?

DATE	VL	CD4	%	HDL
NOV 04	>1000000	31	2.85	4.3
JAN 05	2,038	115	5.0	6.4
FEB 05	165	159	7.8	5.9
MARCH 05	125	202	9.1	6.9
MAY 05	<50	168	10.0	7.0
JUNE 05	<50	199	11.8	7.2
JULY 05	<50	209	11.06	6.4
SEPT 05	56	205	11.9	6.1
NOV 05	<40	204	12%	6.4
FEB 06	<40	260	13.1%	6.7
MAY 06	<40	248	14.4%	6.4
AUG 06	<40	366	15.6%	6.0
NOV 06	<40	356	16.8%	6.2
FEB 07	80	244	17.1%	7.3
MAY07	<40	249	17.9%	6.7
AUG07	<40	326	17.2%	6.2

I became obsessed with my 'numbers' as they were known. In those days, as I was somewhat still at risk, I was tested every month and I rigorously kept a note in a chart of what they were, as if seeing it in writing made it real. Seems a bit sad now, but at the time it made the fact I probably WASN'T going to die more tangible.

I kept it up for three years, but it became somewhat redundant as clearly if I was still writing it, I was still around. Those months, years were very difficult and My Chart was a security blanket, proof of my existence. I pored over those numbers, went into meltdown if my CD dropped, or remained stationery, and examined them for proof that all was well.

What I WASN'T told about however, maybe because it was generally held to be A Good Thing, was 'Immune Reconstitution Syndrome' or IRS. Without going into the medicine and science of it (I can if you want – I became an expert....!) it basically means that when the drugs begin to work, your immune system rebuilds rapidly, as you can see by the numbers, and because of that, it starts to react and attacks things that have lain dormant in your system that it would normally have ignored. So. I got hairy leucoplakia, a severe oral thrush infection, and swollen lymph nodes (more of which later) and....yay!, Shingles. THE most painful thing I have ever experienced. The kind round your head and face and eyes...lovely. The trigeminal nerve that affects the face, jaw, gums, ears, scalp and eyes. The IRS had awoken the herpes virus we all have dormant in the base of our spines and BLAM. I could barely, speak, smile, laugh, lay my head down, wash, chew....anything, any SLIGHT movement which caused my skin to move was agonizing. Plus, I looked like a Klingon.

The result of this, apart from the GUM staff all nodding and going "ooooh, them scabs are coming on nicely, eh?" was drugs. Drugs by the bucketful. I had amitriptyline for the shingles, fluconazole for the thrush, antiviral medication for the leukoplakia, zopiclone to help me sleep through the pain, Tenofovir, Emtricitabine and Efavirenz for the HIV, prochlorperazin for the nausea (which I didn't actually have) and something else for the glands which were swollen, Terbinafine for a fungal infection in my toe, 17 in all, more than I can remember the names of. Everyday. Until the infections disappeared, one by one.

It was the absolute worst time of my life; I am so sorry now for the schadenfreude I felt when I was nursing clients at the respite house, for thinking 'Phew! That's lucky! THAT could've been me!!' when actually, for 18 years...it was!

All this, for a fuck, long, long ago, probably drunken and probably shit anyway.

So, for the next few weeks it was sleep, cry, take drugs, cry, drive on an endless conveyer belt of misery and fear. I had no plan about how to deal with it yet. Still no – one knew, and my whole universe revolved around the GU clinic and my bed, where I could sleep and escape, just for a while. The shock of this was profound and David really didn't know how to deal with it apart from being practical – feeding me, getting me to my appointments and trying to reassure me, mostly failing on that one. I kind of knew that, by now, I wasn't going to die, at least not in the short term. What was SO devastating, so utterly traumatizing was the fact of HAVING it, all these years, through all my travels and adventures, and not having a clue. I cannot describe adequately how this felt to me. The shock, the horror was SO deep, so overwhelming, I had no idea how to move forward. In addition to which, I was beginning to feel pain in my legs and feet, as the IRS continued along its jolly way. The nerves in my extremities had been damaged by 18 years of viral assault and now I had 'peripheral neuropathy' as well. Hurrah! Could it get worse? Well, yes actually – I'll tell you about that in a minute. Its not pretty...

As my system was reawakened, more things became clear. The virus had threaded its stealthy way into my brain – I look back and realized how slow of thought, how forgetful, I had become. As the HAART worked, so my brain function improved. But so too did the knowledge that my hearing had become damaged; I began to be able to drive at night again so it seemed that it was in my eyes too, as my night vision had deteriorated so badly, I couldn't see at night; the pain in my reawakened nerves was getting worse. The only way to describe how it felt is as if boiling water had been poured on them, or bad sunburn. So, joy of joys – more drugs! Pregabablin. Does the trick – I'd have taken anything to stop it hurting. I take them now, still. If I miss one, the pain returns after about 18 hours, distant at first, then more and more insistent until it is unbearable. So, another legacy. Another Forever drug.

I noticed too that I had a small lump in the back of my throat. On telling Nicki, she sent me to ENT (another day, another department) whereupon the utterly GORGEOUS consultant said that he would like a biopsy done on the lump, *"just in case; probably nothing, but better to be safe, eh*?" and was scheduled for three days' time. Bloody hell - that was quick......

So, back to hospital again. Different department, same fear. Bearing in mind I was mid – shingles and I couldn't bear to be touched in any way, here I was, facing throat examinations.....I was put in a 'private' room (as in: 'HE'S GOT AIDS – KEEP HIM AWAY FROM US'. Actually, I HADN'T by this stage, so FUCK. YOU.) and told I'd be first in the morning. Obviously, I didn't sleep as I couldn't put my head on the pillow and my amitriptyline wasn't due yet. I was NBM, and bloody starving.

Morning came and so did a consultant who said, actually, I was to be LAST, because they'd have to disinfect the theatre afterwards so last in the day was best, didn't I agree? I agreed, dumbly. I'm not sure if I understood the implications of what he meant until long after – too full of sorrow and self-pity to think very widely but clearly, they'd decided the AIDS guy should go last. And that's what happened. After a 9 hour wait, they came to get me, put me on the trolley and wheeled me down. Most undignified, those gowns, eh? Arse hanging out. Dimly aware if my arse *hadn't hung out* all those years ago, I wouldn't be here now... I asked what he was injecting me with and he told me it was penguin milk. Before I had chance to answer, I was gone and then woke up in recovery. Sore throat, job done.

I just needed to get the all clear and get on with trying to reassemble my former life, and get back to the time before my whole existence had been blown apart.

Then it got worse.

 It was cancer.

Oh yes, my dear friends. What wonderful news! Still reeling from my HIV diagnosis, still trying to believe my disgusting death was not imminent as I first thought, I get told I have the big C.

I got a letter (from my hunky ENT man) to say my result was with him at Bodmin hospital, nice and local. We could go and get it then nip down ASDA. That was the plan. We went into his office and there he was, all hairy and muscly (I know – some things you just can't help...!) on his swivel chair. He asked me to sit down and then he said: *"Wjf sdofm\cpsdmi\hsgh zdhfoz a4ut 4jsmofjmv\[ej sd\p \of* **CANCER** *moef\sopebnan040ubnt0weitv-]3tn idfzjbrjgp-&^$^^%&%(*Ylo"*

I just stared at him, with the Word bouncing madly off the walls, into my ears, out again, into my head......

Realising I hadn't heard, he repeated what he said:" *I'm afraid it's positive. You have Non – Hodgkinson's Lymphoma, but don't worry!! It's very early, and very treatable...."*

Oh, that's OK then. I must've been REAL bad in a former life to deserve this......AIDS, HIV and now CANCER! How fabulous. Again, it was one of those blank, buzzing kind of moments, where the world grinds into slow motion, just like they say on the telly. I heard nothing more but the hammering of my own heart, saw nothing but the swirly brown carpet as I felt all hope, so recently regained, drain from me into pools of despair ay my feet. Still, I suppose if I was going to die, it would be from a respectable disease and they wouldn't have to lie on my headstone.

I think I said, *"Oh, ok."* But I don't really remember.

So, it began again – same crushing fear, just a different department at the hospital. 'Oncology'. Just a small blue door, innocuous, but holding behind it a mass of suffering; wasting, rotting humans who come with high hopes, some hope or no hope at all and varying amounts of hair and time left in this world.

Amazingly, my consultant had got me a CAT scan for the next day; good and bad. Good because there was no waiting, no time to breed fear, and bad because if it was so 'treatable', what was the hurry?

The next day – it was a Thursday - I went to the scanner department and it was full. Full of defeated people with dull eyes, sitting, waiting for the big white machine to tell them the worst. Somehow, I was taken right to the front, forced to drink a pint of vile milky stuff, which reacts and flags up any tumours or evil within. Slapped on the bed, strapped into place and slid silently into the maw of this thing, this thing that would tell them how long I had left to live. I was, I recall, weirdly calm, intrigued almost. It was quick and painless, not like the death that I was now certain was near would be.

That was that. Another week's wait and back to the blue door, back to confusion, fear, raging hatred against this new thing that was happening to me. Today was 'Bone Marrow Day', which consisted of lying on a bed while the specialist gave me an anaesthetic, for the pain that was to come, although he did say that once he was drilling into the bone, the pain killer wouldn't work but that bit wouldn't last long......I'd rather not have known, thank you. The nurse, who was just lovely, was very reassuring whilst he actually drilled into my hip bone, asking me about Hungary and teaching, but hey, actually, the pain killer really *didn't* work...the massive drill bit removing a piece of bone from my hip was rather more present than the conversation I was trying to have. JESUS BLOODY CHRIST – that was excruciatingly painful, and that was WITH the anaesthetic. *"All done"* he said cheerily, *"Here it is!"* holding up a glass slide with my bone marrow already squashed upon it. *"You may have a little bruising,"* he said. You could say that – it stretched from my behind my knee to half way up my ribs and my arse was completely blue and yellow.

I told my oncologist that I was experiencing sharp pains in the centre of my spine; probing and touching revealed nothing so he arranged an MRI scan for a couple of days' time (again.....bit worrying....) to check. Seven bloody thirty in the morning, though looking back, I realize how much they were doing for me. I suspect, because all the departments are interlinked, Nicki may have told them about me and how horrified and traumatized I had been over my HIV and so they were being especially accommodating and kind to me. Whatever the reason am really truly grateful to you all. It was a horrible horrible time for me and the care you took of me enabled me to cope – I felt I was really being looked after. Anyway, the MRI scan went OK. One good thing – bizarre as it may sound – I heard, for the first time, Carly Simon singing (INSIDE the scanner!) *'Let the River Run'*. What a great song! Not the best place to discover it maybe, but one small victory over death!

Another week to wait. How people who are really in the throes of their disease cope with this staging, this waiting, bit by bit, I don't know. Braver men than I am, Gunga Din. But, as always, the time came round, and we were hospital bound once more. Another wait, seven days. Seven long days and nights full of fear and tears; terror and worst – case scenarios, but somehow, they passed, and there we were in the car, heading back to the Blue Door, to see if the cancer had spread, to where and, as I was thinking, to find out how long I had left. I felt sick with fear, unable to walk properly, being held up like a crippled man.

My specialist sat me down and we began to discuss when we would begin the chemo. (not 'if', but when) and to say it was good news. The tests from the CAT and bone marrow were clear. No metastasis. Nothing from the MRI. No tumours there. Only NHL. Hahahhaaaa ONLY...... He said we should begin next week, with CHOPS, the gold standard of chemo drugs. I knew all about the side effects so that discussion was not to be had. But......I had spent the past few months rebuilding my fucked up, virus – ravaged immune system and I wanted to know what effect the drugs would have PLUS, as no-one was talking about this, whether there would be any contraindications with my ARVs. So I said, *"Will the immune suppression be severe?"* (or something. I'm not sure if I was able to construct a proper sentence, but my meaning was clear. Most of this is kind of pieced together from a memory that was severely compromised during this whole episode.). *"Only, since my diagnosis, I have discovered my immune system has been very weak, as it is."*

"What diagnosis?"

"my ..erm...HIV diagnosis...?"

"Oh. I see. I had no idea. Nobody informed me of this. This puts things in a different light altogether. I have never knowingly treated anyone with HIV with chemo drugs before. I have no idea what will happen."

Wow. That was so *comforting*! So – *what*? I can't have chemo because I have HIV so we'll just let the cancer kill me instead? This was getting better by the minute.

"Excuse me," he said and left the room.

He returned, looking harassed, angry, upset. *"I'm really sorry about this. I should have been told and wasn't and I have to confess to being somewhat under informed in this area. I have just contacted London College Hospital to ask them to look at your biopsy as it may have a bearing on what treatment we can give. I hope you understand that this is not my doing, but am doing all that I can to put it right and ensure the best outcome for you. I have expressed the tissue sample to them and I will contact you by phone when they have given me some advice."*

There wasn't much to say. We left. More waiting.

The days dragged by. We tried to be normal, go and see people, eat, watch telly but there was a massive black cloud, immovable, unforgettable.

Several people rang during those days. Each ring heralded disaster and I made David answer the phone each time. Finally, one afternoon, the phone went at it was him. I picked it up as I was standing right beside it and whispered, "Hello?"

"It's Treliske Oncology here. I have had the result back from UCL and……."

My heart beating. My horizons narrowing. My life span in the balance.

"…….they say it is only a clump of cells, enlarged by one of your autoimmune responses. You actually don't have cancer after all."

"Hello? Hello, Mr Bray? ….Are you there?….Mr Bray…??

I had dropped the phone and it had slid under the desk from where the tinny voice of the consultant could be heard.

David picked it up and spoke to him. I have no idea what was said, what else I needed to know. All I knew was that I had cancer, and now, actually, I didn't. It was a mistake. An error. A booboo. Ooops! It was the weirdest thing – it was like I had planned a massive party and no-one had turned up. It was like a disappointment. I had absolutely NO IDEA how to react. I think I just wept.

No more fear? No more nights of tears and screaming in moonlit rooms, shouting "GODYOU'REAFUCKINGBASTARDLEAVEMEALONEDON'T YOUTHINKI'VEHADENOUGH??????"

into the darkness, sobbing, consumed with self-pity.

It wasn't until a few days had passed that the reality of the situation began to sink in. I had become so convinced, so married to the idea that I had **_CANCER_** and therefore was almost dead, that there was suddenly a massive hole where all the terror used to be. In an instant. They'd made a mistake, had filled me with chemicals, drilled a hole in my pelvis, irradiated me – and it was a _MISTAKE_? And you know what? All I could feel was gratitude. I should be "suing their fucking asses off" apparently, but all I felt was joy, release, love for the unknown doctor in London who had allowed me to live. Yay! I only had AIDS after all!

Actually, no I didn't, not any more. I had been declassified! Check _ME_ out! All of the 'syndromes' that classified me as having AIDS were either being treated, going or gone. The bucket of drugs I had to take at first was gradually decreasing, there was word that those clever people at Gilead had managed to combine two of the antiretrovirals (ARVs hereafter – if you think I'm typing all that every time you've got another think coming) into one pill, thereby reducing the load by another one.....I was feeling quite well, relatively speaking and couldn't wait to tell everyone my good news! YAY! I was going to live! I didn't have it, after all, so you can all stop crying and whispering when I come in to the room and patting me kindly.....

"You've got chemo on Tuesday, remember," David said. What? No, I don't, I'm cured! Well, not _cured,_ as I was never sick in the first place. _"What do you mean, I've got chemo?"_

"You've got chemo the third Tuesday of every month. It's in the diary."

"Whoa.....I DON'T NEED CHEMO. HELLO?"

"Yes you do. We've told everyone now, so we have to stick to it. No answering the phone for a couple of days after, because you'll be sick, but we can go out again by the following Saturday."

I was suddenly in a parallel dimension......I didn't understand.....why would you be doing this? I want to tell EVERYBODY!!! I don't want to have to sit and watch Lou, a Macmillan nurse, all too aware of the endings, quietly weep over dinner for her good friend who has the disease she witnesses every day; to see the terror and hope in my sister's eyes, to watch Mary and Jean be jolly and pretend it's OK when their hearts are breaking; to have my friends speak in that funny way around me – you know, the 'Cancer Voice'......why aren't we just TELLING THEM? Stop their sorrow, ease their pain? *"Because,"* he says, *"it's in the diary. Chemo. Tuesday."*

Looking back, trying to analyse this, I have still come up with no better theory as to why he chose this option. Either he needed to control the situation or was reluctant to be part of the celebration that would surely ensue. WHY that might be, I really cannot make sense of or find a valid reason for. It just was.

Or, maybe, it was that, you know, *CANCER* (whispered, Les Dawson face) is a far more presentable disease. Look! It's even got a Foundation! SO, maybe, by continuing the pretence of me having IT, and knowing I was recovering from my HIV illnesses, having chemo for a few weeks would coincide and voila! I'd be better and nobody would be any the wiser! Well, if that WAS it, it was cruel, both to all of the people crying for me and to me as I was weak and vulnerable and even more likely to agree, no matter HOW outlandish it was.

But, we did it. We're both to blame I guess.

But, looking back at this I am stunned by my passivity, my utter failure in being coerced; I just agreed. It was kind of OK because I KNEW that I would 'get better', that the chemo 'would work', but it was bitterly painful when people, joyfully, would say. *"You're handling the chemo well. Most people have a terrible time".* "Oh, "I'd say, *"I'm just lucky with it"*...

Lies. Dreadful deceiving of the people I loved the most; as 'Chemo Tuesday' came round, it would be: *"Ah, here I go again. It's awful, but don't worry everyone, it's working",* inventing conversations I never had with my Oncologist, staying indoors for four days because I was too sick, too tired.

Lies. What was I thinking? They all deserved better, and yet, dear readers, to this day, that deceit has held firm. As far as they all know, I am a Cancer Survivor. Well done me. But all I feel is shame. Shame. Shame for lying. Shame for allowing such a terrible thing to happen. And disgust at myself for being so led, so controlled, so pathetic. And that, dear reader, was, without a doubt, the thing that caused the breakup of our marriage, and caused my wandering to begin.

One of the strangest threads woven into this awful tapestry was a conversation I had with Anna, and with myself ever since. She was one of the first (and at that time, only) to know. I knew she would not judge. With Anna, everything had a reason and an outcome. As I sat sobbing in her chair, where I had sat so often, batting arguments, learning about the power of herbs, learning how to channel, to deal with ego, how the cerebrospinal fluid moved in waves, like a breath and how the healing crises happened in between its gentle rising and falling, all this back in the good old days before I had become a vile thing, a man of poison and anguish....I was sitting there, hoping she would find something in her heart or from spirit to assuage the tsunami of grief that was constantly overwhelming and threatening to drown me, when she looked at me and said the most fucking stupid thing I had ever heard. Of course, she, as always, was right, and it took much work and much time to see this. After doing that narrow – eyed thing she does when she's listening intently, she said:

"I think you've got HIV as a learning tool. It's a kind of gift, I think".

I was rendered sobless. I stared at her, in disbelief. Anyone else, and I would have laughed and left. But it was Anna.

"What? WHAT? A GIFT?? What do you mean???"

"I think for you to truly be at peace with yourself, to love yourself truly and completely, you need to be in a place where you are faced absolutely with the truth of being homosexual, and it seems that there is nothing more powerful than getting the one thing that characterises the fear and stigma and prejudice of that. Your day to day life had become complacent and you had stopped dealing with the troubling aspect of your relationship with your father. This is a spur to you, the most powerful symbol of all he loathes in you. You have been sent this as a weapon, a way of coming to terms with this. You will live and have good health, I say to you now, but this new struggle is positive outcome for you to truly live at peace with who you are......"

And she suddenly came back to the room and it became clear she had been channelling, I don't know who her guides are, but it was a very powerful message. Now, years later, I see it to be the truth, but then, in that room, at the darkest of all times, it was an utter pile of shite.

My life with HIV and its associated drug use continued, as of course it would have, still does, and will do for ever. The neuropathy increased, strangely always most painful from mid-evening onwards; feet rubbing helped, but it was always a reminder of it. IT. This thing, lurking in my guts, poisoning my heart, my social life, my every day. Nicki's words hadn't yet come true. Yes, I was better, far better, not nearly dead like before (Christ, you saw my passport photo…How could I not have known?) but I was still raging, full of hatred for the cunt who gave it to me (the logic of it having been a consensual shag didn't apply) and it coloured my every moment.

Forgive my indulgence here in a novel but I want to insert the poem I wrote, in the darkest of those times. Maybe it will show you, in a way that my prose cannot, the depths of my feelings at this time.

Lines From A Dark Place.

Stare more into the dark.

Stare more into my dark

- and the sun does not rise, still.

I look at you from the corner of my eye,

Not daring to look at the thing you truly mean

And all I see is my death

> *my despair*

> *my foulness*

and I cannot unknit you form my heart, my DNA

and cannot too learn how to carry your poison.

I hate you for all the things you have robbed me of:

Fearlessness and compassion;

The skills to use my skills;

the beautiful Danube and of wonders undiscovered;

of the time before you ate into my

Tissues and atoms and heart, and man-ness.

You define me – I hate you

You fill me – I hate you

You complicate me – I hate you

You terrify me – I hate you

You steal me – I hate you

I hate you and I hate you.

 I cannot leave you.

 I cannot divorce you.

 I cannot bleed you.

 I cannot kill you away

 And I cannot live beside you.

 I have no therapy

 I have no hope of redemption

 I have no respite from you; all my days ARE you.

I have blue fear.

I have ever more tomorrows of the things you cause.

I have little patience

I am left with songs I can no longer sing,

colours I can no longer paint,

the touch of skin and breath I can no longer feel,

the smells of a past I no longer have,

the rage I can no longer control,

The pain I cause where it is never deserved

And a black hole, and the singularity, into which I pour my losses,

And fear against the dying of the Light.

February 5 2005

This, as I read it back, is all a bit studenty, but it was all I had, the only way to express my sorrow and my rage at what had happened to me. At this stage, we didn't know if David was positive too – it was very likely, as we had been having unprotected sex for over 16 years. So, as well as dealing with my horror and shame, I was overwhelmed with the thought that he TOO was going to be sick, get AIDS, die and it would be MY FAULT.

Or.....actually – maybe he'd been fucking around and HE'D infected ME? Another massive weight to carry – my man had not only been unfaithful, but he'd also given me HIV. None of this was logical or important – who had given what to whom was irrelevant. I had it and that was that. But in those dark days, nothing was certain. I'd escaped death, it seemed, but was condemned to an eternal damnation – no escape, no recourse, no undoing.....

"Hi," he said. *"I'm Bill. A friend of Vince"*. A trace memory; October 87..... Bill. Bill...At Chris's funeral...one OF VINCE'S FRIENDS. WHO ALL HAD AIDS!!! Oh you fool! You drunken bloody fool! A hairy chest, a generous groin, a bucket of gin and a virus. Of course. The Funeral Fuck! The months of searching, trawling my memories for someone or something to blame it on suddenly crystallises here: THIS is the most likely. Does having an answer help? No, actually. It just adds 'STUPID' to the list of self-appellations.

Well played, Mr. Lucky. Well played.

Of course. Bill. He'd given me the reason to move home. And HIV. But, my fault as much as his. Mea Culpa. I have searched and searched over the years for a cause, a point of reference, a reason, and answer. But I didn't come to this until now, until the writing of this story. It makes no practical difference but there's some small comfort in knowing it was actually an amazing shag. Not worth the price, of course, but at least it was meaningful. So now we know. Probably.

So Chris, you bastard, who was most certainly there at that event, watching and grinning from above, probably having an angelic wank as we fucked.....why didn't you stop me? You'd have known. You were supposed to look AFTER me, you fucking fuck. You fucking...you were supposed to be my best.....

...but wait.

Maybe he knew. Like Anna knew. Maybe he knew I'd be OK (in the end) but needed to go through it on my long journey to self-acceptance, as hard and fucking horrible as it was. Maybe he, in the end, engineered that fuck, drew Bill and me onto the same trajectory in order to, finally, enable my true happiness? If so, it was a hard hard lesson, but one, now that I am actually grateful for. I see my life as gift, each and every day, something that I was not aware of before. So, you old cunt. Even after death, you did right by me.

Is this true, or a load of old bollocks? You decide....for me, it provided comfort.

This, from the American author and activist, Bruce Ward, in his memoir, entitled '15 Years' and used here with his permission, encapsulates perfectly the sorrow and loss I felt at this time:

'I wanted to close my eyes and click my heels and be back in that time, a time before AIDS, a time before loss, before fatigue and daily pills and doctor's offices and rejection and more loss. I wanted to return to joy, to hope, to the innocence of romantic love, to possibility. I wanted to be touched. I wanted my circle of friends to magically re-appear, like in the movie 'Longtime Companion', where all the dead gay men come back to dance on the beach at Fire Island. I want this alien ripped from my body.....

.....For over a decade, my primary focus had been to stay alive...one day, one breath at a time. That had been my job. Everything else – career, love, finances, family, friends – became secondary. I had to learn how to live with the stigma *of AIDS, on another planet, in another century, speaking a foreign language, in what Virginia Woolfe described as the 'undiscovered country' of illness....'*

Fortunately, Bruce, we were both granted clemency and we made it, smaller, lonelier, but alive.

Gradually, gradually though, things became easier. I was very lucky with my medication – I didn't shit myself to death like some poor souls did; I didn't turn into the elephant man or the bloke from 'Scream'......the gods were kind. Maybe making up for what they'd done to me eh?

But. But I STILL could not live with the deceit about the *facts*. All my friends and loved ones continued to watch anxiously to see if my cancer would recur – *'Lucky it was only Hodgkinson's Lymphoma, eh?'*, they'd say. Not anything serious like pancreas or prostate. I knew they still were scared, there were subtle changes in the way they spoke to me – kind of hushed, or by overcompensating and telling really shit jokes, the kind usually reserved for kids or old Aunts. Poor them. How I ached to say, to *scream*: *"I DON'T HAVE 'AUTO-IMMUNE DISEASE, YOU KNOW 'LIKE THE ONE BARBRA WINDSOR HAD'. I DON'T HAVE CANCER! IT WAS LIES! ALL LIES!! I NEVER DID. I HAD AIDS. I HAVE HIV. I HAVE H.I. FUCKING V!"* But I didn't. I remained mute. Silenced by embarrassment, fear, humiliation and him. You, reading this, probably have no idea what it is like to have a DISEASE (which is how I couldn't help thinking of it, still in capitals) which was universally feared, despised, judged and caused all kinds of religious, and moral panic; which would cause people – yes even your friends and family – to be repulsed, to stop touching you. Of course, this was only my perception of how it would be. I was probably doing these people a disservice; they would probably be understanding and grown up about it, educated and well versed in the facts. It was all a reflection of how I viewed MYSELF during this time: mendacious, full of shame and disease. It was becoming clear that more and more people were being infected; some celebrities – Andy Bell from Erasure, Holly Johnson from Frankie Goes to Hollywood – were 'disclosing' presumably to say: "Hey, it's OK. It's not your fault", and to spread sexual health awareness. But I couldn't. Just couldn't. I lived in fear and shame with my mouth full of stones.

We were in 2005 now and still my shoe size was the least important thing.

Suddenly I found myself living in a cloaked world, a world of secrets and lies. I was recovering, that was true, and my friends were pleased (if a little surprised at the smooth ride had, given all those 'Chemo Tuesdays' and the havoc they must have wrought) that I was getting better and being out in the world again. But the scales were SO unevenly weighted and with each well – wish, their side rose and mine sank, weighted down with my deception, guilt, self-loathing and degradation. I knew, I just knew, at some point in the not-too-distant future, I would be discovered and my disease riddled secret would be laid bare for all to see and pour their hatred upon. Of course, my rational head knew this would not be so, but I wasn't very big on 'rational' at that precise time. David was monitoring my every move, every word – though what he could have done had I made an announcement, I don't know, but still, he was on Damage Limitation Duty 24/7, particularly when I 'went next door' where inevitably I would get hammered and maybe loose lipped. *In vino veritas,* but not in this case – no one would ever know. Ever. (Except you, gentle readers, who now do!).

So, what did I do? I wrote to my best friends – Marion and Betty. BAM. Just like that. I was suddenly sure that if I didn't release this valve, my heart would burst for sorrow. So I wrote to them and then hid under my bed waiting for a reply, which when it came was so overwhelming and beautiful, so full of love and concern and of practical help on how I could stop being a twat and never to doubt our friendship again. Armed with the hope that it *would* maybe OK, I resolved to tell, actually SPEAK the words to my other friends, the ones nearby. David was absolutely against my doing this – I told him to fuck off. My life, my virus, my choice and maybe if you don't like it, then maybe you shouldn't have lied to them all. I wasn't though in the business of revenge – all I wanted was to have to stop lying.

I rang Louise, the Cancer nurse, and asked to see her, to which she agreed so I drove over and we sat in her lounge, both trembling, but robbed of speech. Eventually, I said:

"Lou, I have something to tell you...."

"......" no reply. Wide eyes, lip trembling.

"Ah! No, it's ok, the cancer hasn't come back... (you lying cunt! Now. EVEN NOW.......) *it's not that..."*

Looking less terrified, she said, *"OK, ...what then...?"*

I couldn't move the stones in my mouth, they blocked the words...

"I......I have....I'm HIV+"

Silence. As I feared. Bracing myself for the rejection, I sat, downcast, waiting.

Eventually she said:

"Thank goodness.....I thought you were having an affair......."

Now, I don't know about you, dear reader, but those two things, in my view, don't carry *quite* the same weight, or stigma, or repulsion factor and the possibility of death, and so her reaction was a bit....unexpected but I came to see that she was less worried about me, as in this case, being in the medical profession, she was educated, knew the state of play with drugs, therapy, survival, prognoses, so actually, when I'd stopped feeling hurt by her apparently cavalier statement, I realised that she was in fact being positive and that I didn't bring news that was going to be awful for me, which (having just had a catastrophic affair herself) she perceived to be a Bad Thing. Big hugs, tears of relief, large gin and tonic, wobbly drive home (yes, I know – don't judge me, I was hardly 'rational' as I said) and the scales had moved back towards the centre, now just weighed down by the biggest lie of all to the two closest friends of all.

My friend came to stay, down from Oop North. We went out for the day, to Polperro, to Looe, to Talland Bay, to Fowey, it was beautiful, it was normal. We took the ferry to Polruan, had a beer, went up the hill to Battery Park and looked out over the sea. How could this be so normal? Nothing, NOTHING would ever be 'normal' again. Not with this this...thing inside me. We found a bench. We sat apart.

"Mads, I wanted to get out today. I have something to tell you" Why? Why did she need to know? I rarely saw her in reality – why fuck up her life? But it was like, now I couldn't help it. I wanted to say it. The Words.

"Oh OK............"What?"

"I......I......"

She looked expectantly...

"...have HIV".

....Just the crashing of the green waves on the rocks below, which five seconds earlier had been beautiful but was now a call to doom, and the gulls all crying: AIDS! AIDS!.....

"Oh. OK. Thanks for telling me." We hugged. Actually hugged! We went home. I told David what I'd done. He was furious – I guess he was unsure exactly how much I'd said, but I assured him I'd said no more than that – and, up till now, I haven't.

Gill, and I respected her hugely for this, had gone off to America, to Boston. I mean PROPER gone, all her stuff and her dog, spotted hankie over her shoulder, to seek a new life. She'd gone to live with Michael (my brother, the one who left, hundreds of years ago) initially and from then to get a better life in the Land of Plenty. It was so hard seeing her go, my ally, my playmate…

Gill's Last Day in Newquay, where we'd spent the day together.

She did good – got some decorating work, made some really good friends and ended up driving a tractor on a tobacco plantation. You go girl! So when all this shit hit my fan, she was 3090 miles away and I could chat on the phone and she'd never know. But then I heard, as usual, the family dynamic fucked up and that she'd be coming back and was bound to see people so it was really important that it was ME that lied to her first. We met in a pub in Penryn and after some bravery water, I said,

"Squiggs, while you were away, I was diagnosed with cancer but I had chemo and check-ups and it's gone so I'm alright. Hey! Don't look so terrified! Really, I'm fine now," all tumbled out in furious rush. *"My round. More beer?"*

OH! OH! OH! PANTS ON FIRE. Why, *WHY*, did I say cancer and not HIV? Because I was a fucking coward, that's why, and was ashamed and scared she'd reject me. That's why. And for that ALONE, I owe her a massive apology. She deserved better, she deserved the truth, but I was in too deep, caught in the web and so I toed the party line. She'd be told, by *somebody* I had cancer so I wanted her to know, from me, I wanted to lie to her *first* so I was able to reassure her that I was OK, that the cancer was gone. Oh! my shame is unbearable; her, of all people.

But I wanted too, to protect her from the truth, because I WAS better and she didn't *have* to know. But I said, in this story, I would tell the truth, the whole truth and nothing but – so, now she *CAN* know, and this very act has been more healing and empowering than you, dear readers, will ever know.

Coming Out. <u>COMING. OUT.</u> In capitals it looks more important. Because it is. The years of jigsaw puzzle making, as documented here by Mr. Lucky himself; the agonies of knowing you were different and that probably meant loneliness / rejection / beatings-up (delete as appropriate); the first time you step through your own Salisbury's Doors into Never Going Back land; the first time you tell someone, *anyone*, but in a whisper so you can pretend you only coughed if the look on the their face wasn't the right one; the opening of your big gay mouth but the words getting stuck behind your teeth every time, so you just say *'Oh, nothing, doesn't matter'*; the standing by the pole, against the wall, blindfolded and handcuffed waiting for the firing squad hired by your parents, waiting for the gunshot that would kill your future and their love for you....all of this, as I look back and compare, WAS a piece of piss, compared to this, *this* COMING OUT, the gayest of all gay signs, attributes, stigmas, targets, *'serves you fucking right, you dirty queer'*, scars, brands...*that* coming out was nothing. And Anna, Chris you were so right - if I could do *this*, I could do anything. But it has taken years, years, dear reader, and here I am, coming out again. To you. From the safety of these pages.

So. The Big One. You, reading this, probably have no idea of the terror I felt as I got in the car later that evening, a bit pissed for courage, a bit pissed so I could avoid being harassed by David to such an extent I'd bottle it. Down the road I'd driven so often, when I was normal, before I became a leper, a thing of disease and fear. Down to the house I'd been so many times, to all those dinners, all those parties, all those times of innocence and joy, to where I would utter words that would never be able to be unsaid and ones that I knew not how they would be heard.

David (no surprise there) had rung to tell them I was coming so they were expectant, fearful but sat side by side on the grey swirly settee, in solidarity as if by their proximity, they could ward off any danger or evil.

I sat. I looked. I said yes, I would like a drink. Large please. We looked.

All the pebbles in my mouth tumbled to the floor and I said: *"I don't have an autoimmune disease, like Barbara Windsor* (oh, to have used Babs as a shield was reprehensible) *I have HIV."*

"We know", said Mary. *"We thought so all along. But we had to wait for you…"*

"It's OK with us", said Jean. *"Want another gin? And a fag?"*

"Yes, and yes", I gasped.

I just sobbed and sobbed and sobbed. We were done. And we never spoke of it again.

Actually, nobody did.

Which is a bit weird.

CHAPTER TWENTY THREE.

INTO THE MADHOUSE.

<u>In which our hero learns new skills, spends some time in Willy World and gets a present from that nice Tony Blair.</u>

.

'Monster'.

by The Automatic. No.4. June 2006.

'Convexed you bend, twist and shout
Twist and shout, twist and shout
Stand up brush off get moving
Get moving, get moving

What's that coming over the hill
Is it a monster? Is it a monster?....'

Bending, twisting, trying to find my way through....

~ ~ ~

Not much changed over the months. It was like nothing had happened. Everyone's life just carried on, as did mine, though I had a Big Secret from most people. Now though, I was in recovery (from Cancer! Lol) so my not being very well was just passed off as 'to be expected'. But it also meant I couldn't work. I really couldn't. My 'gift' was at this point not particularly useful. I had no money and nothing to do. Apart from being online, looking at porn mostly (when David wasn't around) which was ok except that it just made me depressed...Look! Look at those healthy men! Look at their big stiffies! Look at them shagging! Watch them cum! It was now everything I was not. I hadn't had sex since before November last year, 11 / 11 / 11, for all sorts of complicated reasons...I felt ugly and diseased and not particularly shaggable. Also, my libido had shrunk along with my dick – I just had no interest; it felt all wrong and David desperately trying to wank me off and insisting I cum, when I had virtually no hard on, hurt and didn't really help, and it was really embarrassing. A self-fulfilling prophecy...the machinery of erections is so finely balanced it doesn't take much to cause it's malfunction. Great. Fucking ED along with everything else. Back to the clinic. Appointment to see the willy man. Stupid questionnaires about doing sex....homework on how it feels. HORRIBLE, that's how it feels, you idiot, but of course, the more present The Problem became, the worse it got. We were instructed to have sex, every day and write down what happened and how it felt. Really? *'Nothing'* and *'Like shit'* were the answers. How likely was it, Robin, that I was going to want to have sex every day?

"No, it'll be good for the problem."

"I don't have a problem. I'm always rock hard, I am," said David. Not the most helpful interjection, actually.

"No, well, that's good. But its Nigel's problem we have to sort out, eh? Sex every day and keep a diary. That's the ticket."

Well, I did try. And failed. Oh, we did it, him saying, *"You'll never get better if we do don't what he says,"* and of course getting a daily shag, and me really wanting to be anywhere else but there, with his hands on my unwilling cock, trying to make me come. Then writing it down:

'Got erection. 1 minute. Lost it. Didn't come'

'Got erection but not hard.'

'Nothing happened. Kept trying as instructed. Failed'.

It was sad, it was excruciatingly embarrassing and served only to reinforce my loathing of the thing that I believed was cause it all – the foulness inside.

I don't know how it came about but the next thing I know, we're BOTH looking at porn. Tentatively at first, pretending we weren't really that interested, then joining Gaydar ("you know, just to see") and this quickly escalated into having threesomes! HOW? I have no idea, other than I suppose David might have wanted some proper sex, with someone who could get a hard on and come properly, you know, like a Real Man. We found ourselves online all the time and men were coming to the house with increasing frequency. Usually married men, on the way home from 'working late'- builders, high court judges, policemen, teachers, all passing through, all desperate for some anonymous sex, in an anonymous house on an anonymous estate, where it meant nothing after the final panting spurts. And how do you think it went for me, readers? Two virile men, two hard cocks, two loads shot, while I, impotent, infected with HIV, pretending to enjoy it, putting up barriers so that it was safe, safe, always safe, making excuses for my performance, being passed over for the man with the erection. It didn't feel that great, to be honest. But I didn't stop it. I didn't say no. I didn't make an excuse and leave. No matter how awful, there was still a dick to suck, someone to wank off.....and it was this imperative, dear reader, that had brought me to this place of disease and despair in the first place and yet still, the imperative to feel validated by having sex with a man overrode all else. Even then. I cannot explain this.

While all this was going on, I had made a decision to retrain as a...a..I didn't know, but a *something*, something to give my life some purpose, something to do, apart from having sex with strangers, in my bed. I found there was a free Computer Training Course in town and I thought website design might be interesting, if not ever useful. So, I enrolled and went every day. New faces, new activity, new neurons woken. It was a piece of piss actually, but I did the whole course to make it last, finally getting a distinction, a City and Guilds in website design, and a lovely certificate to go in the folder next to my NPQH certificate (the only interesting part of which was, on a weekend away in The Grand Hotel in Torquay, getting pissed in the pub after the day's seminars and having the most amazing sex with a married man (you see? It never stops.) in his room. PROPER amazing, so that the next day, we snuck off and did it again instead of completing the 'Ancillary Staff Training' module) which I have never had any use for or recouped the hundreds of pounds it cost to send me on it.)

It was now Summer, 2006; I was still alive, at least. Against the odds.

So here's the thing:

- I was HIV positive.
- I'd been *THIS* close from starting chemo for cancer I didn't have, which would have destroyed my immune system. Again.
- I am living a lie to everyone I know and love.
- I am living with a man who controls everything I do, and everyone I see. My life is controlled, micro managed, even to only being allowed 1 glass of wine, at 9.00pm, just 1 bowl of crisps from the bag. ('For my own good')
- I am getting very drunk, a lot, as I am very unhappy.
- I am unemployed and we have no money.

- I am having sex with random strangers, having 3somes, being spit roasted, (safe safe safe) even while knowing I am diseased.
- I can't get it up.
- I am full of self-loathing.
- I have constant peripheral neuropathy.

Things are really not great right now, and nobody knows, and I can't get it hugged away.

What to do? What to do?

So. I had a brainwave I know! I know how to fix this mess!

So, having made *sure* that this was a brilliant idea, a few nights later, after our latest shag had gone (it might have been the one who wanted hot wax poured on his bollocks. I remember that one, because he was a High Court Judge (I kid you not, dear reader), he had ginger pubes and no hard on and because it was the very worst to date....), I rolled over in bed, and said:

"David. Will you marry me?"

"Yes", he said. *"I've been waiting for you to ask. Yes, I will. But it's not a marriage of course, it's a Civil Partnership."*

I fucking well KNOW that. That's not the point. Thanks for ruining the moment.

In 1453, someone left the gate open and the Turks got in and sacked Constantinople.

In 1788, the Austrian army attacked itself, by accident, and lost 10,000 men.

In 1812, Napoleon decided to invade Russia. In Winter.

In 1937, the Hindenburg was launched. Filled with helium.

In 1962, Decca records turned down the Beatles, saying 'Guitar groups are on their way out'.

In 2006, I asked David to marry me.

This is up there with the Worst Decisions of All Time, particularly due to the complications it caused further down the line... I *DO* want to say at this point, that I blame him for nothing. He was what he was and in fact, I blame ME because I let it all happen. He was a controller, and I was the controlee. I was totally complicit in this dysfunctional relationship that everyone thought was so perfect and admirable. I am not setting out to diss him – I allowed it all, and so really, it's not his fault, it was mine, but it took years for me to realise it. Years to undo.

My motivation? Fuck knows. Let's see....

Mr Lucky's Motivations:

- Maybe I thought marrying him *("It's not a marriage blah blah")* would make us 'equal'. Really?
- Maybe I thought it would mend all the things that were wrong in my heart and had been fermenting since leaving Hungary.
- Maybe I thought if I had a proper husband, he'd be less likely to leave me for one of the men who came to the house for sex who had a dick that worked.
- Maybe I thought being married would make our relationship – TWO HOMOS! – valid in the eyes of the world.
- Maybe I thought it would make me *normal*. Like *you*.

Ah......getting to the crux. Acceptance. Especially NOW, although that was still my secret to keep. Would I ever disclose? Would I ever be able to say: *'Look here. HIV, in spite of its capital letters, is just a bug. A bug that is no danger to you, or to me actually, if I take my pills, which I do. It's no biggie'*. I doubt it.

Though I was beginning to reach some kind of peace with myself, given that I was getting healthier and healthier, and that because I LOOKED well, nobody had to know (Let's forget the cancer-that-never-was. I'm a 'survivor' and it was, shamefully, a kind of cover story. Forgive me. I was weak. I should've spoken out but I didn't), I didn't expect for it to be common knowledge. Ever. My problems (long resolved) about being gay and the hatred and loathing of my Father would be finally crushed by this act of getting married. I'd be the same as you. See? Normal.

It was, dear reader, the biggest Elastoplast you've ever seen.

I ignored, completely ignored, all the feelings of disquiet as I got swept up in the preparations. Maybe it'd be OK. People were invited. Registered the intention, had Banns read, decided on outfits (Cornish tartan, thankyou), chose the venue, (our house) chose the date...

June 21st 2006. The Longest Day...

June 21st. Summer Solstice. The Longest Day. And I have to say, it was a
wonderful one. I was very proud to be wearing the colours. We got up at
dawn and watched the sunrise from the Beacon, had the service, cried like a
girl, went on the Puffer Train as special surprise, went home, tried to have
sex (married now, you know) and David fell asleep with my soft cock in his
mouth. (About which I didn't feel too good). Got ready, went out to
restaurant, ate till I felt sick. Went home. Stayed up till the Longest Day's
end. Went to bed. My thanks to the two dear friends who made the day so
memorable. Following week, massive party at home, EVERYONE invited,
wedding cake with two grooms (one in tartan kilt. Awwww), food enough to
feed an army, got drunk (no change there then) stayed up till the day's end
again, went to bed. Started married life.

Which was exactly the same as unmarried life, only more trapped. Bollocks. To
quote my Canadian muse (on whom I had been calling often, just lately):

> 'After the rush when you come back down
> You're always disappointed, nothing seems to keep you high
> Drive your bargains
> Push your papers
> Win your medals
> Fuck your strangers
> Don't it leave you on the empty side.'
> (Joni Mitchell, 'Woman of Heart and Mind')

It was true. After all the excitement, it was business as usual – same old,
same old. Trying to get business on the website front, 'fucking our strangers',
and it was, indeed, leaving me on the empty side. I KNEW as I had uttered
those four words, I was being a twat – how would this ever fix anything? I
was getting bits of work, but depressingly few. It was a dying business really:
either people already had a site, built it themselves, or got a mate to do it.
For free, so why would they pay me? But still, it gave me a chance to be
online, away from real life. When I wasn't, I was next door with a couple of
bottles of wine, 'misbehaving' and being disapproved of - *"If you don't stop
drinking, you'll look like Jabba the Hut"*. Thanks for that. My self-image is shit
enough as it is….

We were lost souls, Gaynor and I; her troubled past and my troubled future
came together most synergistically into a troubled present, which we sought
to resolve by blotting it out. Loud music, rollies and red wine – the holy
trinity of escapism. David began to get regular house-sitting requests and

when he was away, the mice did most certainly play, and it wasn't pretty. We got so drunk, we were rendered incapable of speech sometimes, and unable to stand up, but always at hers. Her garden was a fairyland of lights and plants and nooks, quite the opposite of the clinical and anally retentive space next door. It was lovely to be outside there, with the candles in the trees, lit every single evening for the souls of all her animals, the chimenea blazing, the music floating and the wine smoothing out all the edges. It was Narnia, it was Secret Squirrel, it was delicious, I could sa '*Hullo clouds!, Hullo sky*' and skip abut like a gurl',and it was always too short a time. We had no secrets, she and I – all was laid bare*, in vino veritas* was the order of the day, all things spoken of...all, all but one, one that I dared not speak. You fool! You think she would've loved you any less? Judged you? Blamed you? No, stupid boy, she would have given you one of her bone crushing hugs and a kiss, given you a slap for not trusting her enough and then opened another bottle. I am sorry – I should've treated you better. I hope you can understand why? I might've even have found the courage to have told you, but I had been forbidden, by my Master, who didn't want you "*blabbing it all over the place when she's pissed*". Maybe you would've, who knows, but its ME who had it, not him.....or maybe *that* was the problem and he didn't want to be guilty by association. That's why I was forbidden to speak of it, and why he was so angry when I told those dear few, the ones I wanted to know that I wasn't dying and to stop their hearts breaking. So, dear friend, my silence was required and once more, I acquiesced without a murmur.

We partied the nights away, she and I; running, running. We lost whole weekends, but nothing got any better, nothing changed. Her past continued to haunt her and my future continued to be uncertain. But we loved each other deeply; we were connected in ways that nobody else understood. She was loud, brash, rude, often drunk, lairy, but I knew the woman beneath all the bluster, and we held each other up. That old bollocks about crossing paths with the people you were meant to certainly applied here, and was not, in this instance 'old bollocks'. She loved wood, the sea, the hawks and the buzzards, jasmine, beads, Mary Chapin Carpenter and me. And I betrayed her, dear reader, due to being such a weak man; lied to her over and over because I was instructed to. Utterly pathetic. But, for now, we sailed on, having no idea of the tempest that lay ahead.

Unhappy me, internet, time alone...the Perfect Storm.

Typing, alone at night. Just a single lonely light shining on my keyboard. Looking at hairy men on BearWWW. No chance of having a wank, obvs, as much as I'd like to have done.

Click. Click. Click....Oooh, HE'S nice....

The first picture of Si I ever saw. Scrubs up nice, eh?

'Hi'.

Tick.. tick.. no reply. Then, ping!

'Hi'. (Two 'Hi's...what could this mean? Nothing, you twat. He wasn't real.)

'Why are you called 'Shoemaker'?'

'Because I make shoes.'

'Oh. LOL'

'I see you make websites.'

''Yep.'

I was here to see if he had a big one, a hairy chest, what he liked, not to talk about websites.....I was just about to log out and go searching for the next usually faceless profile of a man I would never meet, when he replied:

'Oh that's good then. I need one. For my business. Would you be interested?'

'Um, yes I suppose so......'

There are thousands of men on line, searching gay chat sites, that night and every night; hundreds of sites, dozens of time zones, tens of thousands of profiles. What are the chances of this bloke stumbling across mine, not wanting to see my dick (just as well) but needing a website? Infinitesimally small, I'd say. Or just Lucky

'Your profile says you do reiki too? Is that why you're 'Reikiman?''

Like DUH...*'Yes,'*

'So do I.'

'I'm a bit tired actually. Nice to chat to you. Bye'. And I logged out.

How strange – someone who didn't say 'put your cam on, I'm horny and want a wank with you'. Too drunk to stay up, I went to my large bed, with only me in it. *'The bed's too big, the frying pan's too wide'* as Joni once memorably said.

BUT....

'Woke up this morning feelin' fine

There's something special on my mind

Last night I met a new girl in the neighbourhood, whoa yeah

Something tells me I'm into something good....'

Like Herman, strangely I had something special on my mind. I'd spent so many empty nights online, post wine - quaffing next door, and it was always the same and given my ...ahem...temporary condition, mostly fruitless. Yet last night, I'd met someone who'd actually asked about ME, not how big my dick was or whether I take it up the ass. Like, as a *person*. And that was really cool. Trouble was, being as drunk as I was, I wasn't sure I would be able to find him again, amongst the oceans of flotsam on the gay sites. Or is jetsam? Whatever – I wasn't even sure what site it was now. Gaydar? Silver Daddies – could be; that's where I met the man who came to stay, had sex with us, took us out to dinner and, later saved me......he has become a long standing a dear friend, in spite of finding himself in a not especially pleasant sexual scenario which, dear readers, I will spare you from. DudesNude? No……ah well. Never mind. I'm a married man (*"Civilly Partnered"*. Shut *UP*) so it's irrelevant. It was yet another empty internet night.

'You've got mail!' said Joanna Lumley in her cheery Roedean voice. And there was a message for me, from BearWWW. That's it! Forgot that one. Only ONE bottle of wine tonight, missis! It was still play weekend. I'm allowed….

'Hello. How's you? Nice to talk to you last night. Lovely smile. Don't forget my website. Simon.'

Ohmygodohmygodohmygod….what? What was happening? Be still my beating heart! I think I was so unused to anybody saying anything nice that this seemed very special. *'SIMON!'* So I logged on.

He wasn't there.

'Hi Shoemaker Simon. Got your message. No, I hadn't forgotten (Pants on fire) *so let's talk about it.'*

David came home on Sunday.

"What have you been up to then? Anything nice?" though he knew I would've spent most of it next door, with *'that woman'* (to whom he was more than friendly and pleasant to her face).

"Not much. Oooh, I think I've got a new job though. Website thing. Someone online contacted me."

"Oh that's good. We could do with the money". Not 'Congratulations' or 'Well done'. *"Who is it?"*

"Someone called Simon. From London."

"Gay?"

I'd have to tell him where from I suppose though as he's been picking up trade on Gaydar for months, I think the moral high ground isn't something he could take here.

"Yes. BearWWW. It's a site for….erm….bears."

"Oh."

"Early days yet." I said, moving swiftly on. *"We've got a meeting to talk about it. He's got a business and a house in France or something and he needs all the bits tying together."*

"When's the meeting? It'll be interesting to see him." Yeah, got the subtext.

"I don't know. I just have to see when he's on line and we can put our cams on and chat then."

This happened fairly quickly (though not soon enough for me) and there he was…. better looking than in his profile picture, and the same age as quoted, not in Gay years (which is unusual, believe me.)

I don't remember the chat very well; it was very business-like, things to sort, and being monitored didn't help. It seemed like he was an advocate and activist for gay rights, and disabled people, a theatre designer, a researcher and he also owned a tumble-down house in France. He wanted it put together in one place, and I, still not very experienced, found it quite a challenge. This required me to be constantly asking questions about the how and the where of things, and when David wasn't around, more personal stuff – he'd worked for the Royal Ballet, he'd met Nuryev, Elaine Paige, knew Fenella Fielding…..I was, I have to admit, a bit star struck, and I was being drawn deeper and deeper into his world, a world that spoke to my heart as was he into mine, such as it was….he was the nicest, most gentle, funniest, kindest man I think I had ever met. Well, when I say 'met'…..you know what I mean. He was *'single, 47, moderately hairy and'*…..I'm not telling you the rest, actually. But he sounded wonderful.

Eventually, over time, we began to 'need' to speak on the phone – the messaging 'wasn't immediate enough', and I could then hear his voice. It was soft and utterly engaging, he was funny and inquisitive, respectful of my situation and also professional – he was, after all, paying me for this. By now, I would have done it for free, just to be able to ring him, at what was becoming daily intervals. Still, the website was coming together and everything seemed to be above board and I realised that if it was finished, then so would this…this…thing that was clearly developing far beyond what was actually being said…..

Hardly daring to believe what I was about to do, I said to David, *"This website is proving to be a real sod to finish so we, Simon and I, thought that if he came down to visit with his laptop, where I could actually see what he meant*

– it's really difficult, even on the phone –we could sit together and get it done. Then I'd get paid. You like him, don't you?"

"Hmm not a bad idea. It's been going for ages. Probably time to wrap it up now. OK, yes."

What *his* true motives were, I never discovered. Another shag? Checking out possible competition? Or neither. Maybe it *was* just a good idea.

So, I suggested it to Simon, and we arranged a date. Wednesday April 4th. 18.15 Bodmin Parkway.

And there I met the man who was to mend my heart and break David's.

Simon, in my house. Not knowing what storm will break....

CHAPTER TWENTY FOUR.

JERICHO.

<u>In which everything tumbles down like a tumbling thing at the World</u>
<u>Tumbling Championships, I Come Out (again) and plan The Great Escape (sort</u>
<u>of).</u>

'Breathe Easy'

by Blue. No.6. April 4th 2007.

'I can't breathe easy
Can't sleep at night 'til you're by my side
No, I can't breathe easy
I can't dream yet another dream
Without you lying next to me, there's no air...'

There's no air! I couldn't breathe, or sleep now, without you next to me.

~ ~ ~

After a kerfuffle about not being able to come because he had no money
(*"No its fine! It's fine! I'll pay for everything!!"* Down boy, you're like a bitch
on heat), Simon boarded the 14.06 from Paddington and set off on what
would turn out to be strangest, amazingest, fabulousest journey of his life.
'Cos that's the day he meets Mr. Lucky!

As he speeds towards Bodmin, I am preparing a 47-course dinner; well, OK, 3,
but it's well special. I have shaved, showered and, as Bette Midler once said:
'FDS'd myself into a stupor', only with cologne. I smell like a whore's handbag
'Miss Dior? More like 'Foggy Trollope' as dear Rodney would've said. HAHA!
Geddit? David is bemused, wondering why I am fannying about like a mad
thing, assuming that I'm just looking forward to a shag (which we'd
discussed, agreed and planned – anything to get into Simon's pants) whereas
I in fact, am already giddy with dread and excitement and, well, OK, lust.

We drove to the station, me in a panic, a giddy whirl – I had no idea what to
expect from this meeting only that it was imperative that it had to happen.

Maybe it would be a business meeting and I'd finish the website, he'd pay me and he'd go home; maybe it would be a couple of shags (as we 'always play together', he'd better be up for a 3 – way); maybe it would just be a nice weekend, meeting a new friend. Or all three. Option four was shoved firmly to the back of my mind.

I had already, to backtrack a little – I don't want you to think I'm just anybody's you know – gone up to Devon as Head Teacher on Summer School teaching French exchange students and there I met Bruce, with whom I immediately fell totes in love and wanted to live with. He was only recently (bitterly) divorced and out, - Boy, was he OUT! and he was making up for lost time, astonished that all the subterfuge of shagging behind his wife's back (see?) could stop and he was clearly aiming to win the Mr. Randy trophy in this year's Mr. Randy Competition. I'd leave work, head into town, meet him in the pub and we'd go back to his and have so much sex you wouldn't think we could fit it in (actually, we couldn't but that's another story) before having to get up and go back to work. Bonk, bonk, bonk. I was bleddy knackered. He was a sweetheart, but wouldn't marry me 'cos he had way too much shagging to do and with everyone in sight. I drove away, tear stained and desperate, David Gray's *'Alibi'* shaking the windows of the car.

You have to wonder where my head was at....I had a husband *(CIVIL PARTNER!!!)* at home, a mortgage, a new job with a language school, a house – how could I POSSIBLY live with Bruce? I barely knew him – very nice, great (extremely safe) sex etc, but really?.....Was I *SO* desperate to avoid having to go back to *there*...? I even stopped at Anne's Burger Wagon, in a layby on Bodmin Moor and texted him, begging him to change his mind but one of his clients had just shit himself in Tesco so he was a bit busy...I've heard of some excuses, but really...

Another time, and bizarrely with little protest, I announced I needed to get away for a few days and went to spend the weekend in Windsor with the man who had stayed at ours a few weeks earlier. He'd said, when we parted in ASDA's carpark, *"Look, if you ever need to get away...."*. Wise man. What had he seen? Stuff I was refusing to? *"You're always welcome at mine..."* After a heart-breaking hug he drove away, but a few weeks later, I rang him and went to stay. Same pattern as before. Fell in love, had loads of excellent (and very safe) sex – with an *erection*, thank you very much; a minor detail for you, but a major one for me. I don't think any further explanation is necessary – and then asked, like a twat, if I could move in.

"Erm…no," he said.

"WAAAAAAH! AWWWWWWWWW!! WHY NOT?" I wailed.

Same reasons, as above. Went home, kept texting the poor man, like a stupid child, on the train, but (thank goodness) he held firm. Not that he didn't like me; he did (he does; we're still in touch) but could see a whole shit storm heading his way which he wanted no part of. Right choice. Right choice.

So you see, I had already made two (totally unrealistic and unsuccessful) bids for freedom, and now this Simon was heading my way…..what could it mean? My insides were like jelly, it was like being in love again, right at the start, when you're a bit breathless and you do a small wee. AND I didn't even know the bloke, though it felt like I always had.

"The train arriving on platform 2, is the 14.06 from Paddington…."

'The train arriving on platform 2, is the 14.06 from Paddington.' I (apparently) was running up and down the platform like a fucking eejit, going *"Where is*

he? Where is he? I can't see him! Where is he?......" David was standing, arms folded, by the barrier. What premonitions did he have? And, then, at 18.15, April 4th, 2007, as I said, I met the man who was to mend my heart and break David's. There he was, in his too – small jacket and big red shoes, and I was lost. Gone for good at that moment.

"Oh HIIIIII!" I screeched.

"Hello," he said, in that honey voice and leant in to kiss my cheek.

"I'm David," said David, holding out his hand.

"Good journey? Train's on time. It's been sunny here today. Have you eaten? Would you like some tea somewhere? A café? Or a pint maybe? Are you tired? Do you want to run away with me and keep me close in your heart in a place where no one will ever hurt us?"

I didn't actually say that last bit, but I WAS babbling like an idiot as we walked to the car. I don't remember the drive home, other than I had my hand on his foot all the way, like staking my claim, sneaking my fingers up his trouser leg, or maybe offering comfort. I could see him in the mirror too – and oh FUCK!! He's looking back! Blue eyes fixed on my reflection. I looked away, burned by the intensity of his stare.

We got home, had large gins. Dinner was ready. He'd changed and was wearing very loose pants, Indian style. He was somehow at my end of the table and – dear God - we were able to play footsie under the table. If David detected anything, he didn't show it. Dinner passed in a wine fuelled haze, and the next thing I know, Simon was lying (very provocatively, I have to say, you naughty man) on the settee, and I was right – he wasn't wearing any pants. And David made his move. I was horrified! Mine!! He's fucking MINE!!

The *'we don't play separately'* rule seemed cruelly inappropriate but there it was, so I had to join in and get what comfort I could. We went upstairs, I was drunk, and we had some sort of sex, the three of us, and after, went to bed. Me in the guest room, he in my bed. The only time that the stranger in my bed was welcome and I was in the next room.

The next day, we had a wander round town and then went to the beach and took a lot of photos in which, looking back at them now, there was such a clear and present connection between us; the way we stood, looked, posed, laughed, all pointed towards US being the couple and David the visitor.

Trebarwith, April 2004. Lovers In Waiting. Big Red Shoes.

We had drinks, overlooking the sea, and were joined by Paul, who had happened to be at the same beach, the same time, the same day....planets aligning. He was a sometime acquaintance and also the man who was booked in for reiki the next day.

"Paul, this is Simon. He's a reiki master too, but is trained in Seichem. I'm Usui trained as you know. It might be good for you to have us both treat you tomorrow? What do you think?"

Paul agreed, and we went back home. I can't remember the evening. Did we do anything? I don't know, I was only enthralled to have this splendid man in my house and in my life, even just for a short while. It wasn't long before

Simon went off to bed, early, on his own. I think he wanted to avoid another sex session, which he clearly hadn't enjoyed. Good. Neither had I.

The next morning, we did what ostensibly he had come down for and set ourselves up in the study to try to sort out the website, though it was clear all we wanted to do was to have sex again, on our own, but....'we don't play separately' and my luck was already massively pushed. We fiddled about with pictures and text frames and hyperlinks and CSS and made the best of it. Paul arrived at 2, and we began our reiki session. Paul had no idea of the cataclysm that was about to unfold above his head...

All was going well, Michael turned up on cue, I was treating Paul's neck, Simon his feet. The reiki filled the room and it was both tempestuous and healing. Then, I was bidden to stretch out my hand towards Simon, who did the same and our fingertips touched. I am not linguistically skilled enough to describe what then occurred – if you picture what may have passed between Adam and God, when their fingertips touched, as imagined in the ceiling of the Sistine Chapel, that sort of comes close. A bolt of pure energy exploded between us, through us, each into the other. It was terrifying, and powerful beyond words, but glorious and exultant and exhilarating and magnificent. We snatched our hands apart, both a bit stunned, like we'd been electrocuted by pure love, but unsure about what had just happened. When we eventually talked about it, after we'd stopped pretending it hadn't meant anything, it seemed a clear message from spirit that we had met our true soul mates; both open to spirit in that moment, we were able to transmit the true essence of each to the other. It was indefinable but without any room for doubt. We BOTH knew what had happened, but what the fuck to do about it? NOW what?

Even weirder, the next day David said:

"I'll do breakfast. Why don't you two go out for a walk? 20 minutes?"

"Erm, yeah, OK. You want to?"

"Sure, yeah," said Simon, glad to get me alone whenever he could.

So off we went, through the hedge, where John and I had wee'd so long ago, up to the Beacon; a bit of sightseeing always calmed things down a bit. There's a little area with picnic benches where you can sit and look far down West, where the eclipse had rolled up that day, back in '99, scaring the bejeesus out of us all. We sat. Opposite. Our hands touched and with no prompted thought I said:

"We're going to live in France, and I'm going to help you run a healing centre at your house. Aren't I?" Actually, it wasn't a question, it was a fact, a thing I KNEW.

"Yes. We are," he said, and once more terrified, we leapt apart and said no more.

We went back to the house to finish the website (to sit really really close together). The site wasn't too bad; bit amateur really but it was by now, of course, completely irrelevant.

"I'm just going down the shop. I won't be long," called David, and out he went, leaving us alone. Again. Upstairs. *What the….??* I knew the shop, the local was just a few minutes and so there was no time to make love, not like we were both aching to do. So we kissed. Oh, how we kissed, deeply and completely. Like we would never part. My heart was racing, and my cock growing hard. I have not put that in gratuitously, dear readers; it is actually very relevant. It was getting hard and very visible in the green linen trousers I was wearing. Simon had no idea of the history, the torment, the sadness of my ED, and as he ran his fingers along the length of it, he smiled, and said, *"I am looking forward to when I can have that all for myself."*

"I love you," he said.

"I have HIV," I said.

BAM.

I hadn't planned to say anything. At least not yet. Not till we were somewhere safe, and he was mine, but that would have been absolutely the wrong thing. He needed to know before, so he had a chance to run. To be horrified. Disgusted. Afraid. Like I was.

There was a beat. A silence. And into it, I expected to hear the slamming of laptop lids, hurried excuses, eyes that were just a moment ago boring into mine, now downcast and avoiding meeting, business arrangements made to pay for the work done so far, 'Thanks, but no thanks'….

But not this man. Not this brave, gentle, honest, solid man.

Then he looked at me and said,

"That's OK, It doesn't matter. I love you. That's all that matters," and the front door opened and David was back. We sprang apart, erections wilting, red faced. What have I done? That's that then. Still better to know now than make some stupid mistake and THEN have it go tits up. But I didn't know him, this man. This man of courage, this man who loved me. He meant what he said, and I had to trust it. But it wasn't mentioned again. Is that a good thing or a bad one?

That evening, we'd planned a meal, *en plein air*, round the chimenea, for which I was cooking Mexican. The works. I know it wasn't his last night, but we were planning to go out on the last night, a proper Cornish pub meal. I couldn't bear thinking about it, so I had some more gin. You KNOW what happens, Bray; you and gin are trouble. Anyway, I wanted to quell the panic of him leaving on Sunday. How would we ever put our plan into operation? Then, another weird thing: David said. *"Why don't you two go and have a walk before dinner? I'll do the prep?"* So off we went again. Alarming! What was he playing at? Trying? Trusting? Trapping? Dunno, but I just wanted out of the house, with Simon, for a wee while, probably for the last time, particularly now, after this morning's liddle revelation, before he left on Sunday.

We walked around the back lane to go up to the Beacon again. We sat on a little stone seat, and held hands and looked up as two jets left vapour trails…

it said.

We climbed over the stile, walked up the field to the top and as the sun set over Treningle, my house, and my marriage, we held hands and knew, somehow, we were to be together.

"We'll have to wait, to find a way. I have NO idea how, or how long. But there will BE a way. YOU know what happened in that room," he said. The sun grew redder and the air cooler. *"Come on, let's go back. I'm bleddy starving!"* I said to steer the conversation away from the 'thing', so huge it was uncontemplateable.

"We're back! Ready to eat everyone?"

I put ABBA on full blast, *('The Winner Takes It All')*, poured myself a glass of forget- me- juice and, watching David and Simon sitting chatting, through the window, began to cook dinner. All the red pepper pieces were the same size.

The Garden of Delights...

The tracks went down (*'Dancing Queen'* being caterwauled as I cooked), the wine went down and the sun went down. The chimenea was roaring, the table was set, the fajitas were done, the beans refried, the guacamole whizzed to a fine and spicy delight and....I wanted none of it. I wanted it all to go away, to be over and to be alone in Simon's arms. But. *"HEEEEERE we are!"* I yodelled, carrying out the food. We ate, the music played on, we talked about the inconsequential, the drinks went down.....then we ran out of chat and sat and watched the flames, mesmerised, in a row, with David in the middle.

Deliberate? Just how the chairs were? I don't know. What I DO know is that he was between us and, as I got more and more pissed, I got more and more desperate to touch Simon. What could I do? Lean across? Ask to swap seats? I know. I know - I'll just say, *"Excuse me, David, can I sit next to Simon as we'll be running away together soon."* Fortunately, Simon decided that he really didn't want to share me at bedtime again and excused himself and went to bed. Probably just as well; my gob was gearing up to run away with me, the pressure was so enormous.

"'Night....." Peck on my cheek as he leant in and I could smell him, feel his weight on my shoulder. *"'Night, David,"* and he was gone. Leaving us together alone. I'm not sure why David suddenly started touching me, rubbing his hand up my thighs, proprietorially? Ownership? As a reminder? Just horny? Whatever the reason, and I am ashamed to say, dear reader, that I found his touch offensive and wrong and I pushed his hand off. He put it back, nearer the top of my leg, nearer my balls this time and I said, *"Will you just fucking get off me!"* A little too fierce. A little too tell-tale. But, he did. Then he went and fetched the brandy (Dartington) decanter.

"I'm having a nightcap. I suppose you want one?" he said in that 'don't you think you've had enough already?' kind of voice.

"Yes, please, if that's alright. ... a bit more than THAT. If that's OK with you?" He'd poured enough to just make a film on the bottom of the (Dartington) glass. Remember, *I'M* in in control here..... *"Thank you.!* He poured more. **"More,** *if that's ok?"* By this time the glass was half full of neat brandy (Courvoisier) and we sat in silence, pretending that the flames were interesting. Actually, they were. The brandy was fierce and I was becoming unmoored. The man I adored beyond all else was just 20 feet away, sleeping now no doubt, for now at peace and untroubled. More staring. More silence, as wide as the bed which now held my love.

"I've had enough of this. Shall we go to bed?"

"No, I'm fine. I'm staying for a bit. 'Night."

He picked up the decanter, in a meaningful way - I didn't care, I had enough left in the (Dartington) tumbler to drink myself unconscious.

"OK. Don't be long. And make sure the fire door's shut. And the water feature's switched off. And don't forget the light. And bring your glass in. I'm sure it'll be empty."

Go. Just go.

Alone and drunk, I wondered if he had any idea why I was so unhappy so suddenly? Everything was so exciting a couple of days ago. I supposed not, in a drunken kind of way; we'd done nothing untoward.

I heard a rustling from next door. Then I had a brilliant idea!

"Hey! I can hear you! And I can smell dope, you naughty girl! Roll us one?" Utter madness. A decision that could only be made by someone already robbed of sense and reason. She passed the joint over the wall and I took a drag. Instantly my head began to spin and I felt disconnected from the world.

"Thanks, G".

"Go easy, you twat," came the whispered reply.

Another drag, further from reality. Another slug of brandy. And suddenly. Whoooo. Suddenly I was done. Enough already! I couldn't really see properly and standing was proving a bit tricky as everything was all slopey. I'm gonna slap that Barrie up him head for not laying this patio levelly. I meaned lovely. Ha, Golden Ear Whizz I'll give him. Hee heeeee heeeeee. Oh fuck. Suddenly my head spun really fast and I lost my balance, and toppled over, luckily landing on the steps by the gate and not on the fire. Wait. Pause. Breathe. Breathe.

Everything slowly came back into focus and gingerly I tried to stand. Shut the fire door. 20 paces to the steps. Switch off water thing. 10 steps back to the door. Switch off light. Good boy I am. Fuckity arse. Forgot the glass. Ne'er mind eh? Need a pee now. Like NOW. Fortunately, I had installed a handrail on the stairs. Came in handy as I hauled myself up to the loo, in that being really quiet drunk way. I had to pee like a girl as I'd have needed two hands to wee the boy's way and I had to hold on to the towel rail. Fuck, was I drunk.

And stoned. The whole room was lurching and spinning as the THC in the cannabis thwhacked me in the brain. I felt AWFUL and sorrowful and regretful and my life was shit and nobody loved me and I needed some cheese. Yes, that was it. Cheese.

Hauling myself and then me drawers up, I felt my way back downstairs to the kitchen for cheese.

What was it again? I stared round the kitchen, swaying, and threatening to do that funny run that drunk people do, that we all laugh at when it's not you. I wanted….. um… I don't know now. My eyes stopped swivelling and came to rest on my phone, on the worktop. I moved towards it, oops, bit too fast, misjudged the distance there. Backwards a bit….careful! Now go forward again. What was it??? Oh yes! Phone. I know! I'll write Simon a lovely text so he will see it in the morning when he wakes.

Now, as this is almost 8 years ago now, and given my condition at that time, this is from memory, but I think it's more or less what I wrote:

My darling Simon

You are sleeping not ten feet away and I am in the wrong bed. But don't worry because soon we will be in France together. I love you like I have never loved anyone else. It will be hard to say goodbye on Sunday, but it will only be temporary. I don't know how long, but be strong.

With all my heart. XXX

Aww, that's nice. He'll see that tomorrow. Bed. I now need sleep. Not cheese! That's what it was. Cheese, but I don't want cheese now, I want bed. Not cheese. And I put my Samsung slider phone down on the top. And, before I ended up sleeping on the kitchen floor, wove my way back up the stairs to bed.

Leaving the phone on the bench, open.

With the text unsent.

05.15. A time, easy to remember. Something kicked my foot, and startled me awake and I was facing the clock. That's how I know. Woahhhh, my fucking head……sleep. More sleep. Then something kicked me again. I opened my eye, and swivelled it in the direction of where the pain was now coming from. And there was David. Holding my phone. Not really knowing what was happening, I raised myself, carefully onto one elbow – Jeez, brandy gives you the WORST hangover – and looked at him. What? What you just standing there for? What's that in your hand? What are you showing me? Focus. Focus. My phone. It's my phone.

"What?" What are you doing? Why are you kicking me?"

Silence.

"Why have you got my phone? Has somebody rung?"

"HOW LONG?"

"Uh? What? What are you saying?" Fog clearing....

"HOW FUCKING LONG?"

"What? How long what?"

"YOU AND HIM. HOW LONG HAS THIS BEEN FUCKING GOING ON????"

And he shoved my open phone in my face, where I could blearily discern *'My Darling Simon...'*. The beginning of the text I left on the work top. The one where I didn't press the 'send' key. Oh my days. You know the feeling when you are utterly busted, completely fucked, with no possible recourse or excuse? That moment when the blood drains from all your vital organs, and leaves you with no breath, just a feeling of imminent death? That's what I had and realising that there really WAS no way out, said:

"Three days. That's all. Three days". That was kind of true, but not really, as it had been going on for weeks, even months or even years if you factor in the time the planets have been spinning and bringing us to this moment.

"Down fucking stairs. Now." David rarely swore, so I think he was prolly a bit mad at this point. I stumbled out of bed, feeling really bad. Really sick, hungover, tired, but not scared. That was the remarkable thing. This could have been a trigger for all those times my Dad had thrashed me, but this time I didn't care. I was SO clear in my intentions; he could do or say what he liked – it just WAS.

He was standing silhouetted in the window, the street lights casting an orange halo, making his features indiscernible

"Three days? THREE FUCKING DAYS AND YOU'RE GOING TO FRANCE?"

"Yes."

"How? Where will you live? What on? You don't have any money."

That much was true. I HAD money, but never had any access to it. He always managed the money; when we went shopping for Stuff, he always paid; when we ate out, he always paid. He always joked: *"he's like the Queen – never carries any money. Ha hahaa"* Yes, you control freak. That's because you never let me have any. And again, I let it happen. So. Not really your fault. Mine. Stupid mine, which has led me, finally, to this moment.

"How will you get there? You don't even know him. Are you fucking mad?"

"I don't know how. Or why, or when. All I DO know is that I love him and I WILL be leaving you. For him. Sorry. But that's just the truth."

"He won't love you. Not like I do. Anyway, you've got AIDS."

And that, dear reader, was the end of all things. If Simon had left tomorrow alone, there is now no way I could ever stay here with this man, who had just said the cruellest of things. I had never fully recovered from, or forgiven him for, the Monstrous Lie, but had married him anyway, but that, *that* was the worst thing he could possibly have said.

And it was the end.

"Sorry. Nothing else I can say." Actually, there was, but noticing the clenching fists and increase in breathing decided it was in the interests of self-preservation that I didn't. I just sat, naked and shivering – cold, post adrenalin, fear, all three – on the settee that had seen so many betrayals and waited.

*"WELL HE CAN FUCK OFF. FUCK OFF OUT OF MY HOUSE NOW!! GO AND WAKE HIM UP! AND YOU! YOU FUCK OFF WITH HIM! BOTH OFF YOU! FUCK OFF!! **FUCK OFF OUT OF MY HOUSE!!!!**"*

I thought about reminding him it was OUR house, actually, but given the circs....

So I went back upstairs, found my clothes from where I'd stumbled out of them earlier, and went in next door. The room of more betrayals.

"Simon," I whispered, "*Wake up. Wake **up**.*"

"*Gnnnnnnn..... Oh, good morning. Why's it still dark? What time is it?*"

"*It's early. Come on, get up. We have to go.*"

"*Go where? What's wrong?*"

I'll tell you as we go. Just get up. Can we go to yours? In London?"

"*Uh....*"

"*Here's the phone. Ring your landlady and ask. Do it now.*"

He sat up, this man to whom I was now committed and was risking everything for, rubbed his eyes, and said, "*Has something happened?*" Somewhat of an understatement.....

"*Just ring home and see if I can stay for a couple of days. We have to leave. Now.*"

After a muffled conversation, which I only heard through the bathroom wall from where I had gone to collect stuff, he said, "*She says it's OK. Are you going to tell me what's happened?*"

"*David knows about us. I'll explain as we go. I have to get a cab. Pack your stuff. Hello? Bodmin Taxis? Yes, Parkway please. Immediately. Thankyou. I'll see you downstairs.*"

I went to the kitchen, where David stood staring out the window at the scene of last night's meal.

"*I need my Barclaycard.*"

"*Please.*"

"*My card. I need it. There's a cab coming.*"

No response. Just a back, implacably turned towards me. My card was on the worktop. I picked it up. "*OK. Well.....*"

....."*I'll see you then.*"

Simon came down the stairs and I herded him, dazed and confused, straight out of the front door, and into the waiting cab, driven by, irony of ironies, Mr. Nigel Spank Me. There's always humour in the blackest places, eh?

On the way to the station, I explained about the text and what happened after, and you know what? He just said: "*Well, there you go. Reiki has a funny way of working, but work it does...*"

We were in a bit of a state of shock – I had no idea what would happen now; we were together; it was out in the open; I had no Plan B, But, after a strong coffee, in the café, which fortunately was open, and politely telling a well-meaning, but really really annoying man to FUCK OFF and no, we weren't interested in seeing his model railway, we boarded the 08.20 to Paddington, holding hands all the way to London, as we hurtled towards whatever new life awaited us.

The cafe, where we waited for the train, headed to a new life.

CHAPTER TWENTY FIVE.

MORE UPS AND DOWNS THAN A WHORE'S DRAWERS.

<u>In which our hero goes back and forth and round and round and up and down, walks the red carpet and builds a blanket fort.</u>

'500 Miles'.

by The Proclaimers. No.1 April 7th 2007.

'When I get drunk, well I know I'm gonna be
I'm gonna be the man who gets drunk next to you
And when I haver, hey I know I'm gonna be
I'm gonna be the man who's havering to you...'

The distance doesn't matter. I will fall down at your door.
When you wake up, I'll always come back home to you

~ ~ ~

The train hurtled on, to a strange land, with strange folk in it. I knew nobody, nor where I was headed, but I knew, as I stole a sideways glance at Simon, who had dozed off, that wherever and whatever befell me, with this man beside me, I could slay the dragons and wraiths that might rise up against me. I had a feeling of absolute trust in him, as if I had known him all my life, and I guess I probably had; I just hadn't met him yet. Plymouth, Exeter, Bristol, Totnes, Reading – further and further from the familiarity of the past 19 years, but with a murmuring of joy in my gut. Then, bustling Paddington. After telling a most graceful, stylish and shocked, but delighted, woman that I thought she was beautiful and very elegant, we stopped for a coffee at Ritazza, on the concourse, which became a point of reference for us, the kind of place where lovers met, affairs were designed, partings were wrenched....there we were, all alone, fresh canvases to write our new lives upon. Tube, bus, rush, tube, no time to really absorb was what happening.

We came out of the station, and I, exhilarated, said, in a kind of Vivien Leigh way, (though the skies didn't darken, and I wasn't brandishing a bunch of carrots as the music swelled to a crescendo - though maybe, in my head I was), returning to Tara:

"I am never going to let anybody tell me what to do, ever again!"

And Simon, above the roar of buses and honking of cabs, turned his beautiful blue eyes to me, and said, *"I won't,"* and so it was.

Eventually we arrived at Simon's house, or rather his digs, and let ourselves in and sank gratefully onto the settee in the lounge. Where we fell on each other, like two love starved orphans, and yes – erections burgeoning. Things were becoming clearer in my mind, about cause and effect.... Anyway we snogged and snogged and fondled a bit, like teenagers, wary of an interruption, which came not very long after, and quelled our ardour fairly sharpish.

"Um, hello Wendy. This is...um...this is Nigel. Is it OK if he stays for a couple of days?"

"Hello, Wendy. Thankyou."

"Yes, that'll be fine. Simon, we need some shopping. Will you go please?"

"Yes, of course. The usual?"

"Yes. Don't be long now."

I found myself outside again, then in the car, then in Tesco, doing the shopping. This was getting more surreal by the moment.

"Why are you doing the shopping? By the look of it, they've just BEEN shopping...."

"Oh, I always do it," was all the explanation I got.

Sainsbury's was the first place, over a bunch of coriander, I ever called him 'Si'.

We stopped for a pint afterwards, in the April sun. I just stared at him, just couldn't stop staring at this man, who had saved my life. Astonishing to think that this time, 24 hours ago, we were on the Beacon in Bodmin.....in the blink of an eye, my life had changed. I was not naïve enough to forget I'd be going back soon, and what I would face there I didn't know, but for now, the beer was cold, the sun was warm and the man across the table was utterly astonishing to me.

"They don't seem to have any. Don't worry. I'll ask.."

"No don't! Please don't....Oh god....."

"It'll be fine."

We were in a chemist, on our way home.

"Excuse me? Hello?" Stop chewing your HubbaBubba and serve me?

"Ah, yes I can't see any here. Do you have any extra-large condoms, please?"

Ha! That stopped her chewing! She went 'out the back', and asked. Si was hopping from foot to foot, with embarrassment. Or maybe anticipation? Anyway, she came back with some, wordless and gum-filled and handed them over, stuck her hand out, and I paid. ME! I actually paid. Myself! With *MY* money.

We went back to the house with the shopping, and had some food (which Si cooked) and said some things to some people and then excused ourselves and went upstairs. It was the most thrilling / strange thing. Strange, as I was now alone with him, with nobody to tell me to stop, nobody to shame me, nobody to make me feel guilty, because you know what, dear reader? I felt no shame. No guilt. I had left my husband (CIVIL PARTNER!!!) just that morning, and I could barely remember his face, and nor did I want to. I knew, without any doubt that I was in the right place, that I had waited my entire life for this moment and what would follow from it. Reiki does indeed work in mysterious ways. This was no accident! The timing was perfect. I'd *had* to go to Hungary – a time of shriving; to Germany – a time of coming to understand the kind of life I did *not* want; to get married to understand finally where I SHOULD be. In the heart of *this* man. My HIV, Anna, *IS* a gift, for without it I would never have had to face my mortality, face the demons of my Father, face my place in the world as a gay man. You were right, as you knew you would be so proved.

I AM GAY.

I AM A GAY MAN.

I AM A GOOD PERSON.

I HAVE WORTH.

I HAVE LOVE AND GIVE IT FREELY.

I AM A GAY MAN.

It had taken me 51 years to be able to say this and know it be true. And it was thanks to this extraordinary person beside me.

So we sat, on the bed, cross legged, just looking at each other and then dissolved into each other's soulplace and made love with such intensity of spirit it was utterly astonishing. And when we came, and yes, I did, with no problem whatever, it was with such an outpouring of our very selves nothing would ever be the same again. For either of us.

The Principles Of Reiki

Just for today, do not worry.

Just for today, do not anger.

Honour your parents, teachers and elders.

Earn your living honestly.

Show gratitude to everything.

Mikao Usui.

In that moment, I had achieved half of them.

The four days passed in a blur of lovemaking, tenderly, sweetly, sometimes just shagging with gay abandon (see what I did there?), cooking, and....film making! Oh yes! My man was making a film about the murder of gays in Iraq; not a cheerful subject but nevertheless.... Peter Tatchell was involved and Si had been to interview him. Silly tart that I am, I was all-star struck and wide eyed so when he said on the Sunday, he had to go to the studio to do the final edit, I was well made up. Actually, it was boring as bat shit as the producer was such a pedant, nothing actually got done. Still, it was interesting and I anyway, I didn't care cos I was wiv mah man! I wandered off half way through and went to find a café, sitting under the trees, a tall glass of cold Staropramen, full of such joy and fresh air, hardly knowing who I was.....and trying desperately hard not to think about what was to come.....

...but come it did, and Si came to Paddington with me and it was one of those *'Brief Encounter'* moments although I don't recall either Celia Johnson or Trevor Howard actually sobbing as the train pulled out along the station, but, fuck stiff upper lips! ....we cried and we held hands for as long as we were able until the speed pulled us apart.

Reading, Totnes, Exeter, Plymouth, Saltash, Liskeard, Bodmin and here we are, drab, empty, with David waiting, as he agreed to come and pick me up. Don't ask.

The following week was bizarre; David carried on as if nothing had happened. We ate together, watched telly, went shopping. I don't think we saw anyone – too many awkward questions – but it was if I'd just been away for a couple of days. (further than anyone could possibly know). Except. We both knew it had happened and we both knew it would never go back to how it was and I was now sleeping in the spare room. Awkward. Simon was ringing every night and we'd have long chats, which must have been very difficult but – but, you started this, so.....

"What shall I tell Gaynor?"

Tell her you've got a job and you're going away for a while."

"Why don't I just tell her the truth?"

"Because you won't have to live with her crying and moaning, will you? You'll tell her what I said."

Lies again. Secrets and lies. Deceive my besty. Your fabrications had already lost you any respect I'd ever had for you and now you're asking me do it again!!! But I did. I was so conditioned to do as I was told, I just acquiesced. As always. Beagle boy.

"Hey Gaynor! Guess what! News! I've got news! Can I come over?"

So, we sat in the garden and looking at, or trying to, my best friend I said:

"You know that Simon, that was here? Well, he's got a place in France and a business, and he's offered me a teaching job! Teaching English!"

"Where?"

"In France, you twat!"

"Oh. Don't call me fookin twat, you twat. That's brilliant. How long for?"

"Erm, not sure...about six months I think." How the lies poured off my tongue...

"Aww, that's grand. I'll miss you, but you'll have lots of stories when you get back! Well done!" and she got up to give me one of her Power Hugs that squeezed the air from your lungs and realigned your ribs. *"Let's have wine to celebrate!"* 'When you get back' skewered me to the floor.

And so we drank, toasting my duplicity, to my dishonouring of our friendship and to another lie in the web of deceit I had become part of, while my friend was happy for me. This caused massive harm when she found out later; she was hurt, and angry and unforgiving. And *still* I didn't betray David. I took all her wrath and pain squarely on the chin. It wasn't until much later she found out and switched the source of her anger to the perpetrator and apologised unreservedly to me. But I was as much to blame – I had been weak. I should have said no, and told her. But the abused never stand up, do they?

One night, during one of our late-night calls, a propos of nothing, Si said *'We're going to France for a week! Meet you in Ritazzas tomorrow!"* Just like that! And there I was, back on the train – Liskeard, Plymouth, Exeter, Totnes, Reading, Paddington, his arms. Boom. Coffee at our favourite table and then into the West End because Si had to go home to pay his rent, so we had tea in the Charing Cross Hotel. Very naice. Si went off, I fiddled on my laptop till he came back. It was delightful. It was elegant. It was fucking £38.75! For a cup of tea, two coffees and a tiddly cake? Never mind. New life. Stop moaning....

Train to Stansted, bleddy ansum pasty from The Cornish Pasty Company stall on Liverpool Street station (you can take the boy out of Cornwall...), flight to Tours, hire car and driving in to the night to the place that was to become my home.

It was utterly black when we arrived. The roads from the city had got smaller and smaller and now we turned into a single-track road, and pulled up in front of the house. Well, I say 'house'. After we had managed to get through the six foot high grass and weeds, unsnagged ourselves from the brambles, we opened the front door to find the place all stinky and damp, full of cobwebs and dust. And a dead owl that must have got down the chimney.

And I loved it. Si said he'd brought his former partners here both of whom had said, *"WHAT THE......???"* and he was worried I'd say the same. I didn't, much to his relief, and anyway the die was pretty much cast and I'd have lived in a cardboard box with him, if that's all he had. The place had been locked up for weeks and the cleaners Si had paid clearly hadn't been near the place.

"Bed, eh?" said Si. *"Long day."*

"Can we go to the garden first?"

"It'll be like a jungle, but.....ok then."

There was a torch and we struggled through the undergrowth to the Big Oak. I wrapped my arms round it and, in that moment, knew I'd come home.

We slept on the rickety old bed like babes, lost in the woods, which we were, pretty much.

The next morning, we had a bath, in the bedroom, where there a huge corner bath (handy) and went to town to get some food. 'Foreign shopping' wasn't a problem for me, of course so we just got what we could afford and hunkered down. The week slipped by so smooth, so fast, so full of love and anticipation and then it was the last night and we ate cheese and drank wine and danced together by the single bulb. I quote this here in full because it is OUR song, it is what we danced to, holding each other close, swaying and breathing each other's essence, full of wonder and because it says exactly what Simon has done for me:

> *You've got a way with me*
> *Somehow you got me to believe*
> *In everything that I could be*
> *I've gotta say-you really got a way*
>
> *You've got a way it seems*
> *You gave me faith to find my dreams*
> *You'll never know just what that means*
> *Can't you see, you got a way with me*
>
> *It's in the way you want me, It's in the way you hold me*
> *The way you show me just what love's made of*
> *It's in the way we make love*

You've got a way with words
You get me smiling even when it hurts
There's no way to measure what your love is worth
I can't believe the way you get through to me

It's in the way you want me
It's in the way you hold me
The way you show me just what love's made of
It's in the way we make love

Oh, how I adore you, Like no one before you
I love you just the way you are

It's in the way you want me
Oh it's in the way you hold me
The way you show me just what love's made of
It's in the way we make love
It's just the way you are.

Shania Twain. 'You've Got A Way' lyrics © Universal Music Publishing Group

But again, the time came to face the reality of other people's judgement and scorn and bitterness but I felt much stronger now, invincible in fact, immune to the slings and arrows that were to come my way. By now of course the word was out. When I got back…. Reading, Totnes, Exeter, Plymouth, Saltash, Liskeard, Bodmin….David picked me up (again!), my phone was very busy. *'Is it true?' 'Oh no! Not you two! You're perfect for each other!' 'What happened? Never mind, you'll sort it out'*….if only they knew; a mismatch if ever there was one, and I HAD sorted it out thank you very much. Me and my 'whim' were leaving.

Si, in the honest and admirable way that he has, had agreed to work out his months' notice on his rent and do some decorating, so we had seventeen days to be apart. Actually, that was 17 years, or that's how it felt, anyway. I had a long-standing arrangement to house sit for Anna's dogs and it fell in the middle of this period so at least I was out of the house and David didn't have to suffer the agonies of nightly calls (though by this time, he had a new squeeze of his own and was doing the same thing, which didn't hurt exactly but was just weird. Like the time in a threesome, he was fucking the other bloke – I didn't care, it was just...weird.) and so we could talk long into the night. We didn't have phone sex, (well, maybe once or twice) we had phone *love*. Stop sniggering at the back. It's true. We used to just chat and plan and eventually one of us would talk the other to sleep....I'd hear his breathing change and slow and he'd stop replying and I knew he'd be gone, drifted away from the day.... And then the phone would go again in the morning and there he'd be, all bright and washed with sleep. I had the joy of walking the dogs, the joy of pleasing myself and the joy of knowing it was 17.....16....15...days to go.

CATASTROPHE!! Si has just told me he's got the date for the premier of his film, in London and he's asked me to go...and I'm at fucking ANNA'S!! But, riding to the rescue came my old mate Marion (is there a joke there?) who I'd known since the day I got the job at the school we both went for back in '88.

"Maz!! What can I do? I HAVE to get to London..."

"Stop flapping! Tell me what's wrong..."

I did, breathlessly.

"Oh don't worry. Come and pick me up, and I'll cover for you. Its only one night. Get the early train, and then I'll come and get you from 'Droof station the next day."

"Yes but, what if....."

"Stop being a poof. I said I'll do it. Nobody'll be any the wiser." Although of course they were, because she told her husband who told my husband, who of course is a very close friend of Anna's.....I don't know to this day if she knows or not. I suspect she does, but the dogs were fine, the house wasn't robbed by the stranger, so I guess she figured it didn't matter.

And so it came to pass. On the train again – up and down, up and down – Redruth, St. Austell, Bodmin, Liskeard, Saltash, Plymouth, Exeter, Totnes, Reading....know the route yet? And there he was, fawn linen jacket, new trousers, sexy as.

"Coffee?"

"Yes I think so".

"Ritazza?"

"I think so."

"Thanks for coming."

"I love you".

Ritazza Café, Paddington. Thrills and Sorrows.

Off to the Horse Hospital which was built in 1797 as stabling for cabby's sick horses. The Horse Hospital is now a unique Grade II listed arts venue situated in an unspoilt mews in the heart of Bloomsbury, and it is a really amazing building, with special knobbly floors to stop the horses slipping. So, there we were, a crowd of earnest film enthusiasts, queer activists, lezzers and intellectuals all here to see my man's film. I was SO proud. He introduced me all round as 'my partner', and I was happy to bask in the glow of his success. It was a short film, harrowing and very powerful and evoked much discussion and lit fires. After we got a Subway thingy (oooh! The glamour of the film world) and a cab and then a train back to Wendy's who was not very pleased to see me as of course I was the reason her houseboy and servant was leaving. SO, another long night of joy and love making, and we slept until the alarm went at stupid o'clock and I set off back to the station, all big and grown up, on my own!

Paddington, Reading, Totnes, Exeter, etc etc back down to Redruth where Maz was waiting, and back to the house. Job done. No more trains now, eh?

And so came the last few days at 'home' – the marks are necessary, because it wasn't home now; it was just a place I was sleeping until I could leave. As Rose Royce once said: *"Love don't live here anymore"*......well not for me.

I need to explain a bit here, I think, in case *you're* thinking I'm just a heartless cunt. Well, I'm not. To quote Anne Lamott:

"You own everything that happened to you.

Tell your stories.

If people wanted you to write warmly about them,

they should've behaved better."

This story is how *I* remember it, and how *I* see it. Others can (and certainly did) see it differently but all I can say is 'You were not living inside it and so you really have no right to judge it, or me'. I, without realising, so gradual was it, had allowed myself to be owned, controlled and manipulated. David had replaced my Father and I liked that because he loved me and didn't loathe me, but I hated it too, as he always made me feel stupid, inferior and small. Not unkindly, not with malice, but nevertheless, he did. I had been stolen. All my choices were not actual choices, all the decisions I had made were not really mine. And so when I found an alternative universe (which I had forgotten even existed) in which there was a man who loved me unconditionally, was fair and gentle, interested in equality and justice, and who was not interested in playing power games, why *wouldn't* I choose option B? Yes, of course it was hard, it was painful, it was frightening – I hadn't been in the outside world for 19 years; I had forgotten how to do things for myself and it was terrifying and thrilling in equal measure. There was always going to be collateral damage but leaving the country I'm sure lessened the impact.

In the midst of this sea of sorrows, I went to see Anna, as I didn't know how to proceed. Maybe SHE, with her clear eye and bullshit detector would have something to say that would guide me through. I knew what I wanted, what was right, but didn't know the *how* of it. She as always, made sense of the turmoil. It was like the last hurrah!, where I could weep out all the pain – the pain of separation, the pain of anger having realised I had been duped for all those years; it was like having been kept in a cellar for years and then suddenly someone had prised off the coal cover. And light had flooded in. It was just the *sadness* of it all. Through the snot and the tears, aware of the deep and abiding friendship she had with him, I snivelled:

"But I've really hurt him."

"That's none of your business."

"What? But...."

"No. It isn't. How he feels is none of your business."

Quite a concept to get my head round.

"But the house. There's a mortgage."

"Sell it."

"I can't, it's his home"

"Yes. You CAN. You may not want to, but you CAN. He'll have to find another home."

"But what about all my stuff – we bought it together."

"Leave it. Why would you want to take your old stuff to a new life?"

And that, dear reader, is what I did. In a stroke, Anna (and Jophiel, who was surely there, speaking the truth) cleansed me and healed me.

And THAT is why I was able to leave so calmly, looking outward and toward the man who had come to save me. And *not* because I was a heartless cunt. OK?

That too, was the end of the extremely deep and complex relationship with Anna, a woman of exceptional power and wisdom. We'd met, we'd loved, she'd done what she was supposed to have done, and we moved through. So, thank you Anna, for more than you could ever know. Oh, but wait – of course you do! Medicine Woman, Sage, Healer – I thank you profoundly for the difference you made.

I told David I was going to stay with Debs for the weekend; the house was unbearable now, with an air of impending doom. I packed as much as I could carry, in two suitcases, while David, mute as stone, looked on. I felt powerful, I felt open, I knew that long stored reiki was working for me and that my empowerment was not going to fail.. As the days shrank down from 17, 16,15,... I felt calm, right and ready. This time I thought it unsympathetic to ask for a lift to the station but still, David drove me, not a word was spoken and he left me waiting for the train West. Then, did I mention, Si came too? We had an amazing weekend, full of sun and laughter, beer and sex and it was over too soon, but it was OK because it was just a break, an interlude, an *entre'act*, before the final scenes were to be played out; he was going back to get his stuff and then, soon....soon.....

CHAPTER TWENTY SIX.

THE SUMMER OF LURVE.

<u>In which our hero finds the boy again, makes peace with the Devil, and puts himself out of harm's way.</u>

'Signal Fire'.

by Snow Patrol. No.7, 28th April 2007.

'In the confusion and the aftermath
You are my signal fire

The only resolution and the only joy
Is the faint spark of forgiveness in your eyes...'

I have no fear when you are there, standing in front of me.

Hold me close, 'cause I need you to guide me to safety

~ ~ ~

I had stayed with Debbie the night before, and Si was due the day after. I borrowed Debs' car and went to meet him. Way too early, of course and found myself, in an all too familiar way, *skipping about like a gurl* only this time David wasn't there, oozing disapproval.

Could be, who knows? There's something due any day

I would know right away, soon as it shows

It may come cannon balling down through the sky

Gleam in its eye, bright as a rose

Who knows? It's only just out of reach

Down the block on a beach under a tree

I got a feeling there's a miracle due

Gonna come true, coming to me......

This breathless lyric from *West Side Story* sums up the nervous nearly pooin-me-pants excitement, knowing he was on the train and with every clickety clack he was nearer...

.....heart racing, skipping to and fro....being 45 minutes early wasn't a good idea.....

...text: *'Bodmin'*

...text: *'Lostwhithiel'*

...text: *'St Austell'*

...text: *'Stuck in St Austell'* Oh FFS!!!

...text: *'Left St.Austell'*....

...text: *'Truro next stop'*...

And. There he was. Right there. Hot, tired but there. I swear it was a runn —y thing, along the station in slow mo, into each other's arms. It was hard to believe as it goes, as for the first time so far, there was nobody else telling us what to do, how to be, where to go, judging, criticising, analysing...just us, and the choice to be just how we wanted. And at that moment, it was in bed. My desire for him was overwhelming; not in a pervy, shaggy kind of (well, maybe a bit) but in the way of needing to have a singular intimate connection where nobody could interfere or make us feel that it was wrong. Because it wasn't.

We drove back to Falmouth to let the party of all parties begin. Summer 2007.

We had arranged to meet Gill in town the next day and so we walked down to the City centre and there was my beautiful sister, waiting, a bit nervously, but of course, Si just hugged her and squeezed it all away. He does that, you know. We had a cold beer in the warm sun and everything was perfect. As Si hadn't been to Truro before, we had a little walk round and apparently, unknown to me at the time, in the cathedral with its slanting light and silent air, Gill had taken Si to one side, and said:

"Mum asked me to look after him. Well, now it's your turn and I hand him into your care." Nice, eh?

We went back to Gill's little cottage that she had said we could use if we wanted (we did) and when I say *little*.....we decided we were going to fuck in the shower but after me getting trapped in the door and Si repeatedly banging his head on the shower head, we decided maybe it was a bit *too* small.

"Bedroom, then," he said.

We began again, tenderly, slowly, silently, apart from our breath. After some time, he said,

"I want to fuck you now. Join with you."

"Where are the condoms?"

"We don't need them anymore," and with that and with infinite care he slid into me, making a connection so deep, so intense I thought my heart would burst. I sobbed, I think, with a joy so complete, so grateful, so overwhelming, and he said, *"Did I hurt you?"*

"No," I sobbed, *"No. You just wiped all the hurt away."* I didn't need to explain that. He knew of my trauma with my status, my, shame, my fear and with that one, unselfish act, cancelled out months of agony and self-hatred.

"I've been doing my homework, you know. I've read all the reports and data and studies. I know you've been undetectable for years now, and the risk of infection is negligible, and I wanted to show you how deeply I love you". And I sobbed myself to sleep in his arms. He smelled of soap and sweat.

After, we decided to gate-crash the party at Debs' so we got dressed, got a cab, got some beverages and arrived at Gylling Street. Where we stayed for the next three months. There was room there, there was energy, and most importantly it was in the centre of town. I felt bad after Gill had been so generous, but there just wasn't room – we had two huge suitcases each and no transport. It just made sense, though I knew she was pissed off with me. I hope she knows it was nothing personal. The pasty shop and Threshers the Offy were within sight of the flat. No contest.

The Summer was golden, hilarious and full of possibility. You know that feeling of terror/joy when it's all brand new and sparkly? Everything is wonderful and nothing is impossible? There were always people turning up, always fun to be had and as the Summer wore on, the hurts and the fears were gently smoothed away, by the sun, the sea and his love for me.

Happy happy!

Debs said we could stay on the blow up mattress that first night as there were still people occupying the beds from the weekend. We blew it up and lay it in front of the fireplace, and stumbled to bed. I was on the fireplace side and Si, being a big lad, said he'd have the other side. So, he flopped down on the bed, catapulting me up into the air and into the grate. When we'd finally stopped laughing, we decided to drive back to Gill's and come back the next day.

Debs had a friend who had a thing about Russian gymnasts and it became a Thing, and it developed and we decided there was one called Boris and he lived under the bed in the spare room, useful for housework. And stuff. One day we had a party on the balcony and I decided it was time to meet him. We also had been designing a new recipe book on ways to serve saffron cake, and we had one in the kitchen. Without a thought, I stripped off completely, put on an apron and a Russian accent, and carrying a plate of 'saffron cubes dressed with tomato wedges and chocolate', Boris appeared on the balcony, stark bollock naked, apart from the apron.

"Cake," he said. *"I vant you try cake. Iss very good."*

The reactions were mixed and priceless.

"Mummy!! MUMMY!" said Debs' daughter. *"I can see Uncle Nigel's bum!!"* and she shrieked with delight.

Debs was unable to speak for laughing, that great deep laugh that shakes your soul and renders you helpless.

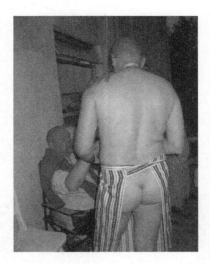

Boris. And his arse.

Debs' straight friend backed in to the corner, as Boris closed in, insisting he had enough cake already, terrified and alone as Debs was no use to anyone.

Si was…..well…both astonished and delighted. He loved this man-child, this man who would do this with such aplomb! He stared in wonder and joy that I was his. HIS. And I was so happy because I would never *NEVER* have done such a thing before, and had never been as free spirited in nineteen years. It was a revelation and a source of undiluted joy.

Eyebrows were raised, pretend laughs were guffawed and Boris just continued to serve, showing his bare arse to everyone, not needing approval or permission from anyone. *"Have cake. Iss nice."*

Wot Larks, eh Pip?

It was wonderful day, as were all the days that summer. My birthday came and we celebrated all day, got kicked out of the bar we were in, tried to blag our way into a concert without tickets, went skinny dipping, me and Debs. Flinging off our clothes, Debs with her tits out, we plunged in to the sea, in the dark, fearless and foolish, but I was so light of spirit, and free, I knew all would be well.

We coulda drowned!

Then fireworks, drunk as skunks, which whizzed and screamed by as they weren't set off properly or safely – shades of Bremen! – then happily to bed, at the start of another brand-new year with my brand-new love. The thought that we were leaving for France soon made the end of that day, month, all the more special and important.

Safely home.

So. To the last task. Unfinished business. There was the only one thing that clouded that blue skied summer. And I needed to resolve it and reach an end. I went to face my Nemesis.

"Hi."

"Oh 'ello boy. I didn't know you were coming. Where's David?"

"Can I come in please, I need to talk to you?"

He sat in the grease stained, fag scented armchair and I stood by the fire place.

"He's not here. We've split up." Beat. *"I'm with somebody else now. His name is Simon. And we're living in Falmouth."*

"Awww, no. That's a pity. I liked 'ee. 'Ee was a good ole boy. What're ee doin' in Falmouth?"

"Staying with Debs for a while. Then I'm moving to France. With Simon. Maybe to teach English. I don't know yet. But there are somethings I need to say before I leave." I was aware that this actually could be the last time I saw him, not that I cared, but there was something unavoidable to be done.

"What're goin' to live on? Got any money 'ave ee?"

"No. Well, not much. That's not why I'm here. Just sit down and don't say anything till I'm finished, OK?

I took a deep breath, no longer afraid of this little man sat before me and opened my mouth and said all the things I had waited years, *years,* to say:

*I want you to know that I don't **care** what you think of my lifestyle, whatever that's supposed to be. I know you find it foul, that you say disgusting things to Gill and Barrie – they tell me, you know... NO! **DON'T** interrupt. I know all you think of is me being in the Shit Shovers Union, as you so hurtfully put it, but I am more than that. I am a good man. I was a good teacher, I am a good son, I am a good partner. I am considerate, and loyal and caring and loving. I work hard, I pay my bills. In fact, I am just like you. Only nicer.*

I was now in full spate, this speech, rehearsed so many times over the years, now just flooding forth...still measured, still calm, still in control of what I was saying. No fear of this man, who had beaten me, betrayed me, belittled me.

"But. I need you to know that I understand why you are so bigoted, so hateful, so ashamed. Given the vile spiteful woman who brought you up, so embittered and full of rage herself, I am not surprised that you deal with anything you don't understand or approve of by being hateful and vengeful yourself. I get it. I do.

I know what you say about me. I know you lie to your friends because you're too ashamed to have a gay son, that you tell them I'm a headmaster! That's just a lie. Why do you SAY that? It's just not true! You spread poison and lies about each of us to the others – do you think we don't talk to each other? That we don't know what you've said about each of us?

I was watching him, so small, so transfixed. Why was I ever afraid of him?

I know your Father left you when you were a baby; he was in South Africa when you were only four. I know you were brought up by an embittered and angry woman. I don't know what that did to you, or being a member of that insane Methodist chapel, but all of these things conspired to make you like you are and to take YOUR bitterness out on an easy target – your 'queer poof of a son'. Especially when he's not around to defend himself.

Well, I am here to say only this. I will NEVER forgive you, or forget, the hurts and damage you heaped upon my sisters and the years of hell you put my mother through. But those are not mine to forgive, I suppose. That is up to them, and now Mum is dead and no longer part of the misery you caused. Still cause...But for me I can say only this: One - I no longer care what you think. I know my worth to the world, to my friends and my partner and, two – I forgive *you. Forgive you for the undeserved beatings, all the hurt and rejection, the shame you made me feel, the self-loathing you made me feel and the desertedness you made me feel. Because I really don't think it was, at heart, your fault. You didn't stand a chance. But you **could've** made a choice. A choice not to judge me, not to loathe me but to accept me, love me and be proud of my achievements. But you didn't. You could've made a better choice.*

I just want you to know it doesn't matter now. I'm done."

Tears were threatening, my pitch was rising. I was spent. All those years of need spat forth and I felt cleansed. Purged. He was just watching, like I wasn't even speaking. Then, do you know what he said?

"You'll need some money if you're going to set up a school in France. You can have your inheritance early. I treat all you kids the same (biting of tongue in incredulity) *so how much do you need?"*

Did you just **hear** anything I said? Were you even **listening**? Or did you hear and for once you were found out? Or was this an attempt to buy me off? Get rid of me? Get me right out of the country – to never need to see your abomination again? Give me money to make up for all the years of hurt? Well, you know what? Fuck it. I don't CARE why, and anyway, I knew better to listen to what he said – I had the real version from my siblings.

"Yes, if you're offering," I said. *I'm sure the others will have something to say, believe I coerced you, but they weren't here, were they? They didn't hear this conversation. They didn't hear you OFFER. They can believe what they like. How much are you thinking?"*

"I can give you £5000 if that will do? That's your share."

"Really? Well, yes, that should be plenty to get me started. Thankyou." And so for the next five days, I travelled over to Truro and he withdrew £1000 a day. Blood money. And I felt not the least bit guilty: he offered, I accepted.

On the last day, he said, *"I would like to buy you and your Friend lunch."* Capital F. After my initial astonishment, given that he didn't speak to David for nearly eight years, I thanked him and the following day, we met. In the British Legion. All Day Breakfast. Congealed bacon and eggs. Classy. But the thought was there, and he met Simon. He kept calling him David, but they got on OK. Maybe he HAD heard some of what I'd said? Who knows? We went to a pub after, where I bought the drinks as he said they were too expensive and he refused to pay that much, after which I went to fetch the car. I arranged to meet them at the main roundabout in town. When I arrived, he saw the car and just dragged Si out in to the middle of the traffic, which was swerving round them, tyres screeching, horns blaring until I managed to pull up, in the middle of the three lanes of traffic as he just flagged me down, opened the doors and they got in, Si visibly white and sweating in fear.

"He tried to fucking KILL ME!!" Si never swears, so he must've been spooked. I wasn't sure to laugh or not. I just waved sheepishly at all the drivers who had narrowly missed being involved in a multiple pile up.

"Home now, eh?" And he lit up a fag, placing the packet next to the sticker that said 'NO SMOKING'. All normal in Trevor land. We dropped him off, with a sigh of relief.

I never saw him again.

He died, from vascular dementia, after months of setting his flat alight, getting nicked for shoplifting, being found wandering round town in his pyjamas, being put in a secure home and running naked in the midnight corridors waving his shrivelled old willy at the nurses, and finally into Hospital, from where he never returned, and at the age of 98, he died. On Christmas Day. Christmas fucking day. Nice one.

Do I miss him? No. Was I upset? No, or, only for Gill, whom he had somehow managed, after *everything* he had done to her, to get her to be his skivvy for the last years of his life – so yes, sorry, only for her, as she was with him when he died and that can't be nice for anyone. I knew too that with the centre of power gone, Shelob, no longer at the centre of the web, holding us all in place with his poisonous threads, that the family would unravel, dissipate, no longer be in thrall. And so it proved – nobody sees anyone else now, has anything to share. We were all, essentially, different people, only connected by birth and once the ties that bound us were gone, so was the dynamic of family.

I have often looked back, from a distance of years, with wonder at Rod's family – all of them loving each other without condition which is what enabled them to thrive. Concern, the desire to protect and nourish each other were all sadly lacking in my family, and so despite the agonies caused by what happened with me and Rod, I would not change a single moment of it, as for those four years, I had a family, a family, all of whom loved and cherished me. That is irreplaceable in my heart and soul.

My Dad died. MY DAD IS DEAD.

I really didn't care.

Does it make me bad? I don't think so….. It makes me *honest*…..

And so, the Days of Summer drew to an end. Ferry tickets were booked, the car was packed; bizarrely Debs was away when we left so there no goodbyes to be said. We locked up and, Betty, with her axles nearly scraping the road, took us north, out of Cornwall….

A30…

M5…..

A35….

M27…

Southampton, Portsmouth, Brighton, Eastbourne, Hastings (fish and chips with our last English money), Folkestone, Dover…..

Bill Bryson once said:

"I can't think of anything that excites a greater sense of childlike wonder than to be in a country where you are ignorant of almost everything. Suddenly you are five years old again. You can't read anything, you have only the most rudimentary sense of how things work, you can't even reliably cross the street without endangering a life. Your whole existence becomes a series of interesting guesses."

My new life was about to begin. Finally.

CHAPTER TWENTY SEVEN.

'THIS ABOVE ALL ELSE: TO THINE OWN SELF BE TRUE'.

In which our hero arrives in a new land, arrives in a safe place in his heart, arrives at the end of the search, meets more people than he knew existed who all think he's fab and plans to become Mr O'Corra-Bray. Or Bray-O'Corra. And, finally, at, Journey's End, he walks into the sun.

'Dream Catch Me'.

*by Newton Faulkner. No11. 1*st *September, 2007*

'You do so much but you don't know it's true
And I know now who I am
Yeah, yeah, yeah
And I know now...'

I know who I am now! Do anything I want!
Be anyone I wanna be!

At last.....

~ ~ ~

Six months ago, almost to the day, I was living in a land of endless horizons with very little appearing on them, apart maybe from the same scene coming round again. Like a kind of zoetrope – same scenes, same people going past, doing the same things. I jumped off. As the Buddhists say: "JUMP! The net will appear!" I did. It did.

September 1st. Now, I am on a boat, watching the white cliffs of Dover, getting smaller, too small to see if there any bluebirds over them, watching England retreat, watching the great churns of the Channel spit and flick and glisten and thinking 'Oh my giddy aunt'. Or something similar. I just said that because as you know I don't swear. Unless it slips out. But that's another story...

On the ferry, bound for France.

There is a very strange pain in my heart. It seems cleft in twain. Half overbursting with joy and anticipation, the other full of anger and sadness at how I had been treated. By my Friends. You know, the ones who promised to love me forever, but haven't spoken to me or contacted me since April, 6 months now, since I met Simon.

These were the people with whom I shared weddings, funerals, birthdays and christenings. Deaths of mothers, fathers, sisters and pets. Sorrows and joys. Illness, fears and joyful recoveries. Nineteen years of intimacy with them all, and who have, since the day I left for London with Simon, *'that bastard, who ate my food, drank my wine and took me as well'*; since I met my 'whim' and had no idea what I was doing, but just fucked off, without a by your leave, with not a backward glance, never spoken a single word to me.

Actually I did. Look back, I mean. Often, and with real sorrow. And as I gave up my homeland, my country, my language, my work and all of *YOU* to be where I knew my true love lay, I would have hoped that you, ONE Of you, might have asked how I was? You may not have agreed with what happened, but you could still have asked…."*Are you OK?"* That's just lazy, taking sides, and not the responsibility of treating us both equally. Just ask this: If it was all so perfect – why did I leave?

It's funny isn't it, the notion of 'break – up', how we all assume the 'left' is the only one suffering and the 'leaver' is having a whale of a time, with nary a care. Well, folks, it ain't so easy. In addition to the agony of separation, of giving up the security that long term relationships and friendships bring, there is a huge burden of guilt. Which is passed on to the new person who has to deal with all the strangeness of a new (if wished for) relationship and to cope with the feelings of terrible guilt of 'what I had done', no matter how blameless, no matter how dysfunctional it had been or how tired and exhausted the relationship was and it being absolutely the right time to go.

It mattered a lot at first. It mattered less and less as time went on. So, Jean, Mary, Richard, Rachel, Kath, Silu, Pauline, Tina, St.John, Chris, Derek, Alwyn, Louise, Judy, Colin, Jo, Pat, Edwin, Karl, Debbie, Mike, Audrey, Edwin, Roger et al......I'm FINE!! Thanks for asking. Oh, wait! You didn't.

Still, the waters close over your head.....

We weren't done yet of course. I had a marriage certificate and house, both of which I no longer wanted. Back away from the Guilty Step.....it's the way of things. So, whilst still in Falmouth I had started the ball rolling and found a lovely solicitor who saw clearly and straight away that there was cause for separation on ground of 'unreasonable conduct'. I of course tried to keep saying "Oh it wasn't THAT bad", trying to assuage my guilt and feelings of failure, but as I told her more and more of my living situation over the years and all the complications arising from my diagnosis and the cancer - that - never- was debacle, it was becoming clearer to me that I had been suffering 'domestic abuse' for years and there were indeed, if I wanted, ground for divorce.

Was it ugly? No. Was it painful? A bit. But I had Si next to me every step of the way, every form, every meeting, supporting, upholding, never judging, always patient when I wasn't very nice, which was quite often, and understanding why.

I still had shed loads of stuff back at the house and once we'd moved, we were forever to and fro to Cornwall in our poor old Vera (Betty was scrapped as Si had written the poor old gal orf) and whilst Si wandered around the shops or stayed back in Falmouth, I went back to the house to collect Stuff. Stuff which in reality, I neither needed nor wanted. It was truly weird seeing David – such little time had passed and I barely recognised him. It was like talking to a really prickly stranger. It WAS of course still my house, though he'd forbidden me to have a key (SEE? See what I mean?) I couldn't be fucked to argue anymore so it had to be 'by prior arrangement'...... MY house! MY stuff! Fucking cheek, but I was able to manage, as it was now just a numbers game: the stuff and the need to go grew less frequent and so the agro quotient fell too.

I'd go, we'd divvy up CDs (yep, really, just like in the films), he'd make me a sandwich, I'd sit on the workbench, just to make a point, he'd ask if I'd like *"some of his crisps"*, I'd have a coffee, pack the car and drive away, over and over till there was nothing left. In all senses. In all ways.

Soon, it was all in France or down the dump.

During one of these times, I bore the brunt, and deservedly so, of Gaynor's anger and disappointment at me having lied to her. It was clear, given the car loads of stuff that was being extracted, I wasn't going 'for a few months'. So, shame faced and sad, I went in for a drink – David was away, so I slept in my house, that night, pissed as a pissed thing, just like the old days. Sort of. - and confessed. The whole story, including WHY I hadn't told her. She was just hurt, hurt and angry, and it was hard for her to have been shat on by, AND to be losing, her best friend, her buddy with whom she shared her heart, her dope and her wine. It was many months before we found peace again, where she had been made aware of just how duplicitous David had been, having nursed *his* heart fiercely after I'd 'deserted him', defended him and screamed at me. But, in *fermentum et veritas,* when the truth came out; when she DID realise how my hands had been tied, my voice silenced, her anger switched sides. Now she adores my man, has apologised twenty thousand times and all is well.

The divorce, amazingly, was uncontested. I don't know whether this was an admission of culpability (I doubt THAT somehow) or if he was just resigned to the fact that for once, he was unable to control what was to happen. I was surprised, and relieved, that he just accepted it – maybe he just took the line of least resistance...but in any event, he agreed and signed it off and hurrah! I was free.

And maybe, just maybe, there was a tacit acknowledgement that we simply weren't right for each other.

The house took longer; he was particularly obstructive, which ended up costing us a considerable amount of money as the market dropped, but I understand why – it was his home and he was probably angry / lost / scared at the prospect of being forced out. Also, probably there was a huge amount of pissed offness as I was in charge of events – an alien landscape for him. Anyway, after much huffing and puffing we found a buyer, split the money and sailed off into our sunsets.

Except of course, we didn't. We were still linked - his Mum, dear Ruth who had promised to be my surrogate Mum and to whom I was close, died so I was involved in that, at least emotionally. I held a little vigil and had a ceremony here in the garden for her. Well, for me, but you know what I mean. As for the multitude of Friends.....nothing. Not a call, not an email, not a question, and it was this that obstructed my healing the most – I was unbelievably hurt by them, by this. *MY* friends – those that were pre-David or from Hungary or NODA Summer Schools were united and with one voice (but with varying amounts and swearing) asked *'How the fuck did you stay with him SO long?'* *'He was a controller, a manipulator, a bully and you were well shot of him'*. How come I saw none of this? All those years....

I am not willing to say they were wasted; they weren't and we DID have some good times; we did lots and saw lots but it was not until I went to Hungary, after my reiki training, that I began to feel wrong, wrong in my **self** and in my heart – so how did it take five more years before I had the courage to leave? What would have happened if Simon hadn't appeared? If I hadn't done the website training? Started inviting strangers to our bed? This is all self-evident of course – all of those decisions, events, agreements (though usually not by me) all led to the point where I WOULD meet him, and by extension, leave. The Universe moves in mysterious ways. Reiki provides, if eyes are open to see and the heart open to receive.

I think now, hand on heart, that we really weren't very good for each other. Fuck know how, or why, we stumbled on for so many years but as Baby Jesus or King James or somebody said:

'To everything there is a season, and a time to every purpose under the sun'

 and I guess things were going to take the time allotted until it became time to do something else. No fault, or fault on both sides. Just ran out of petrol. That's it.

And, DUH, here was the crux. Simon was not, is not, my Father. He is never judgemental, aggressive, belittling or controlling. And he is younger. Look back, you fool! Look back! In all the 'proper' (not necessarily successful or healthy) relationships I'd had, of any length anyway…everyone of 'em was older than me. Rod: +12; John: +23 (Shuddup, yes, really); David: +13. All in their way, controllers, manipulators, bullies – and just like my Daddy. But they LOVED me, just like my Daddy didn't, but just like I wanted him to. How I didn't see this pattern before, fuck knows. Time after time. I just thought I fancied older blokes. When really, I was chasing the illusion that my Dad could like me, didn't mind I was a poof and was nice to me. Except, of course, really not one of them was. All of 'em, just as destructive, just as ruinous to my self-esteem as he had been.

Until now. Until I met, was given, this wonderful man, 4 years my junior with no agenda, who loves me. Unconditionally. With no caveats, other than I love him back.

Lucky Mr. Lucky.

Slowly. Slowly, I adapted to my new life, supported gently, wisely by Simon, who never pushed, never rushed, letting go bit by bit and stepping, wide eyed, into a world where I was allowed an opinion, the answers to whose questions were valued; who was asked questions, where I was never belittled or made to feel inadequate…

…and with that sense of worth, the blood flowed back into my heart and into my penis as surely as the horrors of the previous months had prevented it. I have mentioned stiffies often during this diatribe and you, I bet, have thought 'is that all you think about?' Well, yes actually. But you have no idea how profound a gift it was to be able to be normal again, in all senses of the word, return to a world I had forgotten existed, and was finally blown apart at 11 a.m., on 11/11, 2004 and which I never thought it would ever be fixed.

Well Simon did. Sewed up the rents in my heart, soothed away the bruises. This is the last poem I wrote, not having needed to pour forth pain since we met, only joy.

The Healer

Gentle me, soothe my skin,

Erase the creases the day's bent in.

Unstitch me from the web;

Make me whole – not with plaster or daub,

But close subtly the rents in my heart;

Re-connect me to the lost pathways in which love lived in lives long lost.

Lie with me in astonished silent places,

Brushing off the slough of heavy duty and weighty care,

Till I am clean and open to you.

Then, into these newly cleansed wounds, pour the antiseptic of your love

To heal and suture my wounded pasts -

With high praise and low laughter,

With quick glance and slow caress,

While we join our subtle flesh and rock away our cares

Till we spill them each into the other's most secret places

And we lie, bathed in sweat and joy, seed and light

As we are welcomed home.

April, 2007.

Wedding Pic – the one and only!

In October 2010 we were married, well, *PACSd,* the French equivalent of a Civil Partnership, after a very romantic proposal, down on one knee, on a *boulevard* in the heart of Paris, and soon, thanks to that darling little M. Hollande, we'll marry and this time it will be with a heart so open and eager because I know that this time it will be whole and pure and equal.

We went travelling, my man and I. We went back to Hungary, to Kesckemét, to Bosckai ut, the Tanítóképző Főiskolai, and stood outside my Office door in the *Angol nyelvi osztály,* the English Language Department, where I'd had an engraved plaque with my name; *'Nigel Bray, Angol tanár',* Teacher of English, in gold letters, where I had begun to heal; back to the minutiae of my life there.

Basic, but mine....with a lovely poster of Bradford....

He was fascinated, interested, full of admiration and praise – something I was still quite unused to – and it was amazing to me. We went to the wonders of Budapest, not to lay ghosts, but to see things with different eyes, and I felt a bit of pride to be showing him 'my city' and to do new things, to make new memories and reclaim it as my own, to share with HIM.

We went to Berlin too – it was awful, mostly, but I was able to show him wonders and make new memories and make it ours. Then for our honeymoon, the wonders of Barcelona were ours – new, unsullied and glorious.

Der Fernsehturm, Berlin

Gaudi Park, Barcelona. Full of colour and joy.

By the sea, where my heart resides.

Sixty years have passed since the start of this journey. 532 pages of stuff. 180, 231 words. Photographs. Memories. Years filled with more things than you can shake a stick at. Sorrows, and great joys. Amazing people and those who caused me harm. All necessary to give the tapestry its colours, to construct the man who has told you his tale.

SO, dear kind and patient readers. All that remains then, is to look back see, how it's looking on the old Lucky-ometer and take a reading….

Sure, there were really *really* bad things, - the vileness of my Father, his letters and insults and his actions and the terrible way he treated us and the resulting, lasting damage he did to us all; the terrible mess I made of people's hearts (and my own) as I was just a stupid man/child unwise in the ways of love and how to treat people – you can trace this way way back to the beginning of the book – so I can only, rather late in the day, apologise. I was a twat. *Mea culpa*. My discovery that I had HIV (not very lucky there, eh?) and the terrible damage wrought to my body, my health and my self-esteem. I didn't treat you folks the way I should've and again, I apologise, for the lies I told to the people I loved – not necessarily my fault – but I acquiesced, nonetheless so I am equally to blame and responsible for the pain that weakness caused. *Mea culpa*; the sudden and devastating loss of my Mother and the effect that had on my behaviour as I was suddenly cast adrift; the loss of Chris, wonderful Lager Blagger Extraordinaire, whose presence in my life was of immeasurable value, taken away from me and leaving me to fuck up alone; the enigma that was Rod – the pain he caused and the scars it left.

On the PLUS side, in the other pan – Oh most fortunate me! Contrarily, I was lucky to have had the Father I did, as it was a clear and constant warning to avoid ending up like him; Lucky to have had such a powerful force for good that was my Mother, who, with her unfailing faith in me and her Golden Ear Whizzes, even after death, kept me constant and determined to be the best I could, for her, in return for her loving me, come what may. Lucky to have been well educated and to have had a good and useful career, where I did good and good was done; Lucky to have had those years with Slobbidybobbidy, which though it ended badly, was joyous and full of hope; Lucky for the years I DID have Chris in my life and the fun and joy he brought me, the madness and the sorrow, worth it every bit; Lucky to have had the privilege of having lived in Hungary and be given the massive life lessons I learned there, and for that, I thank you - *köszönöm, Magyarország. Köszönöm szépen*; Lucky to have met Rod, as the joy he brought me, he and his family, far outweighs the mess that was the end. Lucky to have met David for he too, though times were good, was a lesson, in the end, in learning exactly the kind of man I wasn't and didn't want to be; Lucky to have had the special bond with Gill, who has loved me through it all and who is still here, and will be in France again soon where we will get bladdered and cry and tell tales and laugh as we always have; Lucky to have had Ann and Gaynor in my life too, the triumvirate of those Three Tall Women who all made me bigger, better and kinder and wiser and braver; Lucky to have been given the option in so many ways to express my creative side, to be a Luvvie with no fear of ridicule (cos I was good!), at school, at College, with the many children and in Phoenix - we were *mahvellous* dahling, to do good things, to feed the flame; Lucky to have had Anna in my life who kept it real and true and I thank her for her love and wisdom in the very worst of times and of course, Lucky to have met Jim and been granted the gift of reiki and, for Michael who made it possible, eventually, to meet Simon, the love of what remains of my life and whose face I will see as the last breath leaves my body.

Meeting Simon, of course, was very lucky....but it wasn't luck.

Oh, and of course, you lot – for sticking with it to the very end – sharing my fears and joys, my loves and my secrets, my tales and adventures, my fuck ups and my successes – there have been many and often.

That's pretty fucking lucky, I'd say. Now I'll stop swearing. Maybe.

Hope it was worth the effort.

Peaces.

Luv, Mr. Lucky. xxx

CHEERS!

I'm a lucky girl
I found my friend
I've been all around the world
Mission Impossible
Chasing the rainbow's end
Wise guys
Shy guys
And sly lover boys
With big bad bedroom eyes ...
I never loved a man I trusted
As far as I could pitch my shoe
'Til I loved you

You're my lucky star
You're my magician
You make the night prowling disappear
Vanished from the star-war-bars
Empty repetition
I get my heart full here
Playboys
Stray boys
And "Say, hey, hey" boys'll treat you like a toy
I never loved a man I trusted
As far as I could pitch my shoe
'Til I loved you

Cheaters
Woman beaters
And Huck Finn shucksters hopping parking meters
I never loved a man
I trusted
As far as I could pitch my shoe
'Til I loved you

I'm a lucky girl
I found my friend
I been all around the world
Mission Impossible
Chasing the rainbow's end
Wise guys
Booby-prize guys
And sly lover boys
With big bad bedroom eyes ...
I never loved a man I trusted
As far as I could throw my shoe
'Til I loved you

Joni Mitchell. 'Lucky Girl' (1986 © Crazy Crow Music)

Printed in Great Britain
by Amazon

28426886R00294